U0153796

貴州東部村寨物語

Hmub人的日常、情感及語言

簡美玲 —— 著

Narratives of Hmub Village Life in Eastern Guizhou

Everydayness, Emotions and Language
—— Mei-Ling Chien

村寨夜未眠

清水江邊，夜涼如水
吊腳樓旁，水杉英姿
一輪明月，清朗自在
滿天星斗，燦爛輝煌

「阿姐，妳走錯路，到此深山苗寨？」
「不，我跟著夜的聲音來。」

一抹鵝黃，轉深藍
石板古道，夜歸人
村寨裡，我的心情，被濃如墨的黑，渲染，暈開
家屋，亮起盞盞黃燈

月升，夜起，人寂
總有一個聲音
兩個，三四五個聲音
在你耳畔，低吟

遠方，響起，陣陣呼嘯與哨音
此起，彼落，腳步聲近了遠了

張家男孩走唐家
唐家男孩走張家
百年來你聆聽
這交表兄妹
古老的夜訪

指間輕扣輪轉，姑娘房外敲窗聲
嘟嘟嘟咚咚咚，一陣陣劃破沉寂

「阿姐，今晚誰來敲窗，都無妨。此心歸屬，待何時。」

老寨
聽見否
這夜末眠的心意……

———— 簡美玲

目次

序

　　本書初稿在我前往日本京都大學東南亞地域研究研究所（Center for Southeast Asian Studies, Kyoto University），訪學研修期間（2019 年 8 月至 2020 年 1 月）完成。在世界面臨無數變化的時代，民族誌的紀錄，有著多重的角色。本書所記錄的貴州東部高地村寨 Hmub 人的民族誌，始於二十到二十一世紀，跨世紀交替的時代；並論及西南中國周邊族群進入本世紀之後，隨著中國國家經濟的發展所經驗與回應的變遷。人類的書寫文明與口傳文化，不斷的變動與發展。以民族誌紀錄小地方的細微日常，其啓示與顯現的意義，是對人性與人類經驗進行記錄，並給我們的未來世代，留下寶貴記憶與經驗的一部分。本書以「物語」這個日本詞彙爲名，以表達本書的主題概念，帶有此深刻地感受與意涵。

　　在京都大學訪學期間，我常在土曜日（週六）的清晨，散步去京大吉田校園附近一家小小、優雅明亮的「小川 café」。咖啡店位於今出川通路邊，鄰近吉田神社北參道。我喜歡在那裡一邊享用附上咖啡的洋食早餐，一邊展開一天的閱讀與書寫。此店由一對上了年紀的老夫婦所經營。店中也有我喜歡讀的《每日新聞》與《京都新聞》。2019 年 10 月 19 日的《每日新聞》專欄，刊載了村上春樹在義大利發表的小說獲獎感言。村上春樹以「洞窟の中の小さなかがり火」（洞窟中的小篝火）來表述小說是人類遠古以來，說故事的經驗。而通過本書，我想表達這部記錄雲貴高地東部 Hmub 人村寨的民族誌，也是講述人類無數細膩日常與非日常經驗的故事文本，所以將「物語」放入了本書的標題。[1]

致謝詞

　　本書的完成，歷經期刊論文與專書論文之集結、修改、編輯與翻譯。這些作品首次出版於期刊或專書時，感謝每位匿名審查人，以及人類學、史學、哲學、語言學、傳播學界師長與同儕的討論與寶貴意見：Adam Yuet Chau、Shanshan Du、Elizabeth Hsu、William Jankowiak、Paul Kats、Jude Lam、Robert Parkin、Robert Shepherd、James Wilkerson、余舜德、朱炳祥、何菊、何翠萍、李亦園（1931-2017）、施傳剛、施崇宇、張珣、喬健（1935-2018）、徐新建、黃淑莉、鄧育仁、趙綺芳、鐘蔚文、劉子愷、劉塗中、盧彥杰、瞿明安。

　　此書的編輯，感謝陳玫妏、林廷豪、張乃文、潘怡潔、尤士豪、莊文昌，以及四川大學李菲老師所帶領的研究生，在過程中的重要協助。有你們的情義相挺，誠懇相助，此書方得以完備。在此也特別想對已到天上當天使的學生，乃文，說聲謝謝。編輯書稿過程中的討論，讓老師永遠難忘妳的聰慧與對知識的熱情。最後也在此說明，第四章〈田野裡的「聽」〉（"Cultivating the Ethnographer's Ear"）之中文譯版，原擬首刊於《文學人類學》2020 年 12 月號。惟全球發生 COVID-19 疫情，導致出刊有所延遲。是故此文中文譯版之首刊權，仍保留予該期刊。

　　十分感謝在歷經多年貴州人類學研究的過程中，由貴陽省城、台江縣城到清水江畔與高坡的山區村寨，所有協助我的長輩與友人。感謝陸委會中華發展基金會（1998-1999）、中央研究院民族所亞洲季風區高地與低地社會文化主題計畫（1999-2000）、國科會（2002、2004、2006-2007）、科技部（2010-2014）、國立陽明交通大學（2018-2021）、京都大學東南亞地域研究研究所（2018-2020），提供田野研究、書寫，與編輯等經費補助。最後感謝陽明交通大學出版社編輯部程惠芳與陳建安，所給予的溫暖支持，以及編輯、出版的協助。

田野相對位置

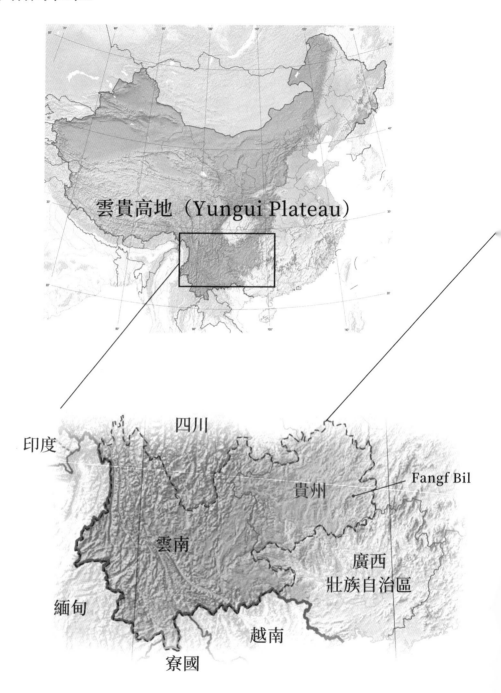

雲貴高地（Yungui Plateau）

四川

印度

貴州

Fangf Bil

雲南

廣西
壯族自治區

緬甸

越南

寮國

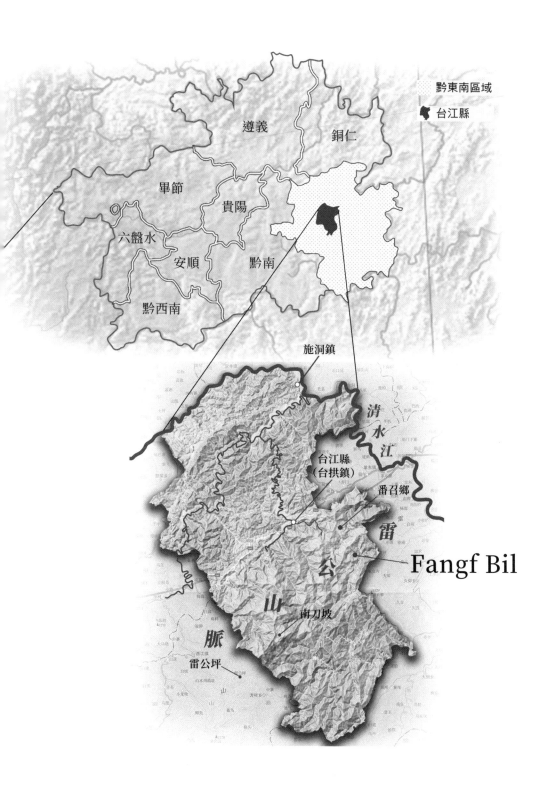

黔東南區域
台江縣

遵義
銅仁
畢節
貴陽
六盤水
安順
黔南
黔西南

施洞鎮
清水江
台江縣
（台拱鎮）
番召鄉
雷
公
Fangf Bil
山
南刀坡
脈
雷公坪

苗文（黔東方言）聲韻調表與國際音標（IPA）對照表

　　本書使用黔東方言苗文聲韻調系統（張永祥 1990）。這套語音系統包括的聲韻調範圍寬，筆者實際進行田野的 Fangf Bil 寨子的地方語音系統，都可以含括其中。苗文的語詞結構爲：聲母＋韻母＋聲調。

聲母：

苗文	IPA	苗文	IPA	苗文	IPA	苗文	IPA	苗文	IPA	苗文	IPA	苗文	IPA
b	p	p	p'	m	m	hm	m̥'	f	f	hf	f'	w	v
d	t	n	n	hn	n̥'	dl	ɬ	hl	ɬ'	l	l	z	ts
c	ts'	s	s	hs	s'	r	z	j	tɕ	q	tɕ'	x	ɕ
hx	ɕ'	y	ʐ	g	k	k	k'	ng	ŋ	v	ɣ	hv	x'
gh	q	kh	q'	h	h								

韻母：

苗文	IPA	苗文	IPA	苗文	IPA	苗文	IPA	苗文	IPA	苗文	IPA	苗文	IPA
i	i	e	əu	a	ɑ	o	o	u	u	ai	ɛ	ee	e
ao	ɑo	ei	ei	en	en	ang	aŋ	ong	oŋ	ia	ia	io	io
iu	iu	ie	iə	iee	ie	iao	iɑo	in	ien	iang	iaŋ	iong	ioŋ
ui	uei	ua	uɑ	uai	uɛ	un	uen	uang	uaŋ				

| b | 33（˧） | x | 55（˥） | d | 35（˧˥） | l | 11（˩） |
| t | 44（˦） | s | 13（˩˧） | k | 53（˥˧） | f | 31（˧˩） |

親屬稱謂代碼

　　本書使用的親屬稱謂代碼，依照人類學親屬研究傳統的英語符號縮寫體系（Barnard & Good 1984）。

F	father（父）	M	mother（母）	B	brother（兄弟）	Z	sister（姐妹）
S	son（兒子）	D	daughter（女兒）	H	husband（丈夫）	W	wife（妻子）
P	parent（父母）	C	child（子女）	G	sibling（兄弟姐妹）	E	spouse（配偶）

相對年齡

　　在相對年齡相關時，以 e 表示年長於，y 表示年幼於。若分別夾在另外兩個符號中間，分別表示其後面那個親人類型年長或幼於其前面那個，如 FeZ 表示父之姐，MyB 表示母之弟。若表示某類親人相對自我之年長或年幼，e 或 y 後置，例如：FBWBy 表示年幼於自我的父之兄弟之妻之兄弟，Be 表示兄，Zy 表示姐。

說話者的性別

當說話者的性別相關時，添加小寫符號（ms）表示男性說話者，（ws）表示女性說話者。例如：FZS（ws）表示就女性說話者而言的父之姐妹之兒子。

相對性別

簡練起見，在有必要時採用相對性別方法：以小寫符號 os 或（os）表示異性，ss 或（ss）表示同性。例如：G（os）表示 B（兄弟）和 Z（姐妹），PosGC 表示全部交表，即 FZS、FZD、MBS 和 MBD，PosGC（ss）表示全部與自我同性別的交表，即 FZS（ms）、MBS（ms）、FZD（ws）和 MBD（ws）。

導言

　　人類學的民族誌書寫以較微觀而具體細膩的風格，展開對人類經驗現象的描述與討論，以及對人類整體知識的探索與開拓，並持續展現其獨特性與重要性。人類學的理論議題、方法論與對區域研究的重視，與民族誌作爲瞭解人類經驗這一獨特的方法論與書寫文類有著緊密關聯。本書即是在區域、族群，以及人類學的理論議題與方法論等面向耕耘多年，並展現關懷的系列民族誌書寫。法國人類學家李維史陀（Lévi-Strauss 1969〔1949〕）指出複雜的聯姻類型在亞洲地區形成一個特殊性的區域。我從 1997 年開始，在中國西南少數民族地區從事人類學研究，至今逾二十年。以貴州東部高地 Hmub 人的親屬研究作爲例子，說明在村落的日常及儀式生活的實踐裡，交表聯姻是此一地方社會之維繫及鞏固的重要基礎。聯姻在此區域與人群經驗的關聯，除了有直接交換及普遍交換等婚姻結構的並置及轉變，也還在個人與集體，情感與結構上，展現聯姻社會的特殊性。亦即，在積極的婚姻體系裡，個人的選擇與情感，始終在面對社會並置的整體確定性與特定曖昧性。

　　通過民族誌來描述與闡述親屬與性別，婚姻與情感的特性、對話性，來探索人類社群在一區域歷史脈絡裡的社會性，以及個人與集體之間的對話張力，是我多年來研究與書寫的主軸。延續此基礎，本書則在三個面向上，持續深入書寫。一是從苗族親屬與情感、身體經驗與日常的村落民族誌書寫，討論看來微不足道的現象，所展現的社群與個人相互協商或積極對話，及其對於族群、社會或個人的瞭解，所凸顯的獨特意義與重要性；其二從身體感官經驗與文化心理的闡述，對人類學的田野方法提出反思與對話；其三則是在我長期進行田野研究的黔東南台江地區，結合生命史研究與語言人類學研究，討論家譜的編撰以及苗族民間口傳文學（古歌），面對書寫體系的介入，在記音與翻譯的過程中，以及展現行動者的主體性與知識的建構性。此三面向的研究成果，都在直面我多年來持續關注的 Hmub 人社群性與個人主體性，在歷史文化脈絡下的建構，及二者之間長久的協商，與持續對話的張力。最後也是面對 Hmub 人文化的傳統制度，習俗與口傳文本，在當代的重組、變遷與再現的歷程。以下從三個主題來簡述本書在西南中國的區域與族群研究的重要性，與人類學理論及方法論上的意義。

一、婚姻外的談情與調情：
民族詩學的人觀、情緒情感與社會理想的對話

　　婚姻與情感之間的複雜性，不僅是當代都會或工業文明的議題。在前工業的山田燒墾或農業社會的村寨社會，及與其通婚交換的區域，婚姻與情感之間，所再現的概念、形式與行動內容的協商與張力，對於瞭解該社會的族群文化有其意義。此一民族誌的材料與個案，對於人性處於婚姻制度與個人情感、情欲中的關係，也提供了一個重要的例子。有關不同文化的婚姻現象與理論，在人類學的親屬研究，十九世紀中葉以來，已然是一個古典議題（如 Lewis Henry Morgan 1871；Claude

Lévi-Strauss 1949；Rodney Needham 1960；Jack Goody 1971；Edmond Leach 1971）。至於情感與婚姻之間論述，則是仍有開展空間的領域（cf. Anthony Giddens 1992；Victor de Munk 1996）。以民族詩學的人觀、情緒情感與社會理想之對話性為主軸，本書第一部（一至三章）將在人類學親屬研究的理論脈絡裡，探討婚姻與情感的對話性與文化意義。

第一章〈婚姻外的談情與調情〉（“Extramarital Court and Flirt of Guizhou Hmub”），是我較初期嘗試以英文書寫村寨 Hmub 人的民族誌材料。[1] 英文書寫使得民族誌材料與人類學理論的對話，有著不同於華文書寫之討論與理解的節奏。村寨 Humb 人以兩種類型的婚姻外遊方談情與調情，面對人類社會普遍的婚姻與情感之間的關係。相對於婚姻，以談情（courtship）為專題的人類學研究較少，雖然人類學家布朗尼斯勞‧馬林諾夫斯基（Bronislaw Malinowski 1982〔1932〕）書寫的美拉尼西亞西北部部落族群的民族誌，已經描述與討論愛、性欲、巫術與神話，與該社會的談情制度。不過談情仍僅視為，為結婚而行之的準備階段，而非獨立存在的層面。貴州東部 Hmub 人的遊方，可能為人類社會相對普遍以專偶婚的文化邏輯解釋婚姻與情感的關係，提出另一種解釋觀點。因為他們所形成的談情與調情的天地，能在寬廣的社會約束裡，讓每個人的一生有較長時間，可在特定場合持續擁有個人情感與情欲的自主性。在村寨日常與儀式的脈絡裡，遊方突顯為兩類談情與調情的區域（two zones）。其一是長期遊方：不受婚姻局限，而能維繫一輩子的調情（flirting）關係；其二是短期遊方：談情（courting）以婚姻終結。

一直到二十一世紀初，貴州村寨 Hmub 人仍努力維持高度結構化與制度化之親屬為基底的社會。對於社會身分、年齡與性別，都有清楚的分類。以身體及語言展示的親密與戲謔，一方面再現交表親的聯姻關係，同時也穿透已婚與未婚的界線，以及稱謂與系譜的輩分關係。換言之，Hmub 人遊方的制度化談情與調情，除了成就婚姻與社會認同，重要的是，也在心理面向，確認情感與情欲是個人認同的重要機制。通過這個材料，Hmub 人在文化上所定義的不貞概念，著重在婚後的談情與調情，一種親密的形式，鮮少導向「性」的關係。透過公開展現情愛的談情，貴州東部高地 Hmub 人表露了人際交流場域的重要性。如亞當‧菲利普斯（Adam Phillips 2000〔1994〕）指出：「調情保持著遊戲的關係。藉此，我們能夠從不同觀點瞭解彼此。」Hmub 人的遊方談情與調情，顯示婚後或婚外遊方，扮演個人內在深處情感表達的出口。

　　第二章〈浪漫愛情與婚姻之間的張力：高地 Hmub 人情歌展演的文化個體性〉（"Tensions between Romantic Love and Marriage: Performing 'Hmub Cultural Individuality' in an Upland Hmub Love-Song"），[2]以高地 Hmub 人的情歌與文化個人性的展演，呼應前一章所述，浪漫情感與婚姻之間所擁有的張力。本章的英文民族誌書寫，是在我的師長，清華大學人類學研究所教授魏捷茲（James Russell Wilkerson），與應邀來訪的英國牛津大學人類學系教授羅伯特‧帕金（Robert Parkin），在 2006 年夏天，於清華大學人文社會學院舉辦的英文民族誌寫作工作坊中形成。此寫作歷程，存在著一個人類學者，面對民族誌描述與討論的孤獨歷程；同時也超越了前者，是西南研究群的師長及同儕，一起討論與實作民族誌材料的再現，以及由華文書寫轉換為英文書寫的差異與對話。這個參與、討論、書寫、改寫的過程，有著探索與再現民族誌知識的深刻意味。

民間口傳文學與情緒情感之表述及地方文化的關聯（Abu-Lughod 1986；Bauman 1977；Bauman and Briggs 1990；Ben-Amos 1971、1972、1998），以及路易・杜蒙（Louis Dumont 1986）所指出的「在地與文化個人主義」，是我關注 Hmub 人情歌與婚姻遊方關係的理論背景。在民族詩學與文化展演的角度裡，即興對唱的四百多行情歌，與社會生活進行了積極的連結。二十與二十一世紀之交的年代，村寨實際展演的形式與行動，以詩學的語言形式，再現農業為主的村寨社會，突出文化上的個人性，並在交表婚姻的社會制度約束裡，再現屬於個人的情感內容。Hmub 人觀點裡的個人性（indivdidulity），展現出一種詩學美感的現代性（the sense of modernity）。我們所能觀察到諸多聯姻的社會理想與實踐；Hmub 人所意識到的個人認同；個人情緒情感與好幾層聯姻結構化脈絡之間的拉扯——都具體表現在情歌歌詞與對歌展演，以及圍觀、聆聽的人群與社會行動裡。然而情歌歌詞所再現之 Hmub 文化下個人主義的現代性，並非朝向西方社會的個人主義發展。Hmub 文化下的文化個人主義的特性，是集體理想（村寨內婚、交表聯姻），與個人情緒情感（戲謔歡愉；若隱若現的婚外遊方調情裡細微的情與欲；個人孤寂的表述）之間，持續、久遠的協商與對話。這些都透過情歌的展演，合法化 Hmub 人社會與個人之間，複雜但確定的關係。並且重要的是，四周圍觀的聽眾裡，通常包含許多村寨年輕人。無論是明白或象徵，在本世紀更為險峻的變遷來臨之前，村寨 Hmub 人的文化與社會理想，個人情感與社會理想的拉扯與對話，仍通過詩學的社會實踐形式與內涵，世代往下傳遞。

　　透過語言人類學的理論視野，第三章〈「你倆是我倆一輩子的丈夫」：情歌語言的兩性意象與結伴理想〉，[3] 討論 Hmub 人情歌語彙的兩性意象與結伴理想。此章的書寫，由初稿到成稿的過程，感謝受過語言人類學紮實訓練的兩位學弟，施崇宇博士與劉子愷博士。電郵往返間的討論，帶給我深刻啓發與寶貴建議。1999 年春天，我與 Fangf Bil 村寨的姑娘，一起去看幾個鄰近村寨聯合舉行的鬥牛。結束後，天色已晚，我與姑娘們仍在附近逗留。此時，環繞四周山坡，大型的跨村寨遊方與對歌正熱鬧展開。在遊方現場，我們幸運的記錄了一場長達四百多句的即興對歌。在聽寫、翻譯、分析這部對歌的過程中，令我印象十分深刻的，不僅是對歌的語意內涵，表達出婚姻理想與個人情感的豐富張力（參第二章）。貴州東部高地村寨 Hmub 人在情歌歌詞裡，還運用大量表徵性別與人的人稱語詞同義字與語彙組合。由此展現多樣、反覆的語彙聚合，傳達情人、夫妻兩類結伴理想的交錯、並置。

語言在人類社會生活，具有參與的積極性與有效性（Bauman and Briggs 1990）。它不僅傳達語意，語言活動本身，也是一種獨特的社會行動。對特定語言活動進行微觀分析，可以達到對特定社會文化情景脈絡（context），進行描述與理解的效力。Hmub 人情歌語言的符號活動，聚焦在結伴與個人兩範疇之並置與流動的性別意象。亦即，在語言的演述場域裡，Hmub 人再現對等的性別意象，而有別於該社會結合從夫、從父居的父系繼嗣體系，以男性共祖爲唯一原則的家屋兄弟群，所展現對於父系理想與男性聲望的堅持。再者有如馬歇爾·牟斯（Marcel Mauss 1979）、米歇爾·羅薩多（Michelle Rosaldo 1980）所示，族群的特性或界線，往往也通過人觀來呈顯個體、自我、社會人，在該社會的分類範疇與意義。通過個人與結伴兩類人稱語彙的對照，以及情人、交表親、夫妻等人稱語彙之間的任意置換，Hmub 人情歌語言展現的性別意象，蘊含以交表聯姻爲核心價值，以及個人與集體之流動的人觀。總而言之，情歌語言的性別意象與 Hmub 人的人觀緊密結合。

貴州東部 Hmub 人的情歌內容，不僅細微一致地唱和著交表聯姻為底層的社群理想，而且語言符號的演述活動本身，讓個人價值在期待聯姻結群的優勢氛圍裡，低調卻穩定地現身。本章指出三種語言符號活動所演述的 Hmub 人性別意象：一、男女歌者有序的輪唱，突出兩性對唱與性別對等意象的象似（iconic）關係；二、親屬稱謂等人稱語彙的組合、解組、替換，標示著歌者在性別認同的主體性與流動性（兩性合一與兩性分立），突顯語言符號與性別意象的指示（indexical）關係；三、通過人稱語彙同義詞的大量群聚與重復，以圖形的象似性，展現 Hmub 人情歌語彙，以語意之外的符號活動，創造出涵蘊 Hmub 人觀的性別意象。換言之，Hmub 人情歌語言符號行動在同一場域演述著性別差異的創造與模糊。差異，不必然是相互排除的對立，也可以在建構兩性有所區辨（分立）的對照中，並存著彼此支援（結伴）的正向力量。

二、身體、感官與遊方的日常性

　　2004 年至今，我長期參與中央研究院民族學研究所研究員余舜德老師召集的身體經驗研究群的定期聚會，進行閱讀、書寫與討論。我們通過人類學、哲學、文學、現象學、史學等跨領域學科，探索以身體感為核心概念的身體經驗與認知、社會、歷史、文化的關聯。我受到余舜德、鐘蔚文、張珣、鄧育仁、羅正心、郭奇正、蔡璧名、丁亮，多位師長與同儕夥伴帶來的啟發。[4] 在此研究群相互學習的機緣與激盪下，我對於雲貴高地村寨 Hmub 人民族誌田野資料的描述與理解，開始將重點延伸至更直接面對田野工作裡所觀察與記錄的情緒、情感與身體經驗的民族誌材料，並據此反思人類學田野研究方法與文化理論構成的歷程與脈絡。

人類學與民族誌對於情緒與情感的研究，基本上以更為人文的關懷，強調社會、文化與歷史，乃至政治、經濟與全球化、新自由主義與情緒及情感的關聯。人類學的田野與民族誌對於情緒及情感的書寫，所展現的材料及論述的村落或都市邊緣的處境或語境裡，其實不僅是情緒與情感單面向的經驗，它們通常也交織著身體的經驗，並通過此（以身體感為名）向外面世界（不論是村落、部落，或都市邊緣）進行探試、闖蕩，或向內在與自我進行獨白式的對談。幾部特定年代與類型的民族誌（書寫作品），如米歇爾·羅薩多（Michel Rosado）的《知識與激情：伊隆戈人的自我和社會生活觀念》（*Knowledge and Passion: Ilongot Notions of Self and Social Life*, 1980）、凱瑟琳·盧茨（Catherine Lutz）的《非自然的情感：密克羅尼西亞環礁上的日常情感及其對西方理論的挑戰》（*Unnatural Emotions: Everyday Sentiments on a Micronesian Atoll and Their Challenge to Western Theory*, 1988）都以各具特色的風格與內容，展現了情緒、情感與身體經驗的交織特性，既是與人類學的學科史、知識論、方法論有其不可分之關聯（一種相互構成的關係），並且也讓我們對於人與社群的書寫與理解，擁有一種更靠近現實（包括想像之現實）的可能性。也就是，如羅伯特·扎榮茨（R. B. Zajonc 1980）[5] 所說的，情緒或情感雖不是那麼精確卻總是在那裡。我們以身體感的觀點來延伸與包含情緒或情感與身體不可分的觀察、體驗與書寫的立足點，試圖掌握住較為「自然」與「實際」狀態下的人與社群。

延續此，本書第二部（四至五章）的核心關懷，在於通過日常生活裡的情緒、情感與身體經驗的人類學研究與民族誌書寫，反思研究方法與書寫的行動與倫理。由此探索身體感的理論概念，如何使民族誌研究與書寫更確實地紀錄、描寫與解釋個人或群體社會生活的複雜性。尤其，當身體與情緒或情感的現象，同處於一種平凡、平淡到近乎無趣，或者分散、流動的脈絡時。在前述的基礎下，討論與闡述身體感與情緒、情感之間的微妙界線。再者本書第二部，也將回到歷史與社會文化的脈絡，說明身體經驗的探索，不僅在於回應文化對個人經驗的模塑與構成。貴州東部高地村寨 Hmub 人的煩悶與解悶的情緒、情感與身體感的日常性，突顯的流動與中介特性，實也標記世紀交疊的年代，雲貴高地深山的農村社會，已靜靜涉入當代中國社會資本主義與市場經濟的轉型與變革裡。

第四章〈田野裡的「聽」〉（"Cultivating the Ethnographer's Ear"），[6] 以我在 Hmub 人村寨田野裡以聽為主的研究經驗，反思民族誌研究方法裡的身體感官經驗與知識論。本章的英文民族誌書寫，是與身體經驗研究群的夥伴，在合作撰寫有關鍛鍊、規訓、練習與身體經驗或身體感之形成與轉變時形成。就理論的關懷，攸關感官人類學（Paul Stoller 1989）、身體經驗與感知的文化研究（Mary Douglas 1966；Clifford Geertz 1973；Pierre Bourdieu 1977；Tim Ingold 2000），以及民族誌田野研究方法與知識論的反思（Carlos Castaneda 1998〔1969〕）。百年來，在人類學的學科史，民族誌田野一直有其核心位置。本章指出民族誌田野不僅積極產出人類學知識，並也涉入身體修練，進而影響個人情緒、人類學者之專業自我與認同。

本章討論在貴州東部大山裡的 Hmub 人村寨，研究者以民族誌學徒之身，進行遊方的田野。以此闡述田野的聽與寫作為一種身體修練，既是關乎個人學習與瞭解的一種靠近人類普遍的經驗，亦是特定文化脈絡下的社會建構。人類學家保羅·斯托勒（Paul Stoller）提醒我們，人類學與民族誌的探索過程中，感官的使用應該是更多層次的。例如，聲調與聲音（tone and sound） 都對於地方文化的描述與闡釋，具有重要的價值。幸運的話，在我們自身的人類學學徒歷程中，也能學到斯托勒在田野工作所習得的經驗：用心傾聽能幫助民族誌學者透過身體感官的溝通與互動，而瞭解地方文化的意義。本章描述我在民族誌田野裡的學徒經驗，探索「我聽」與「我寫」兩者之間的關聯，以及此二者如何影響並轉變我對雲貴高地村寨 Hmub 人文化，與自身的內在瞭解。其意義與細節之所在，不僅來自深夜敲窗聲的內容與音韻風格，更是聆聽與傾聽的經驗本身。後者串起好幾層不同個人情緒，並予以轉變。此情緒經驗的變化過程，也涉及了研究者對於自己作為民族誌田野工作者的認同。深夜敲窗聲的聽與對聽的訓練，使文化挫折、衝擊與害怕、無所適從的感受，到熟悉的情緒轉變得以呈顯，研究者因此感同身受的進入 Hmub 人未當家之年輕姑娘情緒與情感的內心世界。

　　第五章〈煩悶、日常與村寨 Humb 人的遊方〉，[7]與前章寫作歷程相呼應，也是我多年來參與身體經驗研究群的書寫成果。研究群夥伴們以各自的田野民族誌材料或史學、文學資料，以特定理論視角，討論身體感與日常生活在經驗上，與理論上的關聯。我通過貴州東部高地村寨的田野民族誌材料，描述與探討遊方與 Hmub 人的日常生活，與日常性浮現的關聯。遊方的日常性與所開展的社會意義，超越了僅是年輕人的談情說愛，或為婚姻而行的準備階段。遊方文獻可以溯及十九世紀以前（如〔明〕郭子章《黔記》卷 59）。直至 1920 至 1950 年代，就社會科學觀點在貴州進行的少數民族調查，吳澤霖、陳國均等貴州民族學研究的前輩，均關注遊方或跳月等具制度傾向的談情在 Hmub 人社會，相對突顯的社會意義。不過，在過去的遊方文獻尚未從理論的視域涉及兩個重要的屬性：遊方的日常性（everydayness）與社會性（sociality）。本章面對貴州 Hmub 人的個人與社群所經驗的遊方，具體展現與工作、休閒、日常生活、個人主體性的微細關聯——而不僅是作爲婚姻的附屬。這樣的研究取向，既是築基於古典的民族誌敘述與討論，並也深受當代以日常生活作爲探索人類經驗場域的討論所啓發（Lefebvre 1958；Certeau 1984；Highmore 2002）。

換言之，以日常生活、工作及休閒作爲理論視域與探討的經驗範疇，我重返 1998 年至 2000 年在雲貴高地村寨田野記錄的日常遊方與節慶遊方，並通過此對遊方的日常性與社會性，進行描述與解釋。煩悶（rat）與身體經驗，將遊方與日常，以及個人與社會之間被隱藏的關聯予以體現並釋出。煩悶的身體經驗與感受，雖不直接在遊方內，卻是一種特定也實際的身體經驗。一方面它具體表達遊方與地方社會裡特定個人的關聯；另一方面如此流動的，中介在個人與社會的身體經驗，也是形成遊方之特定氛圍與場域的共構者。總之在解讀遊方本質的過程裡，煩悶經驗的呈現，是一個頗爲突出的關鍵。通過它具體的中介，一方面暗示著遊方不僅是一個爲婚姻而儲備的社會機制，同時也可能與工作、休閒、日常生活，以及個人主體性的重構，具體而微建立一種特定關聯。其次，識字與教育或電視與報紙所儲備的文字能力與對外在世界訊息的掌握，影響村寨 Hmub 人的移動 （打工、出外求學、旅行），並也直接與間接影響工作、休閒與日常的內涵與形式。換言之，煩悶以可言說與不便言明之形式並置之際，也就是村寨 Hmub 人重構其主體性的當下：有意識的經驗可消解與轉化的煩與悶。此身體經驗的探索，不僅在於回應文化對個人的影響，煩悶（rat）的消解（或尋趣）所突顯的流動與中介特性，也可能標記出上世紀中葉以來中國國家所經歷的社會主義變革，與社會資本主義經濟自由化增速的當代情境及語境裡，雲貴高地東部村寨 Hmub

人的遊方與個人以及村寨社會之間交錯糾結的關係與變遷。

三、歌師的手稿與 Hmub 人的漢字家譜： 口說與文字對話裡，主體書寫的浮現[8]

口說、文字與邊陲性之構成，是我另一個長期的研究興趣。對於從民間口傳文學來討論社群或族群文化，可以回到 1990 年代初期，我對臺灣阿美族起源神話類型與文化類緣之研究與書寫。[9]這幾年則開始由口說及文字性文本的使用、再現及流傳，探討貴州 Hmub 人社群對於空間、人觀等不同文化範疇的界定；並也討論他們如何通過語言展現地方社會的特性，及其與國家或中心的關係與對話性。本書第三部（六至七章）的核心關懷，即在於此。並分別通過歌師手稿，與環繞一部貴州東部的 Hmub 人與 Kam 人聯譜的漢字家譜為主體，進而展開的民族誌書寫。

第六章〈Hmub 人古歌的記音與翻譯：歌師 Sangt Jingb 的手稿、知識與空間〉[10]的理論關懷之一，是有如寶拉‧魯貝爾（Paula Rubel）與亞伯拉罕‧羅斯曼（Abraham Rosman）在《翻譯文化：關於翻譯和人類學的觀點》（*Translating Cultures: Perspectives on Translation and Anthropology,* 2013）一書所指出的，人類學以揭開不同文化之間的深度關連，為其知識產出與闡釋的獨特性。按理說，翻譯應該在這過程中，扮演重要角色。但一直以來，它在人類學學科史，卻是被忽視的。百年來人類學的研究，並沒有針對民族誌與田野資料的翻譯，建立起有系統的方法論。田野研究法在十九世紀至二十世紀初的人類學雖已日趨成熟，但民族誌資料蒐集過程中的翻譯，則未被重視。延續如是關懷，本章討論記音、翻譯與民族誌文化理解之間的關聯。

記音與翻譯這兩個語言行動，從語意上來看是可以區別的：翻譯（translation）是兩種語言之間的轉換，記音（transcription）則是將聽到的語音或聲音寫下來。本章以貴州東部一位歌師所寫的古歌手稿，作爲民族誌案例，描述與探討，翻譯與記音的語言現象與意義轉換，無法脫離建構與多義本質。這是一位 Hmub 人歌師的生命史與古歌手稿之間的故事。1999 年底至 2000 年初千禧年之際的雲貴高地寒冬與雪季裡，我處於博士論文民族誌田野的後期階段。爲了學習清水江一帶傳唱的古歌，以及古歌所展現的清水江與雷公山一帶人群的遷徙與集聚，因緣際會和一位清水江畔的 Hmub 人歌師 Sangt Jingb，有較深刻的相知與往來。並也因爲跟他學習古歌，得以有緣探入歌師的生命史與古歌之於他的奇幻知性之旅。在民族誌田野的過程裡，閱讀、聆聽、筆記，歌師逐字、逐句對我講述他記音、翻譯的古歌手稿，與即興手繪古歌內容的圖稿。博士論文完成多年後，我才得以回頭思考、整理、分析與重新理解，歌師當初所教我的種種古歌知識。

爲了較有系統的瞭解歌師與古歌之間，所展現的口說與文字之間的關聯，以及此現象流通在清水江一帶的古歌傳唱與書寫文化，2006–2007 年之際，在科技部（當年的國科會）研究經費支持下，我在完成博士論文後，第三度返回貴州東部進行民族誌田野研究。由貴陽、凱里到台江縣城與周邊村寨，再訪 Sangt Jingb 等十餘位黔東南地區的 Hmub 人歌師，並紀錄他們的生命史與對古歌的學習與創作。其中包含家鄉來自台江，後來旅居貴陽，且在貴州的苗文化界，有相當影響力的唐春芳先生（1919–2007）與今旦先生（1930–）。他們是許多人都認識且敬仰的苗文化創作與研究前輩。

　　本章是在前述的探索背景下，轉入以 Sangt Jingb 爲主的個人民族誌書寫。我認識、交往、請益的歌師前輩，都各有其獨特性，也有一些作爲苗族歌師的普遍經驗，Sangt Jingb 亦如是。一方面有其凸顯的個人獨特性，也多少能傳達某些普遍性。本章以 Sangt Jingb 的歌師生命史等民族誌田野資料，以及古歌手稿《跋山涉水》（*Nangx Eb Jit Bil*）爲素材，探討歌師同時作爲口傳民間文學的傳遞者，苗語記音書寫者與漢字的翻譯者，在苗語記音文本與漢字翻譯文本相互構成的過程中，出現的斷裂與縫隙，流瀉與再現的知識，以及跨越時間線性界線的空間意象。再者從民族誌角度探索歌師作爲譯者，以及整理手稿材料多年後，華特・班雅明（Walter Benjamin）對於譯者天職的討論，啓發我不僅在文本語言材料的分析，看到譯者的操作性，並也得以在譯者本性的概念層次，重新整理及思索，研究者與歌師的認識與交往，以及接觸與研究古歌手稿以來的內在衝擊。當譯者同時也是創作者，他所要做的，雖然是從一個文本（原著）轉變到另一個文本（譯本）。但如果引用班雅明的理論觀點，則歌師本身不一定有所本，也不一定是爲讀者而寫。歌師 Sangt Jingb 的生命史經驗與古歌書寫**計畫**，回應班雅明以歷史解釋譯者、譯本與原著之間的神秘關聯。歌師 Sangt Jingb 的個人生命史，歷經 1960 年代的大躍進與文化大革命，中國國家大步經濟改革的 1980、90 年代，直至上一世紀的結束，新世紀的開始。苗人古歌的學習與傳唱，苗語文的學習與寫作，十二部古歌的記音與漢字譯述，以及後期對於出版這批古歌手稿的渴望，共同構成歌師與其記誦口語材料以及文字書寫行動的生命史。換言之，譯者與文本的關係，不僅關乎譯者的美學或哲學處境，更是源於歷史的偶遇：個人的微型生命史與其所生處與糾結的時代、國家、地方、族群，與歷史的處境。

　　第七章〈貴州東部漢字家譜裡的文化政治：無名之聲與作者權威〉（"Anonymous Voices and Authorship Politics in Printed Genealogies in Eastern Guizhou"），[11] 以我在清水江流域 Hmub 人（苗族）與 Kam 人（侗族）的跨族群村寨田野民族誌材料，討論在漢字家譜與漢字姓氏、父系宗族理想結合的社會結構與理想裡，家譜的變裝與作者權力的現身，以及由此所構成及展現的語言與文化政治。本章的英文民族誌書寫，經過較長時間的寫作與修改。過程中感謝多位老師與同僑閱讀初稿，與提供寶貴意見。本文最後完備於康豹（Paul Kats）老師所召集的《亞洲族群研究》（*Asian Ethnicity*）期刊專號：〈宗教與族群〉（"Religion and Ethnicity"）。在面對西南周邊區域，跨族群及語群結盟動員的漢字家譜文本，與行動交錯的複雜現象，本章主要通過語言人類學觀點的分析視域來完成。十分感謝當年在美國芝加哥大學、伊利諾大學求學的施崇宇博士、劉子愷博士與我通過電郵多次往返、討論。兩位學弟對這批語言人類學民族材料的精彩提點，多年後仍令我深刻體認，如是經驗分享與交流，始終是本章靈魂之所在。

　　本章在基礎理論的開展上，擬回應殖民語言研究、社會語言學、語言人類學所關切的議題：邊陲社會的文字性，與語言歷程的差異化（dissimilar linguistic processes）。如戴爾・海姆斯（Dell Hymes）所指出的，語言的雙語化（bilingualism）、混成化（creolization）、國家化（linguistic nationalism）、標準化（standardization）的過程，在在充斥著差別、異質的語言經歷。而這些都與歐洲的擴張以及世界史的發展相互交錯（Hymes 1964；Gal 1989：345-6；Gal 1998: 317-331）。

蘇珊·蓋爾（Suzan Gal 1989）在〈語言與政治經濟〉（"Language and Political Economy"）的語言人類學文獻回顧中也強調，地方的說話行動，不只局限在地方層次，而應該連結到更大的歷史過程與不平等權力系統。邊陲社會或殖民社會文字性所產生的異質語言經驗，不僅出現在說話、會話語言行動（如 Errinton 1998），也表現於書寫文類。延伸戴爾·海姆斯的想法，蘇珊·蓋爾（1989、1998）強調文類多版本特性，權威文類（dominant genres）與被宰制文類（dominated genres）的對比，以及知識分子、精英通過書寫行動，創造與再現文化、政治意識形態，與權力、位置等複雜關聯。

在前述理論脈絡裡，本章探討位於西南中國的邊陲地帶，貴州東部少數民族地方菁英通過文本書寫、編輯，所建立的作者權威與文化政治（the politics of authorship）。這部由地方菁英產出與流通的漢字家譜，不僅公開地連結、跨越族群、語群界線，同時也通過語言現象，有力地構成與宣稱，邊陲族群與國家之間所存在的縫隙。本章要探討，清水江流域的 Hmub 人與 Kam 人，聯合編輯、印刷與流通的《劉氏族譜》（1908年清光緒版的老譜與 1985 年版的新譜）。通過這兩部前後版本的漢字家譜，他們有力地宣稱，住在台江施洞地區的劉姓 Hmub 人，與住在天柱藍田地區的劉姓 Kam 人，都是北方南遷，擁有血緣關聯的漢族弟兄。但是除了積極宣稱彼此擁有父系共祖的關聯，族譜的書寫者，卻同時採取另一種策略，不對族譜內容承擔文責。族譜的整體內容與其他文本（如譜序、譜詩、後世子嗣的字輩與名號）之間，產生文本交錯的互文性（intertextuality）。在鞏固族譜作者權威之際，也策略地將其解構。

一方面，通過出版的家譜，地方菁英對於祖先與父系世系群的敘述，構成一套強而有力的父系血緣價值體系。並以此直接促成文本的作者權威。然而，在此同時，這兩部族譜羅列的子孫名號，卻出現以漢字表述「非人稱」的苗語記音符號，並由此讓 Hmub 人傳統的父子聯名體系，得以現身。換言之，漢字作爲非人稱的苗語語音記音符號，形成包覆在族譜書寫裡的「第三聲音」；以「匿名聲音」潛入與浮現於家譜文本。這讓家譜編輯與流通所構成的文本作者性，呈現流動狀態——由外顯、公開表述之集體作者權威性，轉爲隱密與分散的匿名性。

四、小結

蒂姆·英戈爾德（Tim Ingold）在《對環境的感知：生計、居住與技能》（*The Perception of the Environment: Essays on Livelihood, Dwelling and Skill*, 2000）一書，提醒我們，涂爾幹（Durkheim 1915）所關注的，在一些特定時光與片刻（如儀式之進行），個人私下的感知，如何再現於社群與公眾場域的理論觀點，持續影響著瑪麗·道格拉斯（Mary Douglas 1966）、克利弗德·紀爾茲（Clifford Geertz 1973）與皮耶·布迪厄（Pierre Bourdieu 1977）。道格拉斯偏重時間，與云云眾生對其所在世界之感受；紀爾茲以人在社會空間裡，感知身處的世界，並以此經驗提煉意義；布迪厄指出身體姿勢、行動與多重感官經驗，經由日復一日慣常操演，練就人處身於世的事實。點出多重感官經驗與其所身處世界的關聯，是作爲瞭解人與文化的基礎。就人類學而言，這也和民族誌書寫文類之特性緊密相依（簡美玲 2015）。

我認爲民族誌作爲研究方法、書寫行動或作品文類，靠近人的多重感官經驗。因爲它是一種素樸、草擬手稿的書寫經驗，並由此包容渾沌樣態。情緒情感與多重感官的民族誌書寫，有如米歇爾・傅柯（Michel Foucault 1984）對於檔案的陳述：檔案由物、時間、形式、品味，諸多交錯構成的異質空間，最終關聯著我們所置身的現代性。民族誌的草擬特性，可捕捉或記錄錯綜複雜的情緒與身體感官經驗。我將其稱爲糾纏現象的書寫文類、策略與計畫。尤其在全球化、殖民與後殖民、新自由主義不斷捲入或大或小的個人、地方社會與社群的過往、當下與未來，民族誌對於情緒情感與多重感官身體經驗的紀錄，或許有如一部部的檔案，以交錯之異質空間，再現我們處身於世的時代性（簡美玲 2015）。

在研究與書寫的過程中，民族誌此一獨特性，對我而言正是最迷人之所在。本書七個篇章，一者以微觀的情緒情感與身體感官經驗及日常，闡述對於 Hmub 人村寨地方社會，及其親屬爲底蘊之社會性與個人性的探索；一者以歌師生命史與古歌分析，及探入地方菁英家譜書寫與文本作者特性，表達對歷史民族誌書寫的嘗試。

總之，完備此民族誌專書，對我自 1997 年至 2014 年，跨越十餘年頭，歷經數個階段，進入雲貴高地東部，自有其深刻意義。本書之田野，首先沿著清水江流域與雷公山地區，展開以台江山區 Fangf Bil 村寨，及其鄰近高坡 Hmub 人社群的交表聯姻與情感爲主的親屬人類學蹲點研究。而後隨著我探索 Hmub 人之口語歌謠傳唱，跨越至討論以文字書寫爲媒介的歌師古歌記音與翻譯，以及 Hmub 人與 Kam 人合譜的漢字家譜編寫、印刷、流通。本書所涉及的田野地理空間，還包含靠近清水江兩岸，以 Hmub 人社群爲主的凱里、台江、施洞、黃平，以及 Kam 人社群爲主，鄰近湘黔交界的天柱。我的民族誌研究，是以親屬爲底蘊之社會爲主，進行村寨整體之描述與闡釋。同時關注個人的主體性，情緒、情感、身體感等主觀經驗，及其與社會整體理想的對話性。因此環繞著我的妹妹 Ghaif Wangk 姑娘，我喊舅舅的歌師 Sangt Jingb 的生命史經驗與敘事，可說是本書靈魂之所在。

最後，本書各章節之主題互有關聯，但仍有各自獨立之討論，因而部分描述有所重覆。爲保留各章節主體與原始脈絡，評估過後，仍保留其中重覆之部分，特此說明。

Part I

民族詩學裡的人觀與情感

Extramarital Court and Flirt of Guizhou Hmub

Chapter 1　婚姻外的談情與調情

不會有任何一個社會的女人對她們伴侶婚外的風流韻事毫不關心。[1] 即使是對於兩性中的「性」採取雙重標準的社會，大多數女人面對她們的伴侶與另一位女人發生性關係，仍會焦慮不安與忿怒。多數的女人認為，即使是一段偶然短暫的性關係，亦有可能逐漸地破壞婚姻的束縛。因此，無休止的警戒是必要的。大部分婚外風流韻事的研究，都只著重於所在社群對此的反應態度。本研究注意到有些雙重標準的社會裡，男人牽涉到風流是被容許的，然而女人則否。有些文化則是將感情與性的牽涉作了區別。例如，發展心理學家發現美國女性清楚地區別了感情的出軌與性的出軌之間的差異。對於美國女性，婚姻中情感消逝或其他關係的威脅，大於伴侶與陌生人偶然的一段性關係。概括而言，美國年輕男性較為在意伴侶在性方面的忠貞，相對的，美國女性則較重視伴侶在情感上的忠貞。[2] 然而，仍少有文獻探討女性如何看待伴侶在正式或非正式場合與他人的談情或調情。[3]

　　Fangf Bil 是一個苗族村寨，位於貴州清水江上游處的山腰上，形成黔東中央苗族北方群的一部分。[4] 當地居民自稱為 Hmub，與 Hmong 為同族源的分支。這個村寨在 1998 到 2000 年之間由超過三百三十個家庭組成，約一千五百人。它被區分為十一個小寨（vangf）。每個小寨的居民都歸於某個父系宗族底下後裔的一部分，並共享一個常見的漢人姓氏（如姓張或姓唐）。1998 至 2000 年我到此進行民族誌田野研究。當我第一次聽說這個寨子的男女談情或調情是可以出現在婚姻之外時，十分疑惑當丈夫刻意地在晚間與其他女子談情或調情時，男人的妻子是否會感到忿怒或嫉妒。不過寨子裡的叔伯媽跟我說：「不會的，我並不會因為丈夫在夜晚唱歌給別的女人聽而生氣。因為有女人要聽他唱歌，表示他有副好嗓子。」

本章以談情或調情這兩個詞彙來解釋 Fangf Bil 村寨的遊方。我將會通過民族誌細節，說明遊方在當地如何被定義與使用。簡略而言，遊方對於寨子的 Hmub 人來說，能夠穿透未婚與已婚的界線，創造一個婚姻外談情或調情的區域（flirting zone）。Hmub 人的婚外談情文化，與西南中國的另一支少數民族拉祜（Lahu）形成明顯對比。拉祜族伴侶間的親密關係，與一夫一妻制婚姻為同一事物。愛情表現在婚姻中夫妻兩人的和諧與相互配合。[5] 雖然村寨 Hmub 人的婚姻也行一夫一妻的專偶制，尤其夫妻關係一直持續至往生（這可以從 Hmub 人在各種生命儀禮，都以成對公婆，來喊祖先的信仰與行動看出）。但是一夫一妻的專偶關係，似乎與制度性的婚姻外談情與調情並不衝突。我在這一章將指出貴州 Hmub 人的遊方，可能為人類的婚姻及情感的關係，提出一種特定的解釋。因為他們所形成的談情或調情的習俗，能在村寨整體的社會約束裡，讓每個男人或女人的一生有較長時間，可在特定場合，自主表達個人情感乃至情欲。換言之，在日常及儀式脈絡裡，Hmub 人遊方突顯為兩種類型或特性。其一是不受婚姻局限，而能維繫一輩子的談情關係。其二是短期的談情：後者所指的就是遊方伴侶結為夫妻的婚姻關係。相對的，呼應前者的則有遊方情歌對唱的歌詞所展現的婚姻與談情／調情非一對一的對應性；以及親密的身體語言互動背後，遊方男女的系譜網絡為已婚與未婚可交錯並置的交表姻親身分。本章探討村寨 Hmub 人如何在一個高度結構化與制度化，以及在社會身分、年齡與性別有文化上之清楚分類的社會，仍能爲個人私密的情感與情緒創造一個共享且獨特的天地。換言之，Hmub 人遊方的制度性談情與調情，除了指向婚姻，並也是一種社會機制，讓他們對自我的認同，不只是社會人（這是親屬與婚姻的古典文獻主要探討方向），同時也是心理人。亦即遊方除了成就婚姻與社會認同，也在心理的層面確認情感與情欲是形成與維繫個人認同的重要內容。

一、談情與婚姻

就美拉尼西亞西北部原始族群之性生活，人類學家馬林諾夫斯基注意到「性」這樣的主題，必須放諸所屬的習俗制度背景裡來探討。[6] 在早期的人類學文獻，談情多半未被認爲是個重要的習俗。馬林諾夫斯基是少數的例外。他認爲，愛、情欲、巫術與神話，共同形塑特定的談情文化。然而，他的理論尚未涉及談情在人群的社會生活裡是否自成其特有的完備性。馬林諾夫斯基表示：「談情是一個階段，婚姻的準備階段，而婚姻又僅是家庭生活的一個層面。」[7] 即使馬林諾夫斯基強調談情的功能性，他總是將之視爲較大社會建構的一部分，而不認爲談情在社會功能之外還有獨立存在的面向。談情的社會功能往往被過於簡單的連繫到婚姻的締結。另有一些美國談情文化研究也發現，儘管美國年輕人在挑選伴侶時相對自主，但「在遇見未來伴侶前，他們平均只經歷兩段親密關係」。[8] 根據這項發現我們或可說，美國人的談情與婚姻，與美拉尼西亞人的談情與婚姻，並無太大差異。

相對於前述人類學或社會學文獻，主要討論談情爲婚姻的準備階段；以敘事或展演爲主的文學研究，則指出談情的不同面向，以及談情與婚姻非必然關聯的特性。這些文學作品探究談情與婚姻之間糾纏的關係。[9] 如艾倫・羅絲曼（Ellen Rothman）透過分析日記、書信等史料檔案，強調個人經驗和談情的敘事性，並指出「談情並非線性進程，而是一種參雜期待、經驗、習俗的混合物〔……〕談情的本質抗拒著確切的解釋。愛情的變化、配偶的選擇和面對婚姻時人們的決定，這些對局外人而言，總是神秘且不可思議」。[10]

　　著重於伊莉莎白時期的語言與文學研究，凱薩琳・貝茲（Catherine Bates）也研究談情所展現的修辭性。她認爲談情具有「高度微妙且異常複雜的文學與政治歷程」。[11] 用她的話來說「談情是纖弱、憂慮、危險的過程，依賴眞誠表象的有效性與細心算計。談情需要持續不斷的保持愼重、機智與敏銳」。[12] 如同一個高度系統化的體系，談情使眞誠與欺騙，處於戲弄、糾結並置的模式。[13] 有了對談情的這般理解，由貝茲的作品，就不難明白她指出談請與婚姻之間的矛盾：

　　　　無論談情是否被認爲完全存在於婚姻之外，或者被視爲婚姻之序曲，重要的是，談情絕對與婚姻不同。談情代表著一種與婚姻之間獨特、矛盾，且含混的關連。由於它延續了「初步程序」──指婚姻之前，或配偶關係之外發生的事，因而在象徵婚姻的法律之外，暫時性地存在著。[14]

　　「如果你堅持在談論熱情時，討論婚姻，我們很快地將停止瞭解彼此。」（引用自 Comtesse de Carigliano in Balzac, "At the Sign of the Cat and Rocket"）[15] 婚姻和男性與女性個人幸福的矛盾，是《丈夫、妻子與情人》（*Husbands, Wives and Lovers*）一書的主題。[16] 佩翠西亞‧麥納迪（Patricia Mainardi）在此書討論十九世紀法國藝術與文學所再現缺憾中的婚姻。麥納迪由通姦爭議，檢視婚姻與個人情感之間的矛盾（contradiction）。並通過史學敘述與文學、藝術的再現，探究現代社會之個人幸福所涉及男性與女性之間的理想關係。[17]

經由前述文獻回顧可知，談情與婚姻被視爲功能性的關係，是早已存在於文獻描述中。[18] 部分文獻認爲人們通過談情，從單身轉移到已婚狀態，在身分上是單一的線性發展[19]，部分則指出談情與婚姻爲對話與纏繞的關係，因此談情的制度或習俗，並非通往婚姻的明確路線。[20] 我認爲前述文獻所探討談情與婚姻之間的關係，無論是線性或對話關聯，都在理論化談情的嚴肅性。而本章所探討貴州 Hmub 人遊方的獨特處，則在於他們以制度性的兩種談情或調情的形式，長期遊方與短期遊方，展現談情與婚姻不同關係的並置。

二、*At Khait*（婚姻）

婚外遊方的存在，與 Hmub 人婚姻（*at khait*）的三大結構密切關聯：雙邊交表婚制（bilateral cross-cousin marriage）、村寨內婚（village endogamy）和婚後雙居住制（duo-local post-marital residence，也有文獻稱之爲延遲讓渡婚姻）。這個村寨的親屬稱謂體系，與南亞的達羅毗荼人（Dravidian）稱謂體系相似，結合了指定型的雙邊交表婚的理想與實際。[21] 就類推型的親屬關係，Fangf Bil 的姑娘至今仍和類推的母方交表親，以及類推的父方交表親屬進行聯姻。也就是，父親姊妹的女兒嫁給母親兄弟的兒子（FZD／MBS），或母親兄弟的女兒嫁給父親姊妹的兒子（MBD／FZS）。[22] 不過，交表婚制的實行，與 Fangf Bil 親屬家族如何分類相關。這是一個清楚區別近親與遠親的社群。因此，雙邊交表婚的對象，通常不是系譜上真正的 FZS 或 MBS，而是相隔幾代遠的父方或母方交表姻親；亦就是，他們之間互相有關的，是稱謂上的等同。不論是 FZHBS，FZHFBSS，或 FZHFFBSSS，在稱謂上都等同於 FZS。同樣的，不論是 MFBSS，或 MFFBSSS，在稱謂上都等同於 MBS。與交表聯姻平行的，是 Fangf Bil 村寨的二元體制。全村寨的村人區分為 gad ghat（以父系為中心的結群，或稱主人）和 khait（姻親，或稱客人）。前者的成員之間禁止內婚，後者成員則是優先婚的對象或團體。在 Fangf Bil 村寨內，以 ghat 和 khait 為人群之間的核心關係，標示著親屬關係在此社會的重要性。

村寨內婚亦是考察此村子交表婚姻實踐的另一項重點。Fangf Bil 總人口數中的百分九十，為張家與唐家兩個可相互通婚的婚姻集團。這兩個婚姻集團相互通婚的比率，遠超過與外面村寨的婚姻；而兩個婚姻集團內的六個小寨，大多數的嫁娶皆相互依賴。簡言之，這兩個通婚群組似乎組成了近似明確的二元結構。最終，多數的婚姻經由雙方交表婚制的類別系統發生在村寨內。

婚後雙居住制為影響長期談情制度化的第三個慣習。大體而言，Hmub 人村寨的新娘並不會在婚禮後與新郎同居，反而立即返回娘家與其所出的親屬同住。這個居住習俗稱為 niangt zix，逐字譯為在家坐著，或者在家停留。妻子唯有在節慶期間，或幫忙丈夫家農事才會拜訪夫家，直到第一胎孩子出世為止。這段期間，妻子仍穿著未婚女子的服飾。無論是白天參與農務，或者夜晚參與遊方活動，這些妻子大多與其他未婚女子，亦或其他已婚且同是在娘家停留的女子相聚渡過。[23] 在婚後雙居期間，妻子與丈夫皆可自由、獨立參與遊方。妻子待在自己雙親家時，仍可單獨與夜晚在其房間窗外的男性姻親談愛或戲謔玩笑。投入於婚外遊方（extra-marital courtship），妻子私人的閒聊時間與個體的情感不受婚約拘束，直到她自己成為母親並與丈夫同居。在 Hmub 人的村寨裡，多數的妻子在結婚後一至兩年即會成為人母，極少數在娘家待五年以上。無論妻子或丈夫的年紀多大，若尚未生孩子，他們仍然被認為是年輕女子與單身男子，他們之間的婚姻狀態是模糊、不明顯的。大致來說，交表婚制與村寨內婚的結合，持續一代接一代地，創作出一個小世界，並藉由婚後雙居保留了一個區域，一個穿透談情與婚姻界線的區域。除了制度與規則，我們需要以社會行動者的角度來看 Hmub 人的婚姻。

部分 Fangf Bil 村寨的婚姻可能有相當時日的遊方談情，但也有不少婚姻就發生在一段短暫遊方之後（短則從相識、談情到嫁娶僅僅三、四天）。婚姻可以是公開的婚姻（ghaif zix bat mongf：逐字譯為「新娘由雙親送離家門」），或者私奔（at dlius mongf：逐字譯為「悄悄地離開家」）。近年來多數婚姻，無論是公開婚或私奔婚，主要由年輕人自己決定。核心家庭——包含一對伴侶與他們未當家（未婚且未育子）的孩子，是當代 Hmub 人村寨最常見的家庭形式。

進行物的生產與人的再生產，互相分享見解、知識、情感和合作，是每對已婚伴侶日常生活中的顯著面。夫妻在家經常談話，尤其在進餐時間。他們討論農事和家務的分配，交換如何解決家庭問題與養育孩子的想法，分享在村寨內流傳、耳聞的消息、笑話、謠言、醜聞、八卦、爭議等。我在 Fangf Bil 進行民族誌田野時，時常有機會在家屋內聽到夫妻聊天，但有時亦會聽到夫妻大聲爭吵，或偶爾目睹夫妻打架。夫妻在家裡的互動似乎很平常；但他們在家戶外的空間，對彼此刻意冷淡，卻使我印象深刻。無論是上坡工作、參與儀式活動或走訪親戚，在這些場合夫妻必然分開走出家門，並各自與同性別的本家親屬偕同前行。一對已婚的伴侶在家外、村內走在一起，是被認為不禮貌且不妥當的行為。相反地，在公眾的目光外，Hmub 人實際上追尋著私下的偶然會見，使他們能投入情感的滿足，且與異性間親密的互動——也就是遊方（courtship 或 flirtation）。

三、*Iut Fub* （遊方談情）

在許多社會裡，談情說愛（courtship）是很平常的一種以婚姻為目標的習俗。就 Fangf Bil 村人而言，在遊方期間，男性與女性花費相當長時間相處，藉由談話、唱歌與親密而非（必然）關乎性的身體接觸，表述私人感情。然而，遊方卻並非如此必然與單純。

長期與短期

Fangf Bil 存在著兩類不同期程的談情與調情：長期遊方和短期遊方。長期遊方可說是持續一輩子的時光，而短期遊方則以分離，或者進入婚姻為其結果。不過無論長期或短期，談情或調情的構成特徵都是相似的：它們有別於專屬、排他的浪漫情感。可是，長期與短期遊方的差異，卻沒有被當地觀點嚴密或明確地表達。Fangf Bil 村人將年輕人定義為，青少年至成年人，包含完婚數年仍未育有小孩的中年男女。簡言之，未婚男女（不論單身或離婚），和已婚未生子的男女，皆被認定為年輕人。他們可自由地參與遊方。不過已婚男女參與遊方存在著一些不同的規定：已婚女子可與任何男子遊方直到她成為人母；已婚男子成為人父仍然可繼續參與遊方，直到他的孩子進入十來歲的青少年為止。

村寨裡年輕女孩手工編織的花腰帶，或者母親編織與手工縫製的 Hmub 人衣飾，是遊方場合的男女作為象徵長期遊方情感的交換物。男人通常保留著兩到三條從前愛人所贈的花腰帶。直到他的女兒長到二、三歲，能夠穿著傳統 Hmub 人服飾時，就將先前愛人所送的花腰帶，繫在女兒的圍腰上。如果愛人所送的整套 Hmub 衣是兩人分手的紀念品，無論男人或女人都會將愛人送的衣飾保留著，直到自己三十至四十歲以後，年紀漸長，就穿在自己身上。由這種花腰帶與 Hmub 衣飾交換物的文化表徵，我們看到了長期遊方關係可延續一輩子之所在。

Fangf Bil 村寨 Hmub 語的 *iut fub*，字面上譯為遊方，指到處去走村寨與隨處遊蕩。不過遊方所衍生的語意有性的暗示，所以這個語彙，不會出現在村寨 Hmub 人日常對話中。尤其在談話時，有與說話者不同性別的長輩在座時，更須嚴格謹守語用上的迴避法則。村寨 Hmub 人以 *at zot*（鬧著玩）、*lof vud*（休息一會）、*god*（相聚一塊）、*niangt*（坐著）等日常用語來表達遊方。遊方是社會生活中不可或缺的一部分，具有特別安排的時間與空間，和特定分類的參與者。平常的日子裡，年輕人可每晚遊方。晚餐後，老年人與小孩早早就寢，整個村寨進入黑暗與寂靜，除了每個家屋窗口露出的微弱燈光。經過一段寂靜後，在夜晚不被限制、精力充沛的口哨聲（*kot ghait*）響起，配合著腳步聲，與低聲的談話。男孩呼聲邀女孩進行遊方交流。因此，唐家家族的男孩忙著趕往張家家族的小寨，反之亦然。當腳步放慢，男孩輕敲女孩房間的窗，邀她談話。假若女孩打開窗，他們也許輕聲交談；但若是一群男孩擠在一個女孩窗前，他們的談話必然吵鬧地參雜著詼諧的言辭。

想遊方的男孩們亦試圖找出一群女孩聚集的場所，並加入女孩們的聚會談話。午夜後原先成群的談話，轉為一對一的談情，稱為 *ib laik del ib laik*（一個喜歡一個）。如是場景持續至夜半，直到雞啼一次或兩次，甚至破曉時分。

前文所述，是年輕人的遊方談情。不過，年齡和身分（已婚或單身）的嚴格限制並不存在。不同婚姻狀態（已婚與未婚）和年齡有別的男女遊方亦會發生。年輕女子與非同年齡群組的男人談情時，明顯地較為抑制。例如，有一次在少女們聚會的遊方，我聽見一位年輕少女稱一位將手放在她肩膀的男子為 *daid nenk*（舅舅〔MB〕，遠房的母方姻親），並試圖推開他的手。但另一晚，我觀察到一位十七歲未婚少女，興奮地與一位中年男子相談。這男子已有一位十歲的兒子，她稱呼他為 *but*（姊夫）。第三個例子則是在 *nenk ghait lingf*（姊妹節）期間，一群未婚女孩，邀請了一群已婚且為人父的男子，到村寨附近小坡遊方。這群女孩稱呼這些男子為 Dand 的父親，或 Zent 的父親。Dand 或 Zent 為男子們最年長兒女的名。無疑地，年輕女孩是可以在這種場合，公開地表達她們有興趣與這些成年男子一起進行節慶遊方，不過這僅是短暫的談情。同樣的，對於這群已婚的中年男子，這也是短暫的談情，但卻是婚後的遊方。

遊方時穿著類似的女性可能為未婚或已婚。女性婚後住娘家時，她的穿著打扮相似於其他未婚女孩——同樣地盤起頭髮、配戴花朵、首飾

與穿 *ut Diuf*（漢族的服飾，指在街庄市場買的成衣）。再者如同未婚女子，女性婚後住娘家可自由地在夜晚參與遊方。藉此，制度化的遊方聚會開放給任何人。女性的穿著，象徵流動性的符號，掩飾兩種形式遊方間的界線。

四、身體與親密

　　如同前述女人的服飾，遊方裡的身體與親密交換，也模糊長期遊方與短期遊方的界線。在遊方文化裡，公開表現親密，或調情而肢體接觸，是很平常的。遊方伴侶可將手置於姑娘的肩膀、腰部或腿上。在遊方的適當時間、場合，男女談情或親暱的身體接觸，是可被接受的。若年輕人違反這些規則，會受到年長者的斥責。身體與親密也會跨越婚姻的界限。我曾在一場婚宴後的返程，親眼看到新郎握著新娘好友，並也是父系遠房堂姊妹的手調情。無論這女孩喜不喜歡被新郎拉手調情，只要姑娘未婚（嚴格說是未當家），在遊方的情境下，男孩是可公開地觸碰姑娘的手或身體（如肩膀或腰部）。如是公開展示的身體與親密交換所聯結的人群關係，可以看成是對於村寨雙邊交表婚的積極回應。參與村內遊方的年輕男女，彼此都是姻親關係。一起遊方的男孩可能是姑娘的內兄弟，姑娘可能是男孩的嫂子或弟妹，或者姪子與外甥的妻子。在遊方聚會中，可以聽見姑娘稱呼男孩為 *but*（姊夫）、*daid nenk*（舅）、*bad liut*（大伯，丈夫的哥哥）或者 *bad yut*（小叔，丈夫的弟弟）。這些親屬關係的詞彙，顯示出不同世代遊方男女之間的交表姻緣關連。這套親屬稱謂分類下的人群，完全不違背遊方體制中親密的身體接觸。換言之，通過遊方，Hmub 人有意在道德上迴避性的身體與親密交換，並以公開展示的談情與調情，同時滿足個人的情欲，以及成就雙邊交表聯姻的社會理想。

Diut Hxad Vangt （情歌對唱）

身體之外，情歌二重唱則以詩韻語言的形式與內容，細膩的鋪陳長短期遊方與雙邊交表婚姻並置的複雜與對話關係。如下所述的表演與聽眾所集聚的場景，與對歌的歌詞內容，彷彿跳著同步的舞曲。

> Fangf Bil 村寨的兩位女性歌者，與兩位來自附近不遠村寨的男性歌者，説著相同的 Hmub 語方言，穿著相同的 Hmub 人服飾。兩位男性歌者，約四十歲左右，已婚並為人父；其中一位女性歌者未婚約二十歲，另一位約二十五歲，已婚未成為人母，尚居住在原生家中。兩位女歌者屬於同一父系繼嗣群，但不知她們與兩位男性歌唱者確實的系譜關係。不過，男女歌者在演唱中間休息時與對歌結束後，我們聽見男女歌者彼此以交表親人的稱謂互稱。除了唱歌的四位男女，有兩群觀眾，一群為來自 Fangf Bil 的女性，另一群為來自其他村寨的男性。如同歌者之間為交表姻親關係，男女觀眾也分別來自可通婚的姻親團體。

有關情歌的描述與歌詞的分析，將在本書第二章與第三章，進一步的展開與闡述。在此只討論情歌故事主軸所再現的婚姻與遊方談情的對話性。我在 1999 年所採錄與聽寫的情歌，唱的是兩男兩女在遊方場合遇見。男女皆表達參與遊方的羞澀，與愉悅的情感。但也互相戲弄自身與對方面對婚姻與遊方的複雜與纏繞。在情歌語言裡，遊方的長期與短期並置。一方面唱著：

> 我的交表親呀，人們若思念彼此就來半路休憩。姑娘們欲坐下來與
> 男孩們談話，因而來半路休憩。無論真實與否，我們會說男孩們已
> 有妻子。若是你們已有妻子，男孩們呀，那就回家照顧她們吧！無
> 論真假與否，我們會說男孩們已有妻子，回家並與妻子們分離吧！
> 那麼我倆將會願意與你倆為伴！

　　情歌二重唱展現出婚姻與遊方相互獨立存在的本質，與男女不情願
對婚姻付出完全的承諾。明顯地，許多 Hmub 人願意投入這類的浪漫玩
樂，以使他們自身所欲，具有正當性。這樣的欲望，無疑地造成個體與
其婚姻的配偶間抵觸的關係。

　　另一方面與前述主題相反，也有情歌的詩句凸顯婚姻與遊方間纏繞
的關係：

> 男孩如同言辭字句。男孩與姑娘一同談話唱歌，就像鴨子在水中欣
> 喜地嬉戲。我倆不知為何總是坐在你倆身旁，不知陪伴著的是他人
> 的丈夫。（女歌者唱）
> 姑娘們面貌姣好、談吐優美，但卻有著兩顆心，如同豐饒之地，每
> 年生產兩季黍稷。一顆心伴隨著丈夫，另一顆心伴隨著我們。（男
> 歌者唱）

　　這兩段情歌詩句，通過修辭學創造出相對且戲劇化的隱喻，鋪陳出

婚姻與遊方的對話。這樣的情歌語言揭露了婚姻與遊方之間流動與交錯矛盾的關係。我認為遊方所創造的情感，婚外談情是用來調和個人浪漫與法定雙邊交表婚姻制度對於個體的終身約束。在某種程度上，兩種形式的遊方，面對著社會也面對個人：短期遊方，導向婚姻；長期遊方，則指出了身為人的存在，也包含著以情與欲作為自我肯認的一部分。

五、婚外遊方的在地評論

　　無論在婚姻與婚後雙居的制度與實踐，以及通過 Hmub 歌謠等詩韻語言、身體經驗與表徵、禮物交換，都共同參與了 Hmub 人婚姻外談情文化的創造。它們的意義同時也涉及浪漫與情感的行動，以此回應一個在稱謂分類上所展現的法定雙邊交表婚制。然而如果婚姻外遊方是一個集體的社會理想，個人又如何因應？我在 2004 年的民族誌田野研究，通過訪談 Fangf Bil 男女對於婚外遊方的態度，初步尋得了在地人對於婚姻外談情的敘事觀點。我以此替 Hmub 人之親屬為底蘊的社會結構、文化分類、儀式交換所構成的遊方，作一個註腳。好幾位中年或年長的婦女表示，她們並不會感到嫉妒。一位年老的婦女說：「不。我並不會忿怒，我為他在遊方時的那副好嗓音感到開心。他不過是去玩（參與遊方）。」也許因為感受到我對於她們回答的不確定態度，她們以 Hmub 語唱了段歌謠，試圖在訪談過程中說服我。

　　　　媽媽已變老，因為她生了寶寶。爸爸出門去與其他少女遊方。
　　　　爸爸獨自出門去談情，他的情愛風流韻事，是他自個兒的事。

如同這首歌所敘述的，這些年長的女人也強調，無論是徒步至田地，或參與其他儀式，丈夫與妻子極少一起伴隨彼此出門。「伴侶在外公開地出現，是羞恥的事情」她們強調。「若是丈夫欲外出（去遊方），就讓他去吧。那是他自己的事情。」這些女人以輕鬆心情且帶點好玩的語氣告訴我。類似的議論在村內年長婦女的談話很常見。雖然並非如年長女性輕鬆地談論著婚外遊方談情，兩位年約三十歲的年輕母親也說，她們會讓丈夫夜晚外出與其他女孩遊方談情，直到孩子開始上學（也就是說，當孩子長大後，父親將無法自由地在夜裡出去遊方）。我問她們對於丈夫夜晚外出遊方，是否會感到心碎或生氣？其中一位說：「不。我並不會感到心碎或生氣。就算感到心傷或忿怒，也無法改變任何事情。」另一位強調：「儘管妳會對丈夫生氣，妳也不能在臥房以外的地方斥責他。如果讓其他村人知道妳因為這樣的事發怒，會引起議論，惹人笑話的。」面對集體意識形態的約束與個別的差異，一位村寨內的中年男子告訴我，多數村子裡的男性，對於婚外遊方實際的想法：「若你想在夜晚與其他女孩遊方或對唱情歌，就悄悄背地裡外出。別讓妻子知道。要是她不知道，就沒事。一旦知情，她也許會生氣。」他也提及「有些女人通情達理，不會為這樣的事惱火；有些則否，她們會因此發怒。」

六、討論

概括而論，遊方經由 Hmub 人社會對空間、時間與人群的安排，逐漸制度化。首先，它符合婚姻結盟的規範：所有遊方談情的男女，皆互為姻親。其次，遊方一方面創造出一套並置、固定且二元的交表婚制度；另一方面又與婚姻、婚後雙居，共同展現流動的意象。村寨 Hmub 人的遊方展現談情說愛（courtship）文化的二元性：其一為重視談情交往（courting），其二為注重說愛調情（flirting）。我認為兩者的相似性與差異性值得深入探究。首先，不論是否以婚配為前提，遊方的場域，都被視為一個令人愉悅，且輕鬆的情感區域（類似英文 zone 的概念）。這個特性對於詮釋村寨 Hmub 人如何將他們的社會，著重在制度化的婚姻外調情是重要的。換言之，這個現象指出，人不僅僅只是**社會人**，同時也是**心理人**。再者，無論談情交往或說愛調情的行為，都應定義為嚴肅的事情。例如南希‧唐納利（Nancy D. Donnelly）對於二次戰後移民美國的苗族（Hmong）社會的研究，指出婚前性行為不必然以婚姻交換為目的，而是具有個人社會網絡，與令人愉快的心理和情感經驗的社會含義。[24] 也有社會在道德約束下限制婚前性行為，不過談情交往或說愛調情仍有其嚴肅性。珍‧克里爾（Jane Collier）以西班牙的民族誌例子指出，談情交往所維持的時期可長達十年，並且為了尊重女友與她們的家人，男友會迴避與長期談情交往的女性伴侶有任何性的接觸。[25] 本章探討的貴州村寨 Hmub 人，則同時具有短期的婚前談情交往，與長期的婚後說愛調情；通過花帶、衣飾、身體、語言等交換，建立富有浪漫想像的遊方天地。並且 Hmub 人還簡潔一致的對照著親屬稱謂的分類、村寨內的雙邊交表婚，與婚後雙居。本章提出了伴隨著個人社會網絡與角色的長期與短期遊方的並置，是嚴肅的社會互動。以多元的溝通模式 —— 言語、身體、社會習俗與制度化行為，貴州村寨 Hmub 人的遊方習俗，不只為年輕人情感，創造出一個獨一無二的場域，亦為已婚之成年人，展現出一個制度化說愛調情場域。於此同時也瓦解了談情交往（或說愛調情），與一夫一妻專偶制婚姻的線性關聯。多數人類學文獻，將談情交往描述為婚姻導向，[26] 但也有些文獻強調談情交往與婚姻間不必然有其關聯，[27] 或者指出兩者間的纏繞關係。[28] 這些矛盾顯示了談情交往與婚姻的複雜性。貴州村寨 Hmub 人同時採納兩者。正式的婚配交往過程，和成人間的日常互動中，確實存在著責任，尤其對於公開的已婚夫婦（不包括私下的）。在較寬廣的社會約束下，Hmub 人有著一個談情交往與說愛調情的天地，可延續個人情欲的表達。試問這與十九世紀清朝（或其他階層社會）的城裡人光臨妓院有何不同？前者在公開場合極其正式，私下則非常個人。獨特的是，平權主義（egalitarian）的 Hmub 人，在社會與經濟上都不是一個階序或階層社會。然而，私人的親密區域，則重要且顯著地保持著。在確認人類、社會、心理上的性自我，平權主義的 Hmub 人可說是一個特例。村寨 Hmub 人所實踐的，同時也是西方社會所論述之社會階層、個人主義與浪漫愛情外的另一種選擇。

七、結語

　　最後我們也許可以問，男女之間談情之樂與情愛欲望是否與婚姻無關連？貴州東部村寨 Hmub 人的遊方活動，以結合社會面的法定制度（稱謂的分類系統、雙邊交表婚制、婚後雙居制）與語言及身體符號的交換與展演，突顯個人的情感、欲求與婚姻之間纏繞的對話關係。藉由分析村寨 Hmub 人遊方文化的婚外談情，我探究了這個特定文化中，婚姻內和婚姻外情感表達的界線。經由探究婚後遊方與婚姻制度，在對話關係下如何也能作為一個整合的社會結構，使婚姻外談情或親密存在的流動場域，能夠更嚴密地被檢視。再者遊方文化和婚外談情的民族誌，也突顯「不貞」（infidelity）的概念是文化所定義的。[29] 也就是說，不論是通過言語或身體的親密互動，Fangf Bil 村寨的個人，如何在心理與情感上，回應制度化的婚外情愛？ Fangf Bil 村民是否認定這樣的婚外情愛事件爲不貞？爲人妻，也爲人母的女性，對於她已爲人父的丈夫參與遊方活動的情愛會面，是否會感到嫉妒、生氣、或沮喪？這類問題，涉及性、愛、婚姻三個社會範疇區別的本質。我認爲制度化的婚外談情，補償了過度正式的婚姻與家庭的安排。私底下的「婚姻外」雖充滿親暱言語和行爲，但很難以正式的論點來探索。Fangf Bil 村寨 Hmub 人則少作些逃避，相對的保留更多從年輕到成年人都可戲耍與浪漫想像的場域。在那裡，人在面對婚姻時，不僅是爲法定雙邊交表婚理想之結構所約束的個人，並且也是具有性之吸引力的個人。也或許，在我們身而爲人的人性裡，這樣的欲求，比我們所願意承認的還更強烈。或許，這也是性產業崛起與持續存在於人類文明的主要原因。是的，性的需求是存在的，但除了只有性的解放，其他需求亦該被滿足。Fangf Bil 村寨 Hmub 人的遊方，不直接涉及性這件事，而是供給了承認性是可以正當進行浪漫想象的活動場所。且更重要的是，他們透過公開展現情愛的談情，表露人際交流場域的重要性，以及最終也達到人際間存在的交流。這讓我想到專長於兒童心理精神分析學家亞當·菲利普斯（Adam Phillips）對於調情（flirtation）所下的一個註腳：「調情讓事物可以處於遊戲的氛圍，藉此我們才能夠從不同觀點瞭解這些事物。」[30] 我認爲村寨 Hmub 人的制度化談情，顯示婚後遊方，扮演個體、個人內在深處情感表達的出口。相對地，這也表示人類社會之已婚伴侶，在公開情感表現上的缺乏。

Tensions between Romantic Love and Marriage:
Performing 'Hmub Cultural Individuality' in an
Upland Hmub Love-Song

Chapter 2　浪漫愛情與婚姻之間的張力：
　　　　　　高地 Hmub 人情歌展演的文化個體性

一、前言

皮埃爾·克拉斯特（Pierre Clastres）指出，原始社會即使沒有國家、文字或書面的歷史記錄，也並非是不完整的社會（Clastres 1987）。本章抱持同樣的觀點，探討一個邊陲社會如何透過文化語境中個體性的展演來維持其社會的主體性。值得注意的是，本研究探討的並非普遍存在於現代歐美社會中那種具有道德自主性的個人主義。

本章探討中國西南貴州東部高地苗人（Hmub）社會在情歌表演中對個體性所進行的在地表達，並以一部由兩位女歌者與兩位男歌者以二重唱形式進行，內容包括四百多行歌詞的對歌及其節錄來加以說明 。

情感一直是親屬人類學長期以來關注和爭論的議題，但在過往經常被視為親屬關係的附帶現象（Radcliffe-Brown 1924；Homans and Schneider 1955）。本章試圖另闢蹊徑，從展演的角度探討高地 Hmub 人在情歌表演中所表達的情感。Hmub 人在情歌表演中運用許多不同的詩歌修辭手法，並經常在主題內容上突顯幽默、情感以及社會和親屬關係。我特別關注彰顯「浪漫之愛」（個人情感）和「婚姻」（聯姻群體）之間張力的主題內容，並指出此一類型的 Hmub 人情歌詩意地揭示一個極為普遍的命題：個人認同與社會理想之間的會遇。

涂爾幹、牟斯、杜蒙等人已針對個人與社會之間的對話關係進行過許多的討論。本章將透過個人主義涉及關於人或自我的特定歷史文化概念（Rapport and Overing 2000）此一觀點，指出 Hmub 人的情歌展演及其所體現的社會動力，具有傳達 Hmub 人個體性的作用。

二、人類學對個人與社會的探討

人類學關於個人與社會的爭論由來已久。我將不在這裡重述這段學術辯論史，而是指出法國人類學對此議題的基本取徑（特別是涂爾幹、杜蒙和牟斯），以及英國人類學家瑪麗蓮‧史翠珊（Marilyn Strathern）的研究重點。個人及個人與社會的會遇都是這些學者的研究焦點。我們在這些學者的研究中可以看到個人（individual）、個體性（individuality）和個人主義（individualism）的概念在特定族群、文化和歷史背景下發展的過程。奈傑爾‧拉普伯特（Nigel Rapport）與喬安娜‧奧弗寧（Joanna Overing）在其合編的《社會與文化人類學：關鍵概念》（*Social and Cultural Anthropology: The Key Concepts*, 2000）一書中收錄了一篇探討涂爾幹關於個人觀念的研究評述。本章將以該文作為論述的基礎。艾彌爾‧涂爾幹（Émile Durkheim）是「集體主義敘事的重要提倡者。此敘事將個人行動者嵌入到宏觀社會的運作中」（Rapport and Overing 2000：179）。他將人類視為一種雙重存在（homo duplex）。正如拉普伯特和奧弗寧所指出的，對於涂爾幹來說，個人「是種『雙重存在』，一個紮根於物理有機體，另一個……紮根於社會有機體。……兩者之間一直存在著敵對和緊張狀態，但是透過公共語言和文化的灌輸，人類有能力超越平均（動物）的個體性，成為集體意識的一部分，從中體現社會的（神聖）傳統」（ibid.：180）。

第二章　浪漫愛情與婚姻之間的張力：高地 Hmub 人情歌展演的文化個體性
Tensions between Romantic Love and Marriage:
Performing 'Hmub Cultural Individuality' in an Upland Hmub Love-Song

涂爾幹、馬歇爾・牟斯和路易・杜蒙的敘述觀點，同時結合了個人主義和個體性。拉普伯特與奧弗寧（2000：180）提及，牟斯在〈人類心智的分類〉（"A Category of Human Mind", 1979）一文中，說明「社會如何對生物個體施加壓力：透過集體表徵和集體確定的習慣性行為，進而使個體淹沒在『集體節奏』中」。牟斯結合普世的個體性與特定文化的個人主義兩種觀點，逐步說明不同年齡和社會的人們，如何以不同方式意識到自己作為個體的存在，而其所身處之不同形式的社會結構，又如何造成這些差異。牟斯在文章一開頭就表示他對自我意識不感興趣，認為它基本上屬於心理學，且是一個人類普同的特質：他感興趣的是個人的社會構成。個人的構成，並不具有普世性，不同社會都有自己的表達方式。

　　杜蒙在《個人主義論集》（*Essays on Individualism*, 1986）中同意牟斯的觀點，即「西方的個人概念 —— 具有最高道德價值的自主行動者 —— 是文明發展的一個特殊階段」（Rapport and Overing 2000：181）。對於杜蒙而言，印度教提供的是一種社會見解：「印度教棄世者與現代個人主義者之間的關鍵差異在於，前者的個人只能（在意識形態上）自外於日常的社會世界」，而現代的個人主義卻是西方日常社會世界的核心（ibid.）。

　　瑪麗蓮・史翠珊以美拉尼西亞和英格蘭模式為基礎，探討土著關於個人和社會的概念，在不同文化和歷史時期的不同展現。她在《後自然》（*After Nature*）這本研究英格蘭親屬關係的作品中，清楚闡明她對個人和社會所抱持的理論立場：

〔英格蘭模式〕將二十世紀中葉的英格蘭親屬關係，描述為一種個人的再生產模式，與美拉尼西亞人致力於關係的再生產形成對比。作為個人，英格蘭模式中的人並不象徵整個社會實體，也無法和集體或一系列的關係同構。相反地，人們被認為是存在於眾多不同系統中的一部分──親屬關係系統的一部分，命名系統的一部分，社會的一部分──而且無法完全複製任何一種系統結構。我將此概念稱為「部分圖像」（merographic）。……我認為，我們現在可以藉由「部分圖像」的概念，賦予英格蘭人**美學性**（aesthetic）或**標誌性**（iconic）的意義。……能自主選擇的個人被作為社會慣例縮影的個人所取代。在此過程中，這個圖像將呈現出不同的意象，形成一種關於自身的合成，一種蒙太奇。

（Strathern 1992：125-27，粗體為筆者劃的重點）

上述引文有四點值得提出來討論。第一點是個人與社會之間確實存在著張力或對立；第二點是對個人價值進行界定。史翠珊認為，不同文化對個人的理解截然不同。即使涂爾幹沒有明確說明，但他似乎將個人主義視為一種價值（Lukes 1973：338ff；Dumont 1986：16）。牟斯和杜蒙則把自主性和道德性，視為西方界定個人的價值。史翠珊透過美拉尼西亞模式與英格蘭模式的比較發現，美拉尼西亞人透過個體與個體之間的關係來看待個體，亦即個體之間關係的再生產構成了集體性和社會性。在二十世紀中葉的英格蘭社會中，個人則被簡單地理解為整個系統中各自獨立的一部分。

由於史翠珊探討的英格蘭主體是二十世紀中葉的群體，其引文所突

第二章　浪漫愛情與婚姻之間的張力：高地 Hmub 人情歌展演的文化個體性
Tensions between Romantic Love and Marriage:
Performing 'Hmub Cultural Individuality' in an Upland Hmub Love-Song

顯的第三個重點，是關於現代性的問題。自涂爾幹以來，個人主義便對人類學思潮有著不同程度的影響，明顯存在或隱含於各種革命或進步思想中。長期以來，人們一直認為它是現代西方社會的特徵。後續關於個體本質的辯論也引發對於現代性的探討。如同杜蒙所述：「對於牟斯而言，有時似乎所有的一切，最終都是一種現代性的表現。」（1986：4）事實上，涂爾幹和杜蒙的思想具有演化論的基礎。他們之後大多數的討論都將「傳統」形式與現代形式進行對比，或在結構上具有演化論的色彩。

史翠珊引文的第四個重點，是她對親屬關係所展現的美學或標誌面向的重視。她早期在研究美拉尼西亞社會有關個體性與社會性之間的關係時，受到麥金・萬豪（McKim Marriott）的印度研究（1976）啟發而採取該視角，並特別展現在其所提出之「部分人」（dividual being）的觀點上（Strathern 1988：348–49，f.7）。

> 美拉尼西亞人並沒有被視為獨特的實體，每個人都被視為**部分人**，內在包含著普遍的社會性。人的確經常被視為一個生產社會關係的多元和複合的載體。一個人可以被想像成一個社會的縮影。
>
> （Strathern 1988：13，粗體為筆者劃的重點）

史翠珊提出研究個體性的新視角，無論是美學或標誌性的觀點，都為揭示個人特徵和價值提供一種新方法。本章對語言使用和社會生活展演面向的研究，與這個新方法息息相關。

三、朝向「語言使用」的研究

　　對語言使用的研究有其在哲學和語言學領域發展的根據。路德維希·維根斯坦（Ludwig Wittgenstein）研究普通語言的用法時，「從意義轉向言語習慣」（Urban 1996：xii）。約翰·奧斯汀（John Austin）在遵循這種思路後觀察到——「人們更常使用言語本身（『表現力』）來做什麼，而不僅僅用它來談論世界（『可構想性』）」（ibid.）。俄羅斯語言學家羅曼·雅各布森（Roman Jakobson）提出的目的論語言觀，也推動了此一研究趨勢。對他而言，聲音的變化「因此具有目的性。它必須根據……交流的參照目標來衡量。而如果這個例子來自於詩作，便根據詩意的功能來衡量」。這種多功能、多系統的語言觀點與斐迪南·德·索緒爾（Ferdinand de Saussure）的觀點，有著根本差異——索緒爾認為語言在功能和系統上都是同質的（Caton 1987：231）。此外，巴赫金（M. M. Bakhtin）關於「語言同質與異質的兩極」觀點，也可以被內建到雅各布森的理論模型中（ibid.）。巴赫金對語類（speech genres）之美學體系的重視，值得進一步探討。以下引述邁克爾·霍爾奎斯特（Michael Holquist）對巴赫金思想的介紹：

> 自康德以來，我們始終堅持將系統視為一個封閉的秩序，而不是一連串開放系列的連結。對康德而言，系統不僅是對一套充分發展，且絕對一致的範疇，所進行的嚴格運用。同時還暗示著任何主要問題，都不應被孤立地看待。由此，任何對理性的探討，不僅需要回答邏輯，或認識論上的問題，也必須回答**道德**和**美學**的問題。**只有在後者的意義上，巴赫金的思想才可被視爲一種系統**：他在提出

第二章　浪漫愛情與婚姻之間的張力：高地 Hmub 人情歌展演的文化個體性
Tensions between Romantic Love and Marriage:
Performing 'Hmub Cultural Individuality' in an Upland Hmub Love-Song

……「開放統合」（open unity）時，試圖表達的那種意義。

（Holquist 1986：x，粗體為筆者劃的重點）

伴隨這種實用主義觀點而來的，是一種以批判性觀點，探索語言使用和社會生活在詩學和展演方面 —— 亦即美學面向 —— 的意義。鮑曼和布里格斯（Bauman and Briggs 1990：79）對這種新觀點的評論如下：「對表演研究的重視，標誌著語言學和人類學努力在爲詩學 —— 語言藝術……拓展出更廣闊的空間。對語言表演在親屬、政治、經濟、宗教等社會生活領域的重視，讓我們得以理解表演具有社會性與有效性，而不是次要和衍生的。」

四、地方情歌

1950 年代掀起一股採集、翻譯、整理苗歌的浪潮，出版在《民間文學資料》系列。並於 1980 年代再版。其中如《苗族婚姻歌》（Tang 1986〔1959〕）記錄了 Hmub 人婚姻經驗的集體特性，以及新郎與新娘在婚姻前後切身的「個體」經驗。

Fangf Bil 村寨的情歌分爲兩個範疇：老人歌 hxad lok 與年輕人之歌 hxad vangx。多數的年輕人之歌，表述的主題相近。村寨裡的人，將它們基於展演細節，分成四類：年輕人的對歌 diut hxad vangx，低吟 qint hxad，嘟喝 et hed，吆喝 iof het。這些歌曲類型的區辨，僅在於演唱調子的不同，歌詞則共享相同的語料庫。

老人歌 hxad lok 大多關乎 Hmub 人的神話，與村寨、繼嗣群、氏族或祖先的起源傳說。本章探討屬於年輕人之歌 hxad vangx 的範疇。*Hxad vangx* 有時聽起來是愉悅或戲謔的，但有時則充滿情感，表達一種孤單或寂寞的情緒。傳統交表聯姻與個人情感之間，始終存在的張力，在此類歌謠尤其明顯。

（一）研究方法

我在 Fangf Bil 村寨所蒐集、記錄的歌謠，多數來自於自然情境。亦即這些歌的演唱，本身就屬於節日或儀式後遊方的一部分。我也在諸多儀式與非儀式的場合，記錄 Hmub 人演唱的歌。這部情歌對唱是以錄音機收音記錄，而後用黔東苗文拼音系統來記音、聽寫。

我選擇少數的村人（一位二十歲的姑娘、她的父母親與其他親人或親戚），作為主要報導人（key cultural consultants），協助我進行情歌的記音、聽寫與翻譯。因為記音、聽寫是單調、冗長且費時的工作。要就四百多行的對歌，進行記音、聽寫、翻譯、分析與闡述，需要我與協助的村人間，有著較深的相互理解、信任與熟悉。我們一起工作連續好幾日夜，一再重複播放聆聽錄音帶，才完成這整部對歌的記音、聽寫與翻譯。

（二）情歌展演

本章描述與探討的情歌對唱，展演於 1999 年早春稻作耕種期間的節慶（吃丑節）。這部長達四百多行的情歌，由兩男兩女的歌者對唱。這場對歌的社會情境，是來自周邊鄰近的三、四個寨子，與 Fangf Bil 寨的村人，不分男女老幼，一大群人聚集在 Fangf Bil 寨邊，一塊大山沖上爭看鬥牛。今年第六次吃丑的這場鬥牛比賽，由 Fangf Bil 村寨主辦。鬥牛

第二章　浪漫愛情與婚姻之間的張力：高地 Hmub 人情歌展演的文化個體性
Tensions between Romantic Love and Marriage:
Performing 'Hmub Cultural Individuality' in an Upland Hmub Love-Song

結束後，老人與小孩多半返家。留下的年輕人，以及婚後仍喜歡在遊方場域，與姑娘對歌的少部分中年人，則一道參與跨村寨遊方。來自鄰近不同村寨的青年與姑娘，相互依靠，在坡上或坐或立。有些成群，但多數是兩兩成對。有的愉快交談，也有些對唱情歌。情歌唱得好，會吸引較多人圍觀聆聽。這樣的跨村寨遊方場景，往往見於盛大的節慶儀式之後。

兩位女性歌者來自 Fangf Bil，兩位男性歌者來自鄰近地區，離 Fangf Bil 約四十或五十里的其他村寨。同樣的，除了歌者，這個場合也有兩群聽眾。一群來自 Fangf Bil 的姑娘，以及一群來自其他村寨的青年。青年所說的 Hmub 語言，腔調與 Fangf Bil 相近，服飾的風格款式也相同。男女歌者之間，與男女聽眾之間，彼此都屬於關係較遠的，延展型交表姻親。

兩位男性歌者，年約四十，已經成家且為人父。兩位女性歌者有一位年約二十，未婚；另一位年約二十五，已婚，但尚未為人母仍緩落夫家，與娘家親人同住。幾位與我為伴，並協助我的姑娘與村人，都知悉對歌的兩位姑娘，屬於同一父系繼嗣群。但男女歌者之間，確切的系譜關係，則未明。中場休息與對歌結束時，我們聽到男女歌者，以指定型交表親屬稱謂（prescriptive cross-kin terms）稱呼彼此。

這部情歌從頭到尾，都由男女歌者進行對唱。四百五十行用唱的，二十八行以唸唱形式展現。大約四到八行歌句，組成一首短歌。以六至七行的組合為多數。歌句展演的順序，並無一定的前後規範。四位歌者即興的進行情歌對唱。對於歌者而言，他們共享一個裝載歌詞與詩句的語言資料庫（linguistic repertoire）。但他們並非以記誦的形式，複製一長串的歌句篇章。當彼方歌者演唱時，此方歌者須聚精會神地聆聽。稍不留神他們便可能找不到合適的歌句，來回應對方所唱的歌句及其所組成的短歌內容。只要對唱適當，某些歌句會被重複演唱。部分歌詞或歌句，與歌者性別有關，部分則無關。情歌裡所用的名詞或代名詞可相互轉換，創造並展演出屬於 Hmub 人之民間詩學裡，獨特的性別文化（參第三章）。

這部情歌對唱，長達一小時有餘。整場展演雖有詩韻與對歌的清楚結構，但唱與聆聽的過程，也有其隨意處，並非從頭到尾都顯得嚴肅或正式。當幾行歌句的演唱甫畢，歌者時而彼此交談，或與觀眾開個小玩笑。而圍觀、聆聽這場情歌對唱的姑娘與小夥子們，有時也彼此輕聲交談。在 Hmub 人的民間詩學文化裡，對唱的內容遠比歌聲來的重要。進行對歌的姑娘與小夥子歌者，如果不用心，找不到適當歌詞與歌句來對，一旁意興高昂的聽眾，會私下議論，替歌者安上壞名聲。

（三）情歌語意的焦點

Hmub 人情歌的語意焦點，關注幽默、情感、社會關係與親屬關係。尤為顯著的是，以詩歌美學，展示地方文化所呈顯之個體經驗的浪漫愛情——就是遊方——與地方社會交表聯姻理想之間的張力。

簡言之，這部情歌描述兩男兩女的相遇，就有如傳統以來的遊方談情與調情。一方面男女都表述，進入遊方場合的害羞與愉悅的情緒；另一方面，他們也彼此調侃，身處婚姻與遊方談情的競逐與對話關係。這部情歌，最後止於抒發別離與孤單的愁思情緒與感受。

與前述故事線相互纏繞的，有四個不斷重複出現的主題：（a）婚姻；（b）遊方談情與調情；（c）地方脈絡下婚姻與遊方的兩種關係；（d）

第二章　浪漫愛情與婚姻之間的張力：高地 Hmub 人情歌展演的文化個體性
Tensions between Romantic Love and Marriage:
Performing 'Hmub Cultural Individuality' in an Upland Hmub Love-Song

個體的經驗、婚姻與遊方談情及調情的美學經驗等，通過此展現在 Hmub 人的面前。

（a）**婚姻**是一條明顯的主題絲線，細密的編織入這部情歌的每一角落。婚姻在地方的概念裡，有兩個面向：其一直指個體對締結良緣的渴望，其二為交表聯姻的集體理想。如下面幾行歌句，有別於西方社會的傳統，情歌與歌者是在婚姻結盟，有著清楚方向的傳統裡，展現個體對婚姻的想望（歌句 349 與 157）。

Dat Deik	男歌者
347 *Xud dongf mongf dot jut.*	莫説去嫁別人。
348 *Ninx dongf lel bib mek.*	要説我們來和你們一起。
349 *Ghet benf liangf hvib naik.*	我們無論如何要成夫妻，如此才放心。

Dat Ghaif	女歌者
352 *Ceit daik las baf pent, mul-diangf.*	故意來跟你們對歌，表兄。
353 *Yel bib mongf lab diuf mek zix.*	帶我們去你們家，你們家不要，我們也去嫁你們家。
354 *Nef hfif sax vob diangt.*	飛走的鳥，還是會再靠近籠子。

某幾行歌詞明白表述了交表婚姻的複雜與曖昧細節，例如：

Dat Ghaif	女歌者
154 *Bib mul-diangf naik jut.*	我們彼此是交表親。
155 *Bib def diangf dak niangt.*	我們分開再轉回來，坐在一起談話。
156 *Bib nal diangf dak ghent.*	我們家母親轉來對男孩說話。
157 *Bib naf neif jek dint.*	我們無論如何成為夫妻。
158 *Bib del diangf liak ciet.*	爾後我們又分開，也沒關係。

對於結合村寨內婚的指定型交表聯姻（prescriptive alliance），情歌裡也有著相對內斂與隱微的表述：

Dat Deik	男歌者
359 *Hvid cet liuk lel lait.*	隔了千年，剛剛來到這裡。
360 *Liuk gheb mangk lel ghet.*	下輩子，還是得不到妳們作妻子。
366 *Ghat but vangf hveb bif.*	妳們姑娘出嫁，就嫁在寨子內。
367 *Vob diut dak jut liuk.*	成為別人的妻子。

有如歌詞所表述的，跨村寨對歌的小夥子，往往無法娶得與他們對歌的姑娘。因為 Fangf Bil 及其鄰近地區，直到二十一世紀前十年，中型的自然村寨，仍保有村寨內婚的優先性。男女的婚配，都以自然村寨內部的對象為主。再者指定型交表聯姻的獨特性，也通過對歌的歌詞，與歌

第二章　浪漫愛情與婚姻之間的張力：高地 Hmub 人情歌展演的文化個體性
Tensions between Romantic Love and Marriage:
Performing 'Hmub Cultural Individuality' in an Upland Hmub Love-Song

句結尾反覆唸誦具交表姻親意涵的指定型親屬稱謂（prescriptive affinal kin terms）── 如 *mul-diangf*（交表親、表兄、表妹等）來展現。

（b）**調情**。這部情歌對於調情與遊方，有諸多不同的描繪。我們可將其視爲第二條主軸絲線。通過情歌的短歌、歌句，與歌詞，生動表述遊方調情的情景。換言之，情歌的唱與唸誦，呼應村寨所實踐的遊方文化。其特性有如第 385 行的歌詞。在地人對此的解釋，呈現兩個面向：其一表述男孩與姑娘，相聚在姑娘家火堂房內遊方談情。其二也可表述當姑娘與小夥子，各自嫁娶後，再來多說一些情話。此即緩落夫家之婚後雙居，與婚外談情及調情，相互疊合。

Dat Ghaif	女歌者
343 *Dak lait iauf dak ceit, mul-diangf.*	來到此，就來唱，表兄。
344 *Ceit daik las baf pent.*	故意來跟你們對歌。
Dat Deik	男歌者
383 *Ghaib qub mangk juk ghof, mul-diangf.*	我們彷彿雞，撿拾不完米，表妹。
384 *Bib pot mangk juk jib.*	我們有著說不完的話。
385 *Dleit diut ghab diuk nail.*	留話進家屋內說。

有幾行的歌詞，是描述村寨 Hmub 人因節慶或儀式活動，聚成一個盛大場合。此時此刻，情歌對唱也正展開，周遭充滿遊方談情與調情的歡鬧氛圍：

Dat Deik	男歌者
428 *Bib sint sint ghenf jek wek.*	我們才剛剛坐成群。
429 *Sint sint ninf jek cangk.*	才剛剛坐成一個大場面。
430 *Dit lit deif liuk deik.*	姑娘一會兒就不要男孩。
431 *Deif liud daif rangk dok.*	丟男孩，有如丟柴草。
432 *Qit wab iauf dak ninf.*	男孩生氣的很，才來騙姑娘。

（c）**婚姻與遊方談情／調情的兩類關係**。前面所描述的兩個情歌主題，分別指向婚姻與遊方。然而這部情歌最顯著的語意焦點，是個體所關注的，婚姻與遊方談情／調情的衝突與張力。它們展現出兩種關係。首先，婚姻與遊方談情，彼此有其前後接續的關聯性；遊方談情的合理進程，是以交表婚姻為目標。對歌歌詞第 45 行，所表述的，就是這樣的情感：

Dat Ghaif	女歌者
42 *Naik liat dangk git qet.*	人若互相想，就在半路坐下來休息。
43 *Mul-diagngf eb.*	表兄弟啊。

第二章　浪漫愛情與婚姻之間的張力：高地 Hmub 人情歌展演的文化個體性
Tensions between Romantic Love and Marriage:
Performing 'Hmub Cultural Individuality' in an Upland Hmub Love-Song

Dat Ghaif	女歌者
44 *Niongk liat dangk git qet.*	姑娘想坐下與男孩談，就在半路休息。
45 *Mak dint mongf vux diut.*	男孩你若已有妻小，就回家顧你的妻子吧。

　　另一個有趣的例子是歌詞第 90 至 91 行，與前述的詩學意景，婚姻與情感的對話，相互應和：

Dat Ghaif	女歌者
88 *Daik sat het deif dot.*	真也説男孩得妻。
89 *Hlaib sak het deif dot.*	假也説男孩得妻。
90 *Diangt zix lius mek dint bongf heix.*	回家離了你倆的妻。
91 *Diuf niongk hveb lel ghob.*	我倆才來跟你倆。

　　然而與前述所引述及討論的歌句語意主題有所別，這部對歌也有許多行歌句，對於婚姻與遊方的關係，展現出較為複雜，帶有問題意識的解釋觀點：一種對話性的解釋觀點。整體說來，通過這類歌句所鋪陳的詩學地景（scenarios），遊方談情與調情並非以婚姻為這趟旅程的終點。在這樣的邏輯下，婚姻與個人的情感之間，是相互獨立的。接下來的兩段引述，皆生動表現出，遊方與婚姻的第二類關係。前兩行，第 29 至 30 行，有如希臘歌劇的合音美學效果；第 30 行開始，則提供另一種生動的

比喻，描繪出遊方談情與調情的詩學景致，以及其中的歡愉氛圍：

Dat Ghaif	女歌者
29 Liob huf yiok.	男孩就像話。
30 Ghas hfaf seik.	男孩與姑娘一起談天、對歌，好像鴨戲水般歡欣。
31 Bongt neif meb niangt gait nongt.	不知怎麼的，我們就一直陪你們坐。
32 Bongt lif dak jut liuk.	不知道我們陪伴的，是別人家的丈夫。

另一個有意思的例子是：

Dat Deik	男歌者
263 Benf vux ob vak liuf.	姑娘漂亮會說話，有兩顆心。
264 Lal vux ob vak ghek.	有如豐美的土地，一年熟兩季小米。
265 Ib pit hvib qongk bongf.	一顆心陪家裡的丈夫。
266 Ib pit hvib dak lif.	一顆心陪我們。

（d）**個人情感**。另一條清晰的主題絲線，是串起不同的個人情感、感受與情緒——包含嬌羞、愉悅、孤獨、期盼與熱情。以此連結著婚姻與遊方談情及調情。例如，下面幾行歌詞，展現出男孩與姑娘，想去遊方的害羞心情。

第二章　浪漫愛情與婚姻之間的張力：高地 Hmub 人情歌展演的文化個體性
Tensions between Romantic Love and Marriage:
Performing 'Hmub Cultural Individuality' in an Upland Hmub Love-Song

Dat Deik	男歌者
21 *Lik gif eb pot mal.*	田乾就要水來泡軟。
22 *Naik liuf ment let lab.*	與陌生人說話、對歌，就會相識。
23 *Meit ob lab nit nil.*	就是這樣來說幾句話。
24 *Lab def lab det jaf.*	卻一句話，跟不成一句話。
25 *Xid xeit meb gid weif.*	對你們害羞得很，不知如何是好。

Dat Ghaif	女歌者
72 *Ob lik git ment let xef.*	姑娘我倆話不多。
73 *Naik liuf ment let lal.*	遇到你們這樣的陌生人，我倆話才多。
74 *Diut ux qib ux naif.*	瞧我們衣服沒穿好。
75 *Heb ghaf heb det ghaf.*	一邊穿上衣袖，一半未穿上。
76 *Heb neif heb det rinf.*	一邊穿上衣袖，一半未穿上。
77 *Xid xeit meb gait weis.*	害羞你們的很。

有一些歌詞表達著伴隨遊方談情與調情而來的愉悅與開心。

Dat Ghaif	女歌者
60 *Liuf del let.*	聽到鼓聲,心歡喜。
61 *Deif del ghait.*	聽到男孩說話,也歡欣。

還有其他例子則在充滿比喻的歌詞中,浮現個人心情的表述:

Dat Deik	男歌者
238 *Nef huf yiok.*	姑娘就像話。
239 *Ghas hfaf saik.*	姑娘與男孩談天、對歌,有如鴨戲水般歡欣。

Dat Deik	男歌者
194 *Xongt leif jut dot lif.*	男孩陪別人坐。
195 *Qut das mangk qet liuf.*	能與姑娘一起遊方,死也沒關係。
196 *Dad nef mak qet ninf.*	姑娘會騙人。
197 *Xongx juf daik qet liuf.*	男孩心歡喜。

在愉悅與其他類似的情緒之外,歌詞也傳達強烈的渴望,而這時常混合著一種可預期的孤獨或孤寂。這類情緒通常出現於第二種在婚姻與遊方談情與調情間的複雜關係。

第二章　浪漫愛情與婚姻之間的張力:高地 Hmub 人情歌展演的文化個體性
Tensions between Romantic Love and Marriage:
Performing 'Hmub Cultural Individuality' in an Upland Hmub Love-Song

Dat Ghaif	女歌者
277 *Mek hveb at nit hfuf.*	你們的話就是這樣。
278 *Mek hvib at yat yiok.*	你們的心遠遠的。
279 *Juk eb fat hongx vongf.*	你們的心好像小河流向瀑布。
280 *Juk hob fat hongx bif.*	好像霧坐在山坡間，它要遠遠的走了。
281 *Mek zod but mek bongf.*	你們要走回去跟你們的妻。
Dat Deik	男歌者
284 *Nef cent niangt diek vik, mul-diangf.*	鳥在窩中叫，表妹。
285 *Dliut diut dot jut mongf*	讓姑娘們嫁給別人吧。
286 *Nongf heit ob dak nif*	我倆只能坐一坐，談一談。

最後，渴望與熱情都表達及暗示於此首情歌之中。然而，相對上述情歌所展現較為明確開放的情緒與感受，這首歌則顯得較為幽微。僅有幾行歌詞展現這類描述與暗示，如第 226 行歌詞：

Dat Deik	男歌者
224 *Meb dlab let lil rak renf.*	妳倆的嘴快得很。
225 *Lab qet juf wak wek.*	一顆心遠遠的。
226 *Ment ghad ghuf dek deif.*	姑娘拿身體碰男孩。

Dat Deik	男歌者
227 *Dlek xongx dangf dlek dok.*	跟男孩像跟火。
228 *Diuf xongx nongf wek yef.*	我們這對男孩才孤獨。

另一個例子在第 106 行歌詞：

Dat Ghaif	女歌者
102 *Liat mek gait gof bik.*	非常想念你們。
103 *Mek dak lait dlik vangf.*	你們來到姑娘的寨子。
104 *Jek vob diut deif liuk.*	姑娘變成妻子，作男孩的伴侶。
105 *Jek dint diut lis senf.*	男孩變成丈夫，作姑娘的伴侶。
106 *Mangk hongx xangt bif deif.*	就是不想放開男孩的手。

五、討論

　　透過前述例子，這部對歌所表達的多層主題與情境，展現 Hmub 人婚姻與遊方談情及調情本質的複雜性。這包含在婚姻與遊方談情／調情間的糾結關係，及與之相繫的個人情感。此部分將討論情歌的角色，就如這部對歌所展現的獨特美學與標誌性表演（參第三章），如何建構貴州東部高地 Hmub 人的社會生活與社會再生產。

　　高地 Hmub 人的情歌凸顯 Fangf Bil 村寨視為核心且高度顯現的社會特性：聯姻群體與交表婚姻。而此特性也在部分語言與社會現象中清楚

第二章　浪漫愛情與婚姻之間的張力：高地 Hmub 人情歌展演的文化個體性
Tensions between Romantic Love and Marriage:
Performing 'Hmub Cultural Individuality' in an Upland Hmub Love-Song

顯現，如達羅毗荼人（Dravidian）親屬稱謂，並伴隨著指定型交表婚姻的理想與實踐。引用我之前的研究：

> 指定型婚姻的原則尤其顯現於交表親戚中稱謂用語的變化。未婚的男性說話者被稱作 but，男性交表弟兄，及 mul，交表弟兄；而未婚的女性說話者也被稱作 mul。這是 mul diangf 的一類縮寫。也就是，一位未婚女性與母方或父方交表弟兄的關係。而這也指涉他們可能的婚配關係。而她可能，或者確實被預期與一位和自己有交表親戚關係的男性成婚。

(Chien 1999：46)

實際上，這顯示出在村寨裡延展型交表親屬之間，存在著必須相互成婚的巨大壓力。

此種狀況在情歌對唱，與歌詞的標誌性內容中，有著高度可見的表演特性。歌者之間與圍觀的兩群聽眾之間，均位處於分類系統上，相對性別的交表姻親。而這成為解釋高地 Hmub 人在村寨中，以其稱謂系統及交表雙邊婚姻系統作為核心結構的社會證據。交表親人聯姻的理想型，是歌詞中的語意焦點，並以既明確又幽微的方式強調。例如，前引述第 154 至 157 行歌詞，我們讀到「姑娘與男孩是彼此的交表親戚……我們最終將成為彼此的夫妻。不必擔心如果我們現在必須分開。」又如談及村寨內婚，也在前面引述的第 366 與 367 行歌詞提到「姑娘會嫁給**村子裡的其他人**」（粗體為筆者所加）。在這部超過四百行歌詞的對歌中，這些張力透過男性與女性歌者，對親屬稱謂的反覆使用──主要包括 but、 *mul*、*mul diangf*、*maib yut* 所顯示的交表姻親關係，不斷強調著（參第三章）。

本地寨子交表婚所展現的一致性與再確認，卻與情歌歌詞中明確展現高地 Hmub 人婚姻並存的流動特質，及遊方談情與調情情境下所衍生之衝突，產生對比。來自婚姻與遊方談情及調情的衝突，在村寨是明顯的。私奔婚是其中得以對此提供解釋的社會現象。在高地 Hmub 人村寨裡，相當程度上仍保留著在 1949 年以前，婚姻會發生在一段短暫的遊方談情之後；它不必然經歷浪漫愛情，並幾乎可平均區分成由父母送出門的公開婚姻，與私奔婚。這些都不是在最近或者是 1949 年後才發展而成的現象（簡美玲 2005a）。

公開婚姻多半遵循村寨內婚，且以指稱型交表婚姻為規則積極展開。然而，大多數的私奔婚，則違背了村寨內婚的原則。有些私奔婚的新人，雖屬於不同村寨，但彼此仍屬於較遠的交表姻親關係。有些私奔婚的對象，則是非高地的 Hmub 人或 Hmub 人以外的族群。

私奔婚的發生，不需經過新娘家的父母長輩，事先同意或瞭解，而最終在姑娘與新郎於半夜跨過新娘家門的那一刻，受到肯認。新娘考量私奔婚的決定，必須在眾多不確定之間，及遠較交表聯姻之優先性所展現的高度曖昧裡，進行衡量。也就是面對積極交換婚中，所展現的確定性與整體曖昧。儘管如此，私奔婚在此村寨，仍有其相對的普遍性。以 1998 至 2000 年我在田野期間的觀察與記錄，私奔婚發生於大約半數的婚姻之中。這突出了高地 Hmub 人，對於交表婚姻集體理想的曖昧性。這同時也展現了個體性（individuality）的議題：個體強烈的抵抗，來自交表聯姻，與結合村寨內婚之交表聯姻的強大社會約束力與集體理想（簡美玲 2005a）。

第二章　浪漫愛情與婚姻之間的張力：高地 Hmub 人情歌展演的文化個體性
Tensions between Romantic Love and Marriage:
Performing 'Hmub Cultural Individuality' in an Upland Hmub Love-Song

這部通過記音聽寫的情歌對唱，強調著婚姻與遊方談情及調情之間的眾多不穩定性。尤其，之中所展現的兩類不同的關係，如何為個體所經驗。在一開始，遊方談情與調情的自然展開，是與交表親婚姻的本土理想相互連結。例如，前面引述的第 42 至 45 行歌詞，以及第 88 至 91 行歌詞內容：「如果男孩們想對姑娘求愛，就先回家和你們的妻子分開。如果你們不願意，便停止我們的遊方談情，回家照顧你們的妻子」。在這幾行歌詞中，即使表面上對歌當下，婚外遊方已然進行，但民間詩學的某些內容，卻展現遊方調情與婚姻，無法並存的結構特性。

　　與此完全相反地，有許多行歌詞，展現出在這個高地 Hmub 人村寨，婚姻與遊方談情及調情之間，存在流動與可協商的關係。婚姻不完全依遊方而生，但也不一定會排除它。是故，婚外的遊方談情及調情，也同樣會發生（參第一章）。遊方談情與調情，並不會因婚姻而自然地，或者必須終止。

　　對於參與其中的個人來說，這兩者是互相依存的。由前面引述的女性歌者所唱的第 29 至 32 行歌詞，顯現其中所使用的修辭策略：「姑娘們不明白，為什麼她們總是如此渴望坐在男孩身旁。她們不明白和她們談情的對象，是別人的丈夫」。接著，第 263 至 266 行歌詞運用一種更明確的詩意隱喻：「姑娘們有兩顆心：一顆給丈夫，另一顆給遊方的男孩。」這些歌詞以詩意美學，流露婚姻與遊方談情及調情之間，流動、衝突與對話特性。

　　最後，個體的個人情感，也強調著婚姻與遊方之間的曖昧，是另一個重要的特色與語意焦點。情緒元素是重要的。這些元素也在非儀式性的日常遊方談情及調情的活動中展現。它們不僅展現親屬與聯姻群體，如何受到重視，及之中呈現的社會意涵。更在高地 Hmub 人青年與姑娘們遊方時，以輪流的詩意結構談情說話，創造出獨特的禮貌口吻，以及戲謔、熱情的氣氛（簡美玲 2005b）。

然而，在歌詞中展現的個人情緒，卻比起單純的戲謔互動顯得更為複雜。此外，個人感受包括害羞、開心、孤獨、渴望與熱情，也因表演般的呈現而正當化。相對於通常與婚姻相連之遊方談情及調情所帶來的歡愉情緒，一些包括個人渴望與孤獨的感受，則時常展現於在婚姻與遊方談情及調情間，更為複雜的對話脈絡。如前面引述的第 277 至 281 行歌詞，以隱喻營造出一種強烈的孤寂印象。

在這幾行歌詞中，個人的感受包括孤寂，預見將分離而來的孤單，都透過自然的意象來比喻，如「流往瀑布的小河溪流」及「山嶺間盤旋的雲霧」，也就是行將離開之意。歌詞中也表達出那些參與婚外遊方的人們，如何顯現曖昧，而這次則著重於否定的層面：「你們的言語只是說說而已。你們的心是如此遙遠。你們的心就像流往瀑布的小河溪流。就像山嶺間盤旋的雲霧。你們最終將回到妻子的懷抱」。

這部情歌對唱，所展現的，不僅僅是全人類共享的普同心理與情緒情感，而是以民間詩學的抒情風格，表達屬於個人與個體的領域——他們與在地的遊方談情、調情、婚姻脈絡，所形成的張力及曖昧緊密連結。也正是在如此社會學脈絡中，顯示與展現著高地 Hmub 人個體性的本質。

六、結論：展演 Hmub 人的個體性

本章採取史翠珊在特定文化脈絡下研究個人時，重視其美學

第二章　浪漫愛情與婚姻之間的張力：高地 Hmub 人情歌展演的文化個體性
Tensions between Romantic Love and Marriage:
Performing 'Hmub Cultural Individuality' in an Upland Hmub Love-Song

（aesthetic）或標誌（iconic）意義的取徑，針對 Hmub 人在社會生活中的語言表演進行探討，藉此彰顯 Hmub 人的個體性。

自涂爾幹以來，人類學長期關注諸如個人與社會之間的對立關係、個人的價值、個體性的土著觀點，及其與現代性之間的關係。Hmub 人情歌提供一個重新思考這場辯論的機會——它們通過想像展現個人與其所處社會之間的緊張關係。

在大多數的人類社會，個人和社會之間普遍存在著緊張關係。涂爾幹學派的觀點認為，個人總是在意識形態的層面，掙扎著在集體力量與集體表徵中，認知自己與之相對的個體性。Fangf Bil 的 Hmub 人也面臨同樣難題，並透過婚後雙居和制度化的婚外調情等社會制度，以及強調婚姻和調情之間存在矛盾和緊張關係的情歌，得到淋漓盡致的表達。Hmub 人情歌的內容和主題重點——尤其是調情和婚姻之間的對話關係——清楚呈現個人經驗與情感，和聯姻群體之間所存在的張力。

不同文化對個人與個體抱持不同概念：現代西方的個人概念是道德上具有自主性的人。印度教棄世者只在意識形態上，存在於日常生活世界之外。從社會學的角度來看，他們仍然屬於現實世界的一部分。Fangf Bil 的 Hmub 人藉由語言的使用，在美學意義上展演獨特的個體性：上述所討論的情歌，在突顯個人經驗和情感時，也流露出個人對地方社會之核心價值所抱持的曖昧態度（或矛盾立場）。

拉普伯特與奧弗寧（2000：185）將個體性描述為「與個人意識密不可分，與個人特殊認知，及其對意識的感知能力，緊密相連；這也是人類所體現的記號。……人類透過其獨特的認知、感知、思想、感受和想像力，在現實世界裡認識自己。」Fangf Bil 的 Hmub 人在面對社會集體的婚姻理想時，透過情歌展演表達個人意識，並強調情感與想像力在社會發展動力上，所具有的政治性——亦即個人感受、情緒和欲望的政治性。他們藉由展演的形式來合法化個人經驗，進而抵消社會集體婚姻理想所加諸於個人的強大壓力。

值得注意的是，有如史翠珊在美拉尼西亞社會對於部分人概念的探討，Hmub 人對個體性的概念，是以成對的個體來展現。在這部四百多行的 Hmub 人對歌中，反覆出現涉及成對意象的人。以第 224 至 228 行為例：

Dat Deik	男歌者
224 *Meb dlab let lil rak renf.*	妳倆的嘴快得很。
225 *Lab qet juf wak wek.*	一顆心遠遠的。
226 *Ment ghad ghuf dek deif.*	姑娘們拿身體碰男孩。
227 *Dlek xongx dangf dlek dok.*	跟男孩像跟火（姑娘們渴望靠近男孩，就像渴望靠近寒冬裡的火苗）。
228 *Diuf xongx nongf wek yef.*	我們這對男孩才孤獨。

這幾行歌詞之主題重點是個體的個人欲望、強烈渴求和孤獨感。不過，在每一行中，歌詞所指稱實際上不是一個人，而是兩個人。我認為這種表現手法，除了顯示個人在本質上是一種社會性的存在外，也進一步說明個人願意以這種方式進行自我認同。簡言之，Fangf Bil 的 Hmub 人透過這段歌詞，在展演層面表達其關於個體性獨特的土著觀點。

長期以來，個人主義一直被視為構成現代西方意識形態的一個關鍵

第二章　浪漫愛情與婚姻之間的張力：高地 Hmub 人情歌展演的文化個體性
Tensions between Romantic Love and Marriage:
Performing 'Hmub Cultural Individuality' in an Upland Hmub Love-Song

部分。關於個體性的辯論，也因此包括對現代性的探討（Dumont 1986：4）。本章認為在 Hmub 人的個體性中，也包含一種現代性的表達。透過對情歌表演的分析，我們看到 Hmub 人關於聯姻群體的集體社會理想，對個人身分的意識與覺察，以及在各種制度化的脈絡中，個人情感與聯姻群體之間，所呈現的緊張關係。不過 Hmub 人情歌中所表達的個體性及其現代性，並沒有朝著嚴格意義上的西方個人主義方向發展。Hmub 人個體性的特徵是，集體理想——村內的交表婚——與個人情感之間不斷進行的協商競爭。包括當地 Hmub 人透過情歌歌詞，表達在婚姻外調情中，所感受到的情調和趣味，淡淡的情欲以及孤獨感。Hmub 人有效地透過表演的形式，處理社會與個人之間複雜的關係，並緩解了兩造之間存在的張力。重要的是，不管是現實或象徵層次上，情歌的聽眾正好是即將繁衍孕育下一代的年輕人。

這也與杜蒙對西方個人主義的反思有關。杜蒙將整體主義（totalitarianism）視為一種讓時光逆轉，以修復西方因個人主義崛起而遭到破壞的集體主義（collectivism）：

> 的確，整體主義以戲劇化的方式，表達了我們在當代世界中不斷遭遇的困境：一方面，個人主義的力量是強大的；另一方面，它卻也必然將不斷地受到其對立面的干擾。……在現階段的研究裡，這種在當代思潮，個人主義及其對立面的共存，比任何時候都來得強烈。從這個意義上來說，個人主義所構建的思想和價值具備現代性的特徵，但卻絕不等同於現代性。
>
> （Dumont 1986：17）

透過研究個人主義與人或自我在特定地域、歷史和文化脈絡中的發展過程，我提出 Hmub 人的個體性透過情歌的展演，體現一種美學向度，並形成一股推動社會發展的動力。不管是在 1949 年之前或之後，都以傳統的表演方式在進行傳播；此外，Hmub 人的個體性在本質上也具有現代性的意涵。

　　爲了與人類學在西方個人主義及其現代發展的經典理論進行對話，並採納杜蒙的反思性觀點，以及史翠珊所提出的語言和美學向度，本章進一步論證，貴州東部當代 Hmub 人的情歌展演，開創了一條富有想像力的出路，用來釋放不論是在情感和意識形態上，存在於集體社會的婚姻理想和個人在情感、情欲，以及在生活世界中所體驗到各種自由之間的張力。

　　其次，情歌的歌詞和展演方式也清楚指出，Hmub 人以其獨特方式，在生活和表演中，構建自己的個體性和現代性。Hmub 人所展現的個體性，在在挑戰了西方人類學傳統中關於個體性和個人主義的演化觀點，亦即一種隱晦地預示西方個人主義具有更優越、高級地位的論調。有趣的是，從全球化脈絡來看，當代 Hmub 人努力維護其個體性之獨特表達本身，也成爲一種文化個體性的表達。從這種意義上來說，Hmub 人的個體性，在當代弔詭地成爲一種具有道德價值與自主性的文化個人主義。

第二章　浪漫愛情與婚姻之間的張力：高地 Hmub 人情歌展演的文化個體性
Tensions between Romantic Love and Marriage:
Performing 'Hmub Cultural Individuality' in an Upland Hmub Love-Song

Chapter 3　「你倆是我倆一輩子的丈夫」：
　　　　　　情歌語言的兩性意象與結伴理想

一、前言

Jef nend yeik. 結束一首歌了。

Vef nend dak. 再找歌來唱。

Liob huf yiok. 男孩就像話。

Ghas hfaf seik. 男與女一起談天、對歌，好像鴨戲水般歡欣。

Bongt neif meb niangt ghait nongx. 不知怎麼就一直陪你們坐。

Bongt lif dak jut liuk. 不知我陪的是別人的丈夫。

Jef nend yeik. 結束一首歌了。

Nef huf yiok. 姑娘就像話。

Ghas hfaf seik. 男與女一起談天、對歌，好像鴨戲水般歡欣。

Vef nend dak. 再找歌來唱。

Neif meb niangt ghait nongx. 怎麼就一直陪妳們坐。

Mongf saix mek diuf lel. 妳們回去離了妳們的丈夫，再返回。

　　1999 年一整年，我在貴州東部高地的一個 Hmub 人村寨，進行婚姻與情感為主題的民族誌田野工作。村寨內男女對唱的情歌，是我記錄的重點之一 —— 不僅因為情歌是在遊方的場合下演唱，並且歌詞的內容，也都環繞婚姻的主題與戲謔而唱。[1] 正式對歌的演唱，只有在儀式之後的大型遊方才可能展開，因此要完整記錄一部現場即興對唱的情歌並不容易。1999 年春天，我與 Fangf Bil 村寨的姑娘，一起去看幾個村寨聯合舉行的鬥牛。鬥牛比賽結束後，暮色漸濃，但我與一同前來的姑娘仍在附近逗留。此時，大型跨村寨遊方正熱鬧展開。在遊方現場，我們幸運記錄下長達四百多句的即興對歌。在聽寫、翻譯、分析這部對歌的過程中，令我印象深刻的，不僅是對歌語意內涵表達婚姻理想與個人情感的張力。情歌的歌詞，還大量運用性別與人的人稱語言同義詞及語彙組合，展現多樣、反覆的語彙聚合與表述。經由此傳達情人、夫妻兩類結伴理想的交錯並置。

　　語言在人類社會，具有參與的積極性與有效性（Bauman and Briggs 1990：59-88）。它不僅傳達語意，語言活動本身也是有意義的社會行動。對特定語言活動進行微觀分析，可以有效理解特定社會文化。經由觀察與描述情歌語言的符號活動，如何聚焦成兩性結伴與個人兩範疇之並置與流動的性別意象，本章指出在語言的演述場域，Hmub 人所再現之性別意象的對等，有別於結合從夫、從父居的父系繼嗣體系，以男性共祖為原則的家屋兄弟群所展現的父系理想與價值。個人與結伴兩類人稱語彙的對照，以及情人、交表親、夫妻等人稱語彙之間的任意置換，展現情歌語言之性別意象與人觀的結合。[2] 基於語言的具體分析，本章最後推論情歌的演述，不僅細微一致地唱和 Hmub 人社會以交表聯姻為底層的社群理想，而且語言符號的演述活動，讓個體價值在期待聯姻結群的優勢氛圍裡，低調卻穩定地現身。

二、性別、差異與界線

　　由文化來瞭解性別是本文的基本理論觀點。在這樣的觀點下，我們要討論的是每個社會如何以其特定方式，表達對性別的看法與做法；性別的異、同，如何是每個社會在知識或邏輯上，理論化和歷史化的過程，而非必然的（生物）結果。如丹妮絲・雷麗（D. Riley 1988）所說，將女人與男人視為不同類（賦有不同特性、本質與能力）的概念，純粹是西方文化的產物。雖然不少東、西方社會認為男女兩性由外表到性格，存在著自然的差異；然而，也有社會並不強調兩性外表的明顯差異。東南亞部分南島語群認為，兩性間不存在自然的差異；兩性的差異與其所創造的力量，是以較細膩、隱微的象徵表現。印尼峇厘島的男與女，傳統上圍著紗籠做服飾。雖然在裝扮上他們看起來只有微小差別，但服飾形式上細微的差異，在峇厘島文化的觀點裡，已足以創造顯著的意義，並由此生成該文化所肯定的正向力量。

　　在貴州東部 Hmub 與美國 Hmong 的性別研究，路易莎・謝茵（Louisa Schein 2000）或南希・唐納利（Nancy Donnelly 1994）從日常生活的兩性分工，現代性與社會變遷脈絡下的儀式、身體展演，呈現兩性差異所形成之界線的可移動與複雜。男人鍛鑄銀片、木工和犁田，女人煮飯和織衣——這是該社會傳統之日常與勞動的兩性分工。但由工作內容與場域所創造的性別界線，並非不能移動。即使居住在大山裡的貴州東部高地村寨 Hmub 人，傳統上是男人管田裡的事，女人管家裡的事，不過女人也參與田裡的事，男人在農忙之餘，也幫忙家務。換言之，仍以水稻為主的 Hmub 人村寨，除了織布、鑄銀、木工展現穩定的兩性分工，諸多日常工作其實是兩性互相合作——導致兩性分工所形成的性別界線不是那麼清楚（簡美玲 2016）。再則，日常事務的分工，除了反映內部社會原有生產結構，也受外在經濟環境影響。

路易莎・謝茵（2000）描述 1980 年代到 1990 年代貴州東部西江 Hmub 人面對全球經濟體系和內部社會生活變化的情況，如何產生新的生存適應和策略，並關注在性別與現代性觀點下的族群論述。謝茵（2000：159-160）發現西江男性精英的角色，是促進以女性爲文化象徵的消費。因爲西江婦女在服飾、歌謠、髮型等面向，有著突出的視覺形式。在商業機制和觀光的運作下，婦女的妝扮被客體化爲族群文化的識別。婦女從傳統負責家務的角色，轉換爲詮釋族群文化的鮮明象徵；男人的角色則是這整套機制的背後推手。

南希・唐納利（1994：11-13）比較美國和東南亞老撾（Laos；寮國）兩地 Hmong 人家庭經濟角色的不同，來理解性別關係的轉變。[3] 傳統上，Hmong 人在神話、家庭經濟關係、重要儀式等社會生活上，都透露出理想的性別觀。在小孩養成教育中，男孩被教導射箭、種田、蓋屋和參與部落會議；女孩則學習挑水、搗米、煮茶和織布等。在傳說故事中也述說兩性各自的特質：男性是聰明、務實和有遠見；女性則是保守、服從（obedient）和短視（Donnelly 1994：36-38）。

研究美國 Hmong 人的唐納利發現，根據女性在房間內站立的位置和姿態，以及日常工作分工，女性在傳統 Hmong 社會的地位看似低下。但許多在美國的 Hmong 人卻告訴她，在傳統的思維裡，不同性別的確有不同階級地位，並追求不同的行爲模式，但男性和女性分屬的領域都是生活中必要的（essential）。不同性別所屬的領域都是重要的，彼此之間是互補且一體的。在傳統農業生活上，Hmong 的男性從事農務，是家中經濟主要來源。在美國的新環境中，男性不可能靠種田維生，反而女性的織布具有市場經濟價值。因此，女性的織布漸漸成為家庭經濟的可能來源，兩性在家庭的角色因而有了轉變（Donnelly 1994：185）。而貴州Hmub 人兩性關係的變化不單純是取代，更是一種互補。這關係就如同一個整體中的兩半，缺了哪一方都是不完整。簡言之，Hmub 人兩性的分工關係是跟隨環境而有著動態性地適應和調整。

從以上討論可發現，在不同的社會環境，性別所歸屬的行為和責任，會產生不同的變化。家是傳統 Hmub 人基本的社會單位，日常生活的兩性分工，不同性別有著不同的歸屬。在不斷地相互流動和取代的同時，兩性的關係呈現出互補的特性。從傳統農業社會中，Hmub 人以男主外、女主內為分野。當代中國國家推動民族觀光的機制下，女性成為表徵族群文化的對象，男性則轉變為運作此一再現機制背後的推手之一。在商業的價值上，女性的編織手藝也成為家庭經濟來源之一。性別差異的界線在不同的環境有不同的展現，不過從家的角度來看，呈現的仍是互補的關係。

有越來越多民族誌顯示性別界線與差異的不穩定。亨利耶塔・摩爾（Henrietta Moore〔1993：193-204，1994〕）認為，對於性別的範疇、實質及異同的探討，顯得更重要。我認為現有關於討論性別差異之建構或消解的人類學民族誌，多訴諸儀式或身體展演的行動，而較少關注人的社會生活，密不可分的語言活動與此議題的關聯。語言符號的活動，與身體展演等儀式行動，在建構或解構二元的動力上，雖然無法直接並比，惟個人或集體發聲的語言行動，倘若亦是社會生活基本的環節，作為人群建立其微觀、多元之性別意象的場域，便具備可能性；所創造的性別場域之特性，也有描述與討論的價值。因此，本章主要由語言的現象切入，描述 Hmub 人的情歌語彙之組合等符號活動所表徵的性別意象，以及其中所蘊含的個人與成對結伴之合與分的流動。經由情歌歌詞之語言符號的形式運作，使我們能微觀的面對 Hmub 人社群對性別意象的另一種敘述觀點，與性別意象在符號行動上的具體展現。

三、語言符號的指示與象似性

語言不僅能傳達意義，語言活動本身也是一種社會行動與演述行動（Hymes 1964）。對於語言與文化的探討，語言人類學者所提出的指示性（indexicality）與象似性（iconicity）的理論觀點，[4] 能微觀且具體說明語言與社會文化情景脈絡的關聯。這兩個特性，不僅是人類語言普遍存在的特質，也是個別文化下，展現特定的互動歷程。指示和象似的語言特性，在非語言的文化現象 —— 被視爲自然、必然的社會生活、意識形態、價值規範中，發揮其主動運作的有效性（Irvine and Gal 1999：35-83）。本文經由情歌語言的描述與分析，闡述 Hmub 人如何將語言的指示與象似特性，作爲創造性別意象、差異、認同的社會資源。

Index（指示符號）或 indexicality（指示性），中文可直譯爲指示符號建立的指稱關係。語言人類學者認爲這是人類一種普遍的，與社會情景脈絡相依存之自然語言的發聲活動。查爾斯·帕爾斯（Charles Peirce 1932）、羅曼·雅各布森（Roman Jakobson 1957〔1971〕：130-147）與邁克·西爾弗斯坦（Michel Silverstein 1976）等人致力於語言符號活動的研究和書寫，對此理論概念的出現與成熟有重要影響。以地圖爲例，

帕爾斯指出人類的符號系統是象徵、指示與象似三種符號特性的混合
（Peirce 1932）。雅各布森延伸帕爾斯對符號的全貌觀，以人稱代名詞
爲例，說明語言所具有的指示性。以英文第一人稱代名詞 I（我）爲例，
如果沒有它與客體之間已經存有的關係，I 便無法表示這個客體。換言
之，I 之能用以指稱說話者，是因爲和說話者的發聲，已存在一種關聯。
I 的功能就是指示性的記號。[5] 以人稱代名詞爲例的語言符號指示性，展
現了語言符號不僅有一般意義（a Gesamtbedeutung，general），也有特
定情景脈絡下（a Grundbedeutung，specific）（如說話行動）所實踐的
符號意義。這個著重符號行動的理論觀點，使語言符號特性的觀察與研
究，可以更細微豐富的進行，也使索緒爾主張的語言與說話（language
與 speech）二分，以及語言符號的武斷任意性（arbitrariness），必須重
新評估。語言的指示功能，和主體化過程密切相關（Benveniste 1971a：
217-222、1971b：223-230；Caton 1987：223-260）。 主 體 的 位 置 是
在說話的當下（here and now），運用符號與情景脈絡（context or co-
text）的連接才標定下來。任何可以改變或標示說話主體位置的符號，也
都具有指示的潛力。例如人稱詞（代名詞、親屬稱謂、名字）的效力，
就是在人與人互動時才得以實踐。

　　Icon（象似符號）或 iconicity（象似性），用中文可直譯爲象似符
號建立的表徵關係。象似符號與客體間的關係，主要建立在符號以某種
方式對客體進行複製（Mannheim 2000：107-110）。[6] 圖畫或圖表就是典
型的象似符號。而語言或文字也有其象似性。模擬眞實世界聲音的擬聲
語（onomatopoetic，如英文的 ding-dong，或中文的沙沙作響），就是象
似符號（Duranti 1997a：162-213）。相對於指示符號負載著客體與情景
脈絡的關係，而不描述所指對象；象似符號則以自身具備的特質（quality）

成爲符號（Peirce 1955〔1902〕：98-115）。[7] 即使看起來最自然的象似符號，也和社會的約定俗成，以及特定歷史情景脈絡下符號使用人的解釋習慣有關。例如 Inka（印加）帝國的首都庫斯科（Cuzco）的空間組織，就是以圖形式的象似符號（diagramatic icon），表現社會分層、灌溉權、儀式責任之間的關係。亦即由社會體系的宏觀組織，到詞彙的微觀組織，象似性都可能在語言或文化上展現其影響力。[8]

作爲一種能形成結構的符號形式，象似性也對文化形式的承轉與維繫，有所貢獻。保羅・佛里德里希（Paul Friedrich 1979）指出，符號被個別看待時，它們也許不具有特別的支配力。若將它們看作巨大群聚的一部分（如行動、模式、會話、文法、文化），象似性的概念，特別是圖形象似性（diagrammaticity），就是在瞭解符號群聚、互動的過程與意義。[9] 通過象似符號在形式構成上所表現的力量，可提供我們探討符號的群結、形象化，以及它們所再現的人對其社會生活中一些重要的想法、行動或意識形態的詮釋。甚至能揭開看似自然的非自然與文化歷程。

小結

經由語言符號活動的理論觀點，本章描述與分析 Hmub 人情歌的演述型式、人稱語彙的組合與結構，並討論性別意象的具體敘述，如何經由符號的活動，展現於歌唱的語言現象裡。亦即通過指示符號（index）與象似符號（icon）兩種語言符號的運作，表達 Hmub 人對性別意象、認同及差異的想像與詮釋。特別是在通過對人稱語言符號系統的描述，我們可以推論情歌的演述場合、參與成員、歌的部分語意內容等，雖與交表聯姻、緩落夫家的婚後居制、[10] 遊方談情密切關聯。但情歌作爲語言現象，不僅經由語意，也經由形式符號展現其主動性——對於性別意象的詩學創造——而非僅作爲親屬、婚姻等社會結構的伴隨結果。

四、情歌的演述與符號活動 [11]

（一）短歌的符號組成與詩韻規律

這部對歌的結構由八十首短歌組成。[12] 每首短歌的基本組成包括歌頭（亦稱爲 *dab hxad*〔答歌〕）、歌中（*hxad jat diongx*）、歌尾（又稱爲 *diut ghob yiok*〔唱調子〕），以及添加歌話（*bux hveb hxad*）。以下這例子是一首短歌的基本結構。由上而下，第一句的 *Jet diaut*：是無特定語意的歌頭；短歌中段的第二句至第五句爲有語意的歌中，其中第三句爲歌者即興的添加歌話；最後一句爲歌尾，表示一首短歌結束。

Jet diaut:	歌頭
Mangk lait lait mangk lif,	歌中
mul-diangf.	添歌話
Dak lait ceit daik lif	歌中
Dak lot hxif mek bongt	歌中
Ut:	歌尾

接下來說明組成短歌的基本要素。歌中是每首短歌的主體，它們主要由四到六句有語意的歌句組成。這組對歌之短歌歌中的聲韻結構主要分爲三類：ａｂａｂｃｄ，ｃｄｃｄｃ與ｃｄｃｄ（ａ與ｂ表示三個音節，ｃ與ｄ表示五個音節）。這三類型裡，ｃｄｃｄｃ最爲普遍，其次爲ｃｄｃｄ。這與

在貴州不同方言體系之苗族地區進行歌謠調查、記錄的民族音樂學者李惟白所描述相吻合。呼應李惟白所說的「黔東南地區的苗歌最普遍流行的是五言句式」（李惟白 1996：130）。

歌頭代表一首短歌的開始（在對歌的演述結構下，歌頭也稱爲答歌），歌尾代表一首短歌的結束。藉由此二者，一首首短歌，便可被標示出來。在這組對歌裡，歌頭、歌尾主要是無語意的音，但音本身的差異，則形成輪替的基礎。這點原則在歌頭的表現（以第一音節的子音 /h/ 與 /j/ 的對比來輪替）尤其明顯。

添歌話（插話、裝飾的手法）在情歌的演述，也很常見。這部對歌的短歌裡，添加歌話是在歌中或歌尾加入人稱的親屬稱謂。這組對歌從頭到尾的演唱，添歌話的比例極高。添歌話雖然是作爲修飾的，但它唱的次數多，創造出人稱語彙大量群聚的優勢（參後）。

（二）短歌演述的成對規律與兩性對等意象的再現

這部由男女歌者對唱的四百多句情歌，若依照歌頭、歌尾爲前後標記，一共包含八十多首短歌。除了表現以五節拍爲主的 c d c d c 詩韻規律外，這部對歌所表現另一個優勢的基本結構是成對演唱（song pair）的規律。在歌頭、歌尾的標記下，這部歌至少表現出三類的成對形式。這種成對的演唱規律，明顯創造出兩性意象的對比。以下摘錄第 3 句到第 26 句來說明。第 3 句到第 8 句爲一首短歌，第 9 句到第 13 句爲銜接、應答上一首的短歌。依此往下推。

女歌者：3 *Het:*

4 *Xeit del mongf ghat liok.* 你們夫妻如果喜歡就算了。

5 *Det del diangt zix sait ghat dak meb liuk.* 不喜歡，就回家離了你倆的妻子。

6 *Ghob zis lel bib dangk.* 再轉來，我們作夫妻。

7 *Ses nef dak ghat dliak.* 來娶我這醜姑娘。

8 *Eit: ob dat:* 喂，二位。

男歌者：9 *Jef: diaut:*

10 *Liuf ghaib del*

11 *Liuf deɪ ghaib.*[13]

12 *Ghab buk ghet iauf jat lif let langf.* 老朋友現在才相遇談天、唱歌。

13 *Ut:*

女歌者：14 *Het:*

15 *Meb meit qint qint ghaif nil.* 你倆說甚麼好聽的（話）來著。

16 *Det juk diuf xeif mal: ob:* 沒有花甚麼就來買（一個妻子），二位。

17 *Det ghob niongx ghaif xeif.* 沒有挑甚麼重的來。

18 *Juk nend vus dak niangt.* 只是花點力氣來坐（指遊方）。

19 *Ut: ob dat eb:* 二位。

男歌者：20 *Jet:*

21 *Lik gif eb pot mal.* 田乾就要水來泡軟。

22 *Naik liuf ment let lab.* 跟陌生人來說話、對歌，就會認識。

23 *Meit ob lab nit nil.* 就是這樣來說幾句話。

24 *Lab def lab det jaf.* 但是卻一句話跟不成一句話。

25 *Xid xeit meb gid weif.* 我對你們害羞的很，不知如何是好。

26 *Eit: ob dat eb:* 喂，二位。

　　這部對歌的成對結構，最為顯見的是兩組歌者，對等輪替的成對規律，如（A1，B1）、（A2，B2）⋯⋯的形式。以歌頭、歌尾為區分，輪替交換演唱，是這部對歌突顯的組合。歌頭代表一首短歌的開始（亦稱為答歌），歌尾表結束一首短歌。歌者接歌、答歌，須以交替成對方式添唱歌頭。前面的例子標底色者，就是歌者答歌時唱的歌頭。歌頭無語意，也不作為區辨演唱者性別的標記。歌頭的演唱原則和第一位置的語音異同有關。凡是有 *jet*（包括 *jet diaut*，*maib jet iaut*）被歸為一組，*heb* 單獨一組。原則上兩組輪流搭配，但在演唱過程中，此規則也有鬆動的時候。*Het—jet* 與歌者的對應關係，在演唱的中途可以置換，但是如前所述，Fangf Bil 村寨各類歌謠的演唱都講究有頭有尾。這是必須遵守的原則。

　　年輕人對歌的歌尾比老歌歌尾簡單——這部對歌多數短歌的歌尾 *ut* 就只是一個調或一個音。歌尾的輪替交換類似歌頭，出現的組合類型比較簡單。這部對歌只有 *ut* 與 *eit ob dat* 二個歌尾交替出現，它們與不同歌頭之間，並沒有出現特殊的對應關係。歌尾之一的 *eit ob dat* 具有語意，是在歌者結束一首短歌以前，呼喊與其對歌的對手「喂，兩位」。年輕人對歌裡的歌頭與歌尾，雖然沒有可辨認的語意內涵，但它們規律的輪替，似乎是以音樂交替的形式，提供對歌成對演述的形式基礎。

　　成對規律還可以在插入話語的情形下繼續。在對手演唱時，加入相關或不相關的「話」（如吟誦一段歌詞〔歌話〕，或與一旁的觀眾聊天），當「話」說完後，又回到原先對等、輪替的結構。如：（A1，B1）、（A2，B2[A'2]）、（A3，B3）、（A4，B4[A'4]）、（A5，B5）……。這類型的變化，也包含在（A1，B1）、（A2，B2）的結構中。在輪替演唱的成對結構中，展現的是兩性均衡、對等的意象。

和兩兩相對的輪替類型有所差異的，是在整部對歌演唱的最開頭，先演唱兩三首的是男歌者，然後由女歌者接唱。姑娘唱的第一首歌，只能唱兩句。根據當地姑娘的聽歌經驗，女歌者開頭唱的常是這句："*Dios ob liuk sangf ghet.*"（你倆是我倆一輩子的丈夫）。

除了以歌頭、歌尾當作切割標記，表現三種成對的演述規律；成對規律的再現，也有來自對歌語彙的變化。它是經由人稱語彙以相應和的方式呈現兩性成對意象的輪替、均衡。例如下面三首短歌是由一首短歌所變化。我以底色標示變動的語彙。在不改變短歌結構的情境下，特定語彙的變動，不僅標識歌者性別，也呼應兩性成對之輪替與均衡的意象（對歌語彙的討論，請參下節「歌話的符號活動」）。

女歌者：27 *Jef nend yeik.* 結束一首歌了。

28 *Vef nend dak.* 再找歌來唱。

29 *Liob huf yiok.* 男孩就像話。

30 *Ghas hfaf seik.* 男與女一起談天、對歌，好像鴨戲水般歡欣。

31 *Bongt neif meb niangt ghait nongx.* 不知怎麼就一直陪你們坐。

32 *Bongt lif dak jut liuk* 不知我們陪的是別人的丈夫。

男歌者：237 *Jef nend yeik,* 結束一首歌了。

238 *Nef huf yiok,* 姑娘就像話。

239 *Ghab hfaf seik.* 男與女一起談天、對歌，好像鴨戲水般
歡欣。

240 *Vef nend dak.* 再找歌來唱。

241 *Neif meb niangt ghait nongx* 怎麼就一直陪妳們坐。

242 *Mongf saix mek diuf lel.* 回去離了妳們的丈夫再返回。

男歌者：269 *Jef nend yeik,* 結束一首歌了。

270 *Vef nend dak.* 再找歌來唱。

271 *Nef huf yiok,* 姑娘就像話。

272 *Ghas hfas seik.* 男與女一起談天、對歌，好像鴨戲水
般歡欣。

273 *Nef hfif sat vok liat.* 鳥飛走，就氣鳥籠編的太寬。

274 *Nef hfif niangt mek dief.* 要不到兩位姑娘來一起對歌。

　　詩韻規律、成對結構，不僅突顯這部對歌在語言演述及形式的獨特
性；詩歌之規律或結構的組合變化，亦指向一特定的性別意象。說話、
唱歌的語言行為，是遊方的重要內容。針對遊方說話的研究，我也發現
輪替的現象。[14] 不過這部對歌經由語言形式而來之性別意象的特殊性，不
只展現成對規律，還經由歌話（歌詞），特別是人稱語彙的符號活動，
創造獨特的人觀與性別意象。

（三）歌話的符號活動

另一個形式焦點是人稱語彙重複地群聚、組合、解離，以此指示性別意象與個人意象的連結、個人意象與結伴意象的輪替並置，以及不同範疇之人際關係的流動。[15] 這幾點理解的基礎在於歌話的五種群聚特性。

第一點是以眾多人稱語彙，指示出重重疊疊的男或女，夫或妻之性別與個人意象。語意為男孩或女孩的人稱語彙有穩定的性別表述；語意為伴侶、配偶（妻子或丈夫）之人稱語彙，對性別表述則與歌者以及歌詞內容有關。

Deif、*xongx*、*liob*、*kheit* 的語意都是男孩。除了 *deif* 是指稱兄弟的親屬稱謂，[16] 其他三者是對歌的專門語彙。他們重複出現在整部對歌。*Deif* 出現在十七句歌（其中十一句由姑娘演唱）；*xongx* 出現在九句歌（其中八句由男孩唱）；*liob* 和 *kheit* 的重複不如前二者，但 *liob* 多由姑娘所唱。此符號現象可解釋為：語意為男孩的人稱語彙，有指示著女孩對男孩的他稱；也有指示著男孩的自稱。亦即，符號活動在語意之外，還指示著性別的差異與對比。

Liuk deif、*wangt liob*、*dliok kheit*、*kheit dliok* 是組合的人稱語彙，其語意也是男孩。*Liuk deif* 的 *liuk*，其性別的語意原是不定的（參後），但它與性別語意固定的 *deif* 相連，在性別語意的指稱便確定為男孩。*Wangt liob* 的 *wangt* 不會單獨出現，*liob* 可以，兩者相連後的語意仍為男孩。*Dliok kheit* 與 *kheit dliok* 表現人稱語彙在對歌裡具有可前後對調的組合彈性。詞構上不論是單一的 *dliok* 或 *kheit*，在歌中都表述男孩 —— 亦即兩個單獨的人稱語彙，聯結組合後其語意不變。

Nef、*lis*、*niongk*、*niangk*、*ment*、*wangt nef*、*niangk sint* 的語意都
是女孩。*Nef* 原意爲鳥，*ment* 原意爲井水，是 *Hmub* 人女孩的名字。這
兩個名詞在對歌裡爲指稱女孩的人稱語彙，但平常的談話則不如此用。
這些語彙在對歌裡也重複出現：九句歌唱到 *nef*（其中六次是男孩所唱）；
五句歌唱到 *lis*（全部由女歌者唱出）。*Wangt* 單獨使用時無語意內含，
它與 *nef* 組合成人稱語彙（由男孩所唱）。換言之，*lis* 指示著女孩的自稱，
nef 與 *wangt nef* 則是男孩對女孩的他稱。[17] 這幾個語意爲女孩的人稱語
彙，同樣也在語意之外，以符號活動展現性別意象的對比。

一群語意爲夫或妻的人稱語彙，其指示的性別屬性和情境脈絡有關。
無論是單一的人稱（*liuk*、*dint*、*bongf*、*vob*、*senf*、*benf*），或是語意相
同的人稱組合（*dint bongf*），還是結合動詞與名詞（*jek vob*），語意都
是妻子或丈夫。在當地的觀點，這些人稱用語指示爲丈夫或妻子，需與
歌者的性別對應，或由承載這個人稱語彙的句子，與這個句子所屬短歌，
亦即短歌前後句子交織成的語意情境來決定。例如第 88 與 89 兩句歌的
語意爲「眞也說男孩得妻，假也說男孩得妻」。它們便影響到第 90 句歌
的 *dint bongf* 必須解釋爲男孩的妻子。

88 *Daik sat het deif dot.* 真也說男孩得妻。
89 *Hlaib sak het deif dot.* 假也說男孩得妻。
90 *Diangt zix lius mek dint bongf heix.* 回家離了你們的妻。

第二點特性出現在男女成對結伴的人稱語彙——夫妻與情人。語意
爲夫妻的有 *xeit*、*dangk*、*dint*、*benf*。其中，*dinb* 與 *benf* 不僅可以指示

成對、結伴的意象（夫妻），也可以指示個人伴侶（男人的妻或女人的丈夫）。語意爲情人的有 *ghat buk ghet*、*lek ghengs*、*hment ninf*、*ob dak hfent*、*sint nef jint*。在日常生活中，這幾個人稱語彙所指示之人際間情感，有性別或深淺之別。*Ghat buk ghet* 在日常對話中可泛指同性或異性間有交情的老友。但作爲歌的語彙，其語意僅用作遊方對歌、談話的男女情人。*Hfent*（以 *hfent ninf*、*ob dak hfent* 的組合出現）與 *lek ghengs*，無論在日常談話或歌唱，均爲兩情相悅的戀人（但他們不一定是老朋友——此與遊方男女初次見面，便可談情、相互戲謔之特性相對應）。*Sint nef jint* 是對歌的專門用語，*sint* 是男孩、*nef* 是女孩、*jint* 是鳥叫，組合成的語意爲男女一起對歌談情。

結伴關係的演述，不僅純粹爲單一或組合的人稱名詞，也有動詞與名詞的組合。如 *jek vob*（成爲你的荣，第 104 句）和 *heit dongf dand*（說成夫妻，第 399 句）的語意都是成爲夫妻。對歌也以動詞演述男女在遊方場合裡相互作伴。如 *lif*（陪），*niangt*（坐），*lof vud*（休息）都是男女成對唱歌談情的結伴行動。這幾組語意爲成對結伴的人稱語，以名詞或名詞與動詞組合的比喻、動詞轉喻等修辭效果，指示夫妻或情人的結伴關係。

第三個特點是，人稱語彙指示的性別意含，既有獨立於情境，也有由情境決定。在敘述第一點時，我已說明這部對歌中，有些人稱語有固定的性別表述，有些則無，後者需與歌者的性別相互對應。就語言符號與情境之間的關聯，有些人稱語彙指示的性別意義，不僅對應歌者性別，還被包藏人稱語彙的對歌句子，與包藏這些對歌句子的短歌內容決定。這三種類型交替而成的變動性，緊密地表現在對歌一開始的幾句。我以下面的例子來描述、分析人稱語彙如何在句子與短歌的情境裡創造性別的意象。

女歌者：1 *Het*:

2 *Dios ob liuk sangf ghet.*
是 我倆 丈夫 一輩 情人 （你倆是我倆一輩子的丈夫）

（接下來開始男孩、女孩的對唱。我開始錄音時，現場已由姑娘接唱。）

女歌者：3 *Het*:

4 *Xeit del mongf ghat liok.*
夫妻 喜歡 去   就 算 （你們夫妻如果喜歡就算了。）

5 *Det del diangt zix sait ghat dak meb   liuk.*
不 喜歡 回家   離那   個 你倆的 妻子
（不喜歡就回家離了你倆的妻子。）

6 *Ghob zis lel bib dangk.*
再 轉 來 我們 作夫妻 （再轉來，我們作夫妻。）

7 *Ses nef   ak   ghat dliak.*
結 「鳥」（指姑娘）這個 不好看
（來娶我們這對醜姑娘。）

第 7 句的 *nef* 原意指鳥，在歌中出現不論歌者的性別爲何，都只用來表述姑娘。第 4、6 句的 *xeit*、*dank* 為成對夫妻（無論男、女歌者演唱都有相同用法）。女歌者在對歌正式開始前，必須唱的第 2 句，與對歌開始後的第 3 句都唱了 *liuk*。這個字在語意上，是表述異性的婚姻伴侶，所以 *liuk* 這個語彙，在對歌中一般的語意表述，與歌者的組合關係如下：當男孩演唱時，*liuk* 在歌中指述與男孩對唱之姑娘的丈夫；女孩演唱時 *liuk* 在歌中，指與女孩對唱之男孩的妻。前述第 5 句歌就符合此原則。然而除歌者的性別之外，*liuk* 所表述的語意，還與出現在 liuk 之前的詞彙有關。如第 2 句 *liuk* 前的 *ob*（我倆），就是歌者反身自指的人稱代名詞。若表示為女歌者的自稱，則 *liuk* 表述的便是男性，指對唱者為自己一輩子的情人或丈夫。

　　某些人稱語彙的性別語意，和歌者的性別密切關聯。如對歌第 27 至 33 句、第 237 至 243 句、第 269 至 275 句（參前節引述），三首短歌的內容屬於同一型。三首短歌之人稱語彙的變動，對應歌者性別的變動。例如第 27 至 33 句的短歌，出現在第 29 句的人稱代名詞是固定表述男孩的 *liob*，與其對應的歌者性別為女。與這句歌同一位置的人稱歌話，被唱進第 237 至 243 句與第 269 至 275 句，則轉變為固定表述女性的 *nef*（姑娘）。它們平行地對應第 238 與 273 句的歌者性別為男。

　　第四點是語意為個人或結伴的人稱語彙，在詞構上具有可拆解與倒轉組合的彈性。*Dliok kheit* 語意為男孩，*dliok* 與 *kheit* 也可以分開，或者倒過來組合成 *kheit dliok*，仍維持相同語意。*Dint bongf*（第 90、234、442 句）的組合原則，也是可合、可分，且維持語意不變（妻子或丈夫）。相對的，另一些語彙則是詞構不變，語意可依情境拆解、組合。*Dint*（第 157 句）、*benf*（第 263、309、349 句）、*bongf*（第 265 句）都在詞構不變的狀況下，依歌者性別與對歌的情境，表述不同語意（夫妻、女人的丈夫或男人的妻）。

第五點是男女歌者以歌句或添歌話，唱出兩類相互呼喚的人稱語彙：一類是互稱交表姻親的親屬稱謂，一類是互稱情人的語彙。此二者展現可置換的流動性。以下說明這兩類人稱語彙如何對應著黔東南 Hmub 人社會的親屬稱謂，與其他人稱稱謂原有特性，然後指出對歌裡，展現兩個不同語意範疇之人稱用語間置換的特性。

首先，這部對歌出現幾個 Fangf Bil 村寨常聽到的親屬稱謂，*ob dak maib yut*（兩位叔媽）、*ob dak but*（兩位姊夫）、*ob yol*（我倆的丈夫）、*mul diangf*（表兄弟姊妹）、*bib mul diangf naik jut*（我們是表兄弟姊妹）。它們分別對應著此 Hmub 人村寨親屬稱謂體系裡的幾個特點：世代壓縮（skewing rule）、指定婚姻（prescriptive marriage）、性別、對稱。對歌裡的 *maib yut*（叔媽）雖然與父親弟弟之配偶用了相同的稱謂詞彙（所以我將它譯為叔媽），[18] 但在對歌的情境並不是這個意思。[19] 它是指男性說話者，稱呼同輩的女性交表親為弟的妻或妻的妹。*Maib yut*（叔媽）這個稱謂在此具有兩種特性：其一為世代的壓縮（亦即以同一稱謂指不同輩分的親人）；其二為以稱謂表達指定婚姻的理想（亦即，男歌者以 *maib yut* 的稱謂稱呼女歌者為弟的妻或妻的妹）。這種親屬稱謂稱為指定型婚配稱謂（簡美玲 1999：202-233；2002）。

如同對歌裡的 *maib yut* 主要是男性說話者的用語，*but*（姊夫）、*yol*（丈夫），則是女性說話者專用的稱謂辭彙。它們皆突出稱謂的性別相對原則。*But* 是女性說話者對於比自己年紀大的同輩異性交表親的專用稱謂，語意可以是姊夫、父親姊妹之子，或母親弟兄之子。男性說話者是不用這個稱謂。*Yol*（丈夫）也是女人對配偶的專門用語。相對於前面三個具有性別特性的稱謂，*mul diangf* 是同輩的兩性交表親（表兄弟姊妹）之間相對的稱謂，對應的是此 Hmub 人村寨稱謂體系裡的對稱原則。

　　呼應前述親屬稱謂的相對性別原則：*ob dak but*（兩位姊夫）、*ob yol*（我倆的丈夫）皆由姑娘唱；*ob dak maib yut*（我倆的妻妹）由男孩唱；*mul diangf* 則是男孩與女孩都唱，但由男孩唱得多。*Bib mul diangf naik jut*（我們是表兄弟姊妹）只有女孩唱（如第 154、321 句）。*Mul diangf*（表兄弟姊妹）被重複唱出最多（共有十五句）。若將 *bib mul diangf naik jut*（我們是表兄弟姊妹）計入，便有十七句歌唱到，遠超過其他親屬稱謂在歌中被演唱的次數。

　　換言之，與親屬稱謂對稱原則對應的是：男歌者稱呼姑娘 *ob dak maib yut*（兩位妻妹）（如第 48、66、83 句）；女歌者稱呼男孩 *ob dak but*（兩位姊夫）（如第 401 句）；以及男女歌者互稱呼對方 *mul diangf*（表兄弟姊妹）（如第 43、54 句等，共十七句）。成對稱謂的演唱形式，並非一方唱出後，另一方立即緊連的在下一段歌中對出。但對歌裡的成對稱謂一致地對應著歌者與歌者之間相對的姻親關係、兩性關係，以及稱謂邏輯裡相對稱謂的組合（reciprocal sets）規定。總之，如 *maib yut*（yBW）與 *but*（eZH）的對稱，或者 *mul diangf*（FZD／MBS；FZS／MBD）之間的互稱，無論表現在親屬或性別，都是成對、交錯的組合關係。

　　另一類相互呼喚的人稱語彙，是語意爲情人（或友人）的 *ob dat*、*ghat buk ghet*、*lek ghengs*、*hment ninf*、*ob dak hfent*、*sint nef jint*。*Ob dat* 的語意爲說話者眼前或言說內容裡提及的兩位對歌者。它沒有性別、年齡或身分的規定。因此 *ob dat* 的實際語意內涵與言語情境密切關聯。

如在對歌中，*ob dat* 就是男女歌者相互呼喚對方。相對於本範疇其他指涉情人（或友人）的人稱語彙（如 *ghat buk ghet* 老友、*lek ghengs* 戀人），*ob dat* 在這群歌話的語彙，被唱的次數最多，而且男女歌者都唱（這個現象與 *ob dat* 不僅出現在歌中，並也和它當作歌尾有關）。

　　姻親與情人（或友人）兩類人稱用語，在符號的行動上，有兩點特性值得提出。其一它們皆指示兩性對比、對稱的一致性。其二，經由對歌歌者之間相互呼喚的人稱語彙，表現在交表姻親與情人（友人）兩類範疇之流動、置換，似指示交表親與情人（或友人）兩範疇輪替、流動的意象。這個指示特性，也可在以數首接連的短歌為對象觀察出來。如下面例子，倘若我們將這部對歌的第 1 句至第 88 句當作一個較大的分析單位，便可以觀察到這些指示人際關係之人稱用語（包括自稱與他稱）呈現輪替、回應的流動。例如以老友（第 12 句）回應夫妻（第 6 句），再以妻子、遊方伴（第 16、18 句）回應老友（第 12 句）（參下表）。

男歌者演唱的人稱語彙	女歌者演唱的人稱語彙
？[20]	丈夫（第 2 句歌）
？	夫妻（第 6 句歌）
老友（第 12 句歌）	妻子、遊方的伴（第 16、18 句歌）
陌生人（第 22 句歌）	男孩、遊方的伴、別人的丈夫（第 29、30、32 句歌）
妻（第 37 句歌）	表兄、男孩（第 43 句歌）
妻妹（或弟的妻）（第 48 句歌）	表哥（第 54 句歌）

男歌者演唱的人稱語彙	女歌者演唱的人稱語彙
？	男孩 （第 62 句歌）
妻妹、姑娘（第 66、69 句歌）	陌生人 （第 73 句歌）
姑娘、妻妹（第 82、83 句歌）	男孩 （第 88 句歌）

也就是，人稱語彙在較大範圍的文本間，仍指示著交表姻親關係與情人等其他人際關係的任意置換與流動性；由此創造更大格局之成對結構。

五、符號裡的 Hmub 人性別意象

在前一節描述人稱語彙的五項符號活動特點後，本章接下來要探討這部對歌的演述形式所再現之性別意義，如何有別於人稱語彙的語意組合與解組所再現之性別意象。通過兩類符號活動（指示記號與象似記號）在這部對歌裡的並置與作用，建構出 Hmub 人語言符號世界裡特定的性別意象：（一）對歌裡規律的男女歌者輪流對唱的演述，經由具有象似特性的符號運作，呈現兩性為二元、對等的性別意象。（二）語意為交表親、情人（或友人）的人稱語彙，經由語意組合與解組的符號活動，指示兩性合一之結伴理想與兩性分立之個人價值的並置與流動。

（一）象似性：二元、對等的性別意象

在這部對歌的人稱語言，不論是從語意，或非關語意的語言特性，都可以發現象似記號再現著特定的性別意象。本章雖然以語言符號的結

構關係之描述和分析爲主（注重如語彙的重疊、互換，以及出現的次數），但在前一節的描述裡，其實也已經指出象似性符號的特性，有系統的表現在對歌諸多人稱用語的意義裡。*Deif*、*xongx*、*liob*、*kheit* 的語意都是男孩；*nef*、*lis*、*niongk*、*niangk*、*ment*、*wangt nef*、*niangk sint* 的語意都是女孩。這幾個出現在對歌裡的人稱語彙，在意義上分別指涉特定的性別意象。由於它們的意義與符號之間的關係，並不受任何語境影響，所以是象似符號的作用。

接下來要討論的則是針對非關意義的語言特性。首先是對歌演述的組合、輪流與歌者性別之間形成象似性的指稱關係，以及由此符號活動所突顯的兩性差異，與以輪替爲主軸的兩性對等之意象。象似記號在這部對歌是活躍運作的符號特性之一。有別於指示記號的符號特性依存特定語境（參後），象似記號主要與它所表徵的事物間共享某些特質。

這部對歌以其演述的組合與輪流，肖像般穩定地表徵兩性差異，以及兩性對等輪替的性別意象。對歌的演述過程，歌頭、歌尾的輪替與交換，又形成另一個突出的象似關係。男女歌者在接歌、答歌時，必須以交替的成對方式添唱歌頭。交替的原則，不是依賴語意的區辨，而是以語音的對比（或差異）作爲輪替的規律（H 音開頭與 J 音開頭的交錯）。此項非語意的語言活動，也通過語音組合，展現兩性的差異，以及在差異中對等輪替、交錯的性別意象。

總之，苗歌語言不完全依賴語意表達性別對等的意象，而是通過象似記號的符號活動，在演述、符號運作的層次上，表達以輪替爲焦點之兩性於差異中建立對等意象。此類符號活動所建立的性別意象，也能解釋爲以較大的形式格局，對應著歌的詩韻規律與成對結構。

（二）指示性：「兩性合一的結伴理想」與「兩性分立之個人價值」

　　相對於前述之輪替演述，有如圖像般紋風不動地複製兩性對等意象，這部對歌的人稱語彙，也還展現指示記號的符號活動特性。人稱語彙之所以具有指示性，是因為它們的實踐，總攸關著人與人之間的互動。在這部對歌裡，男孩、女孩、交表親、情人等人稱語彙的出現，指示著對歌的歌者與歌者間之性別關係，與親屬關係的社會情境。

　　這部對歌的人稱語彙，不僅展現同意語的多樣性，還呈現較小語意單位的組合、解離的符號活動。這使得歌者在對歌的過程中，有更多人稱用語的選擇，以此確定自己的主體位置，以及與他人的關係類型。經由微觀地觀察，這部對歌的人稱語彙，可分為四類：1、表述性別區分之個體的人稱語彙；2、表述異性結伴的人稱語彙；3、在語意上呈現個人與結伴可拆解、組合之詞構特性的人稱語彙；4、可相互交替的人稱語彙。

　　第 1 類與第 2 類人稱語彙，指出兩性、個人、結伴三個層次的對比意象。在這部對歌中，並置專門表述男孩（如 *deif*、*xongx*、*liob*）的語彙與專門表述女孩（如 *nef*、*lis*、*niongk*）的語彙。對比於這類指示性別差異之個人的語彙，另一類人稱語彙則指示兩性的結伴：情人（如 *ghat buk ghet*、*lek ghengs*）與夫妻（如 *heit dongf dank*）。

　　相對於第 1 類與第 2 類的人稱語彙在性別、個人、結伴的語意上，指出可區辨的界線，第 3 類的人稱語彙，以詞構上自由的合與分，則提供了個體、結伴及性別三層語意上可拆解、組合的空間。例如，*dint bongf* 的組合或解離原則，可合（*dint bongf*）、可分（*dint* 或 *bongf*），而維持語意不變——皆用以表述夫妻、女人的丈夫或男人的妻子。

第 4 類的人稱語彙，在於由交表姻親與情人兩類稱謂的交替，表現語言符號運作的動態性。這部對歌的歌尾與歌中的演唱，人稱語彙的高度使用是一個不能忽視的突出焦點。例如，男歌者稱女歌者為兩位妻妹，女歌者呼喚男歌者為兩位姊夫，或者男、女歌者互稱對方為表親或丈夫、妻子。與這些親屬稱謂交替呼喊的，則是老友、情人等另一類人稱範疇的呼喚語彙。

　　呼應前述第 4 類人稱語彙在不同的範疇間變換，這部對歌之人稱語彙的指示特性，還可以由數首連續演唱的短歌，觀察到人稱語彙在交表親與情人兩範疇不斷的替換，以此創造性別與結伴的流動意象。例如以這部對歌的第 6 句至第 32 句為一個較大範圍的分析單位（參前一小節），男女歌者所演唱的人稱用語（包括自稱與呼喚語）的變化與轉動：由夫妻（女唱）走向老友（男唱），再轉入妻子與遊方伴（女唱），然後是陌生人（男唱）；再來由女歌者接唱的則是男孩、遊方的伴與別人的丈夫。

　　最後，由稱謂、名字等人稱語彙的實踐，不僅指示歌者在性別認同上的主體性、流動性，以及突顯語言的指示符號（index）特性；Hmub 人的情歌對唱語言，還經由形式的群聚、重複，表現出另一類符號，象似符號（icon）的特性。Friedrich（1979：1-61）所提到的圖形象似性（diagrammaticity）的概念，就是由群聚的觀點，來理解符號行動的支配力量。這部對歌語彙另一項突出的符號行動，就是以符號的大量群聚創造力量。這部對歌由歌者重複唱出同義的人稱語彙，產生一大群專門表述男孩（如 *deif*、*xongx*、*liob*）的語彙，也相對並行一大群專門表述女孩（如 *nef*、*lis*、*niongk*）的語彙。對比於這兩群描述性別差異的個人，另一群聚的語彙，則演述著兩性的結伴：情人（如 *ghat buk ghet*、*lek ghengs*）

與夫妻（如 *heit dongf dank*）。象似記號特性的形成，主要在於大量同意字的群聚，所展現之加強與重複的效果。換言之，經由同意字的群聚、對比，因而也創造了由異性的個人意象到異性爲伴的結盟關係。

六、結語：結伴理想與個人價值

對歌裡的男女輪唱演述著兩性二元、對等意象，對歌的人稱語彙則演述兩性分立的個人價值，以及兩性合一的結伴理想。由 Hmub 人情歌語言所觀察到的性別意象，不僅有別於父系繼嗣理想與實踐所展現之兩性不對等的性別意象，也和 Hmub 人日常（家與兩性分工）生活的觀念和實踐裡的兩性意象或界線，爲適應社會變遷而調整有所對照。[21]Fangf Bil 寨的情歌語言雖無法展現如謝茵或唐納利所聲稱的爲因應社會變遷的美國苗族（Hmong）性別意象與兩性關係之複雜，不過卻和黔東南苗族（Hmub）社會行動中的遊方或聯姻相呼應。

遊方以年輕人爲主，經由多樣的形式，展現社會性與個人性。遊方的社會性展現在時、空、人有序的組成與可變通的規則。尤其在人的方面，多層次交疊的年齡與身分組合的年輕人世界，展現遊方與婚姻間的曖昧。本章面對遊方情歌對唱的形式和符號活動，也反映相似的流動和曖昧。一般而言，在遊方的人群裡，同性之間爲平表親，異性之間爲交表親，不同輩分的同性平表親可結伴同行，不同輩分的異性交表親則彼此遊方。因此，在遊方場域可以聽到同世代、跨世代與指定型等多方雜陳的稱謂組合。這與 Fangf Bil 寨所做的是一種概念上偏向以父方交表婚姻爲理想，但實行的是村寨內婚的雙邊交表聯姻有關。村寨內婚的多元聯姻策略，是爲面對封閉的婚姻市場，以及對父方交表的延遲與隔代交換概念的堅持。在不朝向外在空間拓展婚姻市場（通婚圈不向外發展）的原則下，只能利用人與人的親屬距離符號運作，擴大可婚的對象，亦即，通過稱謂來壓縮世代的距離（不同世代的人，使用同一稱謂），以及允許跨世代異性交表親的遊方與通婚。

遊方的個人特性展現在經由話語、衣及花帶交流的異性相伴情感、自我情緒的抒發，以及對情感內容的小小操弄。個人不僅相對創造遊方、情感與婚姻間的流動與曖昧，也掌握個人的主體性。在異性結伴的遊方天地裡，以花帶與衣的形式，分別表徵女孩與男女對彼此的愛慕情感。此禮物交換系統中，Fangf Bil 寨 Hmub 人以花帶比喻女性，衣比喻爲男和女。姑娘以花帶與衣的相贈，來述說不同的心意。贈物過程要搭配說話來表達心意。因而，同樣是贈花帶，可以表述兩種完全相反的意涵。一是姑娘贈花帶給情人，表示有心跟他結爲夫妻；另一種則是完全相反的心情——遊方一年或兩年後的姑娘，不想再跟男孩維繫穩定的遊方關係，也會以花帶相贈。同樣的贈禮，姑娘必須用特定的話語，才能表明特定的心意。除了花帶的交換，衣的贈與、回禮、退禮等多重組合，也都需配合特定話語才可以作爲遊方行動者對於結伴理想多義的象徵表述（簡美玲 2002、2009a）。

遊方場域裡花帶和布的交換邏輯，類似對歌人稱語彙的特質，有性別區分之個體（花帶喻女）和表述異性結伴的理想，也有用不同的話語和回贈方式，表現語意上個人與結伴的可拆解和組合。姑娘可以透過贈花帶與贈衣給男孩，來表達情感與婚姻的契合，也可以表達兩者的脫離；男孩贈衣給姑娘則通常只表達情感與婚姻理想無法結合。也就是說花帶與衣的交換表達兩種不同的邏輯，一項是通過個人情感走向婚姻理想，一項是個人情感的獨立表現。後者將情人所贈的花帶和衣，作爲個人物終生擁有、保留，由此表明個人的情感，與擇伴理想可以獨立於婚姻之外。

總之，遊方的特質與花帶和衣的交換，正可補充情歌語言裡的個人與結伴理想的實質內涵，以及夫妻與情人的異同。遊方形成個人情感和交表婚姻之間的流動性（表現在遊方對象可能是未來的伴侶，也可能是婚姻之外相互戲謔調情的遊方伴）。個人在遊方的場域具有某種主體性。夫妻和情人的差異，可以透過遊方過程中之定情物的交換清楚區分。結伴的理想包含婚姻和個人情感之期待和延續（雖然，兩者很多時候是有落差）。通過花帶、衣的交換，則表達了在 Hmub 人的社會裡，個人情感與婚姻理想間，相依與非必然相依的並置。

再則，Hmub 人情歌的人稱語彙之所以能演述性別意象的流動（交表姻親與情人兩範疇的流動），係對應著 Fangf Bil 寨 Hmub 人於三個層面所交織擺盪在婚姻理想及個人價值有關的結群制度：其一是親屬稱謂表現出交表聯姻的指定性，其二是婚姻的法則與行動，表現交表聯姻的優先性，其三是遊方。前二者積極指向交表親人與婚姻結伴的社會理想，爲一對一對應的正向關聯。而遊方在行動與結構上，則允諾個人情感與婚姻之集體間的曖昧性（簡美玲 2005a： 347-380、2005b：49-86），對歌的人稱語彙也同樣表現出流動和曖昧性。我認爲 Hmub 人社會在交表聯姻的理想與實踐裡，包含著讓個人情感的自主價值有所出路的遊方世界，這對於人稱語彙能完成性別意象的流動（轉變），交表姻親與情人兩範疇的流動，是個重要機制。而其完成，在於一場又一場互爲交表親男女的遊方情歌對唱，與情歌語言自成一套微體系之符號活動的運作。

　　總之，在 Hmub 人地方社會生活的情境裡，對歌語言蘊含著表徵集體社會價值的主動性。對歌的演述場合、參與成員，乃至歌的語意內容，都與交表聯姻、緩落夫家婚後居、制度化的遊方談情密切相關，但又不僅僅是親屬、婚姻等社會結構的伴隨結果。黔東南 Hmub 人情歌語言的形式與符號活動，在綿密、規律的操作下，自成一套相對細緻、精密的格局，展現 Hmub 村寨人群以特定的詩歌語言形式，創造、融合個人與結伴相互對立亦相互支援的性別意象。對比於 Hmub 人的父系繼嗣社會組織、結構所突顯的單一父系理想，並藉由與遊方、婚姻的對照，情歌的演述和以人稱語言為主的符號活動，展現 Hmub 人所關注的男與女為互補、對等的性別意象；性別的意義，既與結伴的人觀有所關聯，也與體現個人價值的人觀相伴隨。

Part II

身體感與情感

Cultivating the Ethnographer's Ear

Chapter 4　田野裡的「聽」

我還有機會重新體驗那樣的悸動時刻嗎？那時候我手捧筆記本，記下每一秒中所看見的景象，期望有助於將那些變動不居、一再更新的型態凝結記載下來。我現在還是深深執著於這種企圖，還是經常發現自己的手仍然在這麼做。

（Lévi-Strauss 1992〔1955〕：62；王志明譯 2015：83）

那麼，如果是民族誌田野裡「聽」的經驗呢？

（James Clifford 1986：12）[1]

在《憂鬱的熱帶》（*Tristes Tropiques*, 1955）裡，李維史陀不只一次提到了他在巴西與當地印第安人的田野經驗。這些經驗使得他在情感和理智上都同他的人類學家身分聯繫起來。這些田野工作的描述，並不總是贏得同行和同事的讚譽。但作為一個在田野工作中，經歷過文化學習的民族誌學家，我仍為李維史陀那種試圖在腦中尋求一塊淨土，在當地不斷變化的文化背景下探索人類知識的生動描述所感動。我們仍然是他巨大成就的見證人：從巴西多次田野中獲取的六千多張圖紙和大量的田野筆記，以及他提出的這些材料所支撐的資料、觀察結果和假設。

本章將討論我在貴州東部大山的 Hmub 人村寨，以民族誌學徒之身，進行遊方的田野研究。經由描述個人在民族誌田野裡的學徒經驗，我將探索我所聽到的，及我所寫下的，兩者間的互動（或互動關係的缺乏），以及它們如何影響並轉變我對 Hmub 人文化與我自身的內在瞭解。另外，我還將考察一個問題：從我筆尖流動出的紀錄，是否如實反映我的眼睛及耳朵所捕捉到的真實。如果沒有，那我遺漏了什麼？

在田野工作中，我經常詢問自己該聽什麼，以及該如何聽。如同許多人類學研究生，我們的學習著重於如何記錄訪談，卻幾乎沒有受過關於聽的訓練。多數研究生的培訓重點在於觀察，以及與研究對象交談。儘管我缺乏對於聽的正式訓練，然而，除了學習聽見（hearing）以及聆聽（listening to）的方法之外別無選擇。尤其當研究重心轉移到夜間遊方時，更是如此。在分析田野筆記時，我意外發現它們傳達一種混合了視覺及聽覺的細緻描述，這激發了一股領悟：在 Hmub 人遊方中，聽是重要的線索；同時，也促使我面對文化田野調查方法論及認識論的挑戰。這一認識引導我思考，將自己在 Hmub 人村寨的經驗，納入人類學之理解，自我技術及民族誌學徒的討論中。

一、感官

根據保羅・斯托勒（Paul Stoller 1989）的研究，正是通過長期學習桑海人（Songhay）神靈附身儀式的學徒經歷，才發現聲音對理解文化情感的核心地位：

> 1970 年在蒂拉貝裡（Tillaberi）的一個下午，單弦琴動人心弦的琴音把我吸引到一個沙丘上，見證了我初次經歷桑海人的神靈附身儀

式⋯⋯這些樂器的聲音使我印象深刻。以至於在 1971 年,我繼續參與信仰儀式⋯⋯1977 年,我開始在邁哈納(Mehanna)村學習靈歌(spirit poetry)的聲音。兩年後,我作為神靈的僕人,被邀請加入蒂拉貝裡的信徒隊伍當中⋯⋯*在無數次的經歷裡,導師始終提醒我將注意力集中在儀式的聲音上。*

(Stoller 1989:101;斜體為筆者所加)

然而,斯托勒也指出,在當前西方人類學感官訓練中,聲音的維度往往被忽視。我們學會如何訪談和觀察,但關注與事件相關的聲音或語音,並發掘它們如何同民族誌學者的觀察,和對當地文化的解釋相對應,也應當是需要學習的技能。斯托勒和其他學者提醒我們,人類學或民族誌學者所使用的感官應該更為多樣化。在描述和解釋當地文化方面,音調和聲音的價值是無可估量的。如果幸運的話,我們能夠通過我們自己的學徒經歷,學到斯托勒在田野工作中得到的經驗:對聲音保持關注。它有助於民族誌學者通過身體感官的交流和互動,來理解當地文化的意義。

二、自我的技術

傅柯(Michel Foucault 1988:18)用技術(technology)這一術語來展現主體被規訓與修正的手段。他列舉了四種主要技術:生產、符號系統、權力和自我(ibid.)。在強調支配和權力技術後,傅柯的興趣點轉向自我技術,並以認識你自己(know yourself)和關注你自己(take care of yourself)這兩個表達之間的歷史聯繫作為出發點,闡述古希臘羅馬和基督教傳統如何建立關注和自我之間的關係（ibid.：19-20）。傅柯認為，與自我相關的多種關注，使得不同形式的自我得以存在（ibid.：22）。根據他的分析，古希臘羅馬的書寫傳統是創造自我關注此一概念的重要工具（ibid.：27）。例如為日後重新閱讀而做筆記，撰寫文章或書信來幫助朋友，保留筆記本以便日後可以再思索與研究（ibid.）。此時，寫作實踐與自我關注，密切相關。在同一部作品裡，傅柯借助馬庫斯‧奧雷利厄斯（Marcus Aurelius）於西元 144 年或 145 年寫給佛朗托（Fronto）的信件，通過信件中連續不斷地對不重要之日常細節的書寫實踐，闡述自我和身體之間的相互關係（ibid.：28-30）。

三、修練與學徒制：
　　傅柯、斯托勒和卡斯塔尼達的理論關懷

與傅柯和斯托勒的立場相似，我將試著闡釋，通過書寫，我所聽到的是什麼。正如自我關注產生於信件或日記裡，書寫不重要的日常細節；如何陶冶自己的耳朵，和調整自身看法的經驗，也出現在筆記和日記裡對田野經歷的書寫。[2] 我使用 *cultivation*[3] 這個字，是因為它傳達了關於有意識且持續的追求，以及被規訓與修正的某些內在特性。我將此視為類似傅柯所說的自我技術。在田野民族誌語境下，考察書寫的技術或持續練習，是如何影響身體的修練，以及它又是如何打開通向自我揭露，與通過聽與聆聽來學習其他的文化。

斯托勒（1987）和卡洛斯‧卡斯塔尼達（Carlos Castaneda 1998〔1969〕）討論了一個類似的概念，即學徒制。民族誌學者往往將自己

看作學生，或像孩子一樣，通過田野調查來學習他者的文化。但很少有人在民族誌實踐中，明確使用學徒一詞。斯托勒（1987）以學習使用桑海人的視角，及儀式專家的視角，來描述他的兩次學徒經歷。第一段經歷發生在田野調查的早期階段，當時他遇到了挫折，因爲他認爲桑海村民對調查提問的回答，具有誤導性。而後他接受一位村子裡朋友的建議：「保羅先生，你必須學會和人們坐在一起。你必須學會坐下來傾聽」（ibid.：11）。斯托勒承認，他對自己身爲專業田野工作者的身分感到矛盾，並採取一種被動的方式去學習桑海文化。然而，坐下來傾聽，才是他被接納爲一個合格桑海人的關鍵。「親力親爲並眞正成爲村裡的人」（ibid.：17）。

斯托勒（1987：21-41）第二次田野調查的學徒經歷，受益於桑海巫師。經過一段時間密集的記誦儀式文本與讚美詩，和嘗試民俗藥物後，他體驗到同時作爲巫師學徒與人類學家之間激烈的內部衝突。

> 吉博（Djibo）使我沉浸在記誦之中。我忙於記誦文本，以至於根本沒空去理解其中的含義，更不用說它們是如何與變化莫測的桑海文化相聯繫。我擔心作爲人類學家的使命失敗了。
>
> （Stoller 1987：38）

另一個事例是卡斯塔尼達（1998〔1969〕）所描述的，他在一位名叫唐璜（Don Juan）的亞基（Yaqui）印第安巫師指導下的學徒經驗。唐璜迫使他放棄西方思維方式，並採取了某些方式讓卡斯塔尼達去學習和理解亞基人世界的實際情況。卡斯塔尼達說：

在唐璜的信仰體系中，獲得一個盟友僅僅意味著，他通過致幻植物使我體內發生非尋常現實狀態。他認為，通過關注這些狀態和忽略他所教授之知識的其它方面，我會對所經歷之現象有一個連貫的觀點。

（Castaneda 1998〔1969〕：10）

　　卡斯塔尼達遇到了相當大的挑戰。他努力迴避印第安導師禁止的那些專業方法，其中包括訪談、觀察和系統地做筆記。儘管如此，田野筆記對於他內化亞基印第安人的感官體驗，理解他們的世界觀，揭示他對體驗的主觀感知，及唐璜的信仰體系內容，皆發揮重要作用。儘管卡斯塔尼達從未將他的討論，延伸至寫作與其亞基文化學徒身分間的聯繫。但他多次表示，從極端的感官體驗中平靜下來後，撰寫筆記能夠使自己更仔細地審視這些經歷。

　　在討論仔細傾聽作爲一種基本田野技術的重要性之前，我將先介紹自己在臺灣清華大學接受的文化人類學研究方法訓練。而後描述與分析聲音／語音是如何在 Hmub 人的日常生活與儀式生活發揮重要作用，特別是它們在遊方中占據的核心地位。本文中，聲音（sound）（非言語結構）是指一種用於交流的符號系統（Feld 1982），例如敲門或敲窗的聲音。語音（voice）是指人在交流時的語言結構，如人們的交談或其他形式的對話（Keane 2000）。

四、學習和體驗人類學研究方法

　　1990 年代初，我開始進入人類學的養成之路。通過課程的學習、閱讀和討論，我建立了對田野調查工作之要求的理解：學習新語言、繪製地圖、完成家戶人口普查或繪製家譜、進行訪談、親身參與、觀察、撰寫田野筆記與日記。當時羅素・伯納德（H. Russell Bernard）的《文化人類學的研究方法》（*Research Methods in Cultural Anthropology*, 1988）是這方面最廣爲閱讀與教學的著作之一。無論是在學校的課堂上課，還是當年我在臺灣東部進行阿美族民俗醫療之田野研究（1992-93），這本人類學方法論的書籍，都一直帶在身邊。此書的第 7-13 章中，伯納德討論了參與式觀察法；記錄和管理田野筆記；結構化、非結構化、半結構化訪談；問卷和調查；以及直接的、互動性的和非介入性的觀察，所有這些獲取資訊的方法都強調視覺感知。聽見（hearing）和聆聽（listening to）等用語幾乎未出現在伯納德的文本裡。在人類學課程中，如何聽，是極少被論及的。但我認爲，在處理諸如轉錄、翻譯、分類、描述和解釋言語與非言語聽覺資訊或信號等過程時，最好能夠教授聽與聆聽或傾聽的技巧。

　　在清華大學的人類學養成和伯納德著作影響下，觀察、訪談和參與等過程，是我在貴州東部 Hmub 人村寨進行博士論文田野調查（1998-2000）的主要研究方法。最初關注的是村寨社會結構。我對三百多戶家庭進行了人口普查，利用半結構化訪談收集資訊，並爲每個家戶，以及家戶與家戶之間，繪製家譜和族譜。[4] 同時也收集 Hmub 語的親屬稱謂，以及記錄這些稱謂在日常和儀式場合的實際使用情況。這些田野材料除了協助我理解村寨裡的人際關係，還幫助我學習報導人所描述的婚姻概念，以及觀察婚姻的實際狀況，並探索此二者在何處匯合及分歧。對個人情感和社會制度（婚姻、遊方等）之間相互作用的發掘，爲我提供了大量機會去嘗試新的民族誌研究方法與技藝。

在田野調查期間，我居住在 Ghaif Wangk 的家中。當年她 20 歲，未婚。起初，她的家人安排我睡在二樓。但由於二樓的房間在糧倉旁邊，且僅我一人在二樓，後來在我的請求下，才被安排睡在他們女兒的房間裡。我和 Ghaif Wangk 共處了很長一段時間，始終以姊妹相稱。她教我 Hmub 語，協助記音與翻譯村子裡所唱的歌謠、口述傳說及故事，也協助進行訪談。我和 Ghaif Wangk 共處了十五個月以上，因而能較深刻的瞭解她的經歷、情緒，以及對婚姻與感情的觀點。偶爾也能瞭解到她對當地流言蜚語的看法。經由她，我當年作爲一名年輕女性，並被當地傳統所接納。

五、傾聽深夜儀式的聲音

在村寨進行田野時，我察覺到需要採取不同於以往的研究方法。越來越多的情況顯示，如果沒有特別關注那些人們能在黑夜裡聽到的聲音和語音，將可能錯過 Hmub 人社會生活的關鍵面向，和誤解遊方及婚姻習俗。以下事例摘自我 1999 年初的田野筆記：

我聽見公雞在黑暗中打鳴了兩三次。在寒冷的清晨，我仍掙扎著 5 點鐘起床。6 點，我決定去觀察一場立新房的招魂儀式。我叫醒了 Ghaif。但 Ghaif 的母親說，前幾天立新房的主人已經招過魂了。她還說，在四組村（Si-Zu）（延續自集體生產時代，寨子裡編號為四的小寨）有幾戶家屋在招魂，但不知道具體是哪些家。Ghaif 建議我們上去看看（四組位於較高的坡上）。我們出發前甚至沒有洗臉，只拿著手電筒，便在黎明時分出門了。Ghaif 説坡上有聲音，但我什麼也沒聽見。我跟著她到斜坡的四組小寨前。當我們靠近該小寨時，一個人向我們走來。聽 Ghaif 的説明後，他告知我們是哪戶人家在舉行儀式。我感覺他當時臉上微露笑意。後來我們才知道，他就是剛剛招完魂，在回家路上的 *ghet xangt*（鬼師，苗族的巫師或儀式專家）。

田野筆記記錄了我作爲一名田野工作者的緊張和焦慮，尤其是擔心自己失去觀察儀式活動的機會，而正是這些田野筆記，指向了傾聽的重要性。這種不安也可以解釋爲，我對村寨 Hmub 人儀式中聽到的那些獨特聲音和語音感到陌生。無法預測儀式活動會持續多久，也不知道聽到的聲音代表什麼。[5] 除了經歷儀式的家庭成員，村寨裡許多儀式活動（例如保護家屋的喊白公雞鬼儀式、治療儀式，甚至婚禮儀式的某些部分）都是村民們悄無聲息地舉行。我曾經思考，作爲村寨裡唯一的外地人，在 1998 年 11 月到達這個村寨時，是被排除在圈子之外的。在這個圈子裡，大家分享著有關儀式活動的消息。後來才知道，我在這方面並不特別：因爲村民們自身也不一定知道小寨內的每場儀式安排，更不用說其他村寨的家庭了。儘管如此，許多村民告訴我：「如果你想知道儀式在哪裡舉行，只需要仔細傾聽（儀式專家吟唱的）聲音。」然而，對於我，一個人類學學徒而言，分辨出儀式活動豐富多樣的聽覺信號確實是個挑戰。我需要從自己日常生活中那些習慣的聽與聆聽之類型裡，瞭解語境及資訊。

在爲期十五個月的田野調查中，我學到了特定聲音和語音的社會含義：薩滿（鬼師）的吟唱意味有治療儀式或家屋儀式；鞭炮聲意味著新年或婚禮的慶祝，但有時也表示老人家的喪禮儀式；而堂兄弟姊妹在半夜對著門或窗熱情的拍打敲擊，暗示著一場婚禮將會早早地在那天清晨舉行。一直到田野工作後期，我才意識到，自到訪這個村寨以來，就一直生活在這些聲音和語音之中。只有在進入如此情境與覺察，才能致力於探索遊方的深夜聽覺維度。

　　爲了理解在親屬結構和村寨婚姻制度之外的婚姻與遊方的關係，我第二個田野調查的重點是欲望及其情緒情感的語境。通過對制度化求愛活動的研究，瞭解村寨 *vangt*（年輕人）的情感世界。[6]然而，在進行遊方活動調查時，方法論和倫理的衝突使我意識到，聲音及語音對於理解遊方文化有著極爲重要的意義

　　進行這項研究時，我已經是兩個年幼孩子的母親了。這樣的身分，在村寨裡已是 *lok*（年長），也因此需被排除在遊方活動之外。不過，儘管我是已婚的母親，村民們仍將我視爲年輕女孩，也許是因爲研究生的身分和當時上衣搭長褲的簡僕穿著，與村子裡年輕女孩們[7]穿著的服裝很相似。因此，在參與和觀察遊方活動時，有了更大的自由。這種活動的形式是成群的年輕男女聚集在一起，或是夜晚在年輕女孩房間的窗外，進行一對一的談情說愛。我曾是群體聚會的參與者，卻只能是深夜窗邊交談的傾聽者，因而只能隔天對參與窗邊夜談的女孩進行訪談從而補充細節。我瞭解到，遊方活動可以非常開放——具有一些儀式表演的特徵，但有時它們可以是非常私密且個人的。假使沒有村寨內姑娘的幫助，以及願意分享她們浪漫的情感和經歷，我永遠無法理解制度化求愛的遊方儀式，在個別參與者心中的內涵與價值。

六、田野裡聆聽的經驗

正如前文田野筆記中提及的，聲音與招魂儀式相關，聲音也是指向遊方事件的主要索引。在我所寫的將近十五本田野筆記裡，也記載了大量聽到的，有關村寨 Hmub 人遊方活動的內容。它們使我覺察，深夜敲窗的重要性。以下筆記片段寫於 1999 年 1 月，田野調查的早期階段：

今天我匆忙返回田野地點，因為明天會有一個立新房的招魂儀式。我和 Ghaif 的父親討論完費用時，已經 9 點 30 分了。為了早起（喊鬼招魂儀式，將在公雞第二次報曉後開始），而且也感到疲憊，就早些睡了。Ghaif 和我很快就進入夢鄉⋯⋯我是被敲窗的聲音弄醒的。以為天快亮了，但看了看手錶，發現只有 11 點鐘左右。敲窗聲以不同的節奏進行著，並且有著不同的拍子（我突然想到，如果有機會，我應該把這些聲音錄下來）。那時我已經醒了，但仍然想繼續睡。敲窗聲一直持續著。Ghaif 也醒了，她朝著窗子外面的男孩說：「*Nat youl. Det dak youl！*」（我聽到了，但我不想去〔窗邊〕。）她說了兩三次，聽起來有些生氣。後來她告訴我，是因為他們（來唐家村寨遊方的男孩）敲得太響了。敲窗的聲音沒有立刻停止，但過了一會兒後就結束了。我們慢慢地又睡著了。

這段田野筆記，傳達了我對深夜敲窗，最初的感受和經歷。這些聲音常常出乎意料地將人吵醒：有時因敲窗聲，而在睡夢中受驚嚇；有時則是同一個晚上敲了多次。總之，住在村寨裡一段時日之後，我才不對夜半敲窗聲，感到又愛又恨。這種深夜裡突如其來的敲窗聲，總是打斷了人們的睡眠。讓來自他文化的我覺得，這是不禮貌的行為。但於此同時，我也反思，待在村寨裡進行田野所要探索的主題，包含瞭解 Hmub 人的遊方。我逐漸體會到，這些起初不受歡迎的聲音信號，是研究重點，因為它們具有文化與象徵意義。

每一次女孩聽到敲窗聲，她都會根據敲擊聲的節奏、速度和音量來識別敲窗者。對於像我這樣的局外人，這裡的敲窗聲聽起來都很相似；但對於村裡的姑娘們，這些聲音傳達著細微的變化。有一些特定的敲擊策略，是能夠被識別的。例如，其中有一種敲法是：先以正常速度輕敲三次，停頓，再敲三次。聲音也隨之變大，或節奏變快。女孩們尤其期待心上人（ghat mal ghob）的敲窗聲，但心上人並非唯一的敲窗者。事實上，敲窗活動大多來自表兄弟等姻親。因此，女孩們通常需要做的，是區分同一個村寨裡，一般姻親的敲窗聲，和來自村寨外邊陌生人的敲窗聲之間的差異。

我開始將非言語的聲音與特定的人際關係 —— 男朋友、表親、朋友和陌生人聯繫起來，並對此進行分類。起初，敲擊的節奏和頻率似乎都很相似，我便猜想是同一個男孩對 Ghaif 感興趣。後來才明白，實際上那些聲音多半來自不同的遊方男孩。

我由此更加關注這些深夜活動。幾乎每天早上，都會和 Ghaif Wangk 聊聊前一天晚上的來訪者，並盡可能詳細地寫下我們討論的內容，之後才安排當天田野工作的行程。我多數的提問，涉及敲窗遊方者的身分，他們之間的親屬或姻親關係，以及談話的內容。敲窗聲最終成為理解深夜遊方行為的一個關鍵指標。我未能察覺到敲窗聲之間差異的地方，當地村寨的女孩們，則能識別出多樣的類別。這提供了一個重要契機，也就是通過聆聽、傾聽來感受遊方制度，而不僅是從報導人的口語解釋，或經由觀察來獲取地方知識。最終在村寨姑娘 Ghaif Wangk 的協助下，我不僅建立起深夜敲窗的音樂層面與社會層面的觀點，還能用所聽到的意義予以補充、說明。例如，通過 Ghaif Wangk 的親身經驗，我們瞭解到，如果連續幾個晚上都沒有人敲窗，她會感到孤單與悲傷。姑娘通常期待著深夜的敲窗聲，即便她不知道是誰在哪一個晚上，來到她的窗前。

雖然我的研究不是通過模式、頻率、音量等方面分析敲窗聲，但在田野工作裡，所聽到的聲音都是有理解價值的。親身聆聽深夜敲窗的經驗，使我們得以建立起村寨 Hmub 人遊方情感和知識之間的聯繫。對女孩來說，敲窗的聲音，是遊方求愛的明顯標誌。父母和其他家庭成員通常忽視（或假裝忽視）那些聲音，不管其音量、頻率或次數如何。而女孩們會覺得有必要回應，和必須去處理與之相關的情緒及情感。大多數女孩聽到敲窗聲都會感到喜悅。如果好一陣子沒有敲窗聲，她們會低聲唸著：「*Sent feb lel, bib lok yaf.*」（似冬靜且寒，寂寥顏色衰），表達一種孤寂感，擔心自己找不到伴侶。這種感受，解釋了村寨 Hmub 人女孩，能通過敲窗聲，識別來窗邊遊方的人。女孩們聽到來自表兄弟等姻親的熟悉敲窗聲，並打開窗子時，所感受到的情感與情緒，是安全和自信的；若傳來不熟悉的敲窗聲，則會感到不確定，甚至害怕，因此她們不會打開窗戶。

對我而言，產生意義的，並非僅是深夜敲窗的具體內容或模式，而是聽覺體驗，在各種情緒之間建立了聯繫。研究者個人情緒的轉變，由文化衝擊、害怕、無所適從，轉變爲熟悉而規律的日常經驗。這一轉變是戲劇性的。當田野工作接近尾聲時，我已不會去注意那些深夜的聲音，甚至在激烈的敲窗聲中，仍安然入睡。這也已經再尋常不過了。換言之，敲窗的聲音在很大程度上，被認為是友好的，並且是與村寨集體核心價值有關的實踐符碼：親屬制度的維持。如是的情緒轉變，使我們能以同理心感受村寨女孩們的情感世界。體認到半夜醒來的經驗，是如何豐富了她們的日常生活。通過關注聆聽的線索，我們得以重新思考，這些活動關聯著對村寨 Hmub 人遊方文化的理解。我們覺察自身在遊方過程中，傾聽和感受村寨姑娘情感的主體經驗，與研究者經歷最初的文化衝擊，以及在田野後期，感到自在與放鬆之民族誌學者的成長。

七、再次成為田野工作的學徒

1997 年起，開始進行村寨 Hmub 人之人類學研究時，我已非田野工作新手。但卻需要磨練一種新的研究技藝 —— 傾聽 —— 來完備民族誌材料的收集。而這一需求，再次喚醒了頭一回在東臺灣進行阿美族田野時的不安和不確定感。在貴州東部的 Hmub 人村寨田野開始之際，我甚至失去了一些自信，無法肯定自己是受過人類學田野養成的民族誌工作者。除開熟悉的田野研究裡的觀察、參與觀察或訪談，在 Hmub 人村寨語境中，理解未被識別的聲音和語音意義之必要，引發我內心的焦慮與無所適從。這種不安隱隱地動搖著作為民族誌學者的身分。文化衝擊顯然緊密關聯著這些感受。但更重要的討論是，在沒有關於自我感知和地方或空間感等視覺資訊來輔助或協助確認的情況下，如何因應聆聽或傾聽語言和非語言聲音所帶來的直接衝擊。以下引自布林（Micheal Bull）和貝克（Les Back 2003：7）著作中的內容，指出自我感受到的，與認識世界及自我瞭解之間的差異，而此差異正是通過觀看和傾聽，兩條不同的路徑：

在視覺狀態下，主體和客體顯然是「顯現」出來的。經由所見之物來對世界的客觀化予以暗示，正是對該世界的控制。然而正如貝克萊主教（Bishop Berkeley）指出的，「聲音和我們的思想更接近」。那麼，通過傾聽，我們也許能夠感知主客體之間的關係。

換言之，如果我（作為主體）僅僅通過視覺觀察，感知到了村寨 Hmub 人遊方現象（客體），那麼資料、方法和我作為田野工作者的身分之間的關係便顯而易見。從而也消除了對過程的重新思考，和充分體驗村寨 Hmub 人遊方田野工作的所有處境。我之前未意識到的深夜敲窗聲和遊方談話聲，在缺乏熟悉的（視覺）觀察標準的情況下，使研究者在田野裡產生了焦慮和無所適從。但這同時也提供了一個直接的管道，讓研究者感受到我在哪裡，我是誰，和我在村寨裡遇到了什麼。

八、田野裡學習聽

雖然在田野時，我自己認定，已將聆聽、傾聽作為一種特定的材料收集方法。但幾年後，重新翻閱田野筆記的內容時，仍然發現其中反映出難以充分利用聽覺資訊的不確定性。部分原因是由於「眼見為實」的固有成見。這與維特・埃爾曼（Veit Erlmann 2004：20）在《聽覺文化》（*Hearing Cultures*）中的觀點相呼應：「以聽覺為中心的社會實踐形式本身，不能被解釋為權力關係的替代品。因為權力關係是以視覺、監控和大眾媒體形式的視覺生產及消費為基礎。」[8] 儘管如此，當時我還是努力寫下觀察結果，以達到保留和理解田野裡所經歷的一切。田野裡的書寫，除了生產可辨認的語義資訊，其物性的層次，也幫助我們理解所聽到的一切。作爲民族誌學者，我們接受的人類學訓練，要求我們記錄材料，並將其寫成筆記。在進行村寨 Hmub 人遊方的田野研究時，我沒有使用錄音機來捕捉深夜敲窗聲。很大程度是因爲語音和對話常常是聽不清楚的。而且（除敲 Ghaif 的窗戶外），記錄其他屋子的敲窗聲，需要更先進的錄音設備與技術。另一個問題是關乎倫理：夜晚的遊方活動，往往比村寨 Hmub 人社會裡的其他公共活動，更爲私密及個人，而使用錄音機（或攝影機），在一定程度上會介入與影響夜間遊方活動的私人領域。因此，我回到用筆和紙，記錄所聽到的內容。

　　大多數民族誌學者都認識到，在田野中勤奮寫作的必要性，並相信他們的研究工作，會受益於那些記載下來的，和可作爲以後進行分析的意義和資訊。然而，在田野裡，書寫這件事，寫作的過程及其物質性（materiality），並沒有像其他材料的收集與記錄，那樣的被仔細或嚴謹看待。一如我在貴州的研究經歷所顯示，田野寫作是多功能的，換句話說，它也與身體經驗有關。克莉絲蒂娜·哈澤（Christina Haas 1996：24）是爲數不多，專門從書寫工具及其轉變，談論書寫之物質性的學者。她在書中寫著：「從一整疊手稿和對一支全新黑腳牌（Blackfeet）鉛筆的感覺，到明亮、接上電源、呼呼作響的盒子，以及敲擊著放在桌上的鍵盤」。哈澤還發現，對於那些從紙筆寫作過渡到電腦寫作的人而言，文本還存在感官上的問題。例如，有人說，「我必須把它列印出來，才能得到對它的*觀點*」或「我與寫在電腦上的文本之間，沒有出現我所需要的*親密感*」（ibid.：120，斜體爲原作者所標註）。文本感官，被描述爲空間的、活生生的或移動的客體。

　　我認爲寫作存在著兩種物質性：工具的使用和花費的時間，兩者都會在身體裡產生一定的共鳴。哈澤（1996：24）指出，「我們須通過工具的使用，才得以進行寫作。因此寫作在某種意義上是技術性的，也在某種程度上是物性的。」在村寨 Hmub 人的田野工作中，若由工具的角度觀之，我的書寫，也展現一股清晰的物質性：用老舊的萬寶龍（Mont Blanc）鋼筆，在硬皮筆記本上，寫下觀察和聽到的一切。一頁又一頁，一本又一本。由於 Fangf Bil 村寨裡沒有書店，我在寫田野筆記時，盡可能地將漢字、英文字母，以及用羅馬拼音的黔東苗文來記音的文字，都寫得小些，以節省紙張。其次，雖然我隨身帶著一台筆記型電腦進入田野。但在那個年代，村子裡的小水電站，僅在夜晚供電。因此我主要還是使用筆和紙，花費大量的時間，勤快地書寫田野筆記與田野日記。就著窗外的日光，坐在矮板凳上，或床頭，長時間伏案寫作，雖然會帶來身體上的不適，不過一旦習慣了，寫作 ── 就像冥想或者鍛鍊 ── 會幫助我們消解處身在異文化當中，所產生的焦慮、無所適從與困惑的情緒。看著一本本逐漸累積起來的田野筆記，使人感到心安。這種日復一日，重複的寫作，對我專注於聲音和話語的記錄，以及探究它們對村寨 Hmub 人的社會意義，發揮了重要的作用。

語言和非語言的聲音，能夠通過不同的認知過程，被感知、編碼和解碼。兩者也都能在村寨 Hmub 人青年中，傳達社會意義和情緒、情感。因此，出於描述性和分析性兩個目的，本章將英文的 sound／voice 看作和中文的聲／音概念類似。那麼，記錄聽覺、音調，將其轉換為單詞和句子，並把具體的田野材料，通過書寫安全地儲存在田野筆記本裡，就尤為重要。

文學理論家沃爾特・翁（Walter Ong）的文學創作觀，為拓展我們對口語文化和書寫文化之間關係的理解提供了基礎。翁的觀點認為，寫作是「人類最重要的技術發明」（Ong 1982：72）。它將聲音轉化到空間維度，並且「轉變了人們的生活世界」（ibid.：85）。換句話說，翁認為傾聽和書寫之間的相互依賴性，是一種視覺上的優勢回歸。與翁的理論有或多或少地相似，民族誌研究的訓練，涉及身體經驗和共鳴的一種層次分級，其中，視覺通常處於這個層次的頂端，而聽覺則處於較低的位置。

本章試圖講述從傾聽、聆聽經驗和情感共鳴到寫作的這一轉折，是如何運用多重感官去理解村寨 Hmub 人所創造和感知其遊方文化。我們可以追尋到兩種獨特的經驗層次。首先，和傅柯的自我技術並行，我通過田野筆記的書寫，來自我修練。除了看著逐日增加的田野筆記，令人心安外，還通過規律和廣泛的田野書寫來自我訓練與成長。在田野裡對於自我和身分認同的情緒情感世界之轉折裡，逐漸內化我作為一個民族誌學者的田野經歷。此時，這種身體修鍊的經驗，也逐漸明顯。此過程一定程度上貼合利維‧維果茨基（Lev Vygotsky）對於「仲介手段（mediational means）」所提出的概念，即寫作的轉化效力，同時具有物質性和象徵性（Haas 1996：225）。[9]

第二層涉及對非語言之聲音意義的驗證。與斯托勒（1987、1989）的見解相同，我認為，學習如何去傾聽、理解和解釋非語言的聲音，是人類學領域輕忽的一項重要技能。在西方傳統裡，對聽覺文化力量的認知，基本上是較缺乏的。斯托勒是少數關注這類現象的人類學家。而 Hmub人村寨裡的敲窗聲，也許並不能夠算作一個有多獨特與外來的例子。儘管如此，在我自己所屬的東亞華人文化中，那些深夜的聲音，可能攜帶著不同的含義。所以我們必須重新學習和有意識地聯繫聽的技藝，這便是進行研究之關鍵所在。本章指出，聆聽與傾聽的經歷，將各種情緒聯繫在一起（例如透露了村寨姑娘，被人追求時的情感與情緒），而田野筆記的書寫，則能夠讓我們回想和理解敲窗文化，及其相關的遊方談話、事件和參與者。通過田野筆記的書寫，我們能夠將社會價值和情感價值，偕同聽到的聲音，聯繫起來，以便能理解 Hmub 村寨青年們的社會生活與情感生活。

九、結語

除開人類學書中提到的文化衝擊，及其伴隨著的孤獨、思鄉和抑鬱，田野裡自我認同的出現、轉變，及民族誌工作者的身體經驗，則很少被注意。這些情緒、情感與身體感可能對田野材料的深度，以及它被民族誌學者，在更大的社會環境中所覺察的價值，產生深遠影響。我們如何通過聆聽與傾聽，和筆記的書寫，在田野裡練習聽。以及如何在田野工作中，引導感官、情感、認同和作為一個人類學專業自我的轉變，更細微地聚焦到，身體經驗如何可能結合起來，讓民族誌學者感知所研究的對象與事件。這些經歷與體驗都促成了我們作為民族誌學者和研究過程中自我的轉變。同樣的，還有我們對理解村寨 Hmub 人遊方知識的轉變。這或許可以是對傅柯之自我技術觀點（1988：18）的補充：

> ……允許個人以自己的方式，或在他人的幫助下對自己的身體和靈魂、思想、行為和存在方式進行一定程度的操作，從而轉變自己，

來達到某種幸福、純潔、智慧、完美或不朽的狀態。

　　認眞聆聽與傾聽也讓我們體會到對於村寨 Hmub 人遊方知識的瞭解。深夜敲窗，這個「以聲音爲中心的社會實踐形式」（Erlmann 2004：20），通過它的「聽覺即時感」（ibid.）揭示了遊方的制度性、正式性和集體性等特徵，這也促使我對聽到的聲音進行分類。分析其他地區（Chien 2009a，亦參見本書第一章）婚前和婚外調情的長期與短期影響時，我將村寨 Hmub 人遊方理解爲對年輕人有巨大價值的特定情感領域。在本章，強調如何通過仔細聆聽與傾聽，來增補收集到的田野民族誌材料，從而使遊方能夠被更好地理解。但也正如埃爾曼（2004：18）所觀察到的，並向我們提出了一個問題，即需要什麼樣的聆聽與傾聽能力，來收集和篩選日常生活中的聲音，去「拾取所有流動的聲音。在精心限定的，有序的言語交流和音樂區域之外或之間的回聲、殘響、哼鳴和低語」。民族誌方法論在聆聽與傾聽的這一方面，值得進一步關注。將其吸納進人類學的研究技藝中，能夠使我們更好地理解所研究的社會。

Chapter 5　煩悶、日常與村寨 Hmub 人的遊方

一、前言

　　單調、無聊或煩悶是現代人日常生活或工作裡突出的情緒或身體經驗，但如此普通的情緒或身體經驗，其內容與存在或依附的狀態意義為何，卻是頗讓人玩味。它們是現代工業社會才有的情緒或身體經驗嗎？它是怎樣的一種存在狀態呢？研究兒童心理的亞當·菲利普斯（Adam Phillips 2000〔1994〕）認為煩悶或無所事事，是一個處於日常時間內停滯於期待中的身心狀態。存在主義哲學家馬丁·海德格（Martin Heidegger）以等火車等具體的情境，來區辨煩悶是人在不同情境所存在的特定狀態。那是一種與不安或鄉愁相似的存在經驗。本章以貴州東部高地自稱 Hmub[1] 的村寨民族誌為基礎，描述與討論一種近似無聊或煩悶的情緒與身體經驗：*rat*。[2] 我試著通過本章的書寫，來討論在地方文化或地方社會之獨特脈絡裡，*rat* 煩悶的情緒或身體經驗的內容為何；它如何與高地村寨 Hmub 人的工作、休閒，展現具體微細的關聯，並進而披露村寨 Hmub 人日常生活的特性。[3] *Rat* 這個經驗，有被說出的，可稱之語言的經驗；但也有不被說出，而經由身體與情緒流瀉而出的。在貴州東部高地 Hmub 人的日常生活，*rat* 這個語彙是最常用來表述人在心情、生活上煩悶、單調，或無所事事。相對於節慶儀式的熱鬧氛圍，在 Hmub 人的工作與休閒間，流動著的 *rat*，是一種充分展現日常性的無聊或煩悶的情緒與身體經驗。單調與無聊的內容及其存在或依附的狀態與意義，通常被認爲是工業化或資本主義社會之日常生活與工作的特性。而在一個以農作生產爲主，並又和市場經濟已有密切關連的村寨，Hmub 人生活中的 *rat*，和工業社會裡個人的單調與煩悶，是否有別、如何有別。本章在民族誌田野工作的基礎下，以田野筆記、日記爲素材，描述與分析村寨 Hmub 人無聊、煩悶的情緒與身體感官經驗的特性及其轉變歷程。並藉以闡述遊方（*iut fub*，黔東南地區 Hmub 人傳統上具制度化傾向的談情說愛）[4] 所蘊涵之地方社會個人與社群之日常性與主體性，而非僅爲婚姻之附屬。

　　Rat 的發現與記錄是偶然的，不在原先預設的研究問題裡，也未曾出現在與 Hmub 或 Hmong 等不同苗族支系相關的文獻中。是近年來我重新閱讀自己於 1998-2000 年期間，在 Fangf Bil 村寨的田野筆記，才意識到當時留下的諸多書寫，已指出 *rat* 豐富的物性、身體經驗，以及日常、儀式的生活世界，在其中相互的包藏與揉雜。這些也都和遊方、婚姻與親屬所共同形成的社會性有關。但此部分充滿日常、物性的田野材料，在我過去以情感與結構爲主軸的親屬人類學作品裡，並沒有充裕的描述與討論。在這一章，*rat* 不被簡化爲壓抑的情緒，也不以心理學的角度來解釋遊方的材料，而是對田野筆記等民族誌材料重新閱讀與分析。以留有濃厚原始材料之特性的田野筆記爲文本，討論 *rat* 的情緒、身體經驗與日常、遊方的關係。最後藉由以工作、休閒、日常的身體經驗與身體感作爲描述與討論遊方的特性，並檢視遊方與聯姻的關聯與對話性。本章之所以要回到遊方特性，以及遊方與婚姻關聯，乃因這個村寨 Hmub 人的地方社會在當代仍積極實踐著結合村寨內婚理想的姑舅交表聯姻，並在行爲、概念與規範上，展現層層交織的聯姻價值。[5] 而有制度化傾向的遊方談情，基本上突出了與前者兩個不同傾向的關聯：一方面遊方與交表

聯姻爲一對一的關連，另一方面遊方在情感及情緒上所展現的個人性，以及可能延續一輩子的個人浪漫情感，卻不必然與婚姻有一對一的關係。[6] 本章以日常與身體經驗爲切入焦點的書寫，是想面對遊方如何回應集體理想之外的另一面，亦即遊方作爲年輕人夜晚相互爲伴的活動。尤其針對年輕人即興、戲謔的結伴，與抒發、消解個人的煩悶與無聊，進行較細節的描述與討論。

接下來，要講述一個遊方的身體經驗作爲本章的起頭。這個關於 *rat* 的故事，將由 1999 年夏天，我在貴州東部高地 Hmub 人村寨所撰寫的田野筆記說起。那段時間，這個被大山層層圍繞的美麗村寨，一直下著大雨。

在臺灣參加了「雲貴高地親屬與經濟」研討會之後，1999 年六月二十九日，我又返抵 Fangf Bil 村寨。到七月十二日那天，差不多是十三天了。這十來天，Ghaif Wangk（二十歲未婚的唐家姑娘）勤奮地天天陪我整理田野筆記與村寨的家戶資料。十多天了，她夜裡都未曾出去 *iut fub*（遊方）。只有一晚，有男孩來敲窗，她被喊醒，並起來開窗談情。男孩是 Vek Ghas 小寨的 Zangb Jix Dlaid（二十歲未婚的張家後生，Ghaif Wangk 的表兄，他們在小學時曾是同學）。之後二、三晚，我在睡夢中，偶爾也聽到窗外有人喊 Ghaif，但 Ghaif Wangk 都沒有醒。

在七月十二日之前，約三、四天吧，我開始覺得 Ghaif Wangk 有些 *rat*。起初，還很輕微，並不明顯。我便對她說，妳想去 Ghaif Wangf（二十歲左右未婚的唐家姑娘，她是 Ghaif Wangk 的堂妹

〔FFBSD〕）家便去。[7]她是懂我的意思。雖然她常對我說：「我並不喜歡遊方。姊，妳沒在（村寨）時，我也很少去。也很少開窗……」。不過，在我與她說了，要她想去遊方就去的那一天，或第二天下午，她便對我說「今天晚上我要去 Ghaif Wangf 家，妳去不去？」我想了想，決定不去，雖然在決定不去之後，我的內心總有一種研究工作「不落實」的感覺。不過夜晚的遊方如何研究，應否、能否參與觀察？我總是在研究工作及田野倫理間，感到困惑、遲疑。

傍晚，Ghaif Wangk 如常在做家務──挑水、洗菜、煮菜、餵豬，最後再熱一壺洗腳水給全家人在夏季下著雨的涼爽夜裡，晚飯後，睡覺前洗洗手腳。我想今天晚上要出去玩了，Ghaif Wangk 做起家事，會帶勁些。不過，就在我們差不多要吃晚飯，天色已經暗了，近八點或再晚一些，堂妹來喊 Ghaif Wangk。我見她帶著笑臉出現在我與 Ghaif 的臥房窗前。「Ghaif Wangk *dak, wal xuf mongk.*」。堂妹將 Ghaif Wangk 喊出去，講了幾句話便走了。我在窗邊喊堂妹來吃飯，但她說要回家去。堂妹來告訴 Ghaif Wangk，今天晚上不用去她家了，因為有三個巫梭村寨的姑娘來到 Gad Dlongf 小寨。堂妹她們晚上要去陪這三個姑娘作伴。所以，堂妹便不要 Ghaif Wangk 去她家。

這天夜裡，Ghaif Wangk 原本可能的一次遊方機會便消失了。如往常一樣，我們洗淨了手腳，便差不多準備上床睡覺。Ghaif 的父親則還會逛到其他家去談話，休息或看電視。Ghaif 的母親幾乎是沒有在晚上到其他家串門子。而其他家的叔伯媽或媳婦，也少在夜晚上門聊天。婦女的聊天多是在白天工作空檔，或去坡上工作前。她們通常是在家戶外面，一邊梳理頭髮一邊聊，或者縫衣服時，也是聊天談話的。這天她沒去成。往後幾天，她與我一起整理筆記或研究資料時，步履便愈顯沉重，常常是拖著腳步在走路。有時，會對我的發問顯得不耐煩。或是用有些陌生的眼神回應我的注視。也常會呆呆地望著窗外，或倚在大門邊往外看。她的這種狀態，有時會使我覺得心裡有些過意不去……

（1999 年七月十二日田野筆記）

我在本章的開始，放進隨筆、片段風格的民族誌資料，主要有兩點想法。一個是經由初稿風格的田野筆記，留住村寨民族誌的日常生活氛圍，以及在田野當時，所經驗與感受的人與人之間微細的互動；另一個是嘗試以田野筆記的敘述，留住在研究遊方的過程裡，所觀察或經驗到村寨的日常生活，以及穿透、流動在個人工作與休閒之間的煩悶、窒人情緒與身體經驗，rat。這兩點也是本章書寫的主軸。

（一）文獻回顧：從煩悶到日常生活的研究

對於日常生活裡如此微不足道的經驗 —— 煩悶，是何種存在的樣態？它如何界定，不同文獻之間對此的探討，差異何在？以及它與本章的關聯。首先，本章與文化翻譯有關。亦即，村寨 Hmub 語 rat 與中文煩悶或英文 boredom 等字詞之間的關聯，以及它們之間表述此經驗的差異。在漢字古籍裡的煩悶，包含身心的經驗。煩涉及身體的經驗，如頭痛、胸悶、燥熱；[8] 也涉及心裡的經驗，如憂愁、心煩、急躁、思慮紛亂。[9] 悶同樣涉及身體的經驗，如心悶；與心理的經驗，如煩憂、煩懣。[10] 而與中文煩悶相近的英語詞彙 boredom，所代表的則是缺乏興趣所產生的情感狀態，未直接涉及身體經驗。第二版的《牛津英文大詞典》（*The Oxford English Dictionary*）指出，to be a bore 最早出現在 1768 年，用以表述無聊、沉悶的感覺；而 boredom 最早則出現在查爾斯·狄更斯（Charles Dickens）的作品《荒涼山莊》（*Bleak House*, 1852）（Simpson and Weiner 1989a：412-415）。漢語古籍詞彙煩悶所涉及的身與心兼顧的概念，基本上已超過英語辭彙 boredom 僅著眼於內心感覺為主的限制。本章所探討的 *rat*，也非局限於心理的經驗，而是包含情緒與身體的感官經驗。並且，本章還要進一步面對煩悶的由來是如何關聯著人的處境與其社會生活的情境或語境。針對後者，有以下三個例子。

對於煩悶的由來，亞當·菲利普斯以孩童在日常生活的某些片刻所感受到的無聊狀態為例，提出他對 being board 生動的描述與分析。菲利普斯是以兒童心理研究見長的精神分析家。他曾以不同的經驗材料，分析這種非常個人的身體感覺或情緒狀態。他以小孩的內心或身體經驗為例，討論什麼是煩悶。對於小孩處於煩悶、無所事事的身體狀態（being bored），菲利普斯認為小孩與曾經身為小孩的大人不一定明白，但經驗上卻是熟悉的。

> 小孩並非先知，但他們卻不斷地問著這個偉大的存在主義問題：「我們現在該做什麼？」每個成人都記得小時候無聊的時刻。每個小孩的生活每隔不久就會出現一段煩悶的時光：一種停滯於期待中的狀態。此時所有事物皆照常進行，卻沒有發生任何有趣的事情。於是小孩處在一種冗長的躁動情緒下，懷著最為荒謬且矛盾的渴望，也就是對於欲望的渴望。
>
> （Philips 2000〔1994〕：131）

亞當・菲利普斯認為煩悶或無所事事，是一個處於日常時間內停滯於期待中的身心狀態。而且他還指出「我們所應該討論的，顯然不是單一的煩悶，而是許多的煩悶，因為煩悶這個概念本身便包含了許多種無法分析的情緒和感受」（Philips 2000：145）。對於煩悶內容的經驗描述，以及煩悶與人或社群的日常生活之不可分離的特性，因而是同樣必要的。存在主義哲學家海德格也指出煩悶作為人之存在的特定狀態。在《形上學的基本概念》（The Fundamental Concepts of Metaphysics）一書中，海德格以百餘頁篇幅，討論這種經驗。他可能是少數曾以相當篇幅書寫boredom的學者。對他來說，這種無所事事的存在樣態可分為三類，並分別關聯著由特定時間、空間與人所處於之場合組合成的處境。他認為boredom和不安（anxiety）相近，並以鄉愁來詮釋此種經驗。因為鄉愁的宿命分離感與boredom具有被放逐、留放的感覺相同，而這些感覺又和情境的營造有關。他將boredom區分成三種形式。他比喻第一種形式的boredom，好比等待火車的時刻。想像一個人無事可做，就只是為了等候車子到達的那種無趣和孤單的感覺。無法閱讀、無人可交談，任由時光緩慢而明顯的流逝。這種情境充滿壓迫感，海德格強調不是車站本身令人感到無趣，而是時間的拖延，讓人無所適從，徒留空虛。他提出此種形式的boredom，和「對的時間」與「錯的時間」相關。當火車遲遲未來，時光令人感到冗長，此時是錯的時間；當候車時火車即刻來到，此時便是對的時間，而此種形式的boredom便不會產生。第二種形式的boredom，海德格亦以情境來比喻。當我們受邀至某地方用餐，隻身前往，令人感到緊張。雖然食物美味，交談熱烈，充滿詼諧和驚喜感，所有事物都令人感到美好，充滿魅力；然而，此種形式的boredom，雖然看似毫無無聊之感，但相較於第一種形式的boredom而言，這種boredom

則是毫無目的性。而第一種形式的 boredom 則充滿情境空間的無聊感。第二種形式的 boredom，沒有時間孤立不安的壓迫感，卻感到時間無邊無際，不具體，缺乏目標、充滿空洞；好比光陰已經停滯靜止一般，過去和未來的時間皆被掏空。第三種形式的 boredom，海德格將之命名爲 profound boredom（深刻的無聊感）。此種形式的無聊經驗使人感到冷漠（indifference），非個人性（impersonality），充滿遙遠、不確定、無所事事、缺乏價值，帶有空間灰暗耗盡，心理失序之感。顯然，profound boredom 的空洞和前兩種形式不同。它不是等候火車的那種缺乏實踐的感覺，也並非參加宴會特有的情境存在感；而是一種彷彿世界已死，不期望周遭會發生任何事的感覺（Hammer 2004；Heidegger 1995〔1929〕：78-164）。

　　煩悶的由來，也源於特定之生計文明的生產形式所創造的情境。裝配線是其中突出的例子。從日常生活的角度來看，工業化並不限於工廠的生產活動，還包括那些發生在生活中所有面向的事物。大規模的工業化，指的並不只是技術方面的狀況，而是在感官－精神方面的體驗。裝配線之所以成爲日常生活現代性的例證或隱喻，在於它表現出的沉重緩慢、單調無趣的氛圍。如此的一再重複（repetition-of-the-same），將人對日常生活的時間體驗，轉成讓人感覺衰頹的無聊或煩悶（Highmore 2005〔2002〕：12）。以裝配線爲例，煩悶、無聊這樣一種可能被視爲無足輕重的身體經驗或現象，就被認爲是和工業文明之後，人的生活或工作有緊密的關聯。換言之，煩悶與無聊除了被理解爲人存在的特定樣態，它與日常生活之間的建構關係，也成爲一種發問的方向。例如，蘿莉・朗博爾（Laurie Langbauer）以工廠生產線的重複單調，來描述日常生活與煩悶無聊之間的關係。

城市日常生活的無聊，就是裝備（配）線上，那些枯燥動作。一個接著一個，一片接著一片，固定在永無止境的一連串活動上，卻永遠沒有真正的進展。它的變化越多，它就越是沒有變化。

（Langbauer 1993：81；引自 Highmore 2005〔2002〕：9）

《分析日常生活與文化理論》（*Everyday Life and Cultural Theory*）（Highmore 2005〔2002〕）以及《日常生活實踐》（*The Practice of Everyday Life*）（de Certeau 1984）兩部作品，皆試圖將日常生活視為一種美學領域與文化理論，並且認為日常生活所具有之日復一日與無從察覺的特質，正是它最為特殊之處。他們探討此一特殊性的過程，逐步揭露身處於其中的主體，如何在無意識的日常行動中，展現某種自成系統的實踐邏輯與文化。而這樣的實踐又如何反身地形成反抗動能，重組或再生產新的文化意義。班·海默（Ben Highmore 2005〔2002〕：6）以知識考掘的態度，回顧歐陸學界建構日常生活之文化理論的關鍵事件與論辯焦點。貫穿全書的是無聊、神秘與理性思考這三個關鍵概念。狄塞托（Michel de Certeau）則堅持詩學立場，在消費和生產的實踐邏輯中，尋找反抗與顛覆的可能。對他來說，日常生活是一個充滿創造性的集體活動，消費者透過形式變化萬千的戰術（tactics），在無法逃脫的資本主義社會中創造使用商品的新意象，進而組成一個反規訓之網（the network of an antidiscipline）（de Certeau 1984：xiv-xv）。

昂希·列斐伏爾（Henri Lefebvre 1991〔1958〕）則指出日常生活與休閒之間存在著不簡單的對應關係：它們既是一體的，卻又同時是對立的（因此也是辯證的關係）。他認為人其實不可能逃脫日常生活。

因為人努力工作，以便有能力進行休閒，而休閒所擁有的唯一目的，就是為了逃離工作；然而休閒，雖看似是在日常裡呈顯出非日常性（non-everyday），但我們其實並沒有真正擺脫日常生活。因為休閒能對工作進行批判，僅是因為它的非日常。但此部分的實際，主要是以想像為基礎。人的休閒是在日常生活裡，休閒中的人並未徹底脫離物質性的存在狀態。

　　人類學以日常生活為主的民族誌研究，一方面可說是延續列斐伏爾或狄塞托對於日常生活進行反思的取徑，並進一步強調以民族誌的描述探討日常與文化的關聯，以及日常與節慶的對話性。如黛安‧邁恩斯（Diane P. Mines）與莎拉‧蘭姆（Sarah Lamb）編輯的《南亞的日常生活》（*Everyday Life in South Asia*, 2002）對於日常生活的描述，聚焦於人們如何實際進行其日復一日的生活，而此一生活過程即為動態的文化表現。因此他們呼應狄塞托對於日常生活的界定，亦即日常生活是結構與文化實際生產、轉化的場域。另一個文獻的例子是亞努什‧穆查（Janusz Mucha）的《少數族裔在地社群的日常生活與節慶活動：印第安納州南灣的波蘭裔美國人》（*Everyday Life and Festivity in a Local Ethnic Community: Polish-Americans in South Bend, Indiana*, 1996）。穆查指出，那些在時空上可以察覺的活動——如節慶（festivity），也以一種類似日常生活特質——例行、反覆、眾所皆知的方式來進行。因此日常生活與節慶時間，實際上是有所重疊。貴州東部高地村寨 Hmub 人的遊方，中介於日常與節慶。一方面創造出年輕人休閒的歡愉，另一方面又與日常及工作的內容與節奏，有著不可分的關聯，因而是一個可與前述文獻所涉及之日常與非日常的探討，有所對話的民族誌例子。

（二）日常生活的身體感

　　本文延續狄塞托、列斐伏爾、海默等研究日常生活之學者，將日常生活作為問題意識與探索人類尋常經驗之場域，以及人類學者由民族誌來描述與反思日常生活與文化的關聯。但是我們不能忽略前述文獻所涉及的煩悶、日常、工作與休閒，主要是在西方工業社會、資本主義或布爾喬亞社會的脈絡下所進行的議論。它們多半已被西方社會個人主義的傳統所包覆。而如黛安‧邁恩斯與莎拉‧蘭姆（2002）所主編的書討論南亞的族群文化與日常生活，本章則以貴州東部高地的村落民族誌之特殊性為基礎，探討這群以農耕、園藝生計為主，但又已部分被國家與市場經濟捲入的村寨 Hmub 人。描述與分析中介在他們的工作與休閒之間的一種融合情緒與身體經驗的感受，煩悶 rat。這個由民族誌取向來探索煩悶經驗的研究，除了能面對亞當‧菲利普斯所指出的煩悶與日常的關聯，或煩悶作為方法，以瞭解它如何是一種身體與心理的經驗；也與海德格所提到，boredom 因不同的情境，而有不同內涵的內在邏輯，有著延續性。但前述文獻對煩悶與日常的探討，無論是針對孩童或成人（如工廠裡生產線上一個個疏離異化的個體），所指的都是個人的身體或心裡的存在樣態與處境。它們與有意義之集體（社群或社會）的關聯與對話性，並不清楚。相對的，本章對於煩悶 rat 的探討，則通過村寨民族誌脈絡下 Hmub 人的結群，以及個人身體經驗與感受間的對話。並討論 rat 這樣一種特定的身體經驗與感受，如何中介與流動在村寨 Hmub 人之地方社會與日常生活的脈絡裡——尤其是與遊方的關聯。

　　換言之，本章從人類尋常的身體經驗探索，取得與現代社會對話的可能性。這既是築基於人類學古典的民族誌書寫與討論，並也深受當代以日常生活作爲問題意識與人類經驗場域之探索的啓發（de Certeau 1984；Highmore 2002；Lefebvre 1991〔1958〕）。在書寫高地村寨 Hmub 人民族誌材料的過程，我先試著對照華文與英文的相近辭彙，爲 rat 經驗的書寫，提供以文化翻譯爲基礎，進而理解人類尋常經驗的路徑。如前面引述之西方文獻，特定的煩悶或 boredom 經驗的內容（或過程），不僅中介於身心間，並也在日常生活與個人之處境間流動。尤其通過關注現象與存在樣態的哲學家海德格之闡釋，boredom 經驗背後，是沉重的西方工業文明所主導之人類遭逢、居處之現代生活的實際。本章以雲貴高地村寨民族誌爲基礎材料，也在面對當代村寨 Hmub 人之日常生活裡，個人所經驗煩悶的內容，以及可能存在之不同文化範疇的特性或差異。煩悶、無聊、無所事事之特定內涵（具體的概念或行爲），在貴州東部 Hmub 人的個人，或個人所處的地方文化或地方社會之獨特脈絡裡，如何與工作、休閒、日常生活、個人主體性，展現具體微細的關聯，是本章描述與討論的重點。

（三）田野地點與方法

　　煩悶的民族誌書寫，與 Hmub 人村寨之社會理想與實際緊密關聯。貴州省東南部所聚居的族群，以自稱 Hmub 爲衆。本章的研究對象 Fangf Bil 高地村寨，就位於黔東南雷公山系與清水江中游，爲層層山巒所包圍。在當代的行政轄區屬於貴州省台江縣番召鄉，離縣城約二十多公里。現今仍以農作生產爲主，但在政治、教育、消費、生產已和國家與市場經濟有密切的關連。如村長或支書的選舉有政黨的運作與影響。他們也繳稅並向國家承租耕地。台江縣城每六天一場的趕場（diut qangk），是他們將米糧或家禽家畜拿去賣，以及購買日用品的地方。這個現象一直到二十一世紀的當下都還是常見的。

　　1998-2000 年期間，Fangf Bil 村寨人口約一千五百餘人，三百多家戶。這個村寨以父系繼嗣群為家族的核心團體，包含張、唐、楊、萬、邰等漢姓，共居一小寨（*vangf*）的，通常是共享一男性祖先的家族，總共有五個小寨。父系繼嗣群內禁婚。在日常與儀式的生活裡，重視由村寨內婚與廣泛姑舅交表聯姻結合的理想與實際。並且還有與交表聯姻一方面有關、一方面無關的遊方談情，後者指的是私奔婚與婚姻外的遊方談情。如本書前面篇章所述，遊方是具制度化傾向的談情。在日常夜晚男孩敲女孩的窗邊談話或對歌，或是男孩與女孩，三五成群圍聚在女孩家裡談話。節慶的白天則到村寨邊的小山坡或大樹下談話對歌。明清時期成書的黔東南地方誌，文人、官員描述他們所見的思南、黎平府等地的苗族風俗，遊方幾占一半篇幅。可見此風俗在黔東南有其普遍與顯著性。本章將在此地方文化脈絡下，進行煩悶 *rat* 的民族誌描述與討論。

　　針對與 *rat* 有關的民族誌材料，我的研究方法是沉浸在日常的田野，並動用聽、看、嗅等身體的多重感官經驗，進行參與觀察。本章用作分析的材料包含 1998 至 2000 年，我在貴州東部 Fangf Bil 村寨進行田野工作時，當年還未婚，年約二十歲的當地姑娘 Ghaif Wangk 用中文記錄其個人與家人之日常家務的工作日誌，以及我觀察、感受、記錄、書寫 Ghaif Wangk 姑娘，及其家人、親人、親戚之工作、休閒、遊方經驗的田野筆記與日記。以此材料為基礎，接下來三節的書寫在內容的關連與民族誌資料屬性的對照，有必要先指出來。首先此三節的題旨依序為「工作與日常」、「休閒與日常」、「煩悶」。它們雖然沒有直接提到遊方，但工作、休閒與煩悶經驗 *rat*，實質上都涉及日常脈絡裡個人的遊方經驗。

其次，則是此三節的民族誌材料與書寫者的對照。前兩節（工作與休閒）以 Ghaif Wangk 姑娘的工作日誌爲主，後一節（煩悶）則與本章前言的筆記相呼應，是以我自己所寫的田野筆記爲素材，描述煩悶的個人身體經驗、歷程，及其與日常夜晚遊方的動態關係。亦即，rat 的經驗，並未被 Ghaif Wangk 姑娘直接寫出，而是研究者的觀察與通過田野筆記的描述與記錄。[11] 簡言之，經由民族誌材料鋪陳貴州東部高地村寨 Hmub 人的日常、工作、休閒與 rat 的經驗，本章描述與解讀無聊、煩悶的情緒與身體經驗的特性及其轉變歷程，並由此討論遊方雖與婚姻有關，但不必然附屬於婚姻，而是含蘊地方社會的個人與社群之日常與主體性的場域。

二、工作與日常

工作在貴州東部高地村寨 Hmub 人日常生活裡的位置相當顯著。他們的日常生活，不能與土地生產的勞力工作分開。他們將田裡與坡上的生產活動稱之爲 *at gheb*（做工），以此有別於家屋裡面的勞務：*at ghongf ghit*（做家事）。在日常生活裡，高地村寨 Hmub 人的時間配置與空間的移動依其而定；工作也構成及再現人與人的社會關係或社會聲望。比如，有些工作是兩性共同完成，有些是兩性分工；某些工作具體表現年齡的差異，或突顯當家男女的義務；或者也是持續確認他們的社會角色。如稻米的生產，大體上由兩性分工來完成。但整地、犁田、種植杉樹、立屋是男人的事；織布、染布、縫衣、釀酒，則是女人爲儀式而做的活，男人是不插手，並有相當程度的迴避。就大部分的農務與日常的工作，已當家爲人父母的男女，才是勞動的主力；年輕未當家且沒有出外打工的男性，[12] 白天在村寨遊蕩不事勞動，反而是常態。

1998 年十一月至 2000 年二月，我來到這個寨子進行民族誌田野工作，並住進姑娘 Ghaif Wangk 與父母、弟弟共住的家。除了付錢在她家搭伙，並出工資請她協助進行田野工作。由此多少也影響 Ghaif Wangk 家日常工作內容的分配。例如，以白天挑雞到山野放食為例。如果 Ghaif Wangk 不是在協助我進行田野工作，那麼當年初中畢業的她，還沒出嫁也沒到外地打工，[13] 挑雞就是她的日常工作之一。此外在田野工作裡與當地人的互動經驗裡，也反映出村寨 Hmub 人對於工作的認知。我請 Ghaif Wangk 逐日記錄她與家人工作內容的日誌裡，她並不記入參與做研究工作這事。對於協助整理田野資料的事，Ghaif Wangk 在日誌裡總是寫著「在家休息」。這與當地老人對於什麼是工作（*at gheb*）的概念，十分吻合。村寨老人家經常取笑我，天天在家休息（*lel vud*），不用去田裡、山裡做工。雖經我「抗議」說，天天寫字（田野筆記），是在做研究，也是在工作。但直到田野研究告一段落，我返回臺灣了，他們的說法與觀點，始終未變。

（一）Ghaif Wangk 家某幾天的工作

以下是 1999 年六月七日到六月十五日，Ghaif Wangk 寫下夏天插秧農忙時期，家裡的工作日誌。內容呈現出夏季的陰雨天候，父親連著三天犁田，母親與 Ghaif Wangk 則連著三天插秧。犁田、插秧結束後，接著連續數天，父親天天放牛，母親則趕往山坡種辣子、除草，並與看水田等工作，輪流進行。以下是工作日誌之一所記錄的內容。

Ghaif Wangk 工作日誌之一

雨天 6/7（4/24）[14]　今天，父親去「交向」（Jouf Xeix，地名，漢字

讀 Hmub 音)[15] 犁田。母親和我也去「交向」插秧。

陰天 6/8（4/25） 今天，父親去「交向」犁田。
母親和我在「趙向」（Zaut Xeix，地名，漢字讀 Hmub 音）插秧了。

大雨天 6/9（4/26） 今天，父親去「趙向」犁田。
母親和我去「交向」插秧。我家插秧最後一天，就有兩個來搬（「幫」的筆誤）我家的，一個是二組唐偉九（人名，堂姊〔FFBSD〕），一個是一組張娘里（人名，表妹〔FZD〕）。到了吃晚飯後，我們就睡覺了。我們沒有游（遊）方。[16]

晴天 6/10（4/27） 今天，父親去「養機」（Vuk Zib，地名，漢字讀 Hmub 音）放牛。
母親去看水田。
我在家休息。

雨天 6/11（4/28） 今天，父親放牛。
母親去「養嘎林」（Vek Ghad Lingf，地名，漢字讀 Hmub 音）種辣子。
我去搬（「幫」的筆誤）楊格往（人名，堂妹〔FFBSD〕）家插秧。

晴天 6/12（4/29） 今天，父親去放牛。
母親去看水田。
我在家休息。

晴天 6/13（4/30）　今天，父親去放牛。
　　　　　　　　　母親和我去「養機」種辣子。

晴天 6/14（5/1）　今天，父親放牛。
　　　　　　　　　母親也去「養機」種辣子。
　　　　　　　　　我在家挑穀子曬太陽。

晴天 6/15（5/2）　今天，父親去放牛。
　　　　　　　　　母親去「養嘎林」的土，除草。
　　　　　　　　　我在家休息。

晴天 6/15（5/3）　今天，父親去放牛。
　　　　　　　　　母親也去「養嘎林」的土，除草。
　　　　　　　　　我去看水田。
　　　　　　　　　晚上，楊格往來我家跟我睡，我倆都沒有游
　　　　　　　　　（遊）方。

　　工作日誌之一雖然記得簡要，也有少數別字，但她以中文與漢字讀
Hmub 音的「苗文」書寫，清楚包含具體的工作時間、空間、人之間的
互動（夫妻、家人的兩性分工，親人、姻親間輪流幫工）。尤其，家內
家務事、家外的稻田或山坡工作的規律分派，一再地重複著。在此規律
裡，再現工作與休閒於日常生活裡的交錯。但在此重複與規律中，他們
所進行的工作空間則是有所變化 —— 在環繞著村寨的小區域山林範圍內，
有不同名字的小塊耕地間移動。根據父子聯名與口述傳說的推算，Fangf
Bil 村子立寨近六百年。配合著傳統以來世代進行之父系繼嗣制度，理想
與實際上每個當家的男子，都分配到土地。而 1950 年後國家管理土地策

略與多次變更的結果，使得女人與男人一樣配有土地，並改變當代土地與村人的關係。使每個家戶所擁有的耕地，更形零碎與分散。如同村寨裡多數的家戶，以 Ghaif Wangk 家的地為例，有山裡的林地或荒地，也有位於公路邊小壩子上，或河岸邊的小塊平地（可作為菜園），以及山坳內突出的一小塊、一小塊平坦耕地（可種水稻）。

村寨農忙與家務進行的有序與一再重複，或許不完全異於工業社會工廠裝配線工作的重複與單調，不過兩者在本質上，仍存在某些差異。這在日常生活研究的文獻也已提及。如昂希・列斐伏爾（Highmore 2002：227；Lefebvre 1991〔1958〕）指出，區別農夫與工廠工人生活，就在於生產活動是**農夫整體生活裡，必然存在的部分**（筆者註記）。農夫的工作場所，就在家屋的四周，工作不會與家庭的日常生活分離。亦即，裝配線上的工作之於工人，是相對的片斷、零碎；但農村以家戶為單位的工作，則通常對於工作的人，有其整體意義。每天或每季家人之間的工作安排、分工；生產活動的收穫裡，交替豐收、荒旱等等之實際生活經歷；工作者與其所進行的村子裡之家戶內外的工作，存在較可覺察的主體性。而且在自身熟悉之文化範疇下的空間，作為工作場域，勞動之於人的感受，可望有別於單調不變的工廠作為工作場所而產生的異化感。在 Fangf Bil 村寨，每塊環繞村寨四周的土地與山林，都有傳統以來流通於歷代村人間的名字。這使得土地之於人的關係，並非機械式的關係，而是生命史與情感的連結。工作的場域在居家四周，工作的時間脈動與日常生活緊聯。這是村寨的工作所建立的日常性，並以此有別於工業社會都市的工作與其所再現的人與物相對分離、異化的日常性。

三、休閒與日常

在日、月、季、年一再重複的時間脈動裡，貴州東部高地村寨日常的工作氛圍，以其特有的單調形式與內涵，存在於村寨 Hmub 人的生活與生命經驗中。而 *at naud zaif*（作熱鬧）或 *at vuk gad*（作好玩），則是他們半帶戲謔與認真的挪揄日常生活裡的冷清與單調。當錄影帶或電視還不那麼盛行時，在村寨裡的日常，老人、年輕人、孩童，男性與女性的休閒，有其共通也有其差異之處。小孩愛聚成群在家屋附近玩耍，連下雪的日子也不例外。在沒有農忙的冬季，老人愛在屋外曬日或家屋內烤火，取暖，話當年。識字的人也有他們的休閒方式。像 Ghaif Wangk 的父親這樣識字的中年男人，愛蹲坐在主屋的一角，頗有興致的讀一些過期的報紙或廣告、通訊上的文字。這群跑過外面（多數是到過外省打工，少數是求學）見過世面的中年男性，也喜歡閒聊從中央電視臺所看到與聽到的政局時事或國際新聞（在 2000 年前，村寨裡的電視還不普遍時，成年男性在農閒期間的白天，或平日的夜晚，多會擠在有電視的小店鋪前觀看央視新聞或節目）。當家的女人，常見她們在清晨的家屋一側或河壩邊，一邊梳著及腰長髮並盤成髮髻，一邊和住在鄰近的妯娌話家常。在下雨的日子無法到坡上工作，已出嫁的女兒，愛揹著幼娃回娘家，與母親一起坐在屋前，縫衣，話家常。這些都是村寨內頗具休閒內涵的日常。而在平常的夜裡，最突出的休閒，則是年輕男女的遊方。平日的遊方是本章書寫的重點，它有別於較具儀式展演特性與結構張力的節慶遊方（*nenk ghait lingf*，台江地區稱此為姊妹節）（參簡美玲 2009a：31-77）。

本章前節摘錄之 Ghaif Wangk 的工作日誌裡，在工作之外，有她與堂姊妹或表姊妹的日常休閒。工作日誌之一的中間與最後，簡單寫下的兩行內容，指的即是日常生活裡年輕姑娘的休閒。她在 1999 年六月十五日，記「晚上，楊格往（堂妹）來我家跟我睡，我倆都沒有遊方」。在 1999 年六月九日，記「我家插秧最後一天，就有兩個來搬（幫）我家的，一個是二組唐偉九（堂姊），一個是一組張娘里（表妹）。到了吃晚飯後，我們就睡覺了。我們沒有遊方」。所記的，雖然都是「沒有遊方」。但是堂表姊妹間，白天到彼此家戶幫工做農事；來幫忙的姊妹，夜晚留在被幫忙的姊妹家吃晚飯，飯後一起聊天至夜深，留在姊妹的房間一起睡覺，卻就是姑娘在農忙的日常生活裡，主要的休閒。

在入秋收割時節的 1999 年十月十八日到十月二十二日，五天的工作日誌（之二，參後），Ghaif Wangk 則較詳細記錄了收割工作的內容與過程。在工作部分，她同樣以漢字讀 Hmub 語的記音，具體描述工作時間、空間，以及人際之間的互動。夫妻、家人的分工，親屬之間的輪流幫工，家務事、稻田或山坡工作的規律安排，以及重複。這五天的工作日誌，前四天（十月十八日到十月二十一日）記錄白天收割工作的重複進行（雖然收割的地點、參與的人、收割物的米穀物種有部分變動）。十月二十二日，記父親去母親姊姊家，幫忙收穀子的曲折（天雨，以及不同家的親屬，來請父親前去幫工），母親上午做家內的工作，然後到坡上放牛。這天 Ghaif Wangk 寫自己上午「在家休息。傍晚都做家務」。如我前面提過，Ghaif Wangk 在工作日誌裡寫「在家休息」，則通常並不是在家休息，而是協助我整理田野材料與記錄家人工作等日誌的書寫。當天下午，她因為做家務的需要（升爐火，煮晚飯），去小店鋪買點火用的火柴盒。遇到同小寨的堂妹約她晚上來家裡玩。最後表現在這天的工作日誌裡，是以相對較多文字，寫下她參與一晚的遊方休閒。

這段平日夜晚的休閒聚會，她先寫了姊妹伴（包括堂妹的母親）的相聚，談話飲酒的過程。在更平常隨意的姊妹伴平日夜晚聚會，是不喝酒的。這次是因為有姊妹在村寨收割季節，由外地返鄉（有人出外或從外地返回，之於村寨都是件大事。酒的出現，代表人群之聚會，比平常多了一些非日常的特性）。Ghaif Wangk 在日誌（之二）裡提到「我拿一盆酒去她家」，以及閂門喝酒，而後醉酒等情況。此時的休閒都是姊妹伴之間的話家常，而因為堂妹的母親也在一起，所以將大門閂起來。堂妹的母親入睡之後，門閂才拔開。拔開門閂，有如一個指示性（indexicality）的記號，指出從姊妹伴之間的聚會，在此轉為有男孩一起參與談話相聚的平日遊方。前來唐家姑娘遊方的，都是張家男孩。他們與 Ghaif Wangk 這群唐家女孩的姊妹，互為姑舅交表親。並且 Ghaif Wangk 也因為寫這工作日誌是協助我做遊方與婚姻、親屬的研究，還仔細標出一起遊方之表兄的婚姻，以及生養小孩與否的情況。這次遊方人的身分，也沒有局限於以婚姻為界線的單一規範裡。在此 Hmub 人村寨，這算是相當典型的。我將此現象稱之為婚姻外的談情與調情（extra-marital courting and flirting）（簡美玲 2005a：49-86、2005b：347-380；Chien 2009a：135-159）。1999 年十月二十二日這天的日誌，Ghaif Wangk 還寫出這次遊方進行到完成的過程，是一對一對的在家屋外談。以及多人一起在家屋內談；最後，遊方依序結束，姑娘紛紛擠入堂妹 Ghaif Dangd 的姑娘房內入睡。以下是 Ghaif Wangk 工作日誌之二的內容。

Ghaif Wangk 工作日誌之二

晴天 10/18　今天，我家也去「交向」（地名）打穀子，還有美玲、張娘里（表妹〔FZD〕），她兩個來幫我家的忙。美玲、娘里，我們三個專門割，父母親專門打。打到中午母親就下坡去煮菜，煮熟我們都下坡吃飯。吃好飯，我們就休息一下。然後我們都繼續地打，割到六點鐘左右就打完了。美玲、娘里，我們三個就回家呢！到家後我都做家務事，吃好晚飯我們就睡覺。父親也沒回家，還在移穀子。張娘里也跟我一起在我家睡，她不回家。

晴天 10/19　今天，父母親都去「交向」扛穀子。扛完，有車子來，就把穀子（搬）上來了。穀子到家，我跟父母親一起扛穀子回家。晚上的家務事，母親我倆一起做了。

晴天 10/20　父母親去「養機」剪糯米穀，就是 Hmub 話叫「念格」（*ningf ghait*，漢字讀 Hmub 音，意思是糯米穀用小器具剪，有別於粘米穀是用割的）。

今天，剪家糯米穀，都是要那個小小的剪來弄。前一段時間就是打穀子，都打粘米穀了。

我在家休息。然後，美玲和我，我倆去「養機」看父母親「念格」。

陰天 10/21　父母親去「養機」「念格」。早上母親做家務事，做好家務她才去。然後他倆也放牛。

我在家休息，傍晚時就做家務事。

小雨天轉陰 10/22　早上，父親要去伯媽家（母親的姊姊〔MZe〕）打穀子。去她家之後就開始下雨來了，那都打不成穀子。那父親再轉回家，回來他就去「養機」放牛。伯媽二組（指住在二組的伯母〔FFBSW〕，受 Hmub 的語法影響）也叫父親去她家幫忙，然後父親就一定要去伯媽一組（指住在一組的伯母〔MZe〕）打了，因為天下雨就打不成。早上，母親做家務事，做好就去「養機」放牛。我在家休息，傍晚都做家務呢！傍晚我去商店那邊賣（「買」的筆誤）火柴來用。我就碰到唐格當（堂妹〔FFBSD〕），和唐汪歲（堂妹〔FFFBSSD〕）她倆個在半路。格當就約我，今晚上你來我家玩。我就跟（她）說：可以來了。因為她剛從外面（指外地打工）回來一兩天。那我就吃晚飯好後，我拿一盆酒去她家。汪歲已在裡面，我去一下子楊格里（堂妹〔FFBSD〕）就來。我們就休息到十點鐘左右才開始喝酒，格當的母親也跟我們一起喝。我們每一個都醉酒。我們喝酒，就把門閂起來，不讓小伙子進來。喝到十二點鐘就不再喝了。格當母親（FFBSW）去睡覺，我們就把門打開了。然後就有小伙子進來是：八組的張往歲（表兄，已有子。以下皆為遠近不等的旁支姑舅表交表兄弟〔mul diangf〕，他們的名字也都是漢字讀 Hmub 音）、張我翁、張在九，七組是張衣翁、張在榮（已結婚有子）、張抱水，六組張我歲、張翁九，一組張望翁（也有子）。她們三個女人在外面一個跟一個交談，剩下我一個在家裡面跟男人談。我大概到（午夜）二點鐘，我就睡覺了，她們還繼續在（遊方）。然後是汪歲來睡，後來是格當，格里她倆在結束。

　　這晚的遊方和日常生活的工作脈絡，仍是相關聯。其一表現在時間的脈絡上，一方面是夜晚的姊妹伴聚會，接在工作為主的白天之後；另一方面，更多在外省打工的年輕人，在收割稻米的農忙季節，從都市搭長途客運回到村寨幫忙。在白天他們是暫時回流的工作人力，在晚上他們是驟然增添的一群相伴與休閒夥伴。其二，日常遊方或姊妹伴聚會的空間或地方，也與日常生活及工作場域有其重疊或共享的特性。下雨或寒冷的天，在家屋內立有火塘的主屋空間（*ghaif zix jiat dok*）；清朗、溫暖的天，則在家屋前庭，或附近小角落（大樹下，或一段手工原木的半長凳）。這些在夜晚作為日常遊方聚會的休閒場所，白天則是做家務（烹飪，醃製，調理豬、牛、雞、鴨的食料，清掃，洗滌，紡織等等）的地方。這裡也是日常起居的處所。

　　昂希‧列斐伏爾指出，日常生活與休閒之間，存在著不簡單的對應關係：它們即是一體的，卻又同時是對立的（因此也是辯證的關係）。列斐伏爾認為不能以周末（Sunday）與平日（weekday）來區別工作與休閒。因為，儘管人在結束工作之後，其休閒的內容有其特定性，但他還是同一個人。再者平日就是要工作，和周末到了就是要休閒，這所展現的結構特性及其對人的約束與影響，也並無差別。列斐伏爾由此認為，工作及休閒應被看成一體。從全人的立場來看，所謂休閒及工作，就是在每個人可以使用的時間總量內，安排了工作與非關工作的生活（Highmore 2002：226-227；Lefebvre 1991〔1958〕：29-42）。

　　作為列斐伏爾討論的工作、休閒及日常生活的經驗世界，是西方工業社會、資本主義的布爾喬亞社會。生活在貴州東部村寨，以農耕為主的當代 Hmub 人，則是以手工作為生產活動的主要技術。Ghaif Wangk 的工作日誌裡，平表（父親的兄弟或母親的姊妹）親人，與姑舅交表姻親的親屬關係，相對突出在日常的工作與交換，而能與工廠生產線工人非關親屬與交換關係，展現對比的差異。[17]但 Ghaif Wangk 工作日誌的陳述，所表達日常工作的規律性，以及一再重複的特性，也不是完全迥異於西方工業社會生產活動的單調。一方面這種在日、月、季、年重複的日常工作氛圍，以其特有的單調形式或內涵，存在於村人的生活經驗。另一方面當地人也以儀式節慶或休閒的非日常，回應日常的冷清與單調。

　　再者姑娘 Ghaif Wangk 的工作日誌書寫雖然簡單，但重要的是，其間穿插著自己與家人分工的工作，以及自己以日常遊方為主的休閒。在前述 1999 年六月九日與六月十五日兩天的工作日誌（之一），Ghaif Wangk 在最後都寫下她和白天來幫忙農作的姊妹「沒有遊方」這樣的字句。[18]這種否定陳述所指涉的正是日常遊方的類型之一，聚姑娘（*niangt dat ghaif*）。有別於敲窗（*ket kanx xongt*）的遊方，面對面相伴的遊方聚會，是要有姑娘先聚一起，才會成立。六月九日與六月十五日的敘述，雖然沒有遊方，但在一天的農忙之後，仍有姊妹相聚為伴的休閒。而在 1999 年十月二十二日的工作日誌（之二），則是相當典型的唐家姊妹們在白天工作之後，相互邀約於夜晚聚在其中一個姑娘家。這是促成一場相聚遊方的起頭。[19]經由田野民族誌材料所呈現的黔東南高地村寨 Hmub

人日常生活，工作與休閒都是主要的，兩者不是簡單的時間或空間的對立、分離；反而在時間與空間，以及日常與非日常，都具有既是對比，卻又連續的傾向。以如是觀點來解釋村寨 Hmub 人社群日常生活裡的工作與休閒，與列斐伏爾所主張的相近：工作、休閒與日常三者互為一體，且相互間存在著辨證關係；並且它們最終都凝聚在日常生活的場域，共同構成個人與小群體之主體經驗的一部分。

四、煩悶

通過 Ghaif Wangk 為第一人稱觀察者與書寫者的工作日誌之敘述，我們發覺在社會行動的層次裡，工作與休閒的對比與連續，已將 Fangf Bil 村寨的日常生活予以布局，或者某種程度的管制。喬治‧萊考夫（George Lakoff）與馬克‧詹森（Mark Johnson）在《我們賴以生存的譬喻》（*Metaphors We Live By*, 1980）指出，日常生活中口語裡的語言隱喻，充斥在我們生活周遭。他們悄悄地參與，並涉入日常生活的布局、管制與改變。特定的身體感官經驗也影響村寨 Hmub 人日常生活的布局、管制與變遷。這在 Ghaif Wangk 的工作日誌隱晦未明。然而在我本身參與觀察與書寫的田野筆記，則突出了一種遊走其間，並共同形成日常生活整體之一部分的身體經驗與感受，也就是煩悶 *rat*。這是一種在個人層次所展現與體會之無聊、煩悶的情緒與身體感。要覺察此一感覺經驗，需在日復一日，不斷重複之休閒、工作所布局的日常裡，方能得見。因此本節將針對煩悶 *rat* 的身體經驗及其轉變歷程，亦即煩悶到解悶過程的身體經驗，以及此經驗與村寨具有制度性傾向之遊方談情的關連，進行描述與討論。最後本章將由此反思遊方的社會性與遊方人的主體性。希望通過此能給予村寨 Hmub 人的談情文化（courtship culture）另一種註腳。

並不是只有與遊方有關的小姑娘或小夥子，才擁有 *rat* 煩悶的經驗。*Rat* 這個語彙，在貴州東部的 Fangf Bil 高地村寨 Hmub 人的日常生活，是最常用來表述人在心情與生活的煩悶、單調、無所事事的情緒與身體經驗。1998-2000 年，我在寨子做田野期間，與村人在路上碰見，他們愛與我以 Hmub 人的平常話語寒暄。除了村人間相互的問候語句 *Mek denk hangf nif lel?*（妳從哪裡回來）；對我這個從臺灣來的女研究生在村寨裡住了好一陣還不返家，他們最常問候我的一句話是 *Mek niangt bib vangf, mek rat deb rat?*（妳一直住在我們寨子，妳悶不悶啊？）本章將討論煩悶 *rat*，不是無法分析或不被披露的內在感受，而是具體可交換的訊息與經驗。除了前述例子，以 *rat* 作為人與人見面招呼的口語交換；並且 *rat* 也表現在好幾種可以區辨的身體經驗。不同於海德格對於 boredom 的看法，是一種陷入極度荒涼的個人存在處境（有如放逐與被鄉愁所壟罩）；村寨 Hmub 人的煩悶 *rat*，不是走向個人孤獨的存在樣態，而是透過有感受之身，創造一個與他人建立情緒與社會關係相連的存在世界（relational being）。以下幾個例子將說明由聽覺、味覺、觸覺等體現五感的 *rat*，如何中介在村寨 Hmub 人的日常與非日常的儀式裡。

（一）從可言說到不便明說的身體經驗

首先是在聽的經驗上，煩悶 *rat* 通常是較為安靜的氛圍；它有別於饗宴儀式裡滿室話語的熱鬧。在結合生命儀禮的各種宴請姻親之饗宴，充滿歡鬧情緒與整屋的酒歌對唱，以及互為或遠或近姑舅表之姻親關係的主人家族與客人家族間，彼此不絕於耳的嗡嗡話語聲所創造的熱絡與喧囂吵雜的氛圍。它們往往由白日一直穿透到深夜的村寨。這與有點悶的日常在聽覺的經驗上，展現極大的對比。1999 年初下了幾場大雪，平日勤快上坡的唐家叔媽（Ghaif Wangk 的母親），和我們一起在家中烤火。那時我和 Ghaif Wangk 正趕著將寨子的親屬稱謂系統，整理出個頭緒。整個上午在一旁沒說幾句話的叔媽，對著埋頭猛寫字的我說：下雪天，坡上去不成，天天躲在家裡靜靜地烤火，她覺得 rat，悶得很。

　　不過，在身體感官的經驗上，節慶儀式所帶來之熱鬧及非日常性，與 rat 也非完全對立。如與味覺經驗相關的，我曾聽寨子的叔媽說過，2000 年到 2003 年吃鼓藏（nenk jet niuf）祭祖期間，[20] 在殺豬或砍牛後，天天過節，天天喝酒、吃肉，非常 rat。此處的 rat，是對連續數把個月處於節慶氛圍，整天陪來來往往的親戚客人說話、喝酒、吃肉等重覆行動的 rat。在這個例子裡，叔媽的 rat，其實涉入了好幾層不同的身體感官經驗：除了味覺，也有體膚的觸覺與聆聽的經驗。前者如對儀式宴客期間喝酒與吃肉感覺到 rat，因此想喝酸（米）湯煮青菜。後兩者如面對大量湧入的外來人群（來寨子走親的姻親，趁節慶下鄉討酒喝的地方官員、公安，來寨子看民族風情的觀光客，與民族學者），在小寨與家屋間四處往來走動；在家屋內陪客時，身子挨身子緊鄰而坐，或者面對面、雙手互搭彼此的雙肩敬酒；在主人與客人熱切對話的嗡嗡話語聲裡，貼近耳朵大聲說話等多重的身體經驗，都在儀式過節期間，一再重覆。這些令唐家叔媽覺得 rat，因此想回到日常裡的清閒：包括味覺上以酸米湯煮蔬菜，沾辣椒水吃白飯等清淡的飲食；以及在觸覺經驗上，人與人之間在身體的互動與空間，轉回日常裡適度的寬舒。整體而言，rat 是一種與日常有較直接關聯的情緒與多層次身體感官經驗。它也通常反映在細微的生活情境與個人切身的體驗裡。

Rat 也能通過一些身體經驗來進行轉換；用寨子裡的話來說，即是 *ghak rat*（解悶）。以下的民族誌例子涉及解悶的身體經驗，包含觸覺與聽覺，味覺與觸覺等的組合。節慶儀式之非常期間的走親送禮與熱鬧氛圍，必然是一個較大規模消解日常的 *rat*，而且還積極地創造節慶的熱鬧（*naud zaif*）。不過對於村寨 Hmub 人，環繞著農耕生活與生命儀禮的節慶儀式，是在辦正事。在語言上他們少以 *ghak rat*，來指稱如此「重要」的事。相對而言，最常見的 *ghak rat* 行動與觀念，仍是指發生在日常的生活語境與情境之內。在典型的 *ghak rat* 中，比如沒出外打工在村寨內閒著沒事的年輕人，會在村寨入口馬路邊的小店前，或寨子內有屋頂的風雨橋上寬寬的木椅，聚成群。有的打牌，有的圍觀。這種身體經驗是人與人相對親近的觸覺經驗。還有一種比較屬於年輕人常見的解悶把戲，則是集中在聽覺上的經驗。男男女女年輕人，白天去坡上看牛、摘菜、撿拾柴火的姑娘，或是夜晚在村寨內以遊方為名，晃蕩在小寨間的一小群或三三兩兩的男孩（*dat vangx*），也常以吹哨（*kot ghait*）來解悶。*Kot ghait* 創造出響亮昂揚的哨音，尤其容易在夜裡，穿透平日村寨寂靜的氛圍。以 *kot ghait* 解悶有不同吹的方式，所進行的場域也有不同。其中一種是在寨外山坡，面對層層疊疊的群山，孤單一人或兩三人為伴，完全放開嗓音，由胸腔而出，盡情高聲呼嘯。另外一種則是以手指輕置雙唇之間，用力吹出響亮筆直的哨音。年輕人不分男女在白天的坡上，或夜晚村寨內的遊方，都可以這麼吹哨。這種解悶所創造的聽覺經驗，不僅是個人內在煩悶、無聊情緒的抒發，也同時是對外的一種展演。有人在遠處 *kot ghait*，聽者往往不禁意被引出寂寥的心緒。你知有人處於 *rat*，但隨之 *kot ghait* 在聽覺上所創造的短暫熱鬧與喧囂，卻也同時感染聽者，撫平寂寥。

另一種與 *rat* 之轉換相關的用語，是 *deik rat zaf*。那是指，心情正煩悶，想把煩悶丟掉。在寒冷的冬天，無法到坡上工作，在家屋內的火塘，烤個紅薯或糯米粑粑（*jut*）來吃；或者老人家在出了太陽的午後，到小坡上曬日取暖（*dak nat*），聊聊天，也都可以 *deik rat zaf*，減輕或丟掉日常生活中的煩悶與無聊。這裡用來解悶的身體經驗，有味覺與觸覺。

　　在前述較大範圍的日常與非日常之村寨生活情境下的 *rat*，與身體感官經驗的描述後，接下來要討論的材料，是我在 1999 年夏天所寫的田野筆記。這幾頁田野筆記的內容，事件的發生與書寫的時間，銜接著本章一開始所描述 Ghaif Wangk 姑娘的煩悶，以及她遊方不成的挫折心情與身體經驗。有將近一年半的時間，我與 Ghaif Wangk 在日夜起居之日常與私密生活空間內，親近的相處與互動：諸如同住一家屋內，同擠姑娘房內一張 Ghaif Wangk 父親手工製的單人木床，同蓋一床棉被；或者我向她暫借原本收藏 Ghaif Wangk 母親手工縫製的 Hmub 人傳統衣服與珍貴家傳銀飾的檜木箱，來擺放田野研究期間使用的相機與攝影機；乃至她在 2000 年初偷偷走出家門（*at liud mongf*，即私奔婚）的寒冬夜半，身上穿的紅面藍裡的防風外套，脖子上輕繫的咖啡色小圓點圍巾，是我帶進村寨的衣物，並與她平日分享著穿。如前所述 Ghaif Wangk 也是 1998-2000 年間，我在 Fangf Bil 高坡村寨進行民族誌田野研究的重要報導人之一；她也協助部分田野資料的整理，或部分 Hmub 情歌、古歌、鬼師祭辭、深度訪談等逐字稿的聽寫與註記等等。我想如果不是那樣親近的交往，或許無法感受到這股窒人地，在人與人互動間竄動的煩悶與身體經驗的微細與轉變。換言之，有別於前述可以被言說的 *rat*，與遊方有關的煩悶似是不便明說的一種身體感經驗。

約一、二天後，Ghaif Wangk 原本要去堂妹 Ghaif Wangf 家的，但依然不是很順利。原因之一是從（1999 年）七月十三日開始，Vangf Dof 小寨的堂兄弟 Deik Lik 開始在晚上替成人上課。教男人、女人上課——也就是所謂的掃盲。堂妹 Ghaif Wangf 也有去上課。上完回來約近十點了。

七月十四日，那天晚飯時，我覺得 Ghaif Wangk 是帶著想玩的心，找我去 *vax songf dak dongf lik*（看大家讀書）。這幾天，村寨裡的堂姊妹或表姊妹們遇在一起，免不了都在談夜裡讀書（*xif mat dongf lik*）的事。如有誰去了，椅子怎麼坐，發了書啦，一人得一本等等。年輕姑娘與年輕小伙子最顯得興趣的是，哪個孩子的媽（如 Wangk Jeex *menl* 與 Laid Wangk *menl*），及哪些孩子的爸（如 Dingf Wangk *bad*）也去上課的事。其實在第一天夜校開始上課時。*Ghaif* 和我在河邊清洗洋芋，*Bad* Dangd 經過河的對岸，對我們說：「晚上學校那裡『at 晚會』（有晚會表演。）」後來才又更正說，說錯了，是有夜校班。Weif Xeit、Veb Xeit、Daid Nak 等與 Ghaif Wangk 同小寨的堂姊妹都去上課。當時我問 Ghaif Wangk 想去看看嗎？她很堅定的說：不去。（我心中無法不想是因為 Ghaif Wangk 有初中的學歷嗎？）這態度與她今晚興沖沖的想去學校 *vax naud zeif, vax vuk gad*（看熱鬧，看好玩）明顯不同。但我因為天候已晚，沒想去。Ghaif Wangk 知道我的決定，明顯擺下臉色。那晚，她後來對我說她去看電視。但因為大雨，十分鐘後便回家。我拜託她替我收了晾在樓上的衣服。又原本要去堂妹 Ghaif Wangf 家，也因雨作罷，沒去成。夜漸深，我上床寫田野筆記時，她也上床。但並沒有如前幾天夜裡，寫我請她記的工作日誌，便解衣睡了。但她似無睡意，我感覺兩人之間有股冷冷的空氣。Ghaif Wangk 躺在床上，用手輕輕地敲著木屋的板子。不久，她起身抓了小老鼠，並打死它。然後才又睡。

七月十五日下午我和 Ghaif Wangk 去坡上，採摘自家種的蔬菜。此時，Ghaif Wangk 看起來好多了。晚上，做家事時，她也帶勁了些。今天我們要早一點吃晚飯，因為，夜校八點就開始。今天我會與她一起去夜校。晚飯後，洗臉，刷牙，已經八點半。Ghaif Wangk 聽到家屋外面，堂姊妹們正一個喊一個要去上夜校。我們向她弟弟要了手電筒便去學校（這是村子裡唯一的小學）。我們到達時，教室已坐滿人。男孩少些，而其中有許多人是我已熟悉的。Ghaif Wangk 的表妹（FZD），表弟（FZS），堂妹 Ghaif Wangf。遠房姑姑 *Daid* Nak，*Daid* Nak Xik 的兄弟 *Bad* Juk，堂姊妹 Weif Xeit、Veb Xeit、Ghaif Cot 等。還有村寨六組的 Eb Ongx 和她的丈夫 Jix Ongx 也來。不過他們夫妻倆，並沒有坐在一起，而是相隔有一段距離。Ghaif Wangk 的遠房堂叔 *Bad* Zenb 也去，不過他似乎是去找女孩玩。我與 Ghaif Wangk 家附近的遠房姑姑 *Daid* Nak，*Daid* Ghaif 坐在一起。Ghaif Wangk 在我旁邊另一處與他人坐。還有兩位唐家這邊已當媽的婦女也端端正正坐在一起學習讀書、識字。Ghaif Wangk 見到兩位年輕媽媽的模樣，似乎覺得好玩極了，笑得不可抑止。還引我到教室前門去看。之後，Ghaif Wangk 要我一起進去坐，我本不想，但她覺得站外面不好，於是我只好進去了。堂兄 *Deik* Lik 請我上台教苗文。台下的姑娘小伙子學得還很認真。整個上課氣氛十分的輕鬆，也很熱鬧。

上到十點下課，一下子所有學生都走了。她／他們多半還未吃晚飯。我與 Ghaif 回到家，再洗了手腳。她的父親正在看一份《科技通訊》，內容包含一些廣告（有賣農作、賣藥的，賣物品的）。

Ghaif Wangk 姑娘洗淨身體之後，對我說，我去堂妹 Ghaif Wangf 家，看看她睡了沒？如果睡了，我一分鐘就回來。如果沒睡，我今天晚上就留在她那裡。然後，她輕快的消失在夜色中。半個鐘頭過去，我想她順利的在堂妹 Ghaif Wangf 家聚會遊方了。

昨晚十點半就睡。早上，我從兩個夢中醒來，是被蚊子咬醒。七點左右，Ghaif Wangk 回家了。昨天她出門時，父母都睡了，她也不用說聲，就出去了。我今早躺在床上想像：清早，許多姑娘從某一個姑娘家走出來，回家。老人家一見就知，是昨晚遊方的姑娘。我想以前村子裡的姑娘、小伙子還沒出外打工的年代，平日遊方也許夜夜進行地更熱鬧。那麼早晨，是否有更多的姑娘從昨日遊方的姑娘家走出來。

一早，Ghaif Wangk 微笑地推開門，說：*At, fik sot.*（姊，起早。）這種笑容，有些甜蜜、滿足，總是她夜晚遊方之後，回來的表情與心情。波波折折的，Ghaif Wangk 最後去成一次，至少這十幾天以來。我想她的煩悶心情 *rat*，在這樣的遊方相伴的聚會中，已經消解一些了。

（1999 年七月十三日至十五日筆者田野筆記）

這幾段 1999 年夏日的田野筆記，是我在村寨裡，每日書寫之田野筆記的一小部分。那時我已在 Fangf Bil 村寨進行田野工作第九個月。

從 1999 年七月十二日起，我在手寫的筆記頁眉，以英文草體字隨意標上 *The Story of Rat*。在三十二開大小的筆記本裡，以細小的鋼筆字體，寫了將近三十頁關於 *rat* 的內容（本文引述的田野筆記即是其中主要的部分）。我已不太確定是何時開始注意到 *rat*。但進田野以前，並沒有從任何 Hmong 或 Hmub 的文獻，讀過關於這種經驗的描述與討論。1999 年夏天，我在村寨裡以相當篇幅的田野筆記來寫 *rat*。顯然看起來如此無足輕重的它，已成為我在村寨裡進行遊方與婚姻民族誌研究過程中，無意間關注到的重點。如前述引用的筆記片段，*rat* 是書寫的焦點。在研究方法上，書寫的基礎，不是因為訪問得來的材料，而是由事件的參與觀察，以及人與人較親近的日常相處與互動，所獲得對 *rat* 的覺察與探索。

　　前述幾則民族誌筆記，記錄的是村寨夏日夜晚的日常活動。從社會的層面上，我們看到在大山裡村寨成人夜晚的日常，融入通過教育與傳媒介入的文字性活動：年輕男女利用村寨唯一的小學教室上夜校，與中年男性閱讀報紙。這兩個行動展現的，都不只一個層次的社會性。一方面它們是村寨正在經驗現代性的訊息，另一方面也是成人夜晚的休閒。尤其，年輕男女夜晚的習字，雖有嚴肅的教育意義，但在活動過程中所展現的熱鬧氛圍，人群裡的正經與嘻鬧玩笑的交錯，以及口語和身體語言的互動，實際上也就是遊方。相對的，這幾則田野筆記的記錄，也展現特定的個人身體經驗與感受。Ghaif Wangk 姑娘 *rat* 煩悶的潮起潮落，與抒解煩悶的過程，完全是扣連在筆記所敘述的 Ghaif Wangk 姑娘連續幾天的日常生活場域：從無味、無趣的日常夜晚，到夜校班的笑鬧，及夜晚遊方的躍躍欲試與歡愉。

五、*Rat* 觀點下的遊方

　　為解釋與遊方有關的煩悶 *rat*，必須回到在 Fangf Bil 村寨研究遊方的過程與體驗。我自 1998 年起，以村落民族誌的田野研究探索 Hmub 人的遊方，曾經歷過想從此項議題退卻的強烈念頭。那種在田野工作過程中的挫折，也許有點靠近人類學研究方法裡提到的文化震撼（cultural shock）。但又非全然是異文化的撞擊，反而是一種對自己的研究與對自身的否定與晦暗感。事後回想此心路歷程，部分原因可能和遊方密切勾聯著個人私密的情緒與身體經驗有關。遊方的這種特性，使我在研究的過程中，經常在客觀現象、資料，與主觀感受、經驗間掙扎。當初在面對此一困境，最後是憑藉著回到民族誌工作裡原初的做法，也就是每天規律地提筆將對環繞著 Ghaif Wangk 的日常細節（包括她和家人互動的話語，細微的身體語言或身體經驗等等）之所見、所聞、感受，逐字、逐句地刻寫在一本又一本的田野筆記裡。無論那被描述與記錄的現象，是如何的平常，乃至無足輕重。這個經由書寫記錄過程所保留下或產出的民族誌資料，和本章探討遊方的身體經驗有著不可分的關聯性。

　　接著要問的是煩悶 *rat* 究竟能否算是一種遊方（內）不可言說的身體感經驗？這個問題應該分為三部分來說明：其一是 *rat* 與遊方關聯，其二是 *rat* 在遊方的脈絡下是怎樣的身體經驗，最後是 *rat* 的獨特性──特別是經由它，如何呈現我們對於村寨 Hmub 人遊方特性的解釋，而得以有別於過去以儀式或行為為主的理解，並因而能與過去的談情（courtship）研究的文獻展開對話。

　　煩悶 *rat* 與遊方之間，不是制度或因果的關聯。我對此二者的觀察與解釋，和田野過程有關。如果我採取的是「正式的」去參與觀察一場又一場（「成功進行」）的遊方，如此對遊方的探索，應該不會走到 *rat*，也不必然會關注到遊方的前與後，遊方不成的心情與身體經驗。如此所能描述與理解的遊方，或許就止於戲鬧，或浪漫的情與愛（erotic love and feelings）？然而如本章前面三節所引述之 Ghaif Wangk 的工作日誌（之一與之二），以及我的田野筆記，這兩種材料所書寫的，都是環繞著一個姑娘及其家人、姻親與親屬的日常生活。對未當家的姑娘而言，遊方的日常、遊方不成的日常，不同內涵之遊方的日常，既是工作與休閒不斷環繞之生活的必要部分，也是她們在日常裡作為人之所在的焦點。

　　研究過程中所形成的機緣，也影響我對煩悶 *rat* 與遊方的認識與解釋。與 Ghaif Wangk 在村寨日常生活的朝夕相處，有時無法分割是田野的研究工作，還是日復一日在村寨渡過日常生活。但也因此，我才能在一個不被中斷的日常時限裡，看到一種進行中的，走動的，有歡樂與戲鬧，也有沮喪與無望的遊方經驗，與不便被言明的身體經驗與感受。是在這樣的過程中，我才開始記錄 *rat*，並通過田野筆記的書寫，表達出 Ghaif Wangk 不說出的煩悶 *rat* 與身體感。重要的是，這些未被言明的身體經驗和遊方是在村寨日常生活裡，蘊蓄其不可分離的關聯。其二，遊方裡的煩悶 *rat* 是怎樣的身體經驗或身體感？我曾在 2002 年，寫出有如心理學教科書上的語彙：「遊方前的壓抑情緒」來詮釋 *rat*。不過，如本章前節引述的田野筆記（寫於 1999 年七月十二日與十四日）所傳達姑娘 Ghaif Wangk 的煩悶 *rat*，則更多是沉重、窒人的感官與身體經驗（如：她與我一起整理筆記或研究資料時，步履便愈顯沉重，常常是拖著腳步在走路。……用有些陌生的眼神回應我的注視。也常會，呆呆地望著窗外，或立在門口看外面）。遊方人的身體經驗與感受，不只有遊方前或遊方不成的煩悶 *rat*，也有就在遊方裡的身體經驗。例如，調情戲謔時遊方男女彼此「你騙我、我騙你」的 *dlait*（騙）；遊方夥伴群聚之熱鬧經驗與氣圍的 *naud zaif*（熱鬧）；相伴或聚成群之戲鬧、有趣的 *vuk ghad*（好玩）。但也有那種期待遊方的身體經驗與感受。例如，內心很想去遊方，但卻無伴、孤獨的 *nik longf night*（就一人獨坐在那）；很期待或很歡欣的渴望，在遊方時，有那樣一個人能作我伴的 *del wal*（想要有伴，或來與我為伴）。如果這些身體經驗與感受，和遊方的關聯能被歸類的話，煩悶 *rat* 應是歸屬於前述的後兩者。它們雖不直接在遊方內，但卻是一種特定的，也活生生就在那的身體經驗。一方面具體表達出遊方與地方社會裡特定個人的關聯，另一方面如此流動的，中介在個人與社會的這些個身體經驗，其實是一起形成遊方的特定氣圍與場域。再者，在遊方與非遊方的村寨日常生活裡，和煩悶 *rat* 經常彼此勾連，還有一種也涉入身體經驗與感受的 *liat*。我舉一個平常生活裡的例子。前節提到了 Hmub 村寨的唐家叔媽在吃鼓藏儀式期間，因為天天喝酒與吃肉感到 *rat*，因此想喝清淡的酸米湯煮青菜。

這既是一種趨向解悶的過程，也是一種 *liat* 的身體經驗，是在口感與味覺上的身體經驗。常聽到的 Hmub 話的語境是 *Liat het eb jed*（想喝酸湯的很）。亦即，煩悶 *rat* 如果是一種懶散、疲乏的身體經驗，*liat* 所展現之渴求的身體感或經驗，則帶有逃離或消解 *rat* 身體感的積極與潛力。在遊方裡，煩悶 *rat* 與 *liat* 也是這樣的關係，並且二者在幾個不同層次的內涵，都和特定的身體經驗有關。以 Ghaif Wangk 姑娘為例，未當家 [21] 女孩的 *rat* 是一種無力、沉重，也是蠢動、不安的身體經驗與心緒。而 *liat* 也表達好幾層不同的心中欲求，如渴望一場遊方，或對哪個人的想念與思戀。*Rat* 與 *liat* 這兩個身體經驗，雖然都不是直接展現在遊方內，但卻在表達人與遊方之間無可分割的切身體驗。

總之，煩悶 *rat* 除了是和遊方有所關連，它也是我所能理解的 Fangf Bil 高地村寨 Hmub 人身體經驗中，最具體中介在以工作與生活爲主，日復一日之尋常與單調裡的。而且在當地人的觀點裡，無論在遊方或遊方之外的日常，煩悶 *rat* 的展現、舞動與消解，都和村寨社會情境內之物質基礎下的身體經驗有關。例如，女孩在遊方場域裡的談話、相聚；老人家在晴朗寒冬下曬日取暖；孩童在下雪天的遊戲等等爲例的 *ghak rat*（解悶），都在語言與非語言的行動裡，展現幾個不同層次的日常與身體經驗。換言之，這些例子所表達的村寨 Hmub 人遊方之內，或遊方之外的經驗，都不僅單純指向心理的或情緒的經驗。他們對煩悶的感知與消解，都是一種通過身體經驗具體再現的日常性與社會性。

（一）從 *rat* 到 courtship 文獻

最後經由 *rat* 這種特定的與實際的個人身體經驗與感受的探討，使得我們對於村寨 Hmub 人遊方的解讀，有可能與人類學的談情交往（courtship）研究展開對話。過去的人類學書寫，有將談情交往的描述與討論，流瀉出功能、特定或積極正向的傾向。相對於婚姻的研究，以談情交往爲專題的研究較少，我認爲這是因爲傳統上多數社會視談情交往和婚姻爲功能的關係。典型的例子是人類學家布朗尼斯勞·馬林諾夫斯基（Bronislaw Malinowski 1982〔1932〕）注意到，在美拉尼西亞西北部土著族群的生活裡，性必須放在習俗制度的背景裡來探討。愛、性欲、巫術與神話，都與該社會的談情交往有關。雖然馬林諾夫斯基已經是二十世紀早期的人類學家當中，對談情交往現象，提出較多的民族誌細節與關注。不過對他來說，談情交往僅是爲結婚而行的準備階段，尚不具有獨立存在的層面。再者以早期 Hmong 人之談情交往文獻爲例，弗朗索瓦・沙維納（Francoise Savina 1924）、雨果・阿道夫・貝納齊克（Hugo Adolpph Bernatzik 1970〔1947〕）、李穆安（Jacques Lemoine 1972）、蓋瑞・李宜（Garry Yia Lee〔Txawj Yias Lis〕1981）等學者在東南亞的研究，或者葛維漢（David Crockett Graham 1923）、瑪格麗特・波西亞・米基（Margaret Portia Mickey 1947）、鮑克蘭（Inez de Beauclair 1960、1970）在西南中國的研究，同樣都認為談情交往在 Hmong 人社會是婚姻前的儀式過程（參考 Donnelly 1994：115）。而南希・唐納利（Nancy Donnelly 1994：120-124）研究美國境內 Hmong 移民（主要為二次大戰後來自寮國〔老撾〕的難民），則已論及情緒面向的談情交往。她指出傳統以來婚姻是 Hmong 人成年的關鍵，婚前固定的調情是可以公開的，且同時又是一個秘密的遊戲；因而有著令人愉悅的共謀、目擊、興奮的氣氛。也就是說，談情交往即是一個為了情感與愉悅所存在的情緒場域，並且也是個允許婚前性關係的社會場域，以及作為成年禮的一部分。對現居美國的 Hmong 人，在傳統的談情交往裡，雖包含婚前的性，卻並不一定以婚姻交換為目的。它具有個人社會網絡，與令人愉悅的心理和情感經驗的意涵。

　　與早期的民族誌研究對照，唐納利（1994）已能更細節地描述 Hmong 人的談情交往。本章從身體經驗來瞭解並反思黔東南高地村寨 Hmub 人的遊方，也是通過微觀的細節描述與解釋談情交往的另一種特性。這與從文學或文本研究的角度來解釋談情交往的特性，似乎有異曲同工之妙。換言之，相對於多數人類學民族誌的書寫，認為談情交往是婚姻的準備階段；以敘述或表演為主的文學作品研究，則認為談情交往與婚姻間，可能為非直線進行的關係。艾倫・羅絲曼（Ellen Rothman 1984）分析十九世紀末到二十世紀，美國社會戀愛男女的書信及日記，指出談情交往並非線性進程的通向婚姻，而是交織著期待、經驗、習俗的混合物。亦即談情交往的本質，抗拒著確切的解釋。再者通過伊莉莎白時期的英國文學，凱薩琳‧貝茲（Catherine Bates 1992）也闡述談情交往是一種纖弱、憂慮、危險的程序。她認爲依賴著真誠表象的有效性與細心地算計，談情交往需要持續不斷的慎重、機智與敏銳。如同一個高度系統化的體系，談情交往是個真誠與欺騙、戲弄，糾結並置的模式。這兩個文學研究都指出談情交往與婚姻之間具有非線性與非功能的矛盾與曖昧。而本章所展現的村寨民族誌材料，一方面與談情交往之社會本質的探討有關；一方面也探討通過描述個人的煩悶與身體經驗，是在將談情交往與日常，以及個人與社會所隱藏的關聯具體化並釋出。正如前面小節在探討遊方的身體經驗時所指出的，煩悶 *rat* 的身體經驗與感受，雖不直接在遊方內，但卻是一種特定的，也實際的身體經驗。一方面它具體表達遊方與地方社會裡特定個人的關聯，另一方面如此流動的，中介在個人與社會的身體經驗，其實也是形成遊方之特定氛圍與場域的共構者。總之在解讀遊方本質的過程裡，煩悶 *rat* 經驗的呈現，是一個頗爲突出的關鍵。因爲它具體的中介，一方面標示著遊方不僅是一個爲婚姻而儲備的社會機制，同時也與工作、休閒、日常生活，以及個人主體性，具體而細微的關聯著。

六、結語

對於黔東南高地 Fangf Bil 村寨的 Hmub 人，煩悶 *rat* 並不僅與日常的生活或工作有關，它也指出村寨社會所經驗的國家、市場，與全球化的實際。雖然本章並未深入此一特定身體經驗 *rat* 與村寨歷史的關聯，但就田野筆記所載之細節（見第四節 1999 年七月十三日至十五日之筆記），實際上已涉入文字性、教育、傳媒、移動等內涵的社會變遷與全球化的現象。識字與教育或電視與報紙所儲備的文字能力與對外在世界訊息的掌握，影響村寨 Hmub 人的移動（打工、出外求學、旅行），並也直接與間接影響到他們的工作、休閒與日常的內涵與形式。這些不僅涉及村寨的變遷，以及對於現代性的感受與轉化，並也和煩悶 rat 的展現與消解之形式、內容有關。換言之，煩悶 rat 並不是文化建構觀點下，如石像般穩定的文化相對性的再現。它具體的標示出當地人主體的感受，並且也是可以客體化，可以有意識消解與轉變的身體經驗。此身體經驗的探索，不僅在於回應文化對個人經驗的影響，相對的高地村寨 Hmub 人的煩悶 rat 與解悶 ghak rat 所突顯的流動與中介特性，也可能標記出 1949 年之前與之後，中國所經歷過巨大的社會主義變革；乃至 1980 年後期起，隨經濟自由化腳程不斷增速之中國崛起的當代語境裡，貴州東部高地村寨 Hmub 人的遊方與個人，以及村寨社會之間交錯糾結的關係與變遷。

其次，黔東南高地村寨 Hmub 人日常生活裡煩悶的情緒與身體經驗，也是對文化理論新的探討與切入點。如果文化理論在前一典範時期，是以脫離具體性的心智與象徵間的交相影響，作為討論的基礎，那麼本章針對村寨 Hmub 人的煩悶 rat 與身體經驗的研究取向，則是以有經驗能力的身體，所編織的網絡，來面對個人安身立命的群體與世界。換言之，村寨 Hmub 人的煩悶 rat，不是不可逆的悲觀下沉，而是在時間與空間的安置下，規律的消解與重生。因而對黔東南村寨的 Hmub 人，遊方或歲時祭儀都不僅是為成就姻親理想的社會性建構，並也在成就人之何以為人。後者所指的是勇敢的面對情緒，以及有經驗能力之身的存在。以此我們將可望從海德格所述 boredom 的絕望，或個人在現代社會不可逆的孤寂與疏離中，找到出口。第三，村寨 Hmub 人的煩悶 *rat*，並非負面的情緒與感受樣態。它所展現的日常性有其具體的內容。通過可言說與不便言明的身體感等經驗的實作，煩悶 *rat* 對於村寨 Hmub 人之存在，個人與社群的關係、認同與維繫，能被揭露與確認。我們因而能經由這樣一個日常與身體經驗的民族誌個案研究，積極思考文化為何。

Part III
書寫的主體性與社會理想

Chapter 6　Hmub 人古歌的記音與翻譯：
　　　　　歌師 Sangt Jingb 的手稿、知識與空間

一、前言

　　本章要探討的是，一部由我的田野報導人——一位住在貴州東部台江地區（屬黔東方言北部土語〔王輔世 1985：103〕）的苗族歌師（*ghet xiangf diut hxak/hxad*）——以苗文所記音與翻譯的古歌手稿《跋山涉水》（*Nangx Eb Jit Bil*）。[1]根據寶拉・魯貝爾（Paula Rubel）與亞伯拉罕・羅斯曼（Abraham Rosman）在《翻譯文化：關於翻譯和人類學的觀點》（*Translating Cultures: Perspectives on Translation and Anthropology*, 2003）一書指出，人類學涉及不同文化的關連性，翻譯應該扮演重要角色，但一直以來卻被忽視，沒有建立起有系統的方法論。田野研究法在十九世紀至二十世紀初的人類學雖已日趨成熟，但民族誌資料蒐集過程中的翻譯，則未被重視。德裔美國人類學家法蘭茲・鮑亞士（Franz Boas）強調語言總在文化裡。他學地方語音，並以地方語音做記錄來蒐集北美印第安文化各個面向的資料。他也用英文標記地方語音，並注意到研究對象的語言結構和拉丁文或英文的不同，因此特別重視地方或土著語言之語法範疇的特殊性。不過當時的鮑亞士並沒特別討論翻譯的問題。與鮑亞士同屬早期人類學家的布朗尼斯勞・馬林諾夫斯基，被稱為人類學田野研究傳統的建立者。當時他已強調將田野觀察、土著的敘述、詮釋，與觀察者的觀點分開註記。並且強調地方或土著語音的學習，是人類學長期田野的一部分。但同樣地，當時的馬林諾夫斯基也未提及翻譯的問題。換言之，即使人類學家早已認知學習地方或土著語言與瞭解文化的意義有關，但延續到戰後英國和美國的人類學家轉向從象徵與詮釋來理解文化，翻譯與文化理論的關聯，還是未被論及（Rubel and Rosman 2003）。

　　直到 1980 年代詹姆斯·克里弗德（James Clifford）重新檢視田野研究與民族誌資料的生產過程，才提到翻譯對於文化理解的影響。他在 1997 年出版了《路徑：二十世紀晚期的旅行與翻譯》（*Routes: Travel and Translation in the Late Twentieth Century*）一書，書中以 the translator is a traitor 為喻，指出翻譯可能會使真象遭到扭曲或丟失原有價值。正如克里弗德所指出：此前已出版的民族誌都屬於整理過的材料，都有著建構的屬性。鮑亞士勤於保留與重視田野工作中所產出的語言材料，並以原初的面貌，出版他在北美印地安進行民族誌田野工作時的助手喬治·杭特（George Hunt）協助他收集的語言素材。有些人類學家的田野筆記，以自我反思，探討自我如何瞭解他人。也有部分人類學家檢視資料重複出現的行為與觀念模式，並以此呈現他們對當地文化理解的梗概。不管是諸如此類的民族誌書寫，抑或是人類學的分析與理解，翻譯都會以不同的路徑，滲入人類學對文化的探索（Rubel and Rosman 2003）。

　　延續此，本章將討論記音、翻譯與民族誌文化理解的關聯。記音與翻譯這兩個語言行動，從語意上來看是可以區別的：翻譯（translation）是兩種語言之間的轉換，記音（transcription）則是指將聽到的語音或聲音寫下來。[2] 我將以一個民族誌案例，討論與此二者所涉入之語言現象與意義之間的轉換，無法脫離建構與多義的本質。這是一個有關黔東南 Hmub 人歌師 Sangt Jingb 的生命史與古歌手稿之間的故事。我在 1999

年與 2000 年交接之際，博士論文民族誌田野的最後階段，因緣際會和一位台江 Hmub 人歌師來往，並也經由向他學習古歌，而涉入他所記音與翻譯之手稿與圖稿的整理、分析與解釋。2007 年我三度返回貴州田野，再訪 Sangt Jingb 以及近十位黔東南 Hmub 人歌師的古歌與生命史。本章主要經由歌師的生命史等民族誌田野資料，以及古歌手稿《跋山涉水》（Nangx Eb Jit Bil），考掘苗文記音書寫者與漢字譯者同為一人，在苗語記音文本與漢字翻譯文本之形成過程中，所出現之斷裂或縫隙；以及其中所流瀉、再現的知識，與跨越時間界線的空間意象。

二、黔東南 Hmub 人歌師 Sangt Jingb

位於貴州東南並與桂北相鄰的黔東南，是西南中國境內苗族最大集聚地。相對於其他地區苗族居處類型較為分散，此地大範圍的苗族群聚是一顯著特點。研究貴州苗族的人類學家張兆和（Cheung Siu-woo 1995：217-247）指出西方宗教進入苗族地區傳教，西部 Hmong 人比東部 Hmub 人有更高比例的轉宗現象。他認為此與黔東南苗族的群聚，和此地區的自然環境、特殊的歷史背景有關。黔東南的地理水文環境，自成一獨立格局。苗嶺東段的雷公山脈由西南向東北緩降，北邊清水江水系通往長江，南邊都柳江水系通往珠江（貴州省地圖集編輯辦公室 1985）。前貴州大學人口學者呂左教授，在一項清水江幹流沿岸人口經濟環境研究指出，此地區氣候溫和濕潤、土地肥沃、森林覆蓋率較高，資源豐富有如「金飯碗」（呂左 1998：1024）。

西南邊疆內地化的歷史過程中，雖然黔東南地區東、北、西南小部分邊緣地帶，自元代起已與所謂的漢人、侗人等外族有零星接觸，但此區域心腹地帶（今雷山、台江、劍河三縣）直到十八世紀清雍正年間（1726-1731）經略西南，才大規模展開。根據《世宗憲皇帝硃批諭旨》（卷一百二十五之五），雍正年間的雲貴總督鄂爾泰，曾在寫給雍正皇帝的奏摺上，描述黔東南的古州八萬（今榕江）、鎮遠、黎平等地的苗族村寨，及其田土、江河。以下引述的片段，可見其所描述之黔東南地區苗族村寨聚集，以及交通、貿易之樞紐地位與富饒的物產（1983〔清雍正十年敕編〕：420 之 409 頁至 410 頁）。[3]

黔粵之交有八萬古州（今貴州省榕江）。裏外一帶生苗地方千有餘里。雖居邊界之外實介兩省之中。黔之黎平。都云。鎮遠。永從諸郡縣。粵之柳州。懷遠。羅城。荔波諸郡縣。四面環繞。而以此種生苗伏處其內⋯⋯

八萬裏古州。即元時所置古州八萬洞軍民長官司地也。在黎平之西南隅。自府城一百三十餘里抵古州土司所轄寨麻地方。又自寨麻五十里。過八匡沖。即入八萬裏古州之地。其間形勢寬敞。田土膏腴。南自車寨。北抵樂鄉。約長三十餘里。而橫闊之處。或十餘里。或六七里。總計周圍約有八十餘里。除零星各寨不計外。其大寨則有車寨。藏弩寨。頭月寨。口寨樂。鄉寨等處。每寨或千餘戶或數百戶。其小寨則有寨王。麥寨。高達。定達。寨觀。寨晚等處。每寨亦有百餘戶或數十戶。總計約有四五千戶。男婦大小約有二萬餘丁。地勢平衍。戶口稠密。風俗頗稱淳樸⋯⋯

界內有古州江。其高敞處為諸葛營。相傳諸葛亮曾駐兵於此。四望寬平。後倚大山。周圍土垣尚存基址。而古州江臨其前。又有都江縈其右。溶江遶其左。二水迴抱滙合。南流直達廣西懷遠縣界。江內現有小船。裝載鹽貨就近貿易……

　　鄂爾泰經略黔東南新疆後，國家影響力通過派駐屯軍，封賜有戰功將領為地方上的小土官，以及施行保甲等行動進入。位於黔東南最內地的台江、劍河兩地的土官，全都是雍正年間征苗有功的將領。他們多來自湖南西部、黔東南北部等苗、漢長期接觸的地區（羅繞典 1987〔清〕：336-375）。相較於貴州其他區域，國家通過屯軍、土官力量進入黔東南腹地的時間晚，土官管理地方的年代資歷也相對淺。

　　不同於西部支系苗族（近代以來遷移的範圍最為廣遠。中國境外的苗族，主要是這一支系），也不同於北部支系（與彝族的關係最為密切。此支系的早期記錄，主要出現在彝文文獻中），黔東南地區的苗族沒有長期被異族土司治理的歷史經驗。也由於清水江流域自然環境的優越，黔東南苗族較西部支系的苗族有較久的建寨歷史，並在清水江流域內，出現一大範圍內密集的聚落分布（楊庭碩 1998）。這三個苗族支系的差異性也還表現在方言上。以語言學的語音比較研究為例，湘西苗族說的湘西方言，有帶鼻冠音的塞音與塞擦音（mp，nts），但僅出現在單數音節；西部支系說的川黔滇方言，也有帶鼻冠音的塞音與塞擦音，且可以出現在各個調的音節；而黔東南說的黔東方言，則沒有出現鼻冠音的塞音與塞擦音（王輔世 1985：106-107）。黔東方言還可以再區分為北部土語、東部土語、南部土語（ibid.：103-104），本章所討論的這部古歌手稿，主要出自說黔東方言北部土語的台江、凱里地區。

歷史、自然環境造就黔東南地區苗族大量群聚，和此地區婚姻表述的多樣，以及神話與服飾的複雜表現，或許有其關聯。過竹（1988）的苗族神話比較研究指出黔東南神話圈有 422 個神，神系多且複雜。楊鵑國（1997）的苗族服飾比較研究，也提出黔東南型服飾表現在上衣、裙擺、圍腰、綁腿、髮髻的變化，有 30 種之多。苗族文化比較研究，往往以語言學家所分類的苗族支系爲分析單位，將黔東苗先驗地當作 Hmub 文化的原型之一。此雖可能有知識論與歷史疑點，但他們的結果，卻也反映此區域之特殊性。黔東南族群與物質文化的複雜性，堪稱此區域的重要議題。

　　在苗族集聚的黔東南地區，苗族古歌的傳唱，有著相當豐富的歷史。古歌在苗族社會主要是於盛大的祭祖儀式，以及婚禮、喪禮、立新房、新生兒命名等主要的生命儀禮，進行演唱。在儀式的場合需要演唱大部頭古歌時，對唱的姻親（主人群與客人群）兩方，都會分別請來擅長古歌的儀式專家，也就是歌師（*ghet xiangf diut hxak/hxad*），擔任主要的對歌者。古歌的演唱具有對唱競賽的意味，當兩邊實力相當，越是對得起來，姻親雙方的親友越是聽得起勁與專注。一場儀式場合裡的古歌對下來，所演唱的古歌可能多達上千行，實際的對唱則可長達數個日夜。

　　苗族古歌在傳統上都是口頭演唱，古歌的傳承以口耳相傳爲主。古歌的傳承與實際對唱的人群及社群範圍，如同服飾、銀飾、髮式的類型，和通婚圈有緊密的關聯。傳統上以實行父方交表聯姻爲理想的 Hmub 人村寨社群，其通婚圈的地域範圍並不寬廣。學習古歌可以是在家族內的場域來進行，但姑姪、舅甥等主要姻親之間的傳授，也是重要管道。後者呼應著古歌的傳唱、展演與婚姻結盟的緊密關聯。而聯姻與親屬關係，正是黔東南苗族社會維繫其社群理想與實際之所在。雖然至今，以口耳相傳來學習古歌還是主要的方式，不過清代到民國年間，湖南西部與黔東南苗族地區一些上過私塾、義學的男性，就已經會用漢字苗讀的拼音，將苗歌記音在紙張上來學習。例如曾擔任過芮逸夫先生與凌純聲先生在湘西進行苗族研究調查的石啓貴等人，於 1920–1940 期間所蒐集、記錄的苗族民間口傳的儀式念詞、唱詞等文書手稿，[4] 以及我在 1990 年代末於黔東南的民族誌田野，所蒐集到讀書人寫的苗族古歌或情歌，都出現以漢字來記錄苗語語音的現象。

　　就整個貴州地區，目前被記錄並出版較多的苗歌，大多傳唱在黔東南的清水江流域與雷公山區域。1985-1986 年之間，中國民間文藝研究會貴州分會，重新翻印及編印七十二集的《民間文學資料》，當中有二十一集記錄黔東南地區的苗歌。這二十一集資料多數曾出版於 1950 年到 1962 年文化大革命以前。它們包括有苗族古歌、敘事詩（情歌、婚姻、勞動、生命儀禮），以及與近代苗族革命、戰亂有關的歌謠。這些已寫成定本的黔東南苗歌題材廣泛、體裁多樣，涉及到的時空場域極為遼闊。而就本章所關注的苗族古歌而言，在這批《民間文學資料》裡，以較為完整的一部古歌來呈現，並有苗文與中文對照，僅有第六十二集《仰阿莎》（Niangt Eb Sail）（未刊作者名 1984），與第七十二集《苗族古歌：運金運銀》（Qab Nix Qab Jenb）（唐春芳 1985）。前者唱的是一位名叫「清水」（Eb Sail）的美麗姑娘，她的美貌引起太陽的忌妒；後者唱的是運金運銀來致富。這兩部古歌在苗族古歌當中，是最受歡迎的兩部，因為人長得美與多財富，都是苗族的理想。這兩部古歌最常在婚禮中演唱，翻譯與編輯的版本也較多。本章後面將提及的歌師 Sangt Jingb，就是從這兩部古歌開始學。這和此兩部古歌較常被演唱應有其關聯。除了

《仰阿莎》（*Niangt Eb Sail*）與《運金運銀》（*Qab Nix Qab Jenb*），苗族古歌所包括的主題還有：開天闢地、耕地育楓、跋山涉水、四季歌、起房歌、酒曲歌、嫁女歌、誆嬰歌、打茉歌、造紙歌、喪亡歌（王安江2008）。內容包含寰宇天地的創生、祖先的開墾與遷徙，有關人的生產與再生產的生命儀禮及其技術。

從民國時期以來，至今所記錄與出版的黔東南苗族古歌、古詞，多數已立有標題。[5] 我在民族誌田野調查裡，偶也聽到歌師或一般人會以主題來指涉特定的古歌。目前雖然還沒有資料說明古歌的分類與命名從何來，或是否為蒐集古歌的編者所加，但至少本文的研究對象 Sangt Jingb 為他所記音與翻譯的古歌，進行分類或下標題，並非特例，而是地方傳唱與記錄古歌文化的一部分。最後，本章通過苗族歌師的生命史，及其所記音與翻譯的手稿作為撰述與討論的基礎，將闡述在黔東南這個區域裡的民間口傳文學的傳承及其差異的形成與維繫，除了與語言、服飾、婚姻圈等苗族支系的社會文化或歷史等結構因素有關，也與個人的行動與意識有著密切關聯。如文前所述苗族內部有明顯的支系差異，即便是在黔東南能夠用苗語直接溝通的範圍內，各地的苗族服裝和生活習慣，也存在著一定的差異。下一節在介紹 Sangt Jingb 的個人經歷時，將會明確指出，他是向自己的幾位姑媽學古歌。在這樣的基礎上，我們可以推測，苗族古歌的傳承，基本上是以通婚圈為傳承的單位。換言之，燕寶、今旦、唐春芳等前輩業已整理過的苗族古歌，其間存在差異的部分原因，也就可以順利地得到澄清。至於出現差異的另一層原因，則顯然與個人，如 Sangt Jingb 的有意識建構直接關聯。

（一）與歌師相遇：我學古歌

接著在介紹 Sangt Jingb 的生命史，與他以口耳相傳學習古歌，及長達數十載的古歌書寫之前，我想先將這一趟原不在博士論文研究規畫內的田野經歷寫出來。我從作爲第一人稱研究者的書寫角度，來追憶這趟田野歷程，在本文的書寫與討論有其必要性。因爲本章的書寫目的，所涉及的並不僅是語言或文本內的分析與解釋，還關聯著歌師與其古歌作品之間的書寫與創造，以及一個人類學學徒與田野報導人之間互爲主體的師徒交往。後者牽涉到一個人類學者作爲學徒、觀察者與解釋者的多重身分、經驗與立場。在本章的敘述中，也將呈現出多地點的田野經驗（參圖一），以及隱微帶出對於研究者與被研究者之間非單向權力關係的反思。[6]

我稱爲 *daid naif*（舅舅）的歌師 Sangt Jingb，是 1998 至 2000 年期間，我在黔東南進行博士論文田野時，相交甚深的報導人。Sangt Jingb 是台江縣台盤鄉棉花坪的苗族，此地說的是黔東苗語方言北部土語支。我第一次見到他，是在 1997 年的秋夏之交。在台江文藝作家聯合會的文人聚會上，昏暗的燈下，熱絡的談話聲中，他熱切地拿著一部古歌手稿來對我說 Hmub 人的開天闢地。當時，博士論文研究工作還未展開，心情上實在無暇他顧。直到 1999 年底，在 Fangf Bil 村寨所進行與親屬、情歌、遊方（*iut fub*）[7]等相關的田野工作與民族誌資料的蒐集，都已大致有了根底，此時我想由古歌來瞭解口傳系統下 Hmub 人的歷史。但在我蹲點的田野，Fangf Bil 村寨，據說僅有八、九十歲的歌師才會唱鼓藏（*nenk jet niuf*）的歌，[8]而他們不怎麼願意開口。記得寨老 Zhangb Ghat Xiangt Ghet 帶來訊息說，要準備好一隻鴨子、一缸酒才能唱。沒有買鴨子與釀酒，我反而憶起二年前見過 Sangt Jingb 在稿紙上，手寫的古歌《開天闢地》（*Tid Waix*

Xif Dab）的歌詞，以及他手繪的 Hmub 人古歌裡的「渾沌初開」、「生命初始」的鉛筆素描。1999 年天氣轉冷前，我獨自從高坡的 Fangf Bil 村寨[9]來到離清水江較近的棉花坪（Zangx Bangx Hsenb）[10]。記憶中，自己在台盤下了車，走了好長一段路。沿路是翠綠的緩坡、草地及一塊塊小水澤。1999 年底到 2000 年初，當我主動到寨子找 Sangt Jingb 學古歌時，他說，早已料到我會再去找他的。在這段學古歌的過程中，記得曾有幾天是待在台江早期建的公安招待所。在這棟簡樸老舊的屋舍，三十元人民幣一日，待了數日。日以繼夜天天聽歌師 Sangt Jingb 解釋古歌、描繪古歌內容。也有幾天是在 *daid yut*（姑爹）（他的妻子是 Sangt Jingb 的妹）家學，我們買了豬肝與青菜煮了吃。又記得在棉花坪也曾住過幾天，但因為 Sangt Jingb 家沒有當家的女人（當時他的妻子已往生，兒尚未娶媳），所以我去住了另一位 *bad dlat*（伯父，他是 Sangt Jingb 同一房族的兄長）家，在那裡學古歌。那時我的腳已經凍傷，會癢、腫痛。也還記得吃烤粑粑。另一個印象則是 Sangt Jingb 帶我步行（由棉花坪）到相鄰的凱棠村（Ghab Dangx Gix）。[11] 那裡是台江地區古歌傳唱更為普遍的地方。貴州知名的苗歌學者燕寶，就是這裡的人。在凱棠吃了粉（粉條），我們又坐車去旁海（Bangk Hab），Sangt Jingb 的二女兒及女婿家在那。這時，天已經非常冷了，但尚未下雪。我獨自一人住在旁海糧管所的宿舍。有個窗子破了玻璃，僅用報紙貼住。當時夜裡被脊背凍醒的感覺，依然記憶深刻。還有一次受到驚嚇的經歷，是夜半有人來敲門——好像就是 Sangt Jingb 的二女婿，他還不老，小孩也在學前年齡。事後回想，他是來遊方。但當時，我一個人睡在獨立的房間，夜裡整理筆記，在暗夜中僅有火爐還亮著。我因害怕而心跳得很厲害，忘了當時如何回話。他在門外晃了一陣子才離去。我趕緊關燈躲進棉被裡就寢。

我已經忘記是如何又回到棉花坪。但那年學古歌（逐字、逐行的學了二部，《開天闢地》〔*Tid Waix Xif Dab*〕與《跋山涉水》〔*Nangx Eb Jit Bil*〕）是請 Sangt Jingb 唱和解釋，並且一邊繪圖，告訴我古歌的意境。對於這段學歌的過程，最後的印象是天地相連，覆蓋著白白厚厚的大雪。即使之於台江人，1999 年底到 2000 年初的那場大雪，也十分罕見。在這年的寒冬，我跟 Sangt Jingb 學完二部古歌。後來，有幾回在學古歌的過程中，我的內心已十分著急，有時會顯得不安。老人家適時提醒，但總給予溫暖的諒解。至今，永遠忘不了的是學完古歌與歌師 Sangt Jingb 告別時的兩個印象。其一，是在台江的中巴車前，Sangt Jingb 來送我上車，並遞上幾個硬硬的粑粑（他知道這個臺灣來的姑娘，喜歡吃烤粑粑）。那時天已轉冷，但沒有下雪。其二，則是在大雪紛飛的午後，從棉花坪一路走了下來，滿山遍野的銀色景象。一路上，Sangt Jingb 指著起伏的山丘，談論古歌的內容。這原本是我最渴望聆聽的內容，但在大雪中，內心焦慮著如何才能儘快從台盤回到台江縣城，再回到位於高坡的 Fangf Bil 村寨。焦慮與思家之心情（高坡 Fangf Bil 村寨的家，與臺灣的家）交織浮動，使我在雪地裡的行走，無法專注於歌師的激情講述，以至於錯過了在行路過程中，絕好的學習機會。

（二）一個書寫的歌師 [12]

　　Sangt Jingb，1934 年出生，一位經歷文革，會寫苗文的歌師。1954 年自台江城關翠文小學畢業，1955 年經縣教育局介紹到台江泗柳小學任教，後又輾轉到稿午小學、屯州小學等地教書。七年間不斷地在台江縣內移動。1961 年國家困難時期，停課後回鄉，開始和姑媽（*daid*，FZ）學習苗歌。當時除了因工作被迫暫停外，也因妻子過門九年仍未生育，

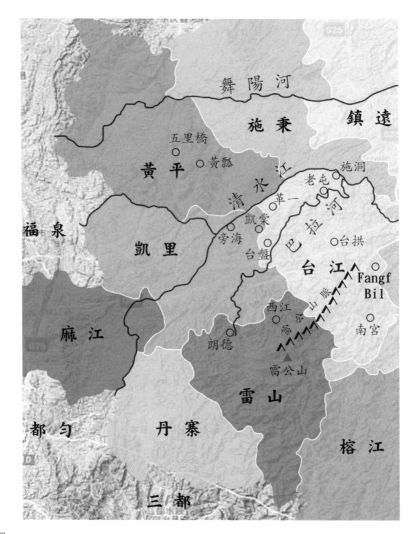

圖一：
在黃平與台江、凱里接壤處，唱古歌的文化區域是沿清水江中段，巴拉河而形成。本
章所提及的多個田野地點、歌師習歌地點、台江及其鄰近的古歌傳唱區域，大抵包含
在此地圖裡（筆者手繪，參貴州省地圖）。

家人催促其返鄉。加上父親的政治立場（老國民黨），幹部不同意讓他教書，認為他不適任，讓他連代課教師都沒辦法當。[13]

關於學習苗歌這件事情，Sangt Jingb 從十二歲起就跟嫁到南窯寨的姑媽學。最早是從《運金運銀》（Qab Nix Qab Jenb）這部古歌開始學起。[14] 此外他也跟另一個嫁到坪水寨的姑媽，學過另一部古歌：《四季歌》（Hxak Dlob Dongb）。Sangt Jingb 的父親據說是不會唱苗歌。1964 年之後，Sangt Jingb 跟隨另一位大坪寨的歌師，從《開天闢地》（Tid Waix Xif Dab）這部古歌學起。那時 Sangt Jingb 已經三十歲，此後長達三十多年，他持續學習古歌與書寫古歌。

1967 年 Sangt Jingb 開始學苗文。起初他的苗歌是以注音符號記音，後來就邊學苗文，一邊學記古歌。Sangt Jingb 學習苗文分成兩個階段，第一階段是 1967 年他自己到學校學習漢語拼音，以及苗文拼音。後來苗文班因為「大躍進」（若依其所述之時間應是指「文化大革命」）而停授。[15]1982 年，台江縣城的人（地方政府的幹部或領導）介紹他繼續去學。縣城的幹部是這麼說的：「Sangt Jingb，縣裡辦了個苗文班，你去學吧。」一個月還有 36 塊錢，他心裡想，那就去試試。他引以自豪的是，「黔東南州當時有幾萬人同時去學，但都學不來，只有我真正掌握了苗文」。

會有學習苗文的想法，是因為雖然他會唱苗歌，但是在村寨內娶親等場合被推上去唱苗歌時，「因為不會苗文，所以沒辦法對歌上酒場」。因此開始學。起初妻子不贊同，還罵他。後來他越學越多，每天上山坡勞動後，回到家就開始整理苗歌。十二部苗文古歌是從《運金運銀》（Qab Nix Qab Jenb）開始學起，[16]《四季歌》（Hxak Dlob Dongb）第二，之後就「每樣」（每部古歌）都學了。有時家裡來了姑爹當客人，姑爹唱歌，他就把歌學起來。有了一、二首古歌的基礎，學其他的就很快。Sangt Jingb 也跟寨上歌師交流古歌。他認為，他們雖然很會唱苗歌，但是「他們不會苗文」，所以在對歌上，很容易因為對不出來，就唱不下去。Sangt Jingb 覺得和他們對歌，「繞來繞去很囉唆」。另外，他也到清水江中下游的劍河、都柳江邊的榕江等地學歌。Sangt Jingb 誇稱全中國有苗族的地方，他都跑遍了。他也曾跟高坡 Fangf Bil 村寨的儀式專家，交流過古歌。他覺得，他們不會把歌總結成一部完整的苗族古歌。換言之，對於歌師 Sangt Jingb，苗文的書寫與古歌的口頭傳承與演出緊密關聯。書寫苗文讓歌師在對唱百餘行乃至千餘行的大部頭古歌時，能確切掌握與回應歌句與歌詞。

關於苗歌的記音與書寫，Sangt Jingb 是從《開天闢地》（*Tid Waix Xif Dab*）開始寫。這部古歌他寫過三次。第一次是「苗語說漢文寫」（漢字苗讀）。在此期間他也曾使用拉丁字母和注音符號來記《跋山涉水》（*Nangx Eb Jit Bil*）等其中幾部古歌，但隔天就忘了怎麼唸。之後他邊學苗文，邊繼續重寫古歌。第一部用苗文寫成的古歌是《開天闢地》（*Tid Waix Xif Dab*），之後寫《耕地育楓》（*Kab Wangs Jangt Mangx*）。最後一部古歌，《喪事之歌》（*Hxak Des*）是在 2002 年完成。他認為注音符號不好用來記歌。雖然苗文不好學，但他到 1982 年就開始用學得的苗文將原先寫成的一些古歌手稿，以苗文重新編寫與整理。書寫的過程中，也會遇到一些翻譯不出來的字，他會同時查閱苗文和漢語字典。在漫長的書寫過程中，1972 年他的妻子去世，家中一個孩子也去世。遭此喪妻與喪子之痛，他停了三、五年沒有寫。後來，因為「看現在大家都在唱古歌，卻不知道意思」，所以他重拾文筆書寫。

而在寫歌的過程中遇到最困難的就是去別人寨子聽到苗歌，有時候不懂爲什麼這樣唱，要先用腦袋記下來，再用苗文書寫。他也曾看過黃平的古歌（集子），但他覺得和家鄉台盤比起來，「較短，東一句、西一句的，要靠專家才能總結」。[17] 他認爲台江縣的苗歌專家有燕寶[18]、今旦[19]、唐春芳[20]和潘定發[21]等人。有些苗歌專家會編輯，會唱，也會用電腦，但是苗歌的故事性不足。Sangt Jingb 說：「『爲什麼天還沒亮就聽蘆笙』？但他們（指歌師或苗歌專家們）卻不知道那是叫大家起床散步和回來吃飯的聲音。」此例展現 Sangt Jingb 偏好以常識爲基底的功能與因果推論，並以此對古歌內容進行解釋 —— 但這也是台江地方的知識分子或苗歌專家們，最常批評 Sangt Jingb 之處（討論參後）。

　　根據我在 2000 年前後的瞭解，除了寨子裡的人在有生命儀禮要進行時，會找 Sangt Jingb 去唱苗歌外，他也教棉花坪的人唱苗歌。對於寫古歌這件事，Sangt Jingb 原本擔心沒辦法完成作品，但他說貴陽有出版社願意幫他出版苗族古歌集。[22]「只是出版社所集中的編輯，幾乎都不會苗文」，Sangt Jingb 以一貫的口吻評論道。寫完古歌後，Sangt Jingb 說，他想繼續寫作張秀眉的故事。張秀眉是清代咸同年間，貴州東部苗族起義的英雄。他的英雄事蹟，被創作爲不同類型的歌謠與民間故事。自清代以來就在黔東南諸多村寨社群間廣爲流傳至今。2000 年台江縣城蓋了一座秀眉廣場，廣場上立了一座高達二公尺的張秀眉威武石雕像。

三、一部古歌手稿的記音與翻譯

　　自 Sangt Jingb 習歌算起，已近四十年。從他由漢字或注音符號作爲標音的苗歌書寫來算，逾二十年。而若以此部苗文記音與翻譯的手稿版本，到 2002 年完成最後一部，則用了 Sangt Jingb 十年時光，將流傳於台江地區的古歌按主題整理，寫成十二部手稿。本文討論的《跋山涉水》（*Nangx Eb Jit Bil*）是古歌第三部。「停留」與「移動」兩個對比的主題，是構築這部古歌的基調。這部古歌約近兩千行歌句，Sangt Jingb 書寫的手稿爲 228 頁，[23] 包括手繪圖的封面、內容提要、序文，以及 141 首短歌（*ot hxak*）。[24] 手稿中偶會出現一些手繪圖，用來解釋古歌的意境；此外還有多處塗塗改改的筆跡。寫作完稿日期爲 1990 年十一月十五日，落款於序文三的結尾下方。Sangt Jingb 在《跋山涉水》（*Nangx Eb Jit Bil*）序文裡敘述短歌（*ot hxak*）的由來。古歌是源自苗族神話敘事長詩，內容描述苗族祖先遷到貴州的故事。Sangt Jingb 說明他所著述的古歌主要是按照長詩在實際演唱中的形式，然後以苗文轉成漢文的方式來表達。每頁手稿的左半，上一行是逐句苗文記音，下一行爲逐字苗漢雙語對照。手稿的右半部與左邊的苗文歌句對齊，將成句苗文短歌，逐句翻譯成規律的五言漢文詩句。[25] 雖然 Sangt Jingb 苗歌手稿之呈現形式（並置苗語記音、漢字逐字直譯或硬譯，以及意譯的五言漢句），在民族誌或語言學的詩歌翻譯並不特殊，但核對手稿的記音與苗漢雙語對譯的文字用語，我們發現 Sangt Jingb 的翻譯，在語意或押韻雖盡力展現「信、達、雅」原則，但也有部分譯句或用語的選擇頗耐人尋味。對於 Sangt Jingb，記音到翻譯是怎樣的書寫任務？本章將由此部古歌手稿裡的一些例子來進行討論。表一的例子是古歌《跋山涉水》當中的第三十四首短歌（Sangt Jingb 手稿第 63-65 頁）。此段短歌的演唱位置，大約在這部二千多行古歌的四分之一處。其內容描述祖先遷移到一處由山頭往下探望江河的地景，並描述祖先遇到擬人化鳥類與碩大魚類。

表一

短歌／行數	苗文記音與中文逐字直譯	中文翻譯
第 34 首／第 1 行	*Lolleit Ngax Dab Diongl*	來到野豬沖 [26]
	來到 野豬 山谷	
	Ob hent Ngax Dab Diongl	我們誇 [27] 山谷
	我們 誇講 野豬 山谷	
	Hsangt deis daib bad lul	哪個大伯父
	哪個 兒女 伯父	
	Bed Wef daib bad lul	鵜鶘大伯父
	鵜鶘 兒女 伯父	
第 34 首／第 5 行	*Niangb ax bob hfud diongl*	他坐在沖頭
	坐 坐著 沖頭	
	Bongf jox eb gid nangl	見江河下（面）[28]
	見 江河 下方	
	Liongx ghenx hlieb jangd jel	大碓杆湧滾 [29]
	湧滾 大 碓杆	
	Nef nox hlieb bad mal	大馬匹青魚 [30]
	青魚 大 馬匹	
	Bongf ax bud gid wil	見不會捉拿
	見 不知 捉拿	

短歌 / 行數	苗文記音與中文逐字直譯	中文翻譯
第 34 首 / 第 10 行	*Bongf seix bud gid gol*	看見會叫喊 [31]
	見　也　知　叫　喊	
	Dlal ib dial ib dial	哥咿哥咿哥
	哥　伊哥　伊哥	
	Lol heik lol heik yal	快撈快撈呀
	來　撈　來　撈　呀	
第 34 首 / 第 13 行	*Ax heik seix faf nail*	不撈魚打脫
	不　撈　都　脫　魚	

　　就這段作爲例子的第三十四首短歌，首先我們要面對的是，中文的翻譯在說什麼。爲此，先將 Sangt Jingb 以五言歌句形式書寫的中文翻譯，作一些增補轉寫爲散文體如下：「苗族祖先在遷徙過程中，來到一個稱爲野豬沖的地方。歌者誇讚山谷，唱到是哪個大伯父，是鵓鴣大伯父。牠坐在山谷上頭，望著江河下面。江河裡彷彿有大碓杆在翻滾，原來是碩大如馬匹的青魚。遷移的祖先們看見了但沒有辦法捉，看見魚會叫喊，哥呀哥呀，快來撈呀，不撈魚就溜走了。」[32] 接著我們再從苗文來檢視 Sangt Jingb 對這段短歌的中文翻譯，可以發現其中有幾個問題作爲我們討論的基礎。其一，短歌三十四首的第七行，苗文原文當中的 *hlieb*（大）字非形容詞，其句法功能不是用來修飾馬匹，而是作句子的謂語使用。故原句的含義應是「仔細一看發現是一條碩大的青魚，它的身軀大得像一匹馬」。Sangt Jingb 可能是受限於五言詩律，將其譯爲「大馬匹青魚」。然而在這行中文翻譯裡的「大」字，就中文的慣用語法，並不能成爲

可以充分理解苗文的基礎。其二，這首短歌在苗文的第九行與第十行，Sangt Jingb 譯文中的「見」和「看見」都出自同一個苗文單詞 *bongf*。而苗文中該詞的含義爲「被感知到」。因而對視覺上感知一種物件而言，應當翻譯爲看見，但對感知聲音而言，應該翻譯爲「聽見」。原文稿都翻譯爲「見」和「看見」，屬於一個明顯的誤譯。然而 Sangt Jingb 本身就是苗語的母語使用者，這個誤譯現象的背後，或許不在於 Sangt Jingb 對於苗語語言知識掌握不正確，問題可能在於翻譯的行動本身。就短歌第三十四首的問題，Sangt Jingb 一方面爲了配合苗文與中文逐字對照的一致性，所以將 *bongf* 都譯爲「見」；又爲了顧全中文翻譯，能配合苗文的五言結構，所以分別譯爲「見」與「看見」。換言之，在檢視這首短歌第三十四首的苗文與中文對照的翻譯裡，我們看到譯者部分的誤譯，主要的原因應是在語言的一般語意（literary meaning）與黔東南苗歌（無論是情歌或古歌）普見的五言詩律結構（吳德坤 1986；李惟白 1996）限制所影響。

除了文字，在此首短歌原稿下方（下接 35：*Ot Hxak* 之間），還有 Sangt Jingb 的親手繪圖，畫著兩座山。兩座山的左半邊，都塗滿黑色（表示山沖），上方有一隻小鳥（表示遷徙的方向），最右則有隻很像山豬的動物，動作像是往山的方向走去。Sangt Jingb 以此圖，示意本首短歌主要的地點：「野豬沖（Ngax Dab Diongl）」。至此，本章以這部古歌的短歌第三十四首作爲例子，將它在手稿出現的文字與圖的配置，以及苗文與中文之記音與翻譯的展現形式進行描述，並且對於苗文與中文翻譯之間進行比對與初步的分析。在這個基礎上，討論的焦點之一是以閱讀古歌手稿的中文翻譯，來作爲第一種閱讀與理解的行動，接著再以同時面對記音與翻譯的分析與討論，來作爲第二種閱讀與理解的行動。我想從這兩套系統來探討翻譯與文化，以及翻譯作為一種行動與主體性之構成的經驗。而這整個討論是從一個有文字書寫與閱讀能力的 Hmub 人歌師 Sangt Jingb 的生命史開始，並涉及黔東南苗族地方社會裡古歌知識的流通與競奪，以及所經歷的近代中國歷史與社會的變遷。

（一）古歌手稿的兩種閱讀方式 [33]

在《跋山涉水》這部古歌，遷徙是貫穿整部手稿的主題。[34] 依 Sangt Jingb 的記音與翻譯的手稿，我們不僅可以閱讀到古歌裡有關遷徙的祖先所行經之空間細節的演述，以及停留與移動交替集成的遷徙經驗；經由歌師的記音與翻譯進行比對，我們將可從兩者之間的斷裂與縫隙中，看到知識的生成與流瀉，知識的建構與多義。

（1）第一種閱讀方式：手稿譯文的閱讀與古歌空間再現

約兩千餘行，141 首短歌所集成的古歌《跋山涉水》能如何被閱讀？方式之一是將 Sangt Jingb 提供的譯文，當作在地版本來讀。Sangt Jingb 作為譯者，在此像是透明、可穿透之攜帶訊息的中介者，不讓讀者看見。苗歌譯文仿若土著觀點，再現古代苗族人群的移動與空間。以下是第一種閱讀的示範，以及分析的細節。

停留與移動兩個對比的主題，是構築這部《跋山涉水》古歌的基調。這一節將經由內容為遷徙前之原居」的短歌第 1–13 首的譯文，以及內容為開始遷徙的短歌第 14–60 首的譯文，比較停留與移動的空間內容差異。

遷徙前的原居地

這部古歌第 1 首至第 13 首短歌所陳述的空間背景是原居地：東方。此時，人群準備往西方富庶之地遷徙。原居地的空間大致有三個特點：想像西方和現實東方的跨界，人群的集體互動，對遷徙的歡樂期待交織對原居地的懷念與不捨。在這 13 首短歌，祖地和想像的西方都不在場，唯有現居地在場。除了第 1 與第 2 首短歌呈現祖地空間，第 3 至第 13 首短歌則主要呈現現實東方與想像西方的空間變換。人群居住在東方原居地，傳聞西方物資豐碩，東、西方在認知上的差異，成為現實東方與想像西方之空間變換的能量來源。原本，得以被直接經驗的在場空間只有現居地，然而，譯文的想像西方呈現具體與象徵兩種層面，使空間產生跨界的流動。其一在第 3、4、8、10、11 首（見表二，以第 3 首短歌為例），呈現西方物產豐盛。用各種常見的物件比喻糧食的碩大：譬如以手指來比喻水稻的管莖 （*Ghongx nax hlieb dad bil*），玉米的秧包大如腳腕，玉米的顆粒跟拳頭一樣大（*Deid laf dol gad nail*， *Ghad dliex hlieb ghongd nagngl*，*Ghab laib hlieb bod liul*）。[35] 對物產實際且生動的描述，使得現實東方和想像西方，同樣具有在場、被經驗的性質。其二在象徵層次上，西方被賦予等同於幸福的符號。向西遷徙，是人群謀求幸福的過程。在此援用跨界一詞，乃因透過歌詞的敘述，空間不斷變換於東方和西方之間，形成一種空間的動態流動。基本上，跨界的前提是，空間被劃定界線並且封閉成相應單位。在這部古歌的歌詞中，東方是現居地，想像的西方被設定為相對應的空間（東方與西方本身代表著對稱的語意，物產豐富與否的落差、實存和想像等等），也就是說，東方和西方間，已經被劃定了分界線。

表二

短歌 / 行數	中文翻譯
第 3 首 / 第 10 行	趕集跑西方
	見那好地方
	窪地水田壩
	莧大如腳杆 36
	手指大稻管 37
第 3 首 / 第 15 行	田萍大碗飯 38
	魚大像雄馬
	黃鱔大碓杆 39
	小米斗五錢 40
	分金一匹馬 41
第 3 首 / 第 20 行	相逢剩玉米 42
	秧包大腳腕 43
	顆大如拳頭 44

　　其次，這部分的短歌也表達人群「互通消息、協商、行前準備」。
這些人群的集體行動都與西方有關：交換關於西方的訊息，協商往西遷
徙，準備行囊往西。這些組構出西方為他方、異地的空間。第三，對比
於往西遷徙之喜悅的集體情緒，第 7、10、11 首則以落寞、低調的歌詞
片段（見表三，以短歌第 10 首為例），顯示即將遷徙的人群，透過對
未能遷徙的親屬與地域的不捨，與對原居地的深厚懷念。尤其，在第 10
首短歌的最後兩句「你們撞叫媽，永世不忘奶」（*Mangx lol mangx hot
mais，Ax dal laib bit wus*）裡，*mais*（媽），指父輩的女性；*wus*（奶），
指祖輩及其以上輩分的女性；撞，指碰見，撞見。此處的用詞習慣承襲

自古代，苗語表達的詞意極為質樸，意在表達朝夕相處，親密接觸之意。這兩句意為：「你們的媽媽會隨你們一道西去，在朝夕相處中，但凡呼喚你們的媽媽時，你們要永遠記住，你們的祖輩還留住在遙遠的東方。」這兩句用詞古樸，而且把女性作為人群的領袖來稱謂。後者在其他部苗族古歌也常被提及，在地的解釋認為此一文化主題是苗族的遠古傳統。我們據此推測這兩句基本上保存了苗族古歌的原有面貌，不像有些句子那樣經歷了 Sangt Jingb 的改寫和潤色（參表三）。

表三

短歌 / 行數	中文翻譯
第 10 首 / 第 1 行	聽孫們向西
	心落如岩塌
	眼淚冒滾滾
	年青們抹目
第 10 首 / 第 5 行	眼淚湧不絕
	像雨降人間
	哪心裡明白
	哪個來喧嚷
第 10 首 / 第 20 行	我走走不到
	安居山坳口
	住在路平面
	成個絆腳石
	你們撞叫媽
第 10 首 / 第 25 行	永世不忘奶

接著，以這部分短歌與空間相關的詞彙來進行一些瞭解。首先，由專稱名詞山或山岰口（*ghongd lot dlongs*，地窪下處），組構出當地主要地景——它們與人群日常生活息息相關。田則是此處最頻繁出現的地物，標示著重要的生產資源。跟空間（想像的西方）有關的形容詞，只在第3、7首出現。在短歌第3首描述想像西方裡肥碩的物資（見表二）；在短歌第7首前二句：「這地好平原，地平像板壁」（*Jox fangb zenx nangl cens，Fangb zenk liek liul bis*），敘述遷徙前，原居地是美好、平坦之地。其次是代名詞頻繁出現，並同時用於指稱西方和東方。例如，第3首短歌前四句：「居住於東方，好得很什麼，來遠這地方，轉移向西方」（*Hext jox fangb gid nangl，Vut jangx gheix xid mongl，Lol dol fangb nongd lol，Lol jox fangb gid bil*），以及第3首短歌第10與11二句：「趕集跑西方，見那好地方」（*Leit jox fangb gid bib，Bongf dol fangb nend lal*），其中「這地方」和「那（好）地方」都是指西方。最後，動詞在此部分也展現人群遷徙的集體與抽象面向。在第4首短歌之第10與11二句：「真也要跋涉，假也要跋涉」（*Deix seix nongt jit bil，Dlab seix nongt jit bil*）；第5首短歌之第11與12二句：「不接祖向西，祖跋涉謀福」（*Ax yangl nals jit jes，Nals nangx bil het dlas*）；第9首短歌之第11與12二句：「我們跑西方，跋涉謀幸福」（*Nax bib mongl jit jes，Bib nangx bil het dlas*）；第11首短歌前二句：「準備已完備，決定要轉移」（*Ait jis ait jangx jul，Max ait mais vax liol*）等等的歌句裡，跋涉、轉移、往某處去、謀福，都是指向遷徙的動詞，呈現人群集體往西的一致性。

開始遷徙

前13首短歌鋪陳人群在原居地集體準備遷徙的過程。緊接的第

14–60 首短歌，則是人群開始遷徙。此部分主軸以地點推移，途經地點依序轉換（見表四）為平行的敘述架構。對於同一地點的描寫，內容的鋪陳以「進到（進入）此地 → 與此地互動，景觀觀察 → 路過（離開，遠觀）此地」為穩定的敘述小架構。路過某地為離開某地，進到某地為到達另一地點。「路過／進到」作為可明確畫分空間界線的動詞，並且同時也指出遷徙空間的跨越。到達某地後，觀察當地的地景，陳述的內容因各自的環境特性而有差異，同時也呈現人群與陌生環境互動過程。對某地的描述以「路過某地」結束、告別。此部分的古歌所展現的空間視角配置為明顯且規律的變換。從遠距的地景印象，到親近接觸的觀察，最後留下一個**可回頭觀看**的印象。

這部古歌手稿所記錄的人群移動與遷徙的內容，和已有的一些苗族研究文獻對於苗族的儀式歌詞內容、生死魂魄移動的宇宙觀，以及地景空間的探討有所關聯。其一是移動的文化母題。如大衛·葛維翰（David Graham 1954）、基恩·莫丁（Jean Mottin 1980、1982）、李穆安（Jacques Lemoine 1983、1987）、王富文（Nicholas Tapp 1989、2003）、帕翠莎·西蒙茲（Patricia Symonds 1991、2004）與凱茜·福爾克（Cathy Falk 1996、2004a、2004b）等人類學者在不同年代，不同地方（四川、寮國、泰國、澳洲）—— 記錄 Hmong 人在喪葬儀禮中，口頭傳唱的古歌。如《指路經》（*Kr'ua Ke*），將死亡當作一場旅行，一趟移動之旅。以下引述李穆安於 1970 年在高地東南亞記錄青苗（Green Hmong）之 *Kr'ua Ke* 當中的片段：「你的祖先們會說：『誰指引你這條路到這裡』？你要回應道：『是一個臉大得像扇子，眼大得像碟子的傢伙……』你的祖先們會接著說：『我們要如何跟著他所指的路走？……』」（Lemoine 1983：38-39）。[45] 本章接下來所要探討的

Sangt Jingb 手稿的翻譯，也將凸顯與此苗族民間口傳文學對於移動之文化母題的相近性。其次 Sangt Jingb 這部古歌手稿的記音與翻譯中，豐富、細膩表述的地景與空間，也很類似凱茜・福爾克（1996：220）所指出的，在東南亞高地的苗族 Hmong 與喪葬死亡相關的古歌內容，不僅是語言的修飾，也是與當地苗族傳統生活的山川河谷等空間地景，以及與農業等物質生活緊密關聯的具體表述。

> 這些與死亡有關的苗歌語言，不僅填之以如花的詞藻，做為比喻與對照，也還包含許多苗族 Hmong 在高地東南亞山區傳統地理環境中的物質文化與充滿農家韻味的生活型態。在苗歌的文本中，有許多關於這地區特有的植物與動物；地形、地貌與地景 河川、溪流、山谷、山沖；農作、工具、備食；生處在這片土地上的神話與傳說的男女主人翁；特有的家屋建築。（Falk 1996: 220）[46]

最後關於苗族的古歌或儀式專家鬼師唸誦的的古詞內容裡，豐富的地景與空間表述，往往也與認同的構成或界限之劃分與再現緊密關聯。通過《跋山涉水》譯稿的閱讀，我們將會發現以停留與移動為基調的地景與空間之表述，再現有如靈媒、薩滿所創造的儀式與神聖、神秘空間，以及與常人日常空間的交疊與轉換（Parkin 1991；Humphrey 1995）。

接著從表四的觀察可以發現，以短歌第 14 首到第 60 首為觀察的對象，除了九金孔與大河床以外，其他十三個地點出現的曲數，至少分別用了三首短歌來陳述同一地點。短歌歌詞的敘述結構，主要如同前文已提到「進到（進入）→ 觀察、互動 → 路過」的時序與空間的移動。從短歌的數量來看，此部分移動空間的描述比較細膩，不僅在於空間視角配置細微的轉換，對移動人群與當地觀察、互動的描寫，也顯得突出。以九石板爲例，短歌第 18 至 21 首，是描述九石板的歌詞。第 18 首短歌交代離開了上一個地點淹雞牛，向大家宣布已經到達九石板（「路過淹雞牛，來呀眞的來，走呀眞的走，進致〔至〕何地方，進到九石板，要告訴大家，人人都聽覺」〔*Fat zat Vib Jid Niel，Lol lol jus deix lol，Yel yel jus deix yel，Lol leit Zat Jex Liul，Nongt xangs dangx ib dol，Xangs dangx dob hnangd jul*〕）。第 19 首短歌的九石板空間是好幾條巷子連接在一起；後來遇到蜈蚣大伯父，對母親不友善，對遷徙有一些後悔；此處所窄小，連烹飪都不方便。顯示出遷徙的人群和當地的蜈蚣大伯父互動的過程，以及對此地的觀感。

表四

短歌	指涉地點、地形或地貌之地名		
	苗文地名	中文翻譯	翻譯歷程[47]
第 14 － 18 首	Vib Jid Niel	淹雞牛	音譯
第 18 － 21 首	Zat Jex Liul	九石板	意譯
第 21 － 26 首	Zhangx Ghaib Vol	漲關峭	音譯與意譯混成
第 26 － 30 首	Dlangs Bib Jil	養壁菊	音譯與意譯混成
第 30 － 32 首	Zhangx Ghaib Mongl	嫜關蒙	音譯
第 32 － 35 首	Niongx Jib Bil	野鴨坡	意譯
	Ngax Dab Diongl	野豬沖	意譯

短歌	指涉地點、地形或地貌之地名		
	苗文地名	中文翻譯	翻譯歷程
第 35 － 38 首	Bil Mut Wus	壁漠武	音譯與意譯混成
第 38 － 41 首	Ghab Vongl Liangl	關溶洋	音譯
第 41 － 44 首	Bil Zat At	壁拶阿	音譯與意譯混成
第 44 － 48 首	Bil Zat Zet	壁砸兆	音譯
第 48 － 52 首	Vongl Hxut Kut	嶸猍苉	音譯與意譯混成
第 52 － 54 首	Eb Fud Dlod	翁湖小	音譯與意譯混成
第 54 － 58 首	Eb Jex Jil	翁玖菊	音譯
第 58 － 59 首	Jux Jenb Khongd	九金孔	音譯與意譯混成
第 60 首	Ghab Saix Eb	大河床	意譯[48]

　　再則根據短歌第 14 首到 60 首的內容，所整理出的表五可以得知，遷徙經過的地點，具有多元的空間景觀，譬如岩壁、沖積地、江河匯流處等等。它們都是古歌描述人群在現居地沒有經驗過的地景空間。因此，相對於前 13 首短歌在原居地停留時，再三強調坳、山、田為主的空間，自第 14 首開始到第 60 首短歌的空間專稱詞，在地景和地物方面的描述，呈現多中心的布局。首先，大量出現「來至」、「趕到」、「路過」等陳述地點之推進的動詞與副詞組合語。其次相較於第 1 首到第 13 首的集體跋涉——僅迴盪於東方和西方之間，此部分古歌內容有 14 個地點的移動，因而表現出更明確的空間推移。再者此部分的空間表述，也展現依地形而有不同行進方式（如渡河、順……江下、繞坡等）。雖然古歌中

的人群主要是以步行走動為前進的方式，但通過不同動詞的運用，卻又表現出移動的人群與空間對應的多元性。最後，從第16首短歌以後，動詞的變化更多樣，遷徙人群因應不同地方，產生互動與生活內容的多樣性（參表六）。

表五

地點	地景與空間
淹雞牛	水域
九石板	廢棄聚落
漲關崤	山
養壁菊	岩壁
嬉關蒙	沖積地
野鴨坡、野豬沖	河岸
壁漠武	山坡
關溶洋	岩瀑
壁拶阿	山林
壁砸兆	黑暗之地
嶸猍芤	懸崖
翁湖小	大江
翁玖菊（九江口）	江河匯流處
九金孔	懸岩
大河床	河床

表六

地點	地景空間	遷徙人群與此地的互動
淹雞牛	湧泉、漁產豐碩	遇動物大伯伯，吹笛聲環繞江流
九石板	多巷弄、住屋狹窄	遇動物大伯伯，欺負媽媽，煮食不便
漲關峭	岰、樹林、坪地	遇動物大伯父，回溯此地的地名由來 種南瓜，爬樹唱歌，烹肉分食
養壁菊	嶺陡直	遇動物大伯父，欺負媽媽，砍木燒飯，休息
嫜關蒙	遍地茅草、野豬野雞、 河水沖積山谷	燒山，熟五穀
野鴨坡 野豬沖	河邊山谷沖積地平坦、 野豬野雞、作物花木花瓜	居住，開田修塘，爭地買地，捉魚
壁漠武	堅硬的山坡、山梁	繞坡巡視，居住，山崩逃離
關溶洋	山岩瀑布	從高山下到瀑布，捉魚蝦
壁拐阿	山谷、竹林、綠色、多紙	賞蟲鳴風景，搬金銀回家，敲銅鑼，吃好
壁砸兆	黑暗無路	劈山開路，架橋跨河，效仿蝙蝠，蟲鳴熱鬧
嶸豿芀	懸崖艱險	過崖受傷跛腳，擰稻藤製草鞋， 親屬和動物陸續到達，齊聚
翁湖小	大江	看到大江很高興，打魚，吃好
翁玖菊 （九江口）	九江匯合、汪洋、礁石、 山林	看太陽起落，沿江奔跑，放草觀察水流 蜘蛛吐絲
九金孔	懸崖	蜘蛛吐絲架橋，眾多遷徙人群淹死
大河床	河床、坡頂、谷底、江流	遷徙人群徘徊哭泣

這一節呈現我們閱讀 Sangt Jingb 的手稿譯文，是在不刻意涉及譯文與苗文記音的對照，而對《跋山涉水》古歌手稿內容進行一種理解。在這閱讀及展現部分我們對於手稿理解的過程與結果——一個微型的人群移動經驗與有著獨特風格之空間美學的再現，只有手稿譯文的現身。在手稿譯文承擔被讀者賦予爲土著觀點的當下，譯者是不在場的。亦即，譯者 Sangt Jingb 似乎不在場，但他的記音與翻譯，已左右著我作爲田野調查人對於古歌的閱讀和理解。因爲歌師按照自己的理解，幫助讀者認識苗族古歌；而且可能賦予了苗族古歌本來不曾有的內容。此部分的資料呈現與分析，是本章接下來討論的重點。

（2）第二種閱讀方式：記音與譯文之間的觀察與譯者的清楚現身

如果我們將苗文記音與漢字譯文進行對比，古歌手稿的某些部分將呈現出記音與翻譯之間的技術與操作。在前一種手稿閱讀裡不在場的譯者，經由記音與譯文之間的不連續或斷裂，我們方能窺見某種形式的譯者現身，並可能得以討論那不連續或出現縫隙的記音與譯文之間的知識與意義。後者是古歌手稿的第二種閱讀方式。

繼續遷徙

《跋山涉水》古歌的第 87 至 104 首，描述人群離開老楓樹以後，繼續向西遷徙。此部分的短歌群，以兩類架構交互穿插。第一類是「路過 A1（某地景空間），來呀來呀來，走啊走啊走，來至何地方，來至 B1（某地景空間）」，緊接第二類開頭是「來至 B1 或 B2（某地景空間）」，兩相交替。在上述兩種類型，A1 僅交代地名，B1 或 B2 的地點，則加以描述。依循這兩種架構穿插的規律，可以將遷徙人群經過的地區分爲 A 地和 B 地兩種（見表七）。

句型規律地表現出「路過某地，來啊眞得來，走啊眞得走，來至何地方，來至某地……（對當地描述）」；下一首續接「來至某地，我們誇聖地（對當地描述）」。以路過代表離開，並以固定的句法，來啊眞得來，走啊眞得走，來至何地方，來至某地作爲緩衝；直到來至某地，遷徙的人群才駐紮於此。例如，短歌第 89 首的前七句：「路過廣濟市，來呀眞的來，走啊眞的走，來至何地方，來至依放坡，這裡好地方，坪地好開田」（*Fat zat Ghab Zat Bil*，*Lol lol jus deix lol*，*Yel yel jus deix yel*，*Lol leit fangb gheix xil*，*Lol leit Vib Fangx Bil*，*Bet nongd vut ghab dlangl*，*Vut ghab zhangx khab wul*）；短歌第 90 首的前六句：「來至依放坡，我們誇聖地，哪個好心腸，翡翠心腸好，起早來窺視，早上起早瞄，[49] 懸崖濱捉魚」（*Lol leit Vib Fangx Bil*，*Ob hent Vib Fangx Bil*，*Dail xil dat vut hxut*，*Nes jit hsaib vut hxut*，*Fal sod fal dat mongt*，*Fal sod fal dat hvat*，*Wil nail ghab but zat*）。

　　整理自短歌第 87 首至 104 首的表七，共有 9 個地名屬於未加描述即離開的 A 類地名，其中 5 個是某某市。「市」[50] 在漢字的書寫體系，雖是可溯及數千年前的典籍，但此手稿所書寫的某某市，可能是指涉現代國家的行政劃分所設定的地名與轄級。何以在古歌的譯文出現這樣的當代語彙？在我與 Sangt Jingb 學歌的過程中，我們工作的桌上，除了稿紙，還擺著我在田野時隨身攜帶的《全國地圖集》。尤其《跋山涉水》（*Nangx Eb Jit Bil*）這部古歌，唱到許多地方與地景。爲了尋找古歌所唱的地方與地景，與苗族人群所處的眞實世界及貴州、湖南當代地名指涉之境間一對一的對照關係，在書寫古歌這許多年來，Sangt Jingb 屢次經由行走、乘車到不同地方，停留數月再返家。旅途中他經由觀察火車窗外景致的變化，思索古歌所唱的地景。他也勤於讀地圖，以確認古歌地點與當代地圖的地名對照。這個過程與我們探索 Sangt Jingb 作爲一個譯者及其對苗歌的翻譯與知識的構築，顯然有其無法分割的關聯。關於此，本文後面還要繼續討論。在此即提出，是要說明在古歌手稿的譯文出現廣濟市、武漢市，隨其所帶出之譯文閱讀上的突兀感，讓我們有一個缺口鑽入譯者的世界。對於譯者的發現，我們還可經由比對這部分的苗文記音與漢字的譯文，發現在苗文記音同爲一個地點，有兩個以上的漢字譯文名字。通常是先出現漢字苗讀的音譯（如：Wub Khangd 烏狂），[51] 然後再出現漢字意譯，後者往往是 Sangt Jingb 考證後的當代或近現代地名（如：Wub Khangd 武漢市）。另外也會出現以漢字苗讀的音譯與漢字意譯的組合，來表達古歌所再現之地景空間的語彙（如：Vib Fangx Bil 依放坡；依放爲 *Vib Fangx* 的音譯，坡爲 *Bil* 的意譯）。

　　從表七得知短歌第 87 至 104 首，指涉地方的漢字譯文共有 19 種，而表八以苗文記音的地名則僅有 11 種。也就是說，由分析者的視角觀之，此部分的短歌，不加描述的 A 類地點和停留描述的 B 類地點之間的差別，其實是譯者將同一地點譯成不同的地名，並且不加描述的 A 類地點多翻譯爲現代地名的某某市（如：武漢、廣濟、鄂州）。這之中所展現的譯者意識，以及通過現代地名的夾帶，隱含著現代性氛圍。漢字苗讀的雙語意象與音的移借，是有意或無意地與歌師的書寫行動，文化認知與生命史經驗，有著什麼樣的關聯？這是頗耐人尋味的。

表七

短歌	苗文地名	中文翻譯	類別	苗文地名	中文翻譯	類別
87	Eb Jex Jil	九江口 [52]	A	Ghangx Jib	廣雞	B
88	Ghab Zat Bil	嘎拶壁	B	無		
89	Ghab Zat Bil	廣濟市	A	Vib Fangx Bil	依放坡	B
90	Vib Fangx Bil	依放坡	B	無		
91	Vib Fangx Bil	黃石市 [53]	A	Eb Zek Dlangl	翁奏	B
92	Eb Zek Dlangl	翁奏	B	無		
93	Eb Zek Dlangl	鄂州市 [54]	A	Fangx Ghangd Dlangl	方放	B
94	Fangx Ghangd Dlangl	方放	B	無		
95	Fangx Ghangd Dlangl	黃岡 [55]	A	Wub Khangd	烏狂	B
96	Wub Khangd	烏狂	B	無		
97	Wub Khangd	武漢市 [56]	A	Jab Wid Dlangl	加宇	B
98	Jab Wid Dlangl	加宇	B	無		
99	Jab Wid Dlangl	嘉魚 [57]	A	Ongd Ful	瀚湖	B
100	Ongd Ful	瀚湖	B	無		
101	Ongd Ful	洪湖 [58]	A	Xox Yangf	小洋	B
102	無			無		
103	Xox Yangf Dlangl	岳陽市 [59]	A	Nangl Hsab Mongl	浪沙蒙	B
104	Nangl Hsab Mongl	浪沙蒙	B	無		

　　另一個牽涉到苗文記音和漢字譯文的議題是聖地。在 Sangt Jingb 的手稿中，指代同一地點的地名，在第二次被提及時，往往冠以聖地或聖坡，這樣的讚語總計出現了六次。也就是說在這部分短歌提及的 11 個地點中，有六個地方被 Sangt Jingb 稱爲聖地或聖坡。若不將 Eb Jex Jil 與 Ghangx Jib 兩地列入（參表八），被稱爲聖地的比例達九分之六。因爲 Eb Jex Jil（九江口）是作爲人群開始移動的地點，它不屬於遷徙過程中對某地的觀察和決定停留與否的脈絡。而出現在《跋山涉水》古歌手稿第 87 首的 Ghangx Jib（廣雞），則可以與出現在第 88 首的 Ghab Zat Bil（嘎拶壁），以及出現在第 89 首的 Ghab Zat Bil（廣濟市）一起討論。若依照古歌歌詞的呈現規律，Ghangx Jib（廣雞）、Ghab Zat Bil（嘎拶壁）和 Ghab Zat Bil（廣濟市）應該是指同一地方，不過出現在這相連的三首短歌，苗文地名並未符合此規律。尤其手稿第 89 首短歌的 Ghab Zat Bil（廣濟市），原本是寫成 Ghangx Jib Vangl（廣雞寨），而後塗改爲 Ghab Zat Bil（廣濟市）（手稿上留下劃線修改的痕跡）。我們推測這也許就是歌師有意或無意地在記音與翻譯之間進行操作的歷程。

表八

短歌	短歌	中文翻譯	苗文地名	中文翻譯
87	Eb Jex Jil	九江口	Ghangx Jib	廣雞
88	Ghab Zat Bil	嘎拶壁	無	
89	Ghab Zat Bil	廣濟市	Vib Fangx Bil	依放坡
90	Vib Fangx Bil	依放坡	無	

短歌	短歌	中文翻譯	苗文地名	中文翻譯
91	Vib Fangx Bil	黃石市	Eb Zek Dlangl	翁奏
92	Eb Zek Dlangl	翁奏	無	
93	Eb Zek Dlangl	鄂州市	Fangx Ghangd Dlangl	方放
94	Fangx Ghangd Dlangl	方放	無	
95	Fangx Ghangd Dlangl	黃岡	Wub Khangd	烏狂
96	Wub Khangd	烏狂[60]	無	
97	Wub Khangd	武漢市	Jab Wid Dlangl	加宇
98	Jab Wid Dlangl	加宇	無	
99	Jab Wid Dlangl	嘉魚	Ongd Ful	潈湖
100	Ongd Ful	潈湖	無	
101	Ongd Ful	洪湖	Xox Yangf	小洋
102	無		無	
103	Xox Yangf Dlangl	岳陽市	Nangl Hsab Mongl	浪沙蒙
104	Nangl Hsab Mongl	浪沙蒙	無	

　　我在表九並置譯者譯為聖地，和沒被譯為聖地之地點，及其所描述的空間圖像。在六個聖地當中，有五個地方的空間地景與田或坪地相關。亦即，聖地是適合人居住，並可以耕耘。若比對苗文記音與譯文，聖地並非直接譯自古歌苗文記音。苗文記音的古歌，僅是將地名複誦一遍，但 Sangt Jingb 將此些再次出現的地名譯為聖地。在 Sangt Jingb 的譯者意識裡，將某地譯為聖地，似乎也呈現一種規律：凡地方具備適合居住

的條件，就譯爲聖地；若此地不宜居，就不會將之譯爲聖地。雖然也有部分例外，如表九的 Ongd Ful 與 Xox Yangf 未被譯者安上聖地之稱，但此兩地名在古歌中的表述，卻也涉及開田、糧熟、立屋、居住等，關乎人群進入文明之進程。不過整體觀之，從聖地圖像的討論中可以發現，不斷地判斷適合居住與否，在人群遷徙中，占有重要的位置。尤其愈接近遷徙的尾聲，從當地的空間圖像判斷宜居與否，就越顯重要。決定某地適合居住與否，除了上述提及的重要空間元素（如坪地、田地）以外，還有另一個與人有關的重要因素，那是母親與當地交涉的情緒與經驗。古歌中的某個地點即便擁有宜居的空間條件，當母親受委屈時，人群就會放棄此地，繼續遷徙。

另外還有三處未被稱爲聖地的地方。Jab Wid Dlangl（加宇、嘉魚）是山海之地。歌詞中對此地的描述，包括來往的船隻、棲息山梁，和不友善的落鰓鬍伯伯。[61] Laib Ongd Ful（來到滃湖、洪湖）則表現出宜居與否的重要性。一開始因爲地處兩濱之間不宜居，決定要早早離開，結果來了一個大伯父宣傳說滃湖有很多熟糧，最後說：「住滃湖好啦」。[62] Xox Yangf（小洋、岳陽市）則是一開始就被遷徙人群認定爲好地方。要居住下來，進行吹蘆笙、[63] 踩鼓和婚禮的儀式。[64] 亦即從譯文「聖地」出現的前後歌句內容來看，聖地幾乎和適合居住劃上等號，但卻又不是必然。因爲未被譯者納入爲聖地者，也可以是宜居之所在。

表九

	苗文地名	譯文地名	歌詞的空間與非人的多物種內涵
稱聖地	Ghab Zat Bil	嘎捯壁、廣濟市	懸崖、山野
	Vib Fangx Bil	依放坡、黃石市	坪地、開田、懸崖、濱、魚
	Eb Zek Dlangl	翁奏、鄂州市	棉、禾、田、稻、泥鰍、五穀熟、山坡、砍柴、（山）嶺
	Fangx Ghangd Dlangl	方放、黃岡	坪地、馬、住
	Wub Khangd	烏狂、武漢市	水、汪洋、河濱、水田、稻穀
	Nangl Hsab Mongl	浪沙蒙	居住
未稱聖地	Eb Jex Jil	九江口	無
	Ghangx Jib	廣雞	懸崖、樹林
	Jab Wid Dlangl	加字、嘉魚	船、山梁
	Ongd Ful	瀇湖、洪湖	兩濱、熟糧、住
	Xox Yangf	小洋、岳陽市	坪地、開田、起屋

　　文化的理解是件不易的事，尤其在作爲讀者的心理狀態裡，從手稿的第一種閱讀方式到第二種閱讀方式，似是一種墜入異質空間的感覺。比對記音與翻譯之間的斷裂，我們看見 Sangt Jingb 作爲譯者，活生生的從譯本裡竄出。使用文字的技術與操作，展現譯者的某種主體性。對此我們或可提問：是否在譯述過程中，Sangt Jingb 不安於記音行動裡，口語古歌某些字眼的單調與重覆？所以，將同一種苗文地名，變裝爲二種或三種化身。又是否對譯者而言，在漢字的書寫裡，無法壓抑從苗文的

口語記音到漢字的文字翻譯，化身為道德的過渡與時代的替換？所以將宜於人群停留的地點，在地名被直接音譯後，轉換成聖地或者武漢市。這翻譯的過程，以及譯者的狀態，我們實無法簡單地判讀與解釋。

　　總之在相對封閉之譯文體系裡的第一種閱讀，古歌手稿表達一種帶有土著觀點，近身距離的 Hmub 人古歌空間文化之再現。而經由記音與翻譯對照的第二種閱讀，讀者可由其中的斷裂與縫隙獲得某種釋放，並由此遇見譯者。本章最後將由 Sangt Jingb 對苗歌的觀點與知識，以及他所身處 Hmub 人古歌解釋權之競奪的地方場域，來探索譯者之職。

四、結論：歌師的譯者之職

　　如本章一開始所述，翻譯的問題早已存在於以文化比較與跨領域為學科本質的人類學研究與民族誌書寫。本章雖不直接討論民族誌研究者作為文化翻譯者的知識與方法論等問題，但卻涉及手稿與文化翻譯的實踐，並也牽涉翻譯者之本體的探問。華特・班雅明（Walter Benjamin 2004〔1923〕：75）曾以「沒有一首詩是為讀者而寫；沒有一幅圖是為觀者而畫；沒有一部交響樂是為聽者而做」，來比喻譯本、原文，以及譯者三者之間的微妙關聯。[65] 他認為譯本與原文之間是一種永遠無法到達的關係（It is plausible that no translation, however good it may be, can have any significance as regard the original.）（ibid.：76）。[66] 他也採用一種擬宗教經驗的比喻，說明譯本、原文的關係。雖然就可譯性（translatability）而言，原文是可以和翻譯貼近，不過他以「下一生」的比喻，則指出了譯本與原著之間的神秘關聯，是由歷史決定，而非作品的本質。以下為其觀點的英文引述：

> The important works of world literature never find their chosen
> translators at the time of their origin; their translation marks their
> stage of continued life... （And for this reason）... the range of
> life must be determined by history rather than by nature. （ibid.）

　　從民族誌角度探索 Sangt Jingb 作爲譯者，以及他的手稿材料多年後，
班雅明對於譯者天職的討論，使我們不僅在文本語言材料的分析，看到
譯者的操作空間，並也得以在譯者本性的概念層次，來重新整理與思索
我與 Sangt Jingb 的認識與交往，以及接觸與研究他的古歌手稿以來的內
在衝擊。我在研究過程中常混淆於 Sangt Jingb 是個平常而規範的古歌記
音與翻譯者，或是一個近乎顛狂與執著的天才？以班雅明自己也是譯者
的身分與經驗，他對於翻譯與譯者的看法，使我們能選擇並意識到從文
化理解的歷程來面對 Sangt Jingb 與古歌手稿。當譯者同時也是創作者時，
他所要做的，雖然是從一個文本（原著）轉變到另一個文本（譯本），
但如果引用班雅明的想法，則 Sangt Jingb 不一定有所本，也不一定爲讀
者而寫。

　　再者 Sangt Jingb 的生命史經驗與其「古歌書寫計畫」（the
Project），也以另類路徑，呼應班雅明以歷史來解釋譯者、譯本與原著
之間的神秘關聯。Sangt Jingb 個人的生命史，有其所生處之時代的複雜
性。他的成長，歷經 1960 年代的大躍進與文化大革命，中國國家大步經
濟改革的 80、90 年代，直至上一個世紀的結束，以及新世紀的開始。苗

歌的學與唱，苗文的習與寫，十二部古歌的記音與漢字譯述，以及對於出版這批古歌手稿的渴望。這些共同構成 Sangt Jingb 與其記誦口語材料以及文字書寫行動的生命史。換言之，譯者與文本的關係不僅關乎譯者的美學風格與哲學處境，更是源於歷史之偶遇：個人的微型生命史與其所生處及糾結的時代、國家、地方、族群，與歷史處境。

（一）「意義」與「道理」

究竟 Sangt Jingb 是怎樣的一個譯者？他的譯者之職，以及記音與翻譯之間的斷裂與隙縫，和 Sangt Jingb 對於古歌的知識是否有所關聯？這首先涉及的就是 Sangt Jingb 對於古歌知識的觀點，並也捲入口語及文字之間的糾葛，乃至競奪。本章前面以歌師的書寫為軸，述及 Sangt Jingb 生命史的小節已觸及此。為何要寫古歌？記音與翻譯的工作背後，實則是一種對於意義與道理的追尋。在肯認古歌為口頭表演與為儀式所用的背後，Sangt Jingb 在意古歌的完整性，並且堅持需安置在可以合理的理解之上。換言之，對於 Sangt Jingb 而言，記音與翻譯古歌這整件工作，就是一個探問口語文化，以及將其意義化的過程。

然而，Sangt Jingb 對於古歌意義的執著，除了依靠書寫文字，還有非文字的手繪草圖。1999 年與 2000 年之交的冬季，我向 Sangt Jingb 學古歌《跋山涉水》，我們師徒之間的訊息傳遞，以及我以學徒之身（apprenticeship）[67] 在田野裡的學習，除了憑藉語言的譯註，還依賴他近兩千幅大小不一的即興插畫繪圖來解釋近兩千句歌。使我除了藉由聆聽歌師的唱與說來瞭解這部古歌，還能通過他的手繪草圖，來學習與紀錄古歌所再現的時、空與人、事、物的情境。歌師的每一小幅隨手創作的插畫，都在解釋特定一行歌句的意義，並由此逐步堆疊出對於更大篇

幅古歌的理解，與意義的再現。本章挑選三幅 Sangt Jingb 手繪的草圖，
藉以表達歌師對古歌的觀點與解釋。圖二爲遷徙的人群在中途的一個坪
壩上，敲鼓、踩舞，進行吃鼓藏（*nenk jet niuf*）祭祖儀式，此圖下方有
龐大的人群集結；圖三爲歌師對於古歌中所提及的一對 Hmub 人男女始

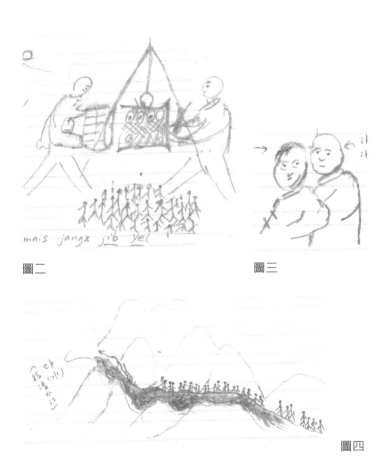

圖二　　　　　　　　　　　　　　　圖三

圖四

祖 （「爸爸與媽媽」）的解釋；圖四為歌師對於古歌中所提及的人群沿山而行的觀點，此圖以遠距離視點進行繪製。

　　Sangt Jingb 對古歌意義的找尋，不僅止於端坐案頭桌前的紙筆書寫與繪圖，還依靠身體的移動與感官經驗。他旅行，以及觀察旅程中所見之天與地。1999 年底我跟隨他學古歌時，他曾對我提到，「昆明的冬天溫暖。我坐火車從貴州一路到昆明。沿途，我一路看著車窗外的風景，那山綿延而去。我一路就思考古歌裡的內容。其實我外出乞討是個幌子。我到處走，到處看，思索古歌裡為什麼要這麼唱，才是我旅行遠方的目的」。2007 年初的寒冬，我和 Sangt Jingb 在台江縣城一家小館子，蹲坐在矮桌前吃火鍋。他對我提到了二次他對一個自然現象的觀察，讓他明白古歌裡的道理。他說：「平常我們白天見到太陽，晚上見到月亮。有一次的清晨（我聽不清楚 Sangt Jingb 說的是在什麼地方，彷彿是一個高山上），看到東邊有太陽，西邊有月亮，下面有一男一女，一對人。有太陽，有月亮，有男女一對。這世界就成了。啊，原來古歌就是在說這個。」此時此刻，此情此景，對我而言，Sangt Jingb 有如一位思索與言說天地根本道理的哲學家。

（二）從記音到翻譯：覓得「解釋」空間

　　相對於高坡地區，由台江往下游至凱里，清水江所流經的這片水域，是苗族古歌的傳唱更為普遍的地區（參圖一）。在這個苗歌傳唱的區域，Sangt Jingb 並不是唯一一位能識字與書寫的歌師。根據 2007 年我在台江的民族誌田野訪談，有的歌師是退休校長，有的曾擔任村裡文書或醫師。有別於 Sangt Jingb，這群同樣有文字閱讀與書寫能力的 Humb 人歌師們，並不以書寫來面對古歌。除了歌師以外，在此古歌傳唱相對普遍的地區，還有另一類古歌專家：古歌蒐集者，或如當地所稱，古歌愛好者。他們共同的特點是都經過短期培訓或自學，學會黔東苗文。他們也會將古歌與書寫連在一起的專家。如，台江地方耆老吳通發在 1978 至 1981 年左右，就和唐春芳[68]一起大量收集古歌，並以苗文記錄。一位住平水寨的小學教師張玉明，在 1980 年代，以苗文記錄並翻譯苗族古歌《開天闢地》。家鄉在黃平，1950 年代起在台江任公職直至退休的潘家齊，也以業餘時間接觸古歌與多種類型的苗歌。他所蒐集的古歌材料，包括已出版的《黃平古歌》。

Sangt Jingb 介於歌師與古歌蒐集者之間。他書寫苗歌，他也是村寨 Humb 人在有生命儀禮與歲時祭儀，姻親送往迎來的場合，會被找去唱古歌的儀式專家。但因為他常在外地旅行、流浪，應該不是村寨最多人找的歌師。Sangt Jingb 自 1968 年起至 2002 年，投入大量時間書寫苗歌。雖然同樣是動用苗文書寫，吳通發做了大量蒐集，並已做好苗文記錄，但大多未翻譯。張玉明完成了一部古歌《開天闢地》（以其堂叔歌師所唱為本），翻譯好，並在 1980 年代出版後，就未再持續。Sangt Jingb 也動用到苗文書寫，也做翻譯。但最大的差別是他持續書寫，以及不斷自問，為什麼會有這樣的古歌內容？為什麼有這些古歌？每一部古歌內的短歌與短歌之間的關係，是如何構成一部歌為何而唱的結構？十二部古歌之間存在何種關係？這些問題都是 Sangt Jingb 在思考的。並且他試著面對這些問題，提出解釋。問為什麼，是 Sangt Jingb 認為重要的。他對我說了多次，「像高坡那裡的人，會吃鼓藏（祭祖儀式）。但是你問他們為何吃鼓藏，他們是不知道。」

對於 Sangt Jingb，口語與書寫之間是一處角力之所在。同樣的，他也評論一般的歌師：「只知道別人唱什麼，然後接著對。一句接一句。

但是爲何唱古歌，古歌爲啥這麼唱，歌師並不瞭解。」換言之，即使同樣擁有苗文與漢字的書寫能力，Sangt Jingb 和台江地區其他會書寫的歌師，或古歌愛好者與蒐集者不同的是——他在作解釋。而 Sangt Jingb 好作解釋的行爲，也是地方上其他歌師，或省城的古歌整理者、苗歌學者（如，今旦、燕寶）最反對之處。他們認爲苗族古歌是集體的，不應添加個人的觀點。而且應具有古代的風格，不應加入現代元素（如汽車、槍砲等之類）。苗族古歌作爲口述文學的特性，即使引入書寫體系，也還是應著重在傳述或敘述，而不能是任意對它作解釋。但 Sangt Jingb 則從書寫（由記音到翻譯），乃至一部古歌之短歌的前後或結構的調整，覓得解釋苗歌的主體性與操作權。他曾說：「歌師們唱歌就是一行一行的唱。聽到對方唱什麼，就會找一行來答。有人就會在那裡繞來繞去，翻來覆去，比較囉嗦。我在和人對歌，就比較精簡，我選擇重要的來唱，很快就上去了。[69]別人也知道，我所唱的是（歌與歌之間的）關係。」對 Sangt Jingb 而言，靠口耳相傳的歌師們，是無法知道一部古歌裡的結構，以及古歌與古歌之間的關聯。他認爲古歌裡的結構，只有被寫下來，才有可能被理解。而瞭解古歌裡的結構，對於 Sangt Jingb 是最重要的，因爲那才可能理解古歌究竟要表達什麼？古歌才有可能被瞭解。歸納與總結是 Sangt Jingb 在提及古歌時，多次用到的語彙。這樣的語彙，我也在聽台江文人張少華談論高坡 Hmub 人唱古歌時提到：「高坡那邊是也可以唱，但他們就是唱個幾句。不像我們那裡（革一、台盤、凱棠、黃平），唱的那麼多，多達上千行。並且也沒有像我們那裡，還會有個總結」。而 Sangt Jingb 透過書寫來面對古歌，則將歸納與總結，運用得更爲有力。他提到《開天闢地》是第一部古歌，他整理過三次才成。這也是他所整理的古歌中，行數、頁數最多的一部。他說，《開天闢地》寫成了，後面的就好寫了。等到《仰阿莎》、《跋山涉水》等寫成，其他就好多了。能一路展開，作爲一個整體來歸納。

　　而在書寫苗歌的過程中，Sangt Jingb 所獲取的操作性不只一個層次。在本章的前面，我以較微觀的方式展現這部古歌裡的部份材料細節，表達出 Sangt Jingb 在記音與翻譯之間，如何加工與動手腳（如音譯與意譯的混成），使得同一個苗文記音的地點，化身爲多種跨越不同時代的漢字翻譯版本。對於台江地區的苗歌愛好者，這樣的作法或可謂挑釁，因爲它破壞了苗歌的古味。在這部聚焦在空間與移動的《跋山涉水》古歌，Sangt Jingb 似乎容許不同時間的錯置雜陳，但卻以另一種辦法追求空間的一致。在時間上，我們看到了過去與現代的並陳。比如，在本章所引述的苗族古歌原文中多次提到，在遷徙的過程中，所到地方的居民一旦對媽媽（遷徙人群的女性首領）不禮貌或者欺負了她，整個人群都會在媽媽的帶領下，繼續跋山涉水尋找下一個理想中的樂土。再如，引文中也多次提到遷徙人群是直接用手去抓魚，而沒有提到使用網、釣鉤、須籠等等更爲有效的工具，以至於碰上很大的魚就束手無策。又如，遷徙所經之處，遇到的當地人首領，都被賦予了動物的名稱，如蜈蚣伯伯、鵂鶹大伯等等。這些內容在歌師 Sangt Jingb 現實生活的時空場域，有的已經過時，有的甚至在記憶中都淡忘了，然而這樣的內容卻呈現了苗族古歌在時間上的古老。而與此並置的，則是當代對長江大河的知識，或將武漢、鄂州、岳陽、九江等在不同時期建立的現代地名貼入譯文的文本中。古今的時間錯置，清楚展現。但在空間上，他則從近代的地理學知識界定的地圖集，來辨認古歌裡的地點；也從他所生長的故鄉，或遠行所觀察的地形、地景來理解古歌。歌師還曾依古歌的情節，在雷公山脈的深山裡覓得古歌所說鬼的居所。他非常仔細的對我描述那整個探訪與發現的經過。總之，相對於在翻譯過程中所展現對時間的包容，但在對於這部古歌的空間探索，Sangt Jingb 卻以一種現代的知識觀，以地圖、旅行、觀察，追求對於古歌所唱的空間與地景的理解及合理的解釋。

（三）結語

面對苗族古歌的記音與翻譯，及其文化上的理解，是項複雜的工程。我在 1990 年代末期在中國大陸所做的田野調查，報導人 Sangt Jingb 不僅與當代的苗族精英有過頻繁的接觸與交流，對所謂的漢族地區也有所瞭解，而且已具備很強的能力，能夠根據時代的變遷和 Hmub 人的情緒與情感的表達形式，對傳統的苗族古歌進行修改、潤色，甚至是附會。這對我們想要揭示苗族古歌原有面貌的研究企圖，構成相當嚴峻的挑戰。本章注意到這樣的挑戰，而且將此挑戰的具體內容予以揭示。苗族古歌的某些本初內容，反映的是對幸福追求的意願，不能理解為苗族的真實歷史。這對引導下一步的類似研究具有其意義。再則，本章所呈現的民族誌材料在收集範圍上，並非在單一的社區，也不僅依賴主要田野報導人，而是與研究過古歌的其他苗族精英保持密切聯繫和交流，以此為基礎，來闡述與討論歌師 Sangt Jingb 在苗族社區的社會背景和地位，以及揭示其他苗族研究者對他的認識與評價。這樣一些關鍵內容是重要的，因為黔東南苗族社會的當代巨變是二十世紀中期興起的社會事實，苗族研究者和非苗族研究者圍繞古歌內容爭議的表面化，就實質性的深入為時甚短。本研究在於及時把握民族誌田野調查背景的變化，從生命史的形式，對 Sangt Jingb 的生平進行有選擇、有層次的說明，並融入我在這複雜的人際交往互動中，親身的感受和理解。最後也是本章的核心關懷，即對古歌語言與人為之意向及其操作之間的複雜性進行分析、呈現與探討。雖然報導人的有意識建構，在人類學者的書寫及相關的田野研究方法早已做出提醒，本章以民族誌的材料，具體呈現在一個當代田野調查的實際經驗與過程。

　　其次本章也關切古歌所處的時空場域與 Sangt Jingb 所處的時空場域存在著鮮明的反差。除了闡述苗族古歌在傳統社會的運行及其與社群之維繫的價值，我也就 Sangt Jingb 所做出的人為建構和解讀的意圖，並以時空場域的差異，來討論苗族古歌經由口說與文字書寫系統之介入的記音與翻譯，所產生的古歌再現與創作及生產過程的差異化與複雜化。換言之，隨著社會的快速發展，族際交往的日趨密切和深入，苗族古歌的文學性與社會性也會引發不容忽視的變遷，對於時空場域之差異與苗族古歌社會功能之關聯性的認定，勢必會成為探討苗族古歌所面對的一項重大挑戰。

　　惟，即使僅就歌師 Sangt Jingb 的生命史及其記音與翻譯的一部古歌手稿所做的建構作為討論的基礎，我們所做的討論與解釋，也僅涉及其中很有限的部分，實際上還有諸多值得持續開展與討論。其一，從這部苗族古歌裡的地名、地景、人、物所表現的空間與時間的錯置，可以發現苗族古歌裡包含著複雜的混入與建構的過程。歌師 Sangt Jingb 並非特例。亦即，即使在口傳文體的本身，其混入與建構也有一個很長的歷史。這點也相對突顯本文所討論的，當記音與翻譯的文字書寫加入，使得古歌的再現與文化理解，變得更為複雜，也有著更大的解釋空間。就以本章前面所引述的「小米斗五錢，分金一匹馬」兩句（短歌第 3 首／第 18-19 行，見表二）為例，其意是指在集市上用貨幣購買物品的價格。這樣的內容顯然是來自中央王朝的影響。文中的「五錢」是指五個銅錢，五個銅錢能夠買到一斗糧食，物品價格的低廉可想而知，而這樣的情況恰好是中央王朝首次直接接觸苗族地區時才出現的現象。主要是用銅錢作為貨幣單位，這在宋代表現得尤為突出。因而從這一計價方式就可以判斷於此相關的內容，反映的可能是宋代時的苗漢關係。下一句「分金一匹馬」，則是以金屬塊作貨幣單位，以銀塊作貨幣用，盛行於明代後期。古歌中這兩句雖然寫在一起，但是其進入苗族古歌的時代，可能是有差異。換言之，交叉對照文書典籍，或可揭示相關內容混入苗族古歌的時代和背景。這是因為自宋代以來，朝廷對苗族地區的經營，甚至是間接的影響，都會滲入傳承下來的苗族古歌之中。不管是有意，還是無意，都會將中央王朝等外來傳入的內容，增補進流傳下來的苗族古歌之中，並傳承到今天。其次，在此部苗族古歌所提到的多種地名，僅就古歌對各地所提供的地理、環境等描述，其實可以將遷徙所過之處分為兩大地理單元，一類是處在山區，也就是當代苗族生活的地區，另外一類則是千里之外的長江中游平原。對於後者在苗族古歌所產生的時代是不可能接觸到的。歷史上苗族要獲得這種類似知識的渠道，主要來自屯軍或漢族移民，而且古歌中所描述遷徙的先後順序，剛好與宋代以來沿長江進入洞庭湖所設置的水驛吻合。這足以證明這部分內容連同相關的地理訊息，是通過漢族屯軍傳到苗族地區，並混入古歌。換言之，其實民間口頭文本從來沒有停止過潤色加工，只不過歌師 Sangt Jingb 所做的建構規模更大、範圍更廣，改動地更多些。

相對於從解構的角度來討論歌師對古歌的記音與翻譯與其中的建構，最後我們其實不能忽視的是，在現實的語言面向，作為一個苗文的記音與翻譯者，有其所面對的局限與困境，而這並非其主觀的意識所導致。其一是苗歌為五言的詩韻結構，歌師的翻譯，有不少處是為配合此詩韻結構與字數的限制，而導致譯文違反中文慣用的語詞順序，而呈現難以理解的局限或困境（如短歌第 3 首的兩句，「手指大稻管，田萍大碗飯」）。另一個兩難則與歌師所使用的黔東方言苗文記音系統（王輔世 1985：145-158；張永祥 1990）的建立過程有關。建立黔東方言的苗文聲韻調系統的語言材料其實是一種選擇的結果。那是在 1950 年代由中國科學院少數民族語言調查第二工作隊，在貴州省凱里市掛丁鄉養蒿寨所蒐集的。他們以此地的語音材料，作為苗語黔東南方言北部土語的代表（王輔世 1985：107；李雲兵 2003）。凱里與台江雖然都屬於北部土語支，但地方語音及詞彙，必然仍有小範圍的區域差異。嚴格說來，歌師所面對的記音工作，除了記音與翻譯的問題，還存在著黔東方言的苗文聲韻調系統，作為一個經過挑選與抽象化的記音系統，其中必然存在再現的問題與困難。換言之，苗文記音系統經挑選與抽象化的建構本質，使得地方語音與苗文之間，非一對一的結構關係所造成歌師 Sangt Jingb 與其他精通苗文的地方知識分子，在面對記音與翻譯的差異與困難，也就可以獲得理解。

Anonymous Voices and Authorship Politics
in Printed Genealogies in Eastern Guizhou

Chapter 7　貴州東部漢字家譜裡的文化政治：
　　　　　　無名之聲與作者權威

一、在黔東南 Hmub 人村寨遇到漢字家譜

　　2003 年，我在貴州東部清水江邊，施洞附近的方寨，進行田野調查。此 Hmub 人集居的村寨，所在的清水江河域，自清代以來，一直被視爲重要的港口，稱爲施洞口，在清朝時以汛著稱。光緒四年（1878），此地建立了渡輪。清水江是通往湖南，進入長江水域的主要水路。由鎮遠到台拱 （台江縣城） 的道路，則是主要的貿易通道。乾隆三年（1738）初期，沿著河壩，在這裡建立了一個有固定趕場天的常態性大市集，吸引許多來自外省的商人。咸豐和同治時期，徐家乾於苗民起義期間，出任湘軍將領蘇元春部書記，隨軍進入湘、黔兩省，並曾駐紮於施洞。徐家乾在光緒四年，所完成的《苗疆聞見錄》，描述施洞口，在當時已是人口繁密、熱鬧的苗疆會市：

> 在鎮遠府南六十里，台拱轄境。後倚高山，前臨清水江，中饒平衍，周數里。八梗峙其西，偏寨附其東，沙灣、岩腳、巴團、平地營蔽其前，九股河依其後，向為苗疆一大市會，人煙繁雜，設黃施衛千總駐之。

（〔清〕徐家乾 1997：75）

2003 年夏天，方寨共有 193 戶人家，是當地最大的一個村寨。除了少數於 1960 年代，移居到方寨村的張姓和吳姓家族外，大多數的村民姓劉。村民在大部分的情況下，使用苗語黔東方言（Hmub）交談。在某次的田野工作，方寨的老支書，引領我到另一位寨老家裡。他們小心翼翼取出了一只木箱，裡面裝著一部 1985 年印刷的漢字族譜（共有五卷）。族譜詳細記載著序言、祖先傳記，和宗支圖譜等，讓人留下深刻的印象。2004-2005 年，我爲了進一步探索這部 Hmub 人所編撰、流通的漢字家譜，返回施洞方寨村，進行民族誌田野研究。接著再由施洞往東行至天柱，進行田野調查。侗族（Kam）村寨的年長頭人，親切地讓我閱讀 1985 年版《劉氏族譜》的舊版（當地人稱它爲老譜）。此一舊版，印製於清光緒三十四年（1908）。

　　這部新舊版本的漢字族譜，是由劉氏家族的兩個不同支系 —— 台江的苗族（Hmub）和天柱的侗族（Kam）—— 共同進行編修和流通。在2004-2005 年田野期間，由台江到天柱，若走公路，須乘坐一整天的客運巴士才到達。而且 Hmub 人與 Kam 人，在語言、族群和文化實踐方面，也存在很大的差異。

　　爲瞭解這個跨族群合譜的現象，我們必須回顧歷史。晚清時期所編修的族譜，與 1980 年代，新版族譜編修的歷史背景，有所不同。明清時期，中央王朝勢力向西南地區擴張，將貴州東部地區，納入帝國的管轄範圍內。1949 年後，中共政府成立了少數民族的行政機構，並推動民族識別運動，以及由官方所制定的苗族和侗族的少數民族羅馬拼音文字的書寫系統。帝國時期地方社會的文本策略，及其對族譜書寫文化的影響，與現代中國國家體制下，有所不同。在帝國時期非漢人群的分類架構下，

Hmub 人與 Kam 人都被歸類為「苗族」。但在 1949 年後所建立的民族分類架構下，兩者屬於兩個不同的少數民族。宗譜是存在於亞洲一種歷史悠久，且使用廣泛的書寫文類，尤其是在過去使用漢字進行書面溝通的國家中。這種書寫文類的特徵和限制，使其產生極強的規範力（Taga Akigorô 1982）。中國南方，非漢貴族家族的族譜彙編，與土司制度的歷史有關。彙編族譜並提交給朝廷，成為明代土司繼任的必要條件。族譜很「自然地」以漢文撰寫（必須如此），並且需要作為土司家族正統繼承人的證明。當時人們遵守中國家族法的壓力越來越大。除了土司家族外，其他的貴族氏族也認為，編修漢式戶籍，宣稱自己具有漢人血統是適當的。這種過程普遍存在於貴州及其他地區。貴州有許多 Hmub 人與 Kam 人，聲稱自己的漢族祖先來自江西（Herman 2007）。

在這種背景下，族譜不必然是這些社會再現其本質或特性（當然並不是整個社會）的知識指標（knowledge index）。另外，根據彭軻（Frank Pieke 2003：120）所說，族譜也不必然代表「一種特殊的心態，標誌其與現代中國的緊密聯繫」。對於土司家族而言，族譜與這種心態無關。這是官僚主義的要求。對於其他人來說，族譜則充當一種保護形式。

基於上述的文獻回顧，以及不同學者之間的辯論，本章企圖瞭解位於邊陲的地方社會，如何因應書寫族譜強大的規範力，同時以論述分析法（discursive approach），來探討族譜在中國邊陲地區的意涵。

首先，我將探討在貴州東部 Hmub 人與 Kam 人的語言社群中，地方菁英如何透過書寫和編修族譜的行為，展現自己擁有的文本權威。其次，根據文本和社會之間的關係，考察《劉氏族譜》新舊兩版的作者身分。再來，在彙編族譜足以創造社會動力或社會關係的前提下，描述族譜的

記錄過程，和不同版本之間的關係。最後，以貴州東部 Hmub 人與 Kam
人的合譜，關注跨族群的差異，和血緣關係或族譜關係之間，相互發明
與構成的過程。

　　我從 1997 年以來，開始在台江山區的 Fangf Bil 村寨從事民族誌田
野研究後，對於 Hmub 人社會網絡的常態結構及其維繫方式，有了深刻
的認識。二十一世紀初，Fangf Bil 村寨，由三百三十多個家戶組成，人
口將近一千五百人，共有 11 個小寨（vangf）。小寨的名稱，都與周遭
地理特徵有關。在 Fangf Bil 村寨的 11 個小寨中，共有 5 個父系通婚群
體，群內禁止通婚。這些通婚群體村寨內婚的比例，遠遠超過村寨外婚。
根據我在山區村寨所進行的家戶系譜關係之普查與紀錄，婦女很明顯有
兩個通婚方向。Fangf Bil 的親屬分類，因此形成一個近乎於二元結構的
事物。這也清楚說明，早期 Hmub 人的社會網絡，或多或少是有限的。
本章關注跨越地區、村寨與族群的合譜，如何產生？過程為何？如何制
定編修標準？是否為相關參與者的共同協議？而從 Hmub 人與 Kam 人的
角度來看，族譜編修與其族群身分之間的認同關係又是什麼？

二、族譜作為一種文化行動

　　自 1949 年，中華人民共和國建國以來，經書、古籍等文本和族譜，
都被視為封建時代的象徵，那是一個印刷品，只在社會各階層菁英之間
流通的時代。文化大革命（1966–1976）期間，大批的族譜被燒毀──這
些行動在中國自 1980 年代開始，快速的文化轉型和經濟發展之後，便消
失匿跡。隨著文化和宗教的復振（透過傳統的家族和社區儀式，以及逐
漸再現的宗教活動），Hmub 人與 Kam 人的地方菁英，恢復了書寫漢字

族譜的地方習俗，用以宣稱過往與所謂「漢族老大哥」的親屬關係。台江方寨和天柱藍田的地方菁英（研究進行的當年，大多為六、七十歲長者）聲稱，許多代人之前，他們從一位當地人都熟悉的漢族祖先那裡，繼承了劉姓。這樣的信念反映在族譜書寫中。這些地方菁英還認為，他們所共享的漢族祖源，是族群兄弟情誼的歷史證明。

一個人的識字能力，是決定他能否參與族譜編修的標準之一。另一個重要標準是資歷。這群地方菁英出生於 1920 至 1940 年之間，同時接受過傳統和現代的漢語教育。劉永亨（1924 年出生），住在方寨的 Hmub 人，是一個在儒家思想主導的時代長大，並於隨後幾十年間，透過適應不同政權的官方思想，得以倖存的典型例子。劉永亨所經歷的教育過程，是老一輩地方菁英的代表。他們當中還有人接受過高等教育。劉耀畢（1940 年出生）在 1963 年自高中畢業後，便進入政府幹部的培訓機構，貴陽市第一公立學院。除了閱讀四書五經，並學習數學、語文、地理等科目外，學寫漢字，也是他們受教經驗的一部分。在這些地方菁英中，有些人比其他人擁有更豐富的漢字書寫經驗。來自天柱的 Kam 菁英劉開軒（1926 年出生），花了一整年的時間，每天進行個人新版《劉氏族譜》的起草工作。在田野工作期間，我親眼目睹，他在家中勤於著述與手繪的巨幅宗族系譜圖。劉開軒在以漢字手寫族譜的勤奮程度，幫助我們瞭解，漢與非漢文字文明與族群界線之間，極為複雜的互動關係。

（一）族譜的編修

以下摘自與修訂族譜有關的序文，說明這群地方菁英如何看待他們的任務。這是由 Kam 的地方菁英，南沖光魁所撰寫的編後語。

這次續修族譜，是聯宗收族，清理世系的盛舉。幸而一創而百和，使得定於本年（1985）六月二十九日在南沖召開修譜籌備會議。會後派人分赴各縣登門聯繫，蒐集材料，籌集資金（可能包括要求捐款）。蒙我熊公各地孝子賢孫，熱忱贊助，積極獻料獻金。不到兩月各地材料，陸續送齊，修譜資金也陸續送到。於農曆九月十一日，我族有文化之士（有識字能力的人），聚集一堂，開始辦公進行初步草稿匯總。經四十天之努力，即進行撰寫樣本。這項工作是很細緻的，很艱鉅的工作。承光禹、光德、光榮、宗淵、光松、榮金、宗來、榮顯、榮桂等。為了上慰先靈，下啓後坤，不辭辛勞，積極苦幹。時經二月，已將樣本順利完成，得以付印。茲刊印族譜貳佰壹拾貳部。隆工告竣，皆是我熊公後裔付出的心血。譜乃家乘至寶，領譜者小心珍藏，不得污損，以免褻瀆祖宗之名諱，貽誤後世之查尋。不得將族譜隨便給同族不同宗者翻閱，以免魚目混珠。更不得將族譜與異姓者翻閱，以免洩漏我族之歷史根源。如是，不惟我個人之願望，亦是我全族之願望。特提數語，與全族共勉。

南沖光魁撰。

（《劉氏族譜》1985：115）

　　除了提到需要細心保護族譜，以獲得祖先的庇佑外，序文裡的另一個重點是，記錄的行爲本身，與文字陳述價值之間的關係。這些 Hmub 人和 Kam 人菁英的自傳敘事，進一步確認教育經歷，是其勝任此項任務的主因。族群界線也透過編修的過程，被打破和重立，藉此促進了族群認同的流動性。

　　遠祖的記錄來源，根據的是分散的族譜。與修訂序中提到的文化人相似，有文化素養的菁英人士，是編輯族譜的關鍵。1981 年退休的劉永亨，是 1985 年版《劉氏族譜》的編輯之一。他花了兩個月的時間，逐戶收集有關遠祖的資料。據他所說，參與族譜編修的人，是根據他們在村民中的社會地位來遴選的。關鍵在於「能寫能唱，這樣才去。那時家裡沒有時間的那些人，都抽不出時間去」。

2003 至 2004 年，我前往貴州進行這項研究之前，老前輩劉光德已經過世了幾年。在田野期間，所拜訪的老人家，無不對劉光德表達敬意和欽佩。人們不斷提到，他受過良好教育，擁有豐富的地方知識。在編修族譜的安排與規畫，發揮重要的作用。事實上，當時所有的族譜內容，都必須經過劉光德的修改，才會出版。他在中文編輯上的地位，與其教育和文化背景有關。據說劉光德本人不通曉 Hmub 語或 Kam 語。在與人溝通時，只說普通話。

由上述的修訂說明中，可以看出，識字是編修族譜必要的能力。劉光德的經歷說明了，識字能力對於地方菁英的重要性。但是，這位編修 Hmub 人與 Kam 人合譜的關鍵人物，卻不說，也可能不理解 Hmub 語或 Kam 語。這表示，所謂受過良好教育的人，主要是會讀寫漢語文字的人。以劉光德為例，如何在記錄 Hmub 人或 Kam 人祖先的內容時，確認其族群的歸屬呢？

修族譜的另一個關鍵是經費。金錢在決定誰能被寫入族譜的過程，發揮了關鍵作用。每家戶根據其記錄在族譜中的人數來繳費（當年每人五元人民幣）。這些費用會作為編修族譜的經費。據聞台江地區黃袍村寨的幾個家戶沒有給錢，編輯們因此將其排除在外，無法列入修訂的族譜內。如果他們想在事後被包括在內，需要取得所有族人的同意。換句話說，那些被遴選來編修族譜的地方菁英，掌握排除未繳費成員參與的權力。以此看來，繼嗣成員的資格，是由金錢和編輯所決定的，而不僅在於擁有父系的親緣聯繫。

（二）族譜的流通

根據報導人的說法，族譜的編修規則和流通情況，決定了它的力量。對於劉姓家族成員來說，每年的曬譜習俗，確保族譜的流通性。老譜（舊版的族譜）被保存在方寨裡，並在每年農曆的六月六日展出。每位劉氏家族成員都會來參加。他們收集捐款，在那天共享一場盛宴。男女都可以參加。這項活動一直持續到五十年前，解放前後才停止。現在，族譜只能在清明節期間展示。族譜有一部永久保存在方寨裡，另一部則在施洞附近的村寨間流通。

與方寨不同，天柱縣至今仍每年都進行一次曬譜的儀式，而且參加的人數很多。劉光松回憶說，在最近一次的曬譜活動，老村長被邀請根據編修好的族譜，來述說劉氏家族的祖源和發展，這是結合識字能力和資歷的一個有力證明。

曬譜習俗的目的，在於提供家族一個機會，以儀式性的方式，對族譜進行公開的傳閱。族譜的流通也賦予或確認了與文本相關的權威——這種現象在施洞很明顯，但在藍田卻不明顯。劉永岳從曾祖父那裡，繼承到這個職位，現在擔任施洞地區流傳之《劉氏族譜》的保管人。族譜保管人的遴選，根據的是一個人在家族中的地位、教育背景和威望。因爲他是整個家族需要對族譜負責的代表。其他姓氏的家族成員，不允許查看此部族譜。相對於方寨 Hmub 人在族譜保存和流通上，採取威權和嚴肅的態度，天柱的 Kam 人菁英對於族譜的流通，則採取靈活且相對寬鬆的態度。中國國家周邊族群在識字水準上的落差，或許是產生這種態度差異的原因。透過比較這兩種展現族譜的方法，可以發現，發行和流通的印刷量，會影響族譜的價值，及其所產生的權威程度。

（三）「發明」的血緣關係：排他性和包容性

羅伯特·帕金（Robert Parkin）在其《親屬關係》（*Kinship*）一書中，提及在使用「繼嗣」（descent）一詞上，所碰到的困難：

> 作為一個專業的學術概念，繼嗣在過去肯定受到一定程度的修正，以致於人類學家有時會在田野中想像它，而不是發現它。這並不表示這個概念沒有用，因為仍然有許多社會對它予以重視。
>
> （Parkin 1997：26）

我也從黔東南 Hmub 人與 Kam 人對繼嗣觀念的理解，來進行《劉氏族譜》的分析。生物學家可能會將繼嗣和血緣關係，視為一種持續不斷且無法被破壞的關係；親屬研究者則會根據特定與有限的條件，來看待社會和繼嗣。關於繼嗣成員的身分，帕金認為「收編」（recruitment）是一個主要的原則。同時具有排他性和包容性的敘事，藉由文本的力量或權威，形成一種特殊的社會關係——血親。《劉氏族譜》在書寫上最顯著的特徵，是排他性。儘管彭軻認為，現代中國族譜的新形式，為界定族群內的同質性和多樣性，提供了靈活的界線（Pieke 2003：120），但在大多數的族譜書寫中，排他性仍然是很普遍的特徵。這個特徵尤其表現在族譜編輯和曬譜活動的參與。正如劉光松所述：「不同姓氏的家族，分開曬譜。同姓的，即使不同譜，也可以在一起（參加曬譜儀式活動），但是要通過邀請。」這解釋了文前關於族譜修訂序,所表述的修譜動機。

相比之下,使用中文書寫的族譜,透過共同作者的形式所展現的**包容性**(*inclusiveness*),使得本地 Hmub 人、Kam 人、漢人之間多民族的身分和界線,變得模糊。其中一個明顯的例子是,採用兄弟情誼的隱喻。以下是有關劉氏家族跨族群紐帶的兩個範例說明:

> 譬如我們兩個原來都是弟兄的。其中一人已經受難,跑到某個地方去避難。他到那邊當家、生了小孩,到了有 Hmub 人的地方,就學 Hmub 語。噢,(但)我那個弟兄,還是弟兄啊。
>
> (台江縣劉永岳)

> (天柱)南沖是有兩個劉氏家族居住的村寨。他們來自於 Kam 的氏族。那裡說著 Kam 話及漢話。在重新編修族譜的過程中,使用的都是漢話。族譜屬於所有劉氏家族的成員。有些人會說漢話,有些人會說 Kam 話,都沒關係。所有人都是親兄弟。對每個人來說,族群問題不重要。
>
> (台江縣劉永亨)

當地許多人對語言多樣性所抱持的看法,創造出一種多元的族群根源,和模糊族群界線的感受。這部《劉氏族譜》的記載,有時也呼應著,我與報導人交談時,所體會到一種族群界線的模糊感。在族譜裡,有些部分的書寫,展現漢人文化作為一種中心的他者態勢,有些部分則將周邊人群的劉姓,推向與漢人/漢族擁有共同的祖源。像是劉泰安這樣的地方菁英的態度,說明人們對地理位置和世代的重視程度,更勝於對於族群分野的關注：

> 有些人說 Hmub 語，有些說 Kam 語，還有一些人說普通話，但大家共譜（或稱合譜）。就看他住在哪個地方，住在哪裡。看他喜歡哪個族，就報哪個族。不強迫，不強求一致。修譜時，不會分彼此是 Kam 族，或是 Hmub 族，是看字輩。不管你是哪個地區，反正都是一個輩，都是一個字。
>
> （天柱縣劉泰安）

根據這種說法，在劉姓的家族成員中，世代取代了地方，而地方取代了族群。換句話說，地方菁英將漢族的共同遠祖，作為 Hmub 人與漢人，或 Kam 人與漢人的跨族群歷史互動的證據，並強調個人選擇，在族群認同中的重要性。結果是，在這份共同編修的族譜中，有關個人的敘事和詮釋，表達出多重身分認同，和模糊的族群界線。而無論是新譜或老譜，《劉氏族譜》的合譜，都是對 Hmub 與 Kam 的語言社群，彼此存在著血緣關係的說法，賦予了權威性。

三、族譜作為一種文本

由族譜的文字內容，以及訪談參與族譜編修，保管族譜的寨老們，我們都可看到創作者的影響力。這是以族譜的口說和書面語言，所展現的權威中心。進一步探索不同文本實踐之間的關係，則將發現另類作者身分，並由此挑戰原有的觀點——作者身分所創造的單一權威。這些地方菁英強調曬譜和族譜的傳閱流通，而編者修訂序，則召喚出祖先的力量──此二者指出多重的文本權威，文本與儀式之間的複雜關係，以及他們所共同促成的，是一種分散的，非集中的影響力。

語言人類學家亞歷山卓・杜蘭帝（Alessandro Duranti）強調，在對話中需要區分說者和聽者。這也意味著，需要重新評估，文本權威和作者身分的概念（Duranti 1994）。在許多實際和潛在作者相互爭鋒的地景裡，通過使用語言或是純粹象徵性的溝通，作者身分的指定，往往取決於說話社群對於文本權威的看法（ibid.）。然而，與語言行動理論，或意圖與語言之間的關係一樣，文本權威也屬於，以人為中心的理論範疇。在說話或語言的活動中，權威可能會轉移到約翰・杜波依斯（John Du Bois）所說，「非人之代理人」的身上。這表示，作者身分不再是第一人稱或第二人稱，而是第三人稱（Du Bois 1992）。接著我將舉出在《劉氏族譜》中，三個「非人之代理人」的例子，並以此探討這部流通在貴州東部的漢字族譜，所展現的無名之聲與作者政治。

（一）例一：個人名字

無名之聲，以親子聯名（透過孩子的名字，來指涉父母）的形式出現。這部總共五卷的家譜，除了首卷是述說始遷祖的故事、各版本的修譜序、家訓等，其他四卷是滕山公、鳳山公、梅山公、正伯公派下父系繼嗣群的世系錄。換言之，在這部家譜中占篇幅最多的，是紀錄以父系繼嗣群為主的每個男性成員個人的名字、娶妻、生子、子再生孫的繁衍過程，偶爾會記錄職業或官職。死亡年齡及埋葬地點，無論知道或不詳，也會清楚標出。

這些環繞著父系繼嗣群成員的個人訊息，全部以漢字來敘述，而在這些漢字書寫的個人記錄裡，每個男人的名字，看來就像是漢人典雅、繁複的命名體系——除了前面的名字有字輩的排行外，還有號或名。下面是梅山公派下子孫的例子（以下粗體字為筆者的標示）：

文陸長子昌海，號寶六，生於 1908 年，卒未詳，葬豹飲梅，配張氏，生卒葬未詳，續張氏，生於 1930 年，生二子：橋、三。昌海長子永德，名橋寶，生於 1954，配張氏，旁壩人。生二子：和平，正橋。

永德長子耀河，名和平，生於 1980 年。永德次子耀政，名正橋，生於 1982 年。昌海次子永清，名三寶，生於 1950 年，任小學教師，配姚氏，名莫瑛，生一子林三。

永清之子耀林，號林三，生於 1982 年。

（摘自《劉氏族譜》1985）

在這個片段的世系錄裡，個人的名字是一個表現三代男性成員繼嗣關係的符號系統。其中並置兩套個人名字的傳承體系，一套是漢字、漢語發聲，另一套是漢字苗讀的發聲。在漢字漢語的系統，上下世代間遵守字派的傳承。「文陸生昌海，昌海生永德、永清，永德生耀河、耀政，永清生耀林」，在這一連串的名字裡，「文、昌、永、耀」，都屬於劉氏族譜所創之 60 字派的一部分。

然而，上下世代名字的關係，出現另一種規律：在有字派的名字之後，每個男性成員都有「號」或「名」。如「昌海號寶六；永德名橋寶、永清名三寶；耀河名和平、耀政名正橋，號林三」。這些名或號，與漢人常見的「雙名」無差別。但若由「寶六生橋寶、三寶；橋寶生和平、正橋；三寶生林三」的關係，我們可以看到相同的字 —— 父代雙名的第一個字，移到子代雙名的第二個字（上面的例子，只有橋寶的長子「和平」是例外）。這個漢字的移動方式，呼應貴州東部 Hmub 人的父子聯名制。他們的個人名字，是單音、單名，如前面的「六」、「寶」、「橋」。每個人完整的名字，是將父親的個人名字，放在自己的名字之後。施洞附近的劉家 Hmub 人的名，至今仍是如此命名，而台江縣高坡 Hmub 人的父子聯名，除了自己、父親之名外，還加上祖父的名。由三個名才組成一個正式而完整的個人苗名。在口傳系統上，只要能記憶，可一直加入父系祖輩的名字。這也是台江縣高坡 Hmub 人口耳相傳，記憶歷史的行動。

在這個完全以漢字書寫的漢字家譜裡，Hmub 人傳統的命名系統，以及每個個人的 Hmub 語發音的名字，仍一世代、一世代完整地記錄在漢字家譜裡。雖然它被漢字書寫所掩飾，加上「名」或「號」，以便與漢語「書名」（貴州 Hmub 人通常稱有字派的名字為書名，也就是到學校受教育用的名字）組合，成為一個有名、有號，類似漢式風格的名字。然而在這多層掩飾底下，漢字書寫還是發出 Hmub 的語音，並且 Hmub 人的父子聯名體系的結構，也再現於漢字家譜內。

漢字和 Hmub 語的這種混合，將個人名字的屬性或聲音，從個人轉變為非人或無名。換句話說，漢字代表了 Hmub 語中，無關乎人的語音符號，是嵌入劉氏族譜書面文字裡的「第三種聲音」。我認為，1950 年代發明的羅馬拼音 Hmub 和 Kam 少數民族文字系統，在 1980 年代地方菁英的族譜彙編中，發揮了作用。相較於 Hmub 人使用漢字，表徵其語音系統，壯族的宇宙觀和儀式語境，例如廣西壯族廣泛流傳的史詩，和傳統文獻《鵝王和祖先王：中國南方廣西的史詩》（*Hanvueng: The Goose King and Ancestral King*）（Holm and Meng 2015），則呈顯出以壯文取代漢字書寫系統的邏輯和方法。

（二）例二：曬譜

台江和天柱的老人家說，族譜僅在每年一次的曬譜儀式中，開放給村寨族人觀看。我將曬譜視爲文本權威的一種延伸。由於《劉氏族譜》不能與其他族譜一起展示，也由此確認了家族之間的界線。年度的曬譜儀式還顯示，文本權威屬於劉氏家族。我所訪問的兩個村寨的老人家，都談到分擔宴席和酒品的費用。儘管這是一次展示族譜內容和文字權威的慶祝活動，但它卻不被認爲是聚會的主要原因。若從語言或儀式角度，來檢視這場年度聚會，很難確定族譜文本、編撰者、曬譜儀式參與者，誰才是主角？

儘管本章沒有全面回顧自清代以來的貴州方志，是否有關於曬譜的記載。但在貴陽和貴州一些地區的方志紀事中，相繼出現了曬書和曬衣的紀錄。他們都在農曆六月六日舉行（丁世良、趙放 1991）。例如，《貴州省普安直隸廳志》記載，該日進行的工作：「六月六日，穫菽，曝書，曬衣，祀青苗，穀神，殺草，儲糞」（曹維祺 1974〔清光緒十五年〕：194）。根據史料，只有當地的士紳家族，才有曬書習俗。《安順府志》指出：「六月六日，祀土地神。曬衣服，士曬書。農夫以酒飯祀田祖，插紙錢于田中，以祈豐年」（ibid.：507）。換句話說，台江 Hmub 人和天柱 Kam 人的劉家，仍在實行的曬譜儀式，代表的是文本和文化，在邊陲社會中複雜的互動。雖然這當中的紀實，是否爲複製他處的訛誤，還需進一步確認。但此處所討論的內容，足以說明曬譜背後存在的廣泛社會連結。例一和例二，也有一個共同點，那就是脫離了以人為中心的作者敘事觀點。

（三）例三：領譜文

以下摘錄，擷自《劉氏族譜》於清光緒三十四年編印的老譜（1908年）。

稽我劉氏原籍江西吉安府太和縣豬市巷，俱係沛公（註：漢高祖劉邦）後裔。至我起祖臣熊公弟兄六人，俱屬顯宦，自經兵燹以後，老譜遺失。我祖初徙山東平地渡州嶺，拜靖州協開，闢天柱文溪所一帶地方，托足重鰲老寨。子孫騰茂，建祠於螃沖，前人幾翻創造，未有成功。眾族捐資買蕭姓宅基，以奉祭祀祠未竣而繼以修譜。共成公譜二十部，各立字號。或腳譜、或公譜，奉熊公為天柱起祖者，皆屬骨肉，自不至視為秦越人也。所謂修族譜以聯疏遠者，即是道也，是為敘。

讚曰：

族譜已修成，祖德流芳百代，與支分派別，子而孫故把吾族譜訂。春秋兩翻祭祀，儼然如見先人，丕承丕顯，庇兒孫瓜瓞，蠢斯衍慶。今夫譜牒所載，實為宗族祖父名諱墓墳所係在，收藏者所珍重，今余等修有總譜二十部，編立字號為據。

以千文為號：天地元黃，宇宙洪荒，寒來暑往，秋收冬藏，紅霞閃電。以上字號，當春秋祭祀執出，符合略無，訊是真宗也。議定每寨能持一部者，另要捐銀十兩，以備祠內公費。若有不肖子孫偷賣譜者，後代不昌，稟祠重罰。

　　本章採取互文性的概念——文本之間的關係，來檢視上述摘錄中，不同段落彼此之間，以及該摘錄和來自同一族譜的其他摘錄引述之間，所存在的對話性。在前述摘錄的第一段開頭，祖先故事確立了以作者為中心的身分。但是，在整個段落中所使用的非人語言（「老譜遺失」和「共成公譜二十部，各立字號」），卻傳達了與以人為中心之作者觀點的分離。第二和第三段的摘錄引述，也包含非人或無名之聲的範例：讚頌族譜，提及二十二卷族譜，以及要求保管者細心維護族譜等。換言之，在前述摘錄中，同時存在著互文性的關係，和雙重的作者身分。

四、結論

　　以往的研究通常根據地方菁英的識文能力來分析族譜的書寫方式，及其流通情況。本章採納近來關於互文性或互語性的理論方法，來探討族譜的「無責性」（nonresponsibility），意指族譜中匿名傳達的聲音，與族譜正文傳達的語意內容，有所不同的現象。祖先或父系繼嗣群體的敘事，所產生的強烈血緣意識型態，有助於族譜文本權威的建立。其他文本中帶有非人語氣的匿名聲音，卻無助於確立文本的權威（Du Bois 1992；Irvine 1996；Keane 1995）。如同邁克‧西爾弗斯坦（Michael Silverstein）所言，文本或話語是一種「過程性的、實時的，與事件有關的社會行為……。溝通的互語性是事件與事件之間的關係，它會根據個人、作者、活躍的訊息發送者、負責任的接收者，或無責任的訊息監督者等，不同的相互位置來予以投射」（Silverstein 2005）。杜波依斯則透過探討中非洲三角地帶的阿贊德族人（Azande），不願「尋求占卜意義的人為或擬人化源頭」，來挑戰「語言的使用，必然具有人為之意識形態」的觀點（Du Bois 1992：57）（民族誌細節參後）。本章採取與討論非人以及言語行為缺乏人為意圖相類似的思路，指出貴州東部 Hmub 人與 Kam 人共享的劉氏族譜，如何透過漢字刻版印刷的兩個版本及相關儀式，表達其特有的無意圖性或無責性，並通過此建構西南邊陲村寨社會關於「外人與親緣」（exclusiveness and relatedness）的意識，並藉此彰顯劉姓氏族成員想像的 Hmub 人、Kam 人與漢人跨越族群界線的族際兄弟情誼，與父系血緣的關係。

其次，本章描述 Hmub 人和 Kam 人地方菁英如何使用漢文字書寫族譜，來彌合族際間的差異，也同時掀開了周邊族群，與中原華夏文明暨國家體系之間的文化知識縫隙。本章以貴州東部 Hmub 人和 Kam 人合譜（共同整理，編排）與印刻、印刷的兩部新舊版本的漢文族譜（老譜與新譜）作為研究對象，並指出這兩部族譜對國家周邊的邊陲語群，所具有共同血緣關係的宣稱，賦予權威性。儘管合作的編輯們援引「我們祖先」的精神，並要求觀看族譜的宗族子孫不可褻瀆祖先的名字，但卻無人對內容負責。換言之，族譜的文本權威，並非總是由狹義的作者來界定。本章指出，當我們將焦點放在寫作活動更廣泛的社會過程，漢文族譜出現了邊陲族群與漢人的族際間，擁有共同血緣的宣稱，而這些宣稱又交互地強調「外人與親緣」的界線。作為一種集體寫作策略，以漢文撰寫族譜的作者身分，變得分散而隱匿。但曖昧的是，這個族譜的文本與社會行動，卻也以此宣稱與華夏中原國家文明，有所區辨之 Hmub 人和 Kam 人族群的族性與邊陲性。

第三，上面的例子顯示，由於這兩部 Hmub 人與 Kam 人合編的老譜與新譜之正文和其他文本間，皆存在由匿名性格所引起的指示現象。是故我們需要仔細斟酌族譜中，其他文本話語的匿名性。上面三個例子流洩的無名之聲與正文中的聲音有所不同。族譜正文關於祖先或繼嗣群體的敘事，形成一種強烈的父系血緣意識形態，對文本權威的建立有直接的助益。這種意識形態是具有意圖性且是人為的。但是其他文本（以及上述三個範例）中的獨特表達，卻帶有非人的匿名語氣，對文本權威的建立沒有幫助。此外，《劉氏族譜》中的匿名聲音，具有明顯不同的性格。曬譜儀式和領譜文本都有助於建立族譜權威。不過在劉氏後裔個人名字的組合中，用漢字表示 Hmub 人的地方語音系統，與父子聯名的系統共存，卻顯示文本權威遭到撼動。其所造成的結果是，作者身分的性質，從公開集體的權威者，變成隱密分散的無名氏。換句話說，在族譜文本中，出現的匿名聲音在兩種指示性格間掙扎不定。

人類學者杜波依斯關於占卜的研究指出，土著族譜中，存在非人的匿名聲音（Du Bois 1992：57）。杜波依斯以其對阿贊德族人占卜儀式的觀察，解釋語言使用中，非人的概念。下述引文來自伊凡－普理查（Evans-Pritchard）在阿贊德部落社群所收集的原始材料：

有毒神諭，那個女人，難道我打算娶她，她就是我的妻子？有毒神諭，聆聽，殺死家禽。如果不是如此，我會感到刺痛的疲倦⋯⋯。我不能擁有她，也不能娶她。有毒神諭，聆聽，饒了家禽。

（Evans-Pritchard 1976：298）

他探討阿贊德人不願賦予占卜意義，擁有人爲或擬人化源頭的意義，並藉此反思語言的使用，向來被認爲具有人爲意識形態的觀點（Austin 1962；Searle 1969）。

如果所有言語行爲，總是具有意義，那麼我們如何在族譜的結構和文本中，解釋非人或無名的聲音？它們是貴州東部邊陲人群想像力的產物，還是一種對國家在禮儀、習性和識文能力之影響的回應？通過重新檢視族譜中，使用具有 Hmub 人語言模式的漢文字符，及朝向 Hmub 人語音符號的轉換現象時，我們可以將此一過程視爲個人在社群集體血緣價值或目的中，所表現之一種分離的個體性。特別是族譜中，通過口傳論述的父子聯名系統。此一觀點，也尤能幫助我們認識 Hmub 文化裡的命名系統，漢人／漢字行輩系統，以及名與字號的雙名系統，相互嵌合、並置的特徵。

最後，儘管姓氏在中華帝國歷史上，有其作爲非漢民族漢化手段的重要性（Wang 2000）。但文化上的學習與模仿，並不一定導致土著的漢化和成爲漢人，更有可能是土著利用他者性，來確認自我及其在地認同的一種重要的本土實踐（Cheung 2012）。本章指出，即使帝國邊陲人群承受在禮儀、習性和識文能力上，必須使用國家語言的壓力。Hmub 人與 Kam 人在族譜中使用漢文，以互文性作爲一種模仿過程，以及藉由他者性，來進行自我的宣稱（Taussig 1993）等，都是邊陲社會，透過共同形成的血緣想像共同體，來表達其地方認同的方式。

附錄
英文原版

Chapter I
Extramarital Court and Flirt of Guizhou Hmub

Generally speaking, no women in any culture and society are indifferent to their partners' extramarital affairs.[1] Even women in societies with double standards in this regard, would become anxious and angry whenever their own spouse or partner is sexually involved with other women. They assume that even a brief sexual encounter has the potential to undermine the marital bond. Thus, continued vigilance is required. Most studies of extramarital affairs focused only on the community's reaction to the affair. These studies note that there are double standard societies where men are allowed to enter into an affair while the women cannot. Some cultures distinguish between emotional involvement and sexual involvement. For example, evolutionary psychologists found that American women make a distinction between emotional involvement and sexual involvement. For them, emotional threat to their marriage or other forms of relationship is more serious than their partner's incidental sexual trysts with a stranger. In general, "young men are more distressed by a partner's sexual infidelity, whereas young women are more distressed by a partner's emotional infidelity".[2] However, there are few studies of women's reactions to their partners' flirtations in either formal or informal contexts.[3]

During my fieldwork in a Hmub village in Guizhou (1998-2000), when

I first heard about "extramarital flirtation", I wondered whether wives became angry or jealous when their husbands deliberately flirted with other girls in the evening. One woman said to me, "No, I am not unhappy at my husband singing for another girl at night. That means he has a good voice." The term "flirtation" is tentatively used in translating the native term of *iut fub* among the Hmub in eastern Guizhou. I will introduce how the Hmub dialectic term of *iut fub* defined locally with details later. Briefly, *iut fub* for the natives can transcend the line between unmarried and married, creating an extramarital flirting zone. This Hmub practice stands in sharp contrast to that of their neighbors, the Lahu, who identify intimacy with monogamous marriage, while love is expressed as harmonious teamwork in marriage.[4] Though monogamous marriage has also been long practiced here and the marital bond will continue to tie the couple as ancestors after life, today, much like before 1949, the Hmub approve and institutionalize extramarital flirtation for men until their middle age (approximately between thirty to forty years old) and for women until they become married mothers. The flirting practices of the Hmub in eastern Guizhou may be offering an alternative in the current theorizing of courtship and marriage, since they have a flirtation zone for continued expression of personal desire within the larger context of social restraint.[5] In this chapter, I will explore how the Hmub may be a special case of allowing for a private personal emotional zone to be created within a highly structured or institutionalized setting that honors social status, age and gender separation. Institutionalized flirting of the Hmub does serve as a means to an end —— marriage, a sociological identity that people in the community will often talk about. It is also the psychological reassurance of one's personal identity as a viable, sexual and desirable human being.

Courtship and Marriage

In *The Sexual Life of Savages in North Western Melanesia*, Malinowski noted that "a subject like sex cannot be treated except in its institutional setting". Courtship was considered one significant customary restraint. For him, love, eroticism, magic and mythology all shape part of a culture's courtship process.[6] However, he did not treat courtship as filling an autonomous niche. In his words, "courtship again, is a phase, a preparatory phase, of marriage, and marriage but one side of family life".[7] Although he emphasized the functional value of courtship, he always considered it an aspect of a larger social construction. He never considered it capable of having an autonomous dimension independent of its social function, which was to bring men and women together in some form of marital arrangement.

Studies of early American courtship found that although young Americans enjoyed relative autonomy in choosing mates, they "had on average only two other relationships before meeting their future husband and wives".[8] From these findings, the relationship between American courtship and marriage is not very different from the Melanesian societies.

In contrast to presenting courtship as a phase preparatory to marriage, other literature, especially those focused on narratives or performances, revealed different facets of courtship and diverse connections between courtship and marriage.[9] These works also explored their entangled relations. Through analyzing historical archives, Ellen Rothman highlighted personal experiences and narratives of courting and found that "courtship was not a linear progression but an amalgam of expectation, experience, and convention... the nature of courtship defies precise explanations. The vicissitudes of love, the selection of a mate, the decisions people make as they approach marriage are always somewhat mysterious to an outsider".[10]

Focusing on Elizabethan language and literature, Catherine Bates also explored the rhetoric of courtship. She described courtship as "a highly nuanced and exceptionally complex literary and political procedure".[11] In her words, "courtship is a delicate, fraught, hazardous procedure which requires constant prudence, tact and subtlety because it depends for its effectiveness upon the appearance of sincerity, an appearance which could (and at times had to be) carefully calculated".[12] Courtship then is like a highly codified system, "a mode which puts sincerity and deception in a teasing and often inextricable juxtaposition".[13] Following such knowledge on courtship, it is not strange to arrive at the following conclusion on the ambivalence of courtship and marriage in her work:

> Whether courtship exists outside marriage altogether or whether it is a prelude to marriage the crucial point is that it is never the same as marriage. Courtship stands in a peculiarly ambivalent indeterminate relation to marriage. For it remains a preliminary process—what happens before marriage, or outside the conjugal unit—and therefore exists temporarily 'outside' the law, which that conjugality represents. [14]

"If you persist in talking passion while I am talking marriage, we shall soon cease to understand each other" (quoted from Comtesse de Carigliano in Balzac's *At the Sign of the Cat and Rocket*).[15] Such ambivalence of marriage and the personal happiness of man and woman was the main theme of *Husbands, Wives and Lovers*.[16] In this work, Patricia Mainardi discussed marriage and its discontents in nineteenth-century France from art and literature. Focused on the issue of adultery, the author attempted to examine the "contradiction" between marriage and individual feelings. Moving from historical narrative to representations in literature or art, at the end Mainardi tried to explore further about personal happiness, concluding that the ideal relations between men and women should be in the modern world.[17]

From these abundant and varying sources of literature, courtship has been described as having a functional relationship with marriage; others view it as serving to highlight a unilineal progression of shifting status arrangements whereby people move from single to married; still others see it as a more fluid or entangled relationship and, thus, not a clear cut route to marriage. Expressing the relationship between or separation of courtship and marriage, these studies significantly theorized the seriousness of court. Linear and dialectical perspectives are both important in understanding complicated courting cultures. This chapter will show that the Hmub may be a special case since they demonstrate the two relationships (lineal and dialectical) between courtship and marriage within one institution by two forms of flirtation, long term and short term.

Field Setting and Research Methods

Fangf Bil is a Hmub village perched high on a hillside on the upper reaches of the Qingshuijiang River. It forms part of the northern subgroup of the Hmub in Guizhou.[18] Fangf Bil is part of Fanzao Township, Taijiang County, southeastern Guizhou Self-Governing District, Guizhou Province. The people in this village call themselves Hmub, which is cognate with Hmong. The village is composed of over 330 households and has a population of almost 1,500 persons. It is divided into eleven hamlets (*vangf*), whose respective names refer to some nearby geographic feature.

The residents of any single hamlet will generally be the agnatic descendants of a lineage sub-segment and share a common Han Chinese surname. The naming system is patronymic. Regardless of gender, a person's name is composed of his or her name preceded by his or her father's name, the father's name being preceded by his father's name in turn. Han Chinese surnames appear to have come into use only in the eighteenth century, with the intrusion of the Chinese State. Han Chinese surnames are seldom heard in everyday Hmub discourse, but they accord with the patrilineal spirit of Fangf Bil naming practices.

The eleven hamlets of Fangf Bil village are organized into five patrilineal marriage groups. Marriage within a marriage group is forbidden. The five marriage groups have the five Han Chinese surnames of Zhang, Tang, Wan, Yang and Tai. However, the correspondence between the Chinese surnames and the marriage groups is not absolute. Hamlets, surnames and patrilineal marriage groups are all organized, one way or another, around ancestor descent groups. These groups are generally localized residentially and share a common male ancestor, corporate ancestral rites and corporate agricultural land. The surnames and hamlets roughly coincide with the marriage groups, but it is only the marriage groups that correspond directly with ancestor descent groups.

This chapter is based on my long term fieldwork in Fangf Bil village. It was started with a pre-field summer trip in 1997, followed by a main fieldwork for my dissertation from November of 1998 to February of 2000, and an additional summer field trip in 2004, I have conducted a village based ethnographical research related to marriage and flirting on the Hmub for more than 20 months. Combining with the anthropological methods of participant observation, in-depth interview and long term residence in the village, I attempted to explore the interplay between personal emotions (erotic, romantic, or flirtatious feelings) and social institutions (marriage and courtship). At the beginning of my fieldwork, I focused on the studying of the social structure of the Hmub village. I did a census of more than 300 households and drew up the pedigrees and genealogical records for each family as discovered through semi-structured interviews.[19] Additionally, I collected the kinship terms employed by native speakers and recorded the actual use of the terminology in both everyday and ritualized settings. This datum outlining of the social networks of the Hmub village enabled me to understand the personal relationships between families and between individuals. It is important to describe the marital ideals provided by my informants, as well as the reality of marriage, to see where they converge and where they differ in detail.

Another focus of this chapter was the private domain of sentiments. By examining how the Hmub behaved in institutional flirting settings as well as analyzing their love songs, I was able to enter into the emotional world of the "young people" (*vangt*).[20] But this entailed a problem: I was already the young mother of two sons when I carried out the research project for my Ph.D. dissertation. For any woman in the village to be a mother meant she would be defined as "old" (*lok*) and, therefore, excluded from most institutional flirting activities. However, the villagers still regarded me as "a young girl", despite my actual social status as defined by their conventions. One of the reasons was probably because of my dress, which was no different from the local unmarried girls.[21] Wearing a youth's clothing combined with being an outsider, plus being a "Han Chinese" doctoral student from Taiwan enabled me to participate in and observe the young peoples' flirting interactions and daily life. The Fangf Bil villagers were accustomed in their encounter with local Han Chinese but it was still a fresh experience for most of them that I, a Taiwanese female graduate, was living in the village with them for more than one and half years continually. Besides asking me about the purpose of my research, they especially liked to ask me about political, economical, cultural, and everyday issues with regards to Taiwan when I had opportunities to chat with them.

Institutionalized flirting activities can take in the forms either of get-togethers or of "talking love" throughout the night underneath a young woman's window. Although I participated directly in many get-togethers, I was able listen to but not directly observe them during their conversations. I was able to interview the girls later as to what was exchanged. Flirting activities in the village can be open, conveying some features of ritualized performance, but they can also be very private and personal encounters. Without the girls accompanying me during fieldwork and their willingness to let me share in their "romantic" or flirtatious emotions and experiences, I would not have been able to understand the content and contextual value of the institutionalized flirtation between individuals.

During my fieldwork, I lived in the home of an unmarried girl. I was able to develop a close fictive relationship with her as evident that we easily and readily called each other sister. In my fieldwork, this girl accompanied me day and night, which enable me to share from her, at times, her friend's experiences, moods and views on marriage and feelings about men.

At Khait ("Getting Married")

The primary structural factors that shape long term (extramarital) flirting are: bilateral cross-cousin marriage, village endogamy, and duo-local post-marital residence. The terminological system of this village is similar to the Dravidian-type structure of the kinship terminology in conjunction with the ideal and practice of prescriptive cross-cousin marriage. In terms of classificatory kin relations, most women in Fangf Bil still marry either their classificatory matrilateral or patrilateral cross cousins: that is, either marriages of father's sister's daughter with mother's brother's son (FZD/MBS) or mother's brother's daughter with father's sister's son (MBD/FZS) occur.[22] Nevertheless, the practice of cross-cousin marriage is still related to how kin are classified in Fangf Bil, a community that clearly distinguishes between near and distant kin. Thus bilateral cross-cousin marriage is not actually father's sister's son (FZS) or mother's brother's son (MBS), but rather between members of patrilineal descent groups who are related to one another. These are either as classificatory patrilateral cross cousin (FZHBS, FZHFBSS, or FZHFFBSSS), who are equated terminologically with the father's sister's son (FZS), or as classificatory matrilateral cross cousin (MFBSS, or MFFBSSS), who are equated terminologically with the mother's brother's son (MBS). This means there are classificatory FZD/MBS and classificatory MBD/FZS marriages. Parallel with the marriage rule, the binary organizations of the groups of Fangf Bil are given classificatory reality in the distinction between *gad ghat* (agnates, literally "hosts" or "us") and *khait* (affines, literally "guests"). Marriage is prohibited between *gad ghat* (or simply ghat), but permitted with *khait*. The centrality of the relationships between *ghat* and *khait* in Fangf Bil village is indicative of the importance of kinship in the village social process.

Village endogamy is also important in exploring the practice of cross cousin marriage in the village. The Chang Family and Tang Family marriage groups have a combined population of over 90 percent of Fangf Bil's total population. The ratio of intermarriages between the two marriage groups far exceeds marriages outside of the village. The six hamlets of the two marriage groups depend on one another for the vast majority of their wives. In short, the two groups seem to constitute something approaching a categorically binary structure. Ultimately, most marriages take place within the village through a system of classificatory bilateral cross cousin marriage.

Duo-local post-marital residence (or delayed transferred marriage) is the third institutional feature to assist the institutionalization of long-term flirtation. Generally, a bride in a Hmub village does not live with the groom after the wedding ceremony but immediately return to stay with her natal kin. This custom of duo-local residence is called *niangt zix* (literally "sitting at home or staying at home"). The wife visits the husband's house only on festival days or to assist in the farm work of her husband's family until their first child is born. During this period the wife still wears the garments of an unmarried woman. Whether doing farm work in the daytime or engaging in flirting activities in the evening, the wife spends most of her time with other unmarried women or other married women who are similarly "staying at her own natal parent's home."[23]

During the duo-local period, both wife and husband can freely attend their own flirting activities separately. The wife still can talk about love or joke along with other boys who flirt with her by her bedroom window in the evening when she is staying at her own parents' home (see the following paragraph for more details of institutionalized flirting activities). Her personal leisure time and individual feelings at engaging in such extramarital flirting will not come to an end until she has become a mother and begins to live regularly with her husband. In the Hmub village, most wives will become mothers one or two years after their marriage. Only a few are still living in their natal homes more than "three, four or five years"[24] after marriage. No matter how old a wife or husband becomes, if they have not yet had children, they will continue to be considered "young" women or bachelors, and their marital status will remain vague, especially in regard to long term flirting activities.

In general, the combination of prescriptive cross-cousin marriage with village endogamy continually creates a small world, generation after generation, which means that the Hmub prefer to form and maintain their social world by production and reproduction within one village, ideologically and sociologically. However, such cohesive social constraint of intra-village affinal alliance leaves a place for duo-local residence, *niangt zix*, which demonstrates the fluidity between flirting and marriage. As described earlier, duo-local residence provides the opportunity for the married men and women to control their extramarital flirting activity. This is an important characteristic in addition to the collective and institutional aspects of the cross cousin marriage of the Hmub. The fluidity of the flirting will be discussed with more details later.

Besides the institutional aspect and the prescribed rules, however, we also need to see Hmub marriage from the perspective of the social actors. Marriages in Fangf Bil occur after a brief courtship, and may or may not involve romantic love. They can be either public marriages (*ghaif zix bat mongf*, literally "to be sent away from home by the bride's parents") or elopements (*at dlius mongf*, literally "to go away secretly").[25] Nowadays, most marriages are decided by the young people themselves, whether public marriages or elopements. To become socially recognized as Hmub adults, they are expected to be married *and* have children. Once the wife and the husband have had their own first child, they will begin to live together. The nuclear family, consisting of a couple and their unmarried children in one household, is the most common form in a Hmub village.

Sharing ideas, knowledge, feelings and cooperation in both the production of resources and reproduction are obvious aspects of the daily life of each married couple. Couples talk to each other often at home, especially during meals. They discuss the division of their farm work and housework, exchange ideas on how to solve family problems and bring up children, and share news, jokes, rumors, scandals or arguments which are circulating among the other villagers. Whenever I visited or stayed in a household I often heard couples chatting, but sometimes I heard them quarrelling or fighting. Interactions between spouses inside their own home seem normal. But what impressed me strongly was the their indifference toward one another once outside their house.

The spouses are expected to walk out separately, ideally with their same-sex relatives, whether they are going to do farm work, engage in ritual activities, or visit relatives. A married couple walking together around the village is considered impolite and inappropriate behavior. Yet, when they are beyond the public's gaze, the Hmub actually seek out private encounters that allow them to engage in emotionally satisfying and intensely intimate interactions with members of the opposite sex. This is the Hmub institutionalized extra-marital flirting.

Iut Fub ("Institutionalized Flirting")

Courtship is very common as an intentional performance with the goal of marriage in many societies. This is also true for men and women of many other Hmub or Hmong villages who spend a great deal of time together, expressing personal sentiments through talking, singing and intimate physical contact. However, it is not necessarily and simply so for the Hmub in eastern Guizhou.

Long Term and Short Term

Classificatory cross-cousins flirt in the Fangf Bil society is similar to a classic symmetric joking relation. Flirtation between Hmub cross cousins demonstrates the marriageability of a potential spouse. Such view is roughly correspondent with that of Mauss, Lévi-Strauss, Dumont, and McDougal.[26] But more than from the perspective of structuralism this chapter explores relationships between marriage and courtship, and between individual feelings and social institutions, through Hmub cross-cousin flirtation. There are two forms of Hmub courtship that can be defined as long and short term flirtation. The long term alliance may last during the lifetime of one's own marriage, while the short term will end in a break up or, if both parties involved are single, marriage. But whether the flirtation is long or short, both may constitute the similar features of flirtation (with details later). It is still different from the conventional ideal of the exclusiveness of one-to-one romantic love (or passion). Yet, this distinction between long term and short term Hmub flirting may not be expressed strictly or explicitly by local views. The indigenous conceptualization of a young person for the Hmub includes teenagers to adults and even middle-aged men and women who have married within the past few years. Briefly, unmarried men or women (whether single or divorced) and married men or women without children are considered young persons who can attend flirting activities freely.

During long term flirtation, love tokens are exchanged to express one's feelings, such as flower belts or coats. Men may tie two or three flower belts from their former lovers over their daughter's Hmub clothing when they are 2 or 3 years old. If the coat is a souvenir of separation with their former lovers, men or women may still wear it when they are in their forties or fifties. Yet, there are boundaries, especially in long term flirtation that cannot be transcended, with rules regulating the flirting activities of married men and women. A married woman can flirt with her male affine until she has delivered her first child. However, married men can participate in extra-marital flirtation after they become a father. Moreover, men are allowed to flirt with his female affine until his children reach their teens. Here exists a gender bias in favor of men.

Iut fub, literally meaning "wandering in the village," is never used in day-to-day conversations among the villagers, because it indicates sexuality. Instead, they use Hmub expressions such as *at zot* ("play for fun"), *lof vud* ("take a rest"), *god* ("get together") and *niangt* ("sit down"), which have nothing to do with sexuality. *Iut fub* is nonetheless an indispensable part of Hmub social life. It occurs during particular time and space, and with a special group of individuals. On ordinary days, *iut fub* may take place every night for the young people. After supper, the old people and the children go to bed early. The whole village falls into darkness and quiet except for the faint lights in the windows of each family. After a period of silence, whistles (*kot ghait*) are blown vigorously and without restriction into the dark night. Footsteps are heard, together with hush conversations. The boys initiate the sounds calling for girls to enter into a flirting exchange. Thus the boys from the Tang family will go to the Zhang family and vice versa. When the footsteps slow down, knocking is heard at a girl's window inviting her to talk to him. If the girl opens the window, they may talk in a gentle voice. If a whole group of boys flirts with a girl, the conversation will be loudly filled with humorous remarks.

The flirting boys also try to find out where a group of girls may be together. Once the girls are located, the boys join them in conversation. At midnight the group's conversation changes into a dyadic or one-to-one exchange called *ib laik del ib laik* ("one likes the other"). Such conversations may continue deep into the night and stop after the cock crows once or twice. Some exchanges may continue until daybreak.

As I have described in the previous paragraphs, the people participating in *iut fub* should ideally be *vangt* (the "young people"). However, there is no strict limitation on their age and status (married or single). These exchanges between men and women from different marital status and age cohorts appear to be conducted, especially by the woman, from a more detached role posture. Young women are clearly more restraint in flirtation with someone outside their age cohort. For example, once, at a "girls' get-together" (*god dat ghaif*) flirting activity, I heard a young girl call a man who had put his hands on her shoulders intimately "maternal uncle" (*daid nenk*),[27] and she tried to push his hands away. Another night, I observed a seventeen-year-old unmarried girl talking heatedly with a middle-aged man, the father of a ten-year-old son, whom she called *but* (literally "sister's husband or brother-in-law"). The third case involved a group of unmarried girls who invited a group of married men, who were fathers, to play or flirt together in a field near the village. During the festival flirting event, the girls constantly called these men "father of Dand" or "father of Zent." Dand or Zent are the first names of men's eldest son or daughter. Clearly, the girls were keen on conveying they were not interested in the men as anything more than a momentary flirtation. For these middle aged married men, there would be a momentary flirtation, too, though in the form of post-marital flirtation relationship.

Women who dress in the same way at the institutionalized flirting gatherings may be unmarried or may have been married for a couple of years. When a woman stays at her natal home, her dress is similar to that of any unmarried girl, coiling up her hair, and wearing flowers, jewelry and *ut diuf* ("Han Chinese clothes" or clothes bought in the downtown market).[28]

Moreover, like unmarried women, she can freely join in the flirting activities in the evening. In this way, flirting gatherings are open to everyone. The fluid display of women's dresses can actually cover up the boundary of these two forms of Hmub institutionalized flirtation.

Physical Intimacies

To display intimate body contacts openly is very common in the Hmub flirting culture. A partner is permitted to put his hands on her shoulders, waists or legs. Flirtatious or intimate physical contact between men and women is acceptable at the appropriate time and place for *iut fub*. The old people will scold the young if the latter disobey the rules. Moreover, only when girls and boys are together in a group can an individual display intimate physical contact flirtatiously and openly. In other words, if there is only one boy flirting with a group of girls, they can only sit down around the hearth and talk to each other; but if there are two or three boys flirting with five or six more girls, the boys can flirt with the girls nearby. However, the other partners will stop them if their physical contacts go beyond the accepted norms. Inappropriate behavior would indicate that the boys look down upon the other girls present in the same *iut fub* activity.

Intimate physical touches do not necessarily indicate a steady relationship between lovers. Even those who meet for the first time in *iut fub* can display intimate physical contact within the accepted boundaries. I remember the first time I went to watch an inter-village water buffalo fight. At the end of the fighting, I saw groups and pairs of boys and girls singing or exchanging intimate love whispers. Some even held each other's shoulders and leaned on each other closely. At first, I thought they were couples in steady relationships. Later on, some girls told me that the girls and boys who were flirting were mainly from different villages near by and were holding an *iut fub* event after the water buffalo fight. Although they looked intimate, most of them had never met each other before. This might be their first flirtatious encounter. For most of them, their personal names remained unknown. Another example of institutionalized flirting was found in a bridegroom's behavior toward my friend Ghaif, a 20 year-old unmarried woman. When Ghaif and I were accompanying the bridegroom's group returning to the Fangf Bil village, I observed the bridegroom was holding Ghaif's hand several times in a flirtatious matter. I felt confused when the other boys did not show any response or comment on the groom's "inappropriate behavior" toward Ghaif, who was the bride's good friend and a sister (they were classificatory patrilateral parallel cousins).

When we arrived at the Fangf Bil village, the groom and his cousins went to repair their bamboo musical instrument, *gik*. I asked Ghaif how could the bridegroom touch her body so openly and flirtatiously? Ghaif evidently found my question funny. She laughed and explained to me: "I don't quite like the way he took my hand, either, Sister. However, he is allowed to take or touch my hands or some part of my body (like the shoulder or waist) openly while I am still unmarried. This is very common in our Hmub society."

Unlike the "strangeness" of the cross village *iut fub* partners, the male and female participants of the intra-village flirting activities are near or distant affines to each other. The boy may be the "brother-in-law" of the girl, and the girl may be the "sister-in-law" of the boy, or the wife of his nephew. At the girls' get-together flirting activity, you may hear the girl call the boy *but* ("brother-in-law"), *daid nenk* ("maternal uncle, mother's brother"), *bad liut* ("husband's elder brother," prescriptive terminology) or *bad yut* ("husband's younger brother," prescriptive terminology). These kinship terms, which reveal the affinal relationships between people of different generations, are used in conformity with the intimate or flirtatious physical touch in the institutionalized extra-marital flirting.

Diut Hxad Vangt ("Love Song Duet")

Besides flirtatious body contacts or heartfelt night conversations, singing love songs (especially duets) is another common feature of institutionalized flirtation. It can occur in day-to-day and festival flirting settings. Here is an example of a love song duet recorded during my fieldwork. This love song performance happened in the early spring of 1999 in connection with the seasonal festival for celebrating the planting of rice in the field. Many people, male and female, young and old, from the neighboring four villages, gathered on the hillside fields to watch bullfights hosted by the Fangf Bil villagers with several other villages in the neighboring area. After the bullfights, most of the older men, women and their children left, but the young men and women stayed for the institutionalized dating. Men and women from different villages were sitting or standing close together, happily talking or singing to each other. The love song performances of some very skilled singers had also attracted a large audience.

The two female singers were from the Fangf Bil village, and the two male singers from another village, not very far from Fangf Bil. The people of the two villages spoke the same Hmub dialect and wore the same style of Hmub clothes. The two male singers, in their forties, were already married and had become fathers. One female singer, in her twenties, was single, while the other, (nearly 25 years old) married with no children, still lived with her natal kin. We knew that the female singers were descendents of the same patrilineal group, but did not know their real genealogical relationships to the male singers. However, during the break and at the end of the song performance, we heard the men and women address each other using prescriptive cross-kin terms. Besides the singers, the audience was consisted of women from the Fangf Bil village, and men from another village. Like the relationships between the male and female singers, the male and female audiences were also classificatory affines.

The whole performance took the form of a spontaneous competition among the singers. They had to listen carefully to what their opposite side was singing. If they were careless, they might get lost among the verses and fail to respond correctly. The 400 verses sung by the four singers as a duet lasted for more than an hour. However, the performance was not really serious or formal. The singers talked to each other, or joked with the audience when they had finished their own verses. The audiences also talked to each other while they were enjoying the show. They liked to make comments on the performance, comparing the skills of the singers, or discussing the contents of the verses with the other members of the audience. The contents of the verses were more important than the voices. Any singer who did not pay attention to his or her turn to sing, or who did not look for a good verse with which to respond, might be criticized and receive negative comments or be given a bad "name" (reputation) by the audience.

The story line of this love song duet is about an encounter between two women and two men who meet each other at an institutional flirting event. On the one hand, the men and women both express the same shy but joyful emotions in attending *iut fub* occasions. On the other hand, they tease themselves and their partners about the dialectical relationship between marriage and extra-marital flirtation. Finally, they express their own solitary sentiments and lonely emotions. Expanding from the story line, there are four thematic emphases in the song: "marriage," "*iut fub*," "two kinds of relationships between marriage and *iut fub*," and "individual sentiments." These form the aesthetic and sentimental dimensions of marriage and flirtation for the Hmub.

In this chapter I pay special attention on the singing of love songs which reveals the often entangled relationship between marriage and flirting in Hmub society. The love song duets address the autonomous nature of marriage and flirting as well as the reluctance of men and some women to make a total commitment to their marriage. Clearly, many Hmub want to engage in some sort of romantic play which serves to validate their own desirability. This intention is not without its problems as it may result in fostering conflicting relationships between individuals and someone else's spouse. These themes are evident in the following love duet: "People who are thinking of each other come to rest in the middle, my cross cousin. The girls want to sit down and talk with the boys, so they rest in the middle. No matter it is true or not, we will say the boys have wives. If you have wives, boys, then go home to take care of them. No matter it is false or not, we will say the boys have wives. Go home and separate from your wives. Then we two will be willing to accompany both of you."

In contrast to the previous themes, other love song verses highlight the separation between marriage and flirting. The female singers sing one of the two verses as follows: "The boys are like 'words.' The boys and the girls are talking and singing together like ducks playing joyfully in the water. We do not know why we are sitting next to you all the time. We do not know why we are accompanying husbands of others." While the male singers would sing "The girls are good-looking and speak well, but with two hearts. Like the good field grows millet twice, yearly. One heart accompanies their husbands; another heart accompanies us." All the verses vividly show the same dialectical relations between marriage and flirting. Using rhetorical strategies to create contrasting and dramatic metaphorical expressions, the verses uncover the hidden, fluid, conflicting, and dialectical features of marriage and institutionalized flirtation, both poetically and symbolically.

Local Comments on Extramarital Flirtation

Interviews (2004) with Fangf Bil women and men about extramarital flirtation found a range of attitudes. Several middle-aged or older women noted that they were not jealous. An older woman added that, "No, I am not unhappy. I am also glad of his good singing voice during extramarital flirtation. He only goes (flirting) for fun." Perhaps because of being aware of my uncertain attitude toward their answers, these women even sang a Hmub folk song to convince me during the interview: "Mom has become old, because she has given birth a baby. Dad under such situation goes out to flirt with another girl. Dad goes to talk about love by himself. Dad's flirting affair is his own business." Like the description of the song, these older women emphasized that husband and wife hardly ever accompany each other out of doors, no matter whether walking to the fields or attending ritual activities. "It's a matter of shame for (married) couples to appear together openly," they emphasized. "If a husband wants to go out (for extramarital flirting) let him go. That's his business," these women said in an amused fashion. These comments are very common among the aged women of this village.

Although not as light-hearted as the older women when talking about extramarital flirting, two younger mothers (30 years old) in this Hmub village also said that they would allow their husbands to go out and flirt with girls in the evening until their children begin to go to school (i.e. when the children have grown up and the father will not be expected to flirt with girls freely). I asked them whether they felt heart-broken or angry about their husband's flirting activity in the evening. "No, I am not heart-broken or angry. Even if you feel hurt or angry, you just could not change anything at all. My kids' daddy still keeps going out flirting with another young women alone," one mother said. "Although you may be unhappy, you cannot scold him outside your bedroom. That would cause shame among other villagers if they know that you are unhappy at such a thing," the others emphatically added.

In trying to conform to the collective ideas about extramarital flirtation, there still exist individualized actions or perceptions. One middle-aged man in the village told me how most of the male villagers perceive extramarital flirting in a practical manner: "If you want to go flirting with girls in the night time by talking or singing duets, you go ahead secretly. Do not let your wife know. If she does not know, nothing will happen. If she knew, she might get angry." He also mentioned "some women are 'reasonable,' they don't get mad at this; but some are 'unreasonable,' they do get mad." It seems clearly that there is a double standard for men and women in terms of permissible flirting after marriage. In some of the informants' quotes, it seems very salient, with the focus being on women left behind while men pursue extramarital gratification. Though this chapter does not aim to explore the practice of gender bifurcation of the extra-marital flirtation, we still may wonder about how this practice might relate the tradition of polygyny in the history of the Hmub or Hmong,[29] or how it might relate to the role of motherhood.

Discussion

I have described the relations between marriage and flirting and also the practice of extra-marital flirtation both verbally and no-verbally. There are two points that I will elaborate further: First, what the characteristic of the *iut fub* can be explained as an institutionalized extramarital flirting; and second, how the *iut fub* can be depicted as an alternative to functional courtship or courtship with lineal relation to marriage which also sheds light on certain specific features of "courtship," e.g. the duality of flirting and courting, or the "serious" flirting culture with regards to extramarital as well as non-extramarital relations.

Institutionalized Flirting Zone

In general, *iut fub* in the Hmub village has become institutionalized through the ritualized social arrangements of place, time, and the grouping of people. On the one hand, it conforms to the rules for affinal alliance: all girls and boys of the Fangf Bil village who flirt together are *khait* affines towards one another. On the other hand, *iut fub* also creates a juxtaposed, solid, binary structure for the institution of cross-cousin marriage, as well as an image of fluidity when integrating the institutions of marriage, extramarital flirting and duo-local residence. Ultimately, the textual description of duets does not necessary have a lineal relation between marriage and flirting. With the hybrid display of intimately physical contacts among flirting men and women marked with diverse genealogical ties, affinal relations and marital status, this creates fluidity between personal emotions and the social constraints of the institution of marriage. Among the emotions created by *iut fub*, extramarital flirtation is a way of reconciling personal "romantic" and "intimate" encounters with a lifetime of constraint through the institution of prescriptive marriage. In a way, there are two forms of *iut fub* in this flirting zone: one leading to marriage and another leading to validation of the self as a sexual being.

The peculiarity of this zone of the Hmub can be highlighted furthermore when compared with other societies. In addition to the literature quoted above, which is divided over the exact nature of the interplay between courtship and marriage, the study of Jane Collier on the Los Olivous in Spain elaborates how market economy, individual intention, and self-management techniques related to the senses and emotional workings of the "modern" individual, plus varying gender conceptions, move a society from one based on courtship to dating, especially as it pertains to the shift between duty to personal desire.[30] Unlike the Spanish cases, where duties shift with heighten individuality to personal desire, the Hmub adopt both. There is duty indeed in the formal processes of flirting and the everyday interaction between adults, especially married couples in public (but not in private). The Hmub also have a flirtation zone for continued expression of personal desire within a larger social restraint. How different is this from 19th Qing dynasty (or maybe many other stratified societies) where ordinary men went to brothels, and social elites seek the company of courtesans, all started in the form of entertaining in a public place, but ended with personal gratification when in private. Yet what is unique among the egalitarian Hmub is the absence of a stratified society where a very well off class is nonexistent. But the personal zone for intimacy remains important and salient. In this way, the Hmub may be a special case for validating the sexual self of a human being, socially as well as psychologically, with the provision of an alternative in theorizing romantic love from the Western social stratifications and heighten individualism.

Duality of Flirting and Courting

However, can the *iut fub* be explained in terms of flirtation culture rather than courtship culture? The *Oxford English Dictionary* defines courtship as "the action or process of paying court to a woman with a view to marriage; courting, wooing." It is also defined as "behavior or action befitting a court or courtier; courtliness of manners," or "the paying of court or courteous attentions; *esp.* the paying of ceremonial or complimentary acts of courtesy *to* a dignitary".[31] As such, the meaning of courtship seems to be identical with manners or politeness. In contrast flirtation seems considered less serious than courtship.

Flirtation is defined as "a quick, sprightly motion, a cant word among women;" and "the action or behavior of a flirt; flighty or giddy behavior, frivolity; the action of playing at courtship".[32] In reviewing the Hmub institutionalized flirting data I will shed light on its seriousness, and argue that the boundary between courtship and flirtation may not be so obvious. For our discussion, I will draw on three other ethnographies with regards to courting and flirting cultures to demonstrate that seriousness is a specific feature commonly seen in other institutional courting and flirting customs, though with diverse levels of seriousness. Long term and formal obligations or institutions create one type of serious courtship and flirtation, while the other is related to premarital sexuality.

The socially constrained Hmub flirtation, enhanced with entertaining devices, creates a leisurely and socially playful zone for the community. Similarly, Collier also addressed the conventional courtship of a Spanish village in the 1960s' as a long, formal institution and a pleasing emotional zone for young persons. In this case, the seriousness of courtship is derived from its formal asexual manners, reputation, and long-term courting activity before marriage.[33] There is a vivid description about how the boy was permitted to enter into the girl's house formally, successfully transforming his interest from informal street courtship, that I would label "flirtation", to courtship.

The boy, hair plastered and shoes polished, enters the kitchen and accepts a chair. Suegro (father-in-law) and novio discuss crops or the weather until the girl's father, uncomfortable in this social situation, retires to the café for some coffee and male companionship. The mother however must sit close by her daughter, hacienda la cestact (literally, 'basket weaving') while the novios 'pluck the turkey.' Physical contact is forbidden at any time, and the rule is generally respected. [34]

Parallel to the long term flirtation of the Hmub, the seriousness of the conventional Spanish case was related to its long term premarital courtship. Prior to the 1960's it was common that courting partners in the Spanish village would marry only after courting more than ten years. Furthermore, sexual desire is carefully separated from romantic or emotional desire during the formal courtship process.

In contrast to the "asexual", long term post-marital flirtation of the Hmub and the serious pre-marital courtship in a Spanish village in the sixties,[35] the courtship customs of the Hmong in Laos[36] and Chinese villages in Northern China are quite different. In both cases courtship allow "pre-marital sexuality," though with different connotations for each community. In *Changing Lives of Refugee Hmong Women*, the conventional Hmong courtship in Laos is an important part of its culture because marriage is the "natural stage" to becoming true mature adults, and the pleasant counterpoint to a hard working life.[37] Regular flirtatiousness could be in public and also as a "secrecy game, with its pleasing air of conspiracy, witness, and excitement".[38] In other words, the Hmong courtship is not just an emotional zone for casual emotional enjoyment, but also an arena for engaging in physical enjoyment and experimentation. Donnelly mentioned that, "There is another reason for shyness and desire for privacy. My respondents (except the converted Christian Hmong) seem to agree with other sources that Hmong girls and boys play sexual games together, and that fidelity to one friend is not expected".[39] The *iut fub* of the Hmub appears to have captured both the serious, respectful atmosphere of the Spanish and some of the light hearted, experimentation of the Hmong. Focusing on love, intimacy, and family change in a Chinese village from 1949 to 1999, Yan Yunxiang gave an interesting alternative example of the relations of courtship and marriage: post-engagement dating and premarital sex. Yan argues that there are two important effects of this custom: first, securing a marriage contact, especially, for the groom's family; second, creating mutual affections and emotional ties between the two. In other words, Yan emphasizes the seriousness of the intent of extra-engagement dating and premarital sex for the rural Chinese, which achieve a twofold goal: the emotional outlet and development of mutual affection for the couples; and the social capital for the bride's and groom's families, positively attained from engagement toward marriage.[40]

Either in terms of "courting with emphasis on courtship," or "flirting with emphasis on courtship," I suggest that there are both commonality and diversity to be further highlighted. Firstly, all four cultures display a specific zone as being a pleasing and relaxing emotional zone regardless of courtship as a precursor to marriage (such as in the Spanish or the contemporary rural Chinese villages) or an indirect result (such as flirtation in the subgroup Hmong of the Miao in Laos or the subgroup Hmub of the Miao in eastern Guizhou). This commonality is especially significant when interpreting how the Hmub place their social focus on institutionalized extramarital flirtation. In other words, based on these ethnographies of courtship or flirtation, human beings are psycho-emotional beings, not just social beings.

Additionally, all four cultures define "courting with emphasis on courtship" or "flirting with emphasis on courtship" activity as a serious matter. For the rural Chinese villagers, premarital sexuality is presented as an effective social strategy to solidify the marital contract between the families of the bride and groom. In contrast, the practice of premarital sexuality of the Hmong does not necessarily aim for marital exchange, but has significant social implications for an individual's social networks as well as having pleasant psychological and emotional experiences.

Though restricting premarital sexuality, the other two cultures make flirting with emphasis on courtship serious with long term flirtation. The conventional Spanish cases are amazing for the length of courtship, often enduring for 10 or more years, and avoidance of sexual contact with their long term courting partners fulfilling the social obligation of respect for both the girl and their family. The Hmub, on the other hand, conduct both short term premarital courtship as well as a long term extra-marital flirtation simultaneously. This chapter asserts that the juxtaposition of the long term and short term flirtation is a very *serious* social interaction with important implications for an individual's social network and standing in the Hmub society. By means of multiple modes of expression: verbal, physical and use of social conventions and institutionalized behavior, the *iut fub* creates not only an exclusive arena for emotional expression for the young, but also presents itself as an institutionalized flirting zone for the married adults, providing an approach with a result that is different from the lineal relation between flirtation and monogamous marriage. It provides a transitional phase for the young to have role models and gradually assume the responsibilities of mature Hmub adults in their social networks and obligations.

Conclusion

Most of the literature quoted describes courtship will lead to marriage, but some do point out that there is no necessary connection or entangled relations between them. These contradictions suggest the complications involved. Is erotic desire or the flirtatious happiness of men and women relevant or irrelevant to marriage? The *iut fub* of the Hmub in eastern Guizhou further underscores the entangled relations between flirting and marriage created by the integrated marital institutions, cross cousin marriage and duo-local post-marital residence, the entertaining devices, singing of love songs and intimate physical contact. In general, by analyzing extramarital flirtation of the Hmub, I have sought to explore the boundaries of emotional expression, both within and outside marriage of this specific culture. By looking into *iut fub* as an integrated social structure in a dialectical relationship within the institution of marriage, the fluid situations for extramarital flirtations or intimacies can be more closely examined.

Besides documenting erotic encounters outside the institution of marriage, this ethnography of Hmub extramarital flirtation suggests that we can pay more attention to the concept of infidelity as it is defined culturally.[41] In other words, how does an individual in Fangf Bil village respond psychologically and emotionally to institutionalized extramarital eroticism, whether verbal or physical? Do Fangf Bil Hmub villagers regard such extramarital erotic happenings as infidelity? Will a young mother feel jealous, angry or sad as a result of the erotic encounters of her middle-aged husband in Hmub flirting activities? Such questions may touch on the nature of the distinctions between the three social domains of sex, love and marriage. I suggest that institutionalized extramarital flirtation is a compensation for an overly formal marriage/family arrangement, which may not necessarily result in an aloof relationship, but an intimate one instead. So, the practice of the Hmub extramarital flirting is less an escape but rather the establishment of a safe setting where people can satisfy themselves of being sexually attractive. Maybe this desire is stronger than what conventional wisdom should have acknowledged. Whereas the primary reason for the existence of the sex industry in other parts of China is to meet the need of sexual satisfaction which can go beyond just a physical intercourse. The Hmub practice is not sexually motivated but just the provision of an arena for sexual validation and that in the end may be an alternative but important encounter that constitutes a person's own emotional gratification. The Hmub's culturally defined conceptions of infidelity would focus on extramarital flirtations, but without ending with sexual intercourse as a result. Through the public display of erotic flirtation, the Hmub of eastern Guizhou demonstrates the existence of significant arenas for interpersonal exchanges. Recalling Adam Phillips's suggestion that "flirtation keeps things in play, and by doing so lets us get to know them in different ways",[42] I suggest that the Hmub's extramarital flirtation serves as an outlet for individual, personal expression of deeply held emotions. This stands in sharp contrast to the lack of public emotional expression allowed to married couples.[43]

Chapter 2

Tensions between Romantic Love and Marriage: Performing Hmub Cultural Individuality in an Upland Hmub Love-Song

Introduction

Pierre Clastres notes that primitive societies are not 'incomplete', even without a state, literacy or written historical records (Clastres 1987). In line with this way of viewing and understanding non-modern or non-Western society, this chapter focuses on a peripheral society that has retained its autonomy by performing individuality within its own cultural contexts. This, however, does not imply an approach towards the morally autonomous individualism found in modern Euro-American societies.

This chapter explores the local expression of individuality in the love-song performance of an upland Hmub society in eastern Guizhou in south-west China, illustrated using extracts from a song of over four hundred lines performed as a duet between two female and two male singers.[1]

Sentiment has long been a topic of both attention and contention in the anthropology of kinship, but it is often treated as following from kinship relations (Radcliffe-Brown 1924; Homans and Schneider 1955). This chapter adopts an alternative performative perspective, exploring the sentiments expressed in the love-song performances of upland Hmub people. Hmub love-songs place thematic emphasis upon humour, sentiment, and social and kin relationships by employing the rhetorical force of various poetic devices. I give special attention to a thematic analysis of the tensions between 'romantic love' (personal sentiments) and 'marriage' (affinal alliances), and outline how this Hmub love-song poetically reveals a very common theme: the encounter between individual identity and social ideals.

The dialogic relationship between the individual and society has long been discussed by Durkheim, Mauss, Dumont and others. Examining further the claim that 'individualism pertains to a particular historic-cultural conceptualization of the person or self' (Rapport and Overing 2000), this chapter concludes that Hmub individuality is expressed within performances of Hmub love-songs and the social dynamics they embody.

The Individual and Society in Anthropology

There is a long history of debate on the topic of the 'individual' versus 'society' in the anthropological literature. I will not review the entire debate here but concentrate on outlining the general approach of French anthropology, in particular Durkheim, Dumont and Mauss, as well as the work of the British anthropologist Marilyn Strathern. Much of this work gives a significant role to the individual, and to the encounter between the individual and society. From their work, one can see how the concepts of 'individual', 'individuality' and 'individualism' developed by considering them within their specific ethnographic, cultural and historical contexts. An article by Rapport and Overing in their *Social and Cultural Anthropology: The Key Concepts* (2000) reviewing Durkheim's notion of the individual is my starting point.

Émile Durkheim was the 'key exponent of collectivist narratives which subsumed the individual actor within grand-societal workings' (Rapport and Overing 2000: 179). He saw human beings in terms of the concept of *homo duplex*. As Rapport and Overing note, for Durkheim the individual 'led a double existence; one rooted in the physical organism and one ... in a social organism. ... Between the two there was constant antagonism and tension, but through inculcation into a public language and culture humankind was capable of rising above mean (animal) individuality and becoming part of a collective conscience in which the (sacred) traditions of a society were enshrined' (ibid.: 180).

The narratives of Durkheim, Marcel Mauss and Louis Dumont all combine individualism and individuality. Again citing Rapport and Overing (2000: 180), in 'A Category of the Human Mind' (1979), Mauss shows 'how society exerted its force on the physiological individual: how, through collective representations and collectively determined habitual behaviours, it submerged the individual within "a collective rhythm" '. Combining universal individuality with cultural individualism, Mauss proceeds to outline an evolutionary account of how people in different ages and societies have been aware of themselves differently as individual beings, and how these differences can be traced back to different forms of social structuration. Mauss dismisses self-awareness early on in his paper as of no interest to him, considering it to be basically psychological and a human universal: what he is interested in is social constructions of the person. What constitutes 'an individual' is not a universal —— it has its own expression in different societies.

In his *Essays on Individualism* (1986), Dumont agrees with Mauss that 'the Western notion of the individual —— an autonomous actor, bearing supreme moral value —— is an exceptional stage in the evolution of civilisations' (Rapport and Overing 2000: 181). For Dumont, Hinduism offers a social insight: 'the crucial difference between the Hindu world renouncer and the modern individualist is that the former can [*ideologically*] continue to exist only outside the everyday social world', while the notion of the modern individual is central to Western society (ibid.).

On the basis of Melanesian and English models, Marilyn Strathern discusses how indigenous conceptualizations of the individual and society differ in different cultures and in different historical periods. Her theoretical position regarding the individual and society is clearly articulated in *After Nature*, a work on modern English kinship:

[The English model] depicted mid-twentieth century English kinship as a model for the reproduction of individuals and suggested a contrast with the Melanesian interest in the reproduction of relations. As individuals, persons in the English model do not symbolize whole social entities and cannot be isomorphic with a collectivity or a span of relationships. Rather, individuals are held to exist as parts of numerous different systems—a part of the kinship system, part of a naming system, part of society—and do not replicate in total any one systemic configuration. I referred to the conceptualization as merographic. ... We are now in a position, I think, to give this merographically conceptualized English person its *aesthetic* or *iconic* dimension. ... The individual person who is the microcosm of convention becomes elided with the individual person who makes his or her own choice. In the process, this figure will present a different kind of image, a composite, a montage, of itself. (Strathern 1992: 125–27, *my emphasis*)

Four points follow from the above quote that deserve to be highlighted. The first is that there is a tension, or antithesis, between the individual and society. The second is the valuing of the individual. Strathern found that different cultures understand what an individual is quite differently. It seems that Durkheim saw individualism 'as a value', although not explicitly stating this (Lukes 1973: 338ff.; Dumont 1986: 16). Moreover, Mauss and Dumont address autonomy and morality as the defining values of the Western individual. Comparing the Melanesian model with the English one, Strathern found that in Melanesia individuals are seen in terms of the relationships between them, that is, as producing the relationships which constitute their collectivity, their sociality; in mid-twentieth-century English society individuals were simply understood as being various discrete parts of the whole system.

Given that her English subjects were a 'mid-twentieth-century' group, a third point Strathern's quote raises is the question of modernity. Individualism has to different degrees underlain anthropological thought since Durkheim, being explicit or implicit in revolutionary or progressive ideas. It has long generally been considered a feature of modern Western society. Subsequent debate on the nature of the individual brought about a consideration of modernity. As Dumont notes, 'for Mauss it is sometimes as though everything else were leading up to modernity' (1986: 4). In fact, Durkheim and Dumont himself both have an evolutionist basis to their ideas. Most subsequent discussion contrasts 'traditional' forms with modern ones, or is evolutionist in structure.[2]

The fourth point of interest in Strathern's study of contemporary English kinship is the shift towards the aesthetic and iconic dimension. Her considering the relations between individuality and sociality from such a perspective might also be traced back to her earlier study of Melanesian societies: Strathern's notion of the 'dividual' being was drawn originally from McKim Marriott's work on India (1976), and she applied this notion to Melanesia (Strathern 1988: 348–49, f.7).[3]

> Far from being regarded as unique entities, Melanesian persons are as *dividually* as they are individually conceived. They contain a generalized sociality within. Indeed, persons are frequently constructed as the plural and composite site of the relationships that produced them. The singular person can be imagined as a social microcosm. (Strathern 1988: 13, *my emphasis*)

This novel perspective on the individual addressed by Strathern, aesthetic or iconic, offers a new method for uncovering the characteristics and value of the individual. In fact, this perspective is closely related to what I am doing in this chapter, namely examining language in use and the perfomative dimension of social life.

The Turn to 'Language in Use'

The turn towards 'language in use' has its roots in the fields of philosophy and linguistics. Wittgenstein examined ordinary language usage: he 'turned away from meanings and toward speaking habits' (Urban 1996: xii). Picking up this line of thinking, John Austin observed that 'people do much more with words ("performativity") than merely talk about the world ("constativity")' (ibid.).

The Russian linguist Roman Jakobson's teleological view of language also contributed to this trend. For him, change in sound 'therefore, is teleological. It must be measured ... against the referential goal of communication, or if the example is from verse [*sic*], against the poetic function.' Such a multifunctional, polysystemic view of language is a radical departure from Saussure, for whom *langue* was homogeneous in both function and system (Caton 1987: 231). Moreover, M.M. Bakhtin's 'homogeneous versus heteroglossic poles of language' could also be built into the Jakobsonian model (ibid.). Bakhtin's emphasis on the system of aesthetics in speech genres deserves more attention. Michael Holquist introduces Bakhtin as follows:

> Since the time of Kant, we have with ever increasing insistence perceived system as a closed order rather than as an open-ended series of connections. System for Kant meant not only the rigorous application

of a fully worked out and absolutely coherent set of categories. System also implied that no major question should be treated in isolation: thus, any consideration of reason had to answer demands not only of logic or epistemology, but of *ethics* and *aesthetics* as well. It is *in this latter sense only that Bakhtin's thought might be labeled systematic*: the sense he seeks to invoke when he calls ... for an 'open unity'. (Holquist 1986: x, *my emphasis*)

Following the development of this pragmatic view, a critical perspective has emerged which explores the poetics and performance of language and social life, the aesthetic aspect. Bauman and Briggs (1990: 79) comment on these new perspectives as follows: 'the turn to performance marked an effort to establish a broader space within linguistics and anthropology for poetics—verbal artistry... . A focus on the artistic use of language in the conduct of social life—in kinship, politics, economics, religion—opens the way to an understanding of performance as socially constitutive and efficacious, not secondary and derivative.'

Background

There are roughly nine million Miao currently spread across a large part of the massif that covers the Yun-Gui Plateau in south-west China and surrounding uplands in both south-west China and northern parts of South-East Asia (in Vietnam, Laos and Thailand). The Miao within China are usually divided into five groups on the basis of their language and geographical distribution.[4]

The earliest known relations of the central Miao group with the Han

附錄

Chapter 2   Tensions between Romantic Love and Marriage:
            Performing Hmub Cultural Individuality in an Upland Hmub Love-Song

Chinese occurred during the Song dynasty (Yang 1998). From the Yuan dynasty onwards, Chinese written records refer to Miao in this area as 'Black Miao'. The region where the central Miao are located, 'an unbroken strip of Black Miao', did not become widely known until the Chinese forced their way into Miao territory in the Qing dynasty period of the Yongzheng (雍正) reign (1724–1736).

Fangf Bil is a Miao village perched high on a hillside in the upper reaches of the Qingshuijiang River.[5] It forms part of the northern subgroup of the central Miao (Yang 1998: 99), and administratively is part of Fanzao township, Taijiang County, in South-Eastern Guizhou Self-Governing Autonomous District in Guizhou Province.[6] Local people speak an eastern Miao dialect of the Miao-Yao subfamily of Sino-Tibetan. The people of Fangf Bil call themselves Hmub (cognate with Hmong, the usual self-designation). The village is composed of over 330 households with a population of almost 1,500 (1998–2000). It is divided into eleven hamlets (*vangf*), whose names refer to various nearby geographical features. The residents of any single hamlet are generally the agnatic descendants of a lineage subsegment, and share a common Han Chinese surname. The naming system is patronymic. For both males and females, their name is composed of their individual name preceded by their father's name, and their father's name preceded by his father's name. Han Chinese surnames came into use only in the eighteenth century and are seldom heard in everyday Hmub discourse. They are nevertheless in keeping with the patrilineal spirit of Fangf Bil naming practices.

The eleven hamlets are organized into five patrilineal marriage groups within which marriage is forbidden. The five marriage groups are designated by the five Han Chinese surnames of Zhang (張 , *Zix Zangb*, literally 'Family Zhang'), Tang (唐 , *Zix Tangf*), Wang (王 , *Zix Uangd*), Yang (楊 , *Zix Iangf*) and Tai (邰 , *Zix Taif*). There is no exclusive correspondence between the name of a marriage group and the surnames of the households and people belonging to it. For example, not everyone in the Zhang marriage group has the surname 'Zhang', and there may be people in other marriage groups with this surname. Hamlets, surnames and patrilineal marriage groups are all, in one way or another, organized around ancestral groups. Those in a marriage group generally live in close proximity, share a common male ancestor, and act as patrilineal descent groups in relation to ancestral rites and the possession of agricultural land. The surnames and hamlets coincide roughly with the marriage groups, but only the marriage groups correspond directly with the ancestral groups.

The combined population of marriage groups 2 and 4 composes over 90 percent of Fangf Bil's total population. The proportion of intermarriages between them therefore far exceeds the proportion of intermarriages between any other marriage groups and marriages outside the village. The statistics in Table 2.1 are based on the family genealogies of the *Vangf Dof* and *Ghad Dlongb* hamlets. It is clear that women marry in both directions. The affinal classifications of this village seem to constitute something approaching a binary structure.

附錄

Chapter 2 Tensions between Romantic Love and Marriage:
          Performing Hmub Cultural Individuality in an Upland Hmub Love-Song

Table 2.1 Marriages into and out of the *Vangf Dof* and *Ghad Dlongb* hamlets of marriage group 4

Other marriage group	Marriages into *Vangf Dof* and *Ghad Dlongb*	Marriages out of *Vangf Dof* and *Ghad Dlongb*
1	4 (4.2%)	2 (2.2%)
2	84 (89.3%)	71 (80.06%)
3	0 (0.0%)	0 (0.0%)
Zix Hot hamlet of marriage group 4	0 (0.0%)	1 (1.1%)[7]
5	2 (2.1%)	3 (3.3%)
Marriages out of Fangf Bil village	4 (4.2%)	11 (12.4%)
Totals	**94 (100%)**	**88 (100%)**

Most marriages take place within the village, and the society is organized around classificatory bilateral cross-cousin marriage. The kinship terminology of this village has a similar structure to the Dravidian-type kinship terminology in its ideal and practice of prescriptive cross-cousin marriage. Most women in Fangf Bil still marry either their classificatory matrilateral or patrilateral cross-cousins: that is, both FZD/MBS or MBD/FZS marriages occur.[8]

Nevertheless, the local practice of cross-cousin marriage is still related to how kin are classified in a community which clearly distinguishes between near and distant kin. Thus for female ego, bilateral cross-cousin marriage is not with actual FZS or MBS but occurs between members of patrilineal descent groups:

- who are related to one another as classificatory patrilateral cross-cousins (FZHBS, FZHFBSS, or FZHFFBSSS); or
- who are equated terminologically with the FZS; or
- who are related to one another as classificatory matrilateral cross-cousins (MFBSS, or MFFBSSS); or
- who are equated terminologically with the MBS.

That is, there is again both classificatory FZD/MBS and classificatory MBD/FZS marriage. The binary organization of Fangf Bil is given classificatory reality in the distinction between *gad ghat* (agnates) and *khait* (affines).[9] These are relative categories of the sort found in virtually all societies, rather than sociocentric groups; there is no true dual organization here, despite the quasi-'binary organization' in this village. Marriage is prohibited between *gad ghat* (or simply *ghat*) but permitted with *khait*. The centrality of the relationships between *ghat* and *khait* in Fangf Bil is indicative of the importance of kinship in village social processes.

Traditional formalized flirting and what I call 'delayed transfer marriage', that is, duolocal post-marital residence, are the last specific Hmub cultural phenomena I introduce here, though they are far from being the least important. They significantly demonstrate some fluid aspects of Hmub marriage which exist simultaneously with the system outlined above, and seem to have done so for a long time.

附錄

Chapter 2 Tensions between Romantic Love and Marriage:
            Performing Hmub Cultural Individuality in an Upland Hmub Love-Song

Courting is commonly understood in the Western tradition as an activity performed with marriage as its goal. Hmub flirting is a far more complex phenomenon and is certainly not solely linked to the goal of marriage. Flirting in a Hmub village is an institutionalized cultural practice, an expression of local social and cultural arrangements of place, time and person. It partly fits in with the stipulations of the affinal alliance pattern and partly gives expression to the fluid nature of the interplay between personal sentiments, as well as the relatively rigid cross-cousin marriage which is the social ideal.

In contrast with some other Hmub villages in eastern Guizhou that permit daytime flirting, in Fangf Bil this traditional activity is only permitted in the evening, but it is also allowed during the daytime following certain ritual activities such as New Year or harvest festivals. Evening flirting takes place in the living room of the house of the young woman being flirted with, or outside but close to the house. Daytime flirting activities take place at different 'flirting places' belonging to specific marriage groups, where opposite-sex affines flirt with each other in conjuction with affinal alliances.

Formal flirting is the most important social activity in Fangf Bil village and is practised exclusively by 'the young'. The local indigenous conceptualization of 'the young' who may and do participate encompasses those from as young as ten years old, as well as adult men and women who have married within the previous few years. The latter do not usually flirt with their spouses, though this does occasionally occur. This inclusion of recently married people is a critical difference from the Western idea of courting, or courtship, and will be discussed further below. Flirting involves young men and women spending a great deal of time together, sometimes in groups, sometimes in single pairs, talking, singing and exchanging gifts.[10] Sex is expressly prohibited.

Hmub flirting is clearly not simply a prelude and pathway to marriage: married people also participate in this quite distinct cultural activity (Chien 2009a). There are, however, specific rules for married men and married women. A married woman can flirt with her opposite-sex affines until she has delivered her first child. In contrast, a married man can participate much longer than most women: he is not prohibited from flirting with his opposite-sex affines until his children reach their teens. Unmarried men or women (single or divorced) are considered to be 'young persons' who can attend flirting activities freely, as long as they flirt with someone appropriate, that is, in conformity with prescriptions of affinal alliance. There is some fluidity in the kinship terminology – for example, sometimes a particular person can be described by two different kinship terms, each having different practical implications.

Like 'flirting', duolocal residence also demonstrates the complex nature of local marriage. The bride does not usually go to live with the groom immediately after their wedding but returns to stay with her natal kin soon after it instead. She only visits the groom's house on festival days or to assist her husband's family do farm work. She does not live with her husband in his house until she has her first child. During the duolocal period, the bride and the groom can both freely attend flirting activities —— interacting with other opposite-sex cross-cousins —— on their own as they did before they married. The solid, clear binary structures of cross-cousin marriage are juxtaposed with the fluid aspects of marriage, flirting and residence that are clearly seen in the customs of traditional formal 'flirting' activities and duolocal residence. This

附錄

Chapter 2   Tensions between Romantic Love and Marriage:
            Performing Hmub Cultural Individuality in an Upland Hmub Love-Song

juxtaposition and the complexity of the social domains associated with flirting and marriage find clear expression in Hmub love-songs.

Local Love-Songs

Many Miao songs were published during the 1950s in the series *Minjian wenxue ziliao* (民間文學資料 , 'Miao folklore data'), reprinted in the 1980s. The lyrics of these and the Miao songs published in *Miaozu hunyin ge* (苗族 婚姻歌 , 'Marriage Songs of the Miao', Tang [1959] 1986) are public records expressing the Miao collective experience of marriage, including the personal 'individual' experiences of bride and groom before and after marriage.

Songs in Fangf Bil fall into two categories: 'old' songs, *hxad lok*, and 'young' songs, *hxad vangx*. Most 'young' songs present similar themes; the villagers further classify them into four subcategories based on performance details.[11]

The 'old' songs are generally about Hmub mythology, the origins of villages, lineages, clans and ancestors. The song discussed below is in the 'young' song category. These generally have a joyful, joking tone, but at times the tone can also be sentimental, lonely or forlorn. Among other things, they present the inherent tension between traditional marriage and individual personal sentiments.

Methodology

Most of the Hmub songs I collected in Fangf Bil village came from natural settings in the sense that almost all were performed as part of the 'flirting' activities in conjunction with the celebration of certain festivals or ritual activities. I recorded such songs on many occasions in both ritual and non-ritual settings. This love-song performance was recorded with a tape recorder, and then transcribed using the Hmub phonetic system.[12]

I chose to rely on a small number of local villagers as key cultural consultants to assist me with this —— a twenty-year-old girl, her parents and some other relatives —— because transcription is extremely tedious, time-consuming work, and the interpretation, translation and analysis of the more than four hundred lines required mutual understanding, trust, familiarity and patience on behalf of both the cultural consultants and myself. We worked together for several days and nights replaying the tapes many times, and transcribed the entire performance.

Love-Song Performance

The extracts cited below come from a love-song performance that took place in the early spring of 1999 in connection with the seasonal festival celebrating the planting of rice. The song, of more than four hundred lines, was performed as a duet between two female singers and two male singers. The social context was that many people, male and female, young and old, from Fangf Bil and four neighbouring villages gathered on the hillside fields to watch bullfights. The event was hosted by Fangf Bil. After the bullfights most of the older men and women and the children left, but the young men and women stayed for the traditional 'flirting'. Men and women from different villages sat or stood close together, some in groups, most in single couples, happily talking, and some, though not all, singing to each other. Love-song performances by some of those

附錄

Chapter 2   Tensions between Romantic Love and Marriage:
            Performing Hmub Cultural Individuality in an Upland Hmub Love-Song

who were skilled singers attracted a large audience. More than one of these performances could be happening at any one time.

The two female singers were from Fangf Bil, the two male singers from another village, not very far from Fangf Bil —— about 40 or 50 *li*. Similarly, apart from the singers, there were in effect two audiences: one of women from Fangf Bil, the other of men from the other village. The people of both villages speak the same Hmub dialect and wear the same style of Hmub clothes.[13] Like the male and female singers, the men and women in the audience were also classificatory affines to each other.

The two male singers (both forty years old) were already married and had become fathers. One female singer (twenty years old) was unmarried; the other (nearly twenty-five years old) had married but not yet become a mother and was still living with her natal kin. We —— myself and some young ladies, Fangf Bil villagers, who were accompanying and assisting me —— knew that the female singers were descendants of the same patrilineal group, but did not know their actual genealogical relationships to the male singers. During the break, however, and at the end of the song performance, we heard the singers address each other using prescriptive cross-kin terms.

This particular love-song was sung entirely by men and women as a duet.[14] In total, 450 lines were sung and 28 lines were spoken. They were grouped into verses of various lengths from 4 to 8 lines, mostly of 6 or 7 lines. The sequence of these lines was not prescriptive. This love-song performance took the form of a spontaneous competition among the singers. They had a 'data bank', a store of lyrics and verses, but they did not simply memorize and reproduce a long set sequence. They had to listen carefully to what their competitors, the other singers in the duet, were singing. If they did not do so, or were careless, they could get lost among the possible responses and so fail to select an appropriate response to what had just been sung. They could repeat some lines if appropriate. Some lines or verses were gender-specific, some were not. Nouns or pronouns could be changed to express gender-specific contents (Chien 2007).

The duet performance lasted for more than an hour. It was not at all serious or formal. The singers talked to each other, or joked with the audience when they had finished their own lines, and the audiences talked to each other while enjoying the show. They mostly liked commenting on the performance, comparing the skills of the singers, and discussing the contents of the lines with the other members of the audience. The content was much more important than the quality of the singing delivery. But any singer who did not pay attention to when it was their turn to sing, or did not come up with a good line with which to respond, left themselves open to being criticized and commented on negatively by the audience, something not good for their reputation.[15]

Thematic Foci

Hmub love-songs place thematic emphasis upon humour, sentiment, and social and kin relationships. A particular feature is their performative expression of the local culturally determined tension between the individual experience of 'love' —— equated with the flirting setting —— and local cross-cousin marriage, which is the ideal.

To summarize briefly, this love-song describes an encounter between two women and two men meeting each other at just such a traditional flirting event. On the one hand, the men and the women both express the same shy but joyful emotions they experience when attending such occasions. On the other hand, they tease themselves and their partners about the dialogical relationship between marriage and flirting. They finish the performance by expressing their feelings: forlornness about parting and being alone.

Interwoven with the 'story line' outlined above are four recurring themes: (a) marriage; (b) flirting; (c) the two different local relationships between marriage and flirting; and (d) individuals' experience, through which the aesthetic dimensions of marriage and flirting for the Hmub are brought to the fore.

(a) *Marriage* is an obvious thematic thread permeating the love-song. Two particular aspects of local marriage are directly referred to: the individuals' desire for marriage, and the collective ideal of cross-cousin marriage. The following lines are an example of the song and singers expressing individuals' longing for marriage. Viewed somewhat paradoxically from the Western tradition, this longing occurs in the context of assured marriage in keeping with tradition, as referred to in line 349, and line 157 further below:

Dat Deik	Male Singers
347 *Xud dongf mongf dot jut.*	Do not say that you will marry others.
348 *Ninx dongf lel bib mek.*	Just say you will be with us forever.
349 *Ghet benf liangf hvib naik.*	We have to become husbands and wives, anyway.

Dat Ghaif	Female Singers
352 *Ceit daik las baf pent, **mul-diangf.***	We come here intentionally to sing with you, **cross-cousins.**
353 *Yel bib mongf lab diuf mek zix.*	Bring us to your homes. They (your parents) do not like us, but we still want to marry you.
354 *Neff hfif sax vob diangt.*	The flown bird will return to the cage.

Some lines more explicitly refer to or articulate details of cross-cousin marriage, for example:

Dat Ghaif	Female Singers
154 *Bib **mul-diangf** naik jut.*	We are **cross-cousins.**
155 *Bib def diangf dak niangt.*	We separate temporarily then return to sit together again and talk a while.
156 *Bib nal diangf dak ghent.*	Our mothers come to say something to the boys.
157 *Bib naf neif jek dint.*	We will become husbands and wives anyway.
158 *Bib del diangf liak ciet.*	Do not mind if we have to part right now.

There are implicit allusions to the prescriptive alliance involving village endogamy:

附錄

Chapter 2   Tensions between Romantic Love and Marriage:
            Performing Hmub Cultural Individuality in an Upland Hmub Love-Song

Dat Deik	**Male Singers**
359 *Hvid cet liuk lel lait.*	We come here just now as done for thousands of years.
360 *Liuk gheb mangk lel ghet.*	We still cannot take you as our wives even in our next lives.
366 *Ghat but vangf hveb bif.*	You girls will marry someone else within your own village.
367 *Vob diut dak jut liuk.*	Become other men's wives.

The young men cannot marry the young women they are singing to; village endogamy requires that both parties marry within their own village. The emphasis on the relatively prescriptive cross-cousin alliance aspect of marriage is realized both by the lyrics and also by the repetitive use of the prescriptive affinal kin terms throughout the entire song, indicated in bold in the extracts.

(b) *Flirting*. There are various illustrations of flirting and institutionalized formal flirting occasions, this being the second thematic thread. Some lines vividly describe the flirting scene. Descriptions of the singing and talking mirror what occurs in real life. Line 385 can be understood in two ways: as a reference to how flirting also occurs in the living room of the flirted girls, or to talking more 'after we marry':

Dat Ghaif	**Female Singers**
343 *Dak lait iauf dak ceit, **mul-diangf.***	Once you have come here, come and sing together, **cross-cousins**.
344 *Ceit daik las baf pent.*	We come here on purpose to sing with you.
Dat Deik	**Male Singers**
383 *Ghaib qub mangk juk ghof,* ***mul-diangf.***	Like chickens, we cannot stop pecking the rice, **cross-cousins**.
384 *Bib pot mangk juk jib.*	We cannot stop talking to each other.
385 *Dleit diut ghab diuk nail.*	Leave something to be said inside the house.

Some lines describe a scene of everyone gathered for an event such as the one where this performance was underway, and the playful atmosphere that is characteristic of such flirting events:

Dat Deik	**Male Singers**
428 *Bib sint sint ghenf jek wek.*	We just sit together in groups.
429 *Sint sint ninf jek cangk.*	Just sit together creating this spectacular scene.
430 *Dit lit deif liuk deik.*	The girls do not want the boys immediately.
431 *Deif liud daif rangk dok.*	They throw the boys away like straw or firewood.

附錄

Chapter 2　Tensions between Romantic Love and Marriage:
　　　　　　Performing Hmub Cultural Individuality in an Upland Hmub Love-Song

Dat Deik	Male Singers
432 *Qit wab iauf dak ninf.*	The boys are very put out, so they come to tease the girls.

(c) *Two Relationships between Marriage and Flirting.* The two themes outlined above address marriage and flirting. The most pervasive thematic focus in the song, however, is the conflict inherent in the relationship between marriage and flirting experienced by the individuals concerned. Two different relationships are presented. In the first, marriage and flirting are sequentially connected; the logical progression of flirting is towards cross-cousin marriage. This is the sentiment expressed in line 45:

Dat Ghaif	Female Singers
42 *Naik liat dangk git qet.*	People thinking of each other come to rest midway.
43 **Mul-diangf** *eb.*	**Cross-cousins**.
44 *Niongk liat dangk git qet.*	The girls want to sit and talk with the boys, so they rest midway.
45 *Mak dint mongf vux diut.*	If you have wives, boys, then go home and take care of them.

Another example is at lines 90 and 91:

Dat Ghaif	Female Singers
88 *Daik sat het deif dot.*	No matter what the truth is, we will say the boys have wives.
89 *Hlaib sak het deif dot.*	No matter whether it is false, we will say the boys have wives.
90 *Diangt zix lius mek dint bongf heix.*	Go home and part with your wives.
91 *Diuf niongk hveb lel ghob.*	Only then will we two be willing to accompany both of you.

In contrast with the themes outlined above, many lines present a more complex and perhaps problematic model of the relationship between marriage and flirting, a dialogical one. Generally in these scenarios, the flirting does not lead to marriage; in that regard both are simply independent of each other. The next two extracts both vividly express the second complex relationship between marriage and flirting. The first two lines, 29 and 30, are like a Greek chorus in their effect; line 30 offers another vivid metaphor portraying the flirting scene, and the pleasure of those there:

Dat Ghaif	Female Singers
29 *Liob huf yiok.*	The boys love to talk to us.
30 *Ghas hfaf seik.*	The boys and girls are talking and singing together like ducks playing joyfully in the water.

附錄

Chapter 2 Tensions between Romantic Love and Marriage:
            Performing Hmub Cultural Individuality in an Upland Hmub Love-Song

Dat Ghaif	Female Singers
31 *Bongt neif meb niangt gait nongt.*	We do not know why we sit next to you all the time.
32 *Bongt lif dak jut liuk.*	We do not know we are accompanying others' husbands.

Another example is:

Dat Deik	Male Singers
263 *Benf vux ob vak liuf.*	The girls are good looking and speak well, but have two hearts.
264 *Lal vux ob vak ghek.*	Like the good fields, which can grow millet twice each year.
265 *Ib pit hvib qongk bongf.*	One heart accompanies their husbands.
266 *Ib pit hvib dak lif.*	Another heart accompanies us.

(d) *Personal Sentiments*. Another obvious thematic thread is the various individual personal sentiments, feelings and emotions —— including shyness, joy, solitude, longing and passion —— in connection with marriage or flirting. Some lines describe the shyness with which both the boys and girls approach flirting, for example:

Dat Deik	Male Singers
22 *Naik liuf ment let lab.*	Strangers will become familiar with each other by singing and talking.
23 *Meit ob lab nit nil.*	Just come to say a few words.
24 *Lab def lab det jaf.*	But we do not know how to talk to you.
25 *Xid xeit meb gid weif.*	We feel very shy to you.

Dat Ghaif	Female Singers
72 *Ob lik git ment let xef.*	The girls do not love to talk.
73 *Naik liuf ment let lal.*	Until meeting the strangers like you.
74 *Diut ux qib ux naif.*	Look, we do not wear our clothes appropriately.
75 *Heb ghaf heb det ghaf.*	Put on one sleeve of our coat only.
76 *Heb neif heb det rinf.*[16]	Put on one sleeve of our coat only.
77 *Xid xeit meb gait weis.*	We feel very shy to you.

Some lines describe the joy and delight associated with flirting:[17]

Dat Ghaif	Female Singers
60 *Liuf del let.*	When we hear the drums, we feel delighted.
61 *Deif del ghait.*	When we hear the words of the boys, we feel happy.

Other examples are:

Dat Deik	Male Singers
238 *Nef huf yiok.*	The girls love to talk to us.
239 *Ghas hfaf saik.*	Like ducks joyfully playing in the water.

Dat Deik	Male Singers
196 *Dad nef mak qet ninf.*	The girls will fool people.
197 *Xongx juf daik qet liuf.*	The boys are happy about that.

In addition to joy and similar emotions, the lyrics also express strong longing, often in combination with a sense of anticipated solitude or forlornness. These sentiments mostly arise in contexts of the second, complex relationship between marriage and flirting:

Dat Ghaif	Female Singers
277 *Mek hveb at nit hfuf.*	Your words are just talk.
278 *Mek hvib at yat yiok.*	Your hearts are far away.
279 *Juk eb fat hongx vongf.*	Your hearts are like a river flowing to the falls.
280 *Juk hob fat hongx bif.*	Like a fog in the midst of the hillsides which has lifted.
281 *Mek zod but mek bongf.*	You will go back to be with your wives.
Dat Deik	**Male Singers**
284 *Nef cent niangt diek vik,* **muldiangf.**	The bird is singing in the nest, **cross-cousins**.
285 *Dliut diut dot jut mongf.*	Let the girls marry others.
286 *Nongf heit ob dak nif.*	We two can only sit together a while, and talk a while.

Finally, desire and passion are expressed and alluded to in the song. This, however, is not done as explicitly as are the emotions and feelings outlined above. Only a few lines have such descriptions and allusions, for example, in line 226:

Dat Deik	Male Singers
224 *Meb dlab let lil rak renf.*	You two are good at talking.
225 *Lab qet juf wak wek.*	Your hearts are distant.
226 *Ment ghad ghuf dek deif.*	Girls touch the boys with their bodies.
227 *Dlek xongx dangf dlek dok.*	You desire to be close to the boys, as you desire to be near the fire in the winter cold.
228 *Diuf xongx nongf wek yef.*	We two boys are all alone.

Another example is line 106:

Dat Ghaif	Female Singers
106 *Mangk hongx xangt bif deif.*	We just do not want to let go the boys' hands.

Discussion

The various themes and scenarios presented in the lyrics of this love-song, examples of which are given above, provide complex expressions of the nature of Hmub marriage and flirting, and more. They include both the entangled relationships between marriage and flirting, and associated individual personal sentiments. This section discusses the role of love-songs such as this one —— with its specific aesthetic and iconic performance —— in constructing Hmub social life, as well as social reproduction.

The Hmub love-song emphasizes a central, highly visible social feature of Fangf Bil village: affinal alliance or cross-cousin marriage. This is clearly noticeable in certain linguistic and social phenomena, such as the Dravidian kinship terminology, in conjunction with the ideal and practice of prescriptive cross-cousin marriage. Citing my own earlier research,

> the principle of prescriptive marriage is particularly obvious in the changes in address terms for cross relatives. Unmarried male speakers are addressed as *but*, male cross-cousin, and *mul*, cross-cousin; unmarried female speakers are also addressed as *mul*. This is an abbreviated form of *mul diangf* (FZS/MBS), that is, an unmarried woman whose relationship with her cross-cousins —— including potential husbands —— is thereby indicated. She may, and indeed is expected to, marry a male having the same relationship with her. (Chien 1999: 46)

In effect this means that classificatory cross-cousins within the village are under very strong pressure to marry among themselves.

This situation is highly visible performatively within the love-song duet and the iconic content of certain lines. Singers and audience are all classificatory opposite-sex affines. This is social evidence that instantiates the core structure of the Hmub terminology system and its bilateral marriage system within the village. The ideal of affinal alliance is a thematic focus within the text, highlighted both implicitly and explicitly. For example, in lines 154 to 157, we read: 'We are cross-cousins to each other. ... We will become husbands and wives anyway. Do not mind if we have to part from each other for now', as in village endogamy, for example, lines 366 and 367: 'You girls marry someone else *within your own village*' (emphasis added). The lyrics reinforce this with the repetitive use of affinal kin terms by both male and female singers —— mainly *but, mul, mul diangf, maib yut*, indicating cross-cousins —— throughout the more than four hundred lines.

The consistent presentation and reaffirmation of local cross-cousin marriage contrast with lines which make highly visible the coexistent fluid nature of Hmub marriage and the associated conflict in flirting contexts. The tension inherent in marriage and flirting in this Hmub village is obvious. Elopement is a social dimension that throws some light on this. In this Hmub village, much like before 1949, marriage occurs after a brief period of flirting; it may or may not involve romantic love and is divided more or less evenly between public marriages and elopements. This is not just a relatively recent or post-1949 development (Chien 2005a).

Public marriages are conducted according to —— and must comply with —— the positive rule of prescriptive cross-cousin marriage with village endogamy. Most elopements, however, violate village endogamy. They may or may not be between cross-cousins; they are very occasionally with non-Hmub. They occur without the prior consent or knowledge of the bride's family and are finalized when she crosses the threshold with her groom in the middle of the night. A bride considering elopement must weigh the uncertainties and far greater ambivalence of a cognatic marriage against the alternative: the certainties and normal ambivalence of a restricted marriage. Nevertheless elopements do occur —— in fact, in approximately half of all marriages —— highlighting Hmub ambivalence about the collective marital ideal. This also raises the issue of individuality: individuals strongly resist the severe social constraints represented not just by cross-cousin marriage, but by cross-cousin marriage with village endogamy (Chien 2005a).

The recorded love song performatively highlights the uncertainties about marriage and flirtation, in particular, the two different relationships between marriage and flirtation as experienced by individuals. In the first the natural development of the flirting is towards the local ideal of cross-cousin marriage: they are connected. For example, lines 42 to 45 and 88 to 91: 'If you want to court the girls, go home to separate from your wives first. If you don't, then let's stop our flirtation and you guys go home and take care of your own wives.' In these lines, flirting and being married cannot exist at the same time, even though on the surface it seems that extra-marital flirting is in fact underway at that moment.

In complete contrast, there are lines which express the much more fluid and negotiable relationship which also exists between marriage and flirting in this Hmub village. Marriage does not necessarily follow flirting, nor preclude it. Similarly, extra-marital flirting occurs (institutionalized extra-marital flirtation; see also Chien 2009a); flirting simply does not naturally or necessarily stop because of marriage. The two are simply independent of each other for the individuals involved. Lines 29 to 32, sung by the women, illustrate this using a rhetorical strategy: 'The girls do not know why they desire to sit next to the boys always; they do not know their flirting companions are somebody else's husbands.' And again, lines 263 to 266 use a clearly poetic metaphor: 'The girl has two hearts: one is for her husband, and the other is for the boy.' The lyrics poetically reveal the fluid, conflicting and dialogical features of marriage and flirtation.

Finally, individual personal sentiments, which also highlight the ambivalence between marriage and flirtation, are another major feature and thematic focus. The emotional element is significant. These elements are also seen in non-festival flirting activities. These not only index how kinship and affinal alliance are valued, and their social connotations: a polite tone and playful, cheerful atmosphere is also created as Hmub boys and girls take conversational turns while flirting (Chien 2005b).

The personal emotions presented through the lyrics, however, are more complicated than simply playful interaction. In addition, personal feelings such as shyness, joy, solitude, longing and passion are also performatively presented, and thereby legitimated. In contrast to the joyful emotions that are mostly linked to marriage-connected flirtation, sentiments such as personal longing and feeling solitary are usually expressed in the context of the more complex dialogical relationship between marriage and flirtation.

Lines 277 and 281 create a strong impression of such lonely feelings using metaphors:

Dat Ghaif	Female Singers
277 *Mek hveb at nit hfuf.*	Your words are just talk.
278 *Mek hvib at yat yiok.*	Your hearts are far away.
279 *Juk eb fat hongx vongf.*	Your hearts are like a river flowing to the falls.
280 *Juk hob fat hongx bif.*	Like a fog in the hills which has lifted.

Dat Ghaif	Female Singers
281 *Mek zod but mek bongf.*	You will go back to be with your wives.

In these lines, the personal feelings —— forlornness, anticipation of parting and loneliness —— are expressed metaphorically by images from nature such as the 'river flowing to the falls' and the 'fog in the hills which has lifted', that is, gone away. They also express ambivalence over how those who participate in the extra-marital, 'flirtation'-style of Hmub courtship feel, this time focusing on the negative aspect: 'Your words are just talk. Your hearts are far away… . You will go back to be with your wives.' The emotions lyrically expressed in this love-song, which belong to the personal, the individual sphere, are not simply a panhuman or universal psychological 'thing' – they are closely linked to the tension and ambivalence inherent in the local flirting and marriage context. And it is this sociological context which informs and celebrates the nature of 'Hmub individuality'.

Conclusion: Performing Hmub Individuality

Following Strathern's aesthetic and iconic approach, studying individuals in their specific cultural context, this chapter has focused on an example of the performative use of language in the conduct of social life, thereby foregrounding Hmub individuality.

Tensions such as the antithesis between the individual and society,

附錄

Chapter 2   Tensions between Romantic Love and Marriage:
            Performing Hmub Cultural Individuality in an Upland Hmub Love-Song

the value of the individual and the modern sense related to the indigenous conceptualization of individuality have been discussed in anthropology since Durkheim. Hmub love-songs offer an opportunity to rethink this debate: they imaginatively expose the tensions between local individuals and their society.

Tensions between individuals and society are common, it would seem, in most human societies. A Durkheimian view suggests that the individual is always struggling with an awareness of his or her individuality as opposed to collective forces and representations on the level of ideology.[18] The Hmub in Fangf Bil face this dilemma too, as is clearly demonstrated by certain social institutions, such as duolocal residence and institutionalized extra-marital flirtation, and brought into high relief performatively in the contrast and tensions between marriage and flirting, expressed in the lyrics of love-songs. The content and thematic emphasis of Hmub love-songs – particularly the dialogical relationships between flirtation and marriage – make the tensions between individual experience and sentiment and affinal alliance clearly visible.

Different cultures have different concepts of the 'individual': the Western notion of the modern individual is of someone morally autonomous. Hindu world renouncers ideologically exist outside their social world but sociologically remain part of it. Fangf Bil Hmub have their individuality, which has its own aesthetic linguistic dimensions: the love-song discussed above highlights individual personal experience and sentiments, while at the same time showing the ambivalent position of the individual with regard to a central aspect of local society.

Rapport and Overing (2000: 185) describe individuality as 'tied inextricably to individual consciousness, to that unique awareness and awareness of awareness, which is the mark of human embodiment. ... human beings come to know themselves within the world by way of cognition and perception, thoughts, feelings and imaging, which are unique to them.' Faced by the collective social ideal of marriage, Fangf Bil Hmub villagers address their consciousness to performatively highlighting the political nature – in the sense of social dynamics – of feelings and imagination, that is, of individuals' sentiments, emotions and desires. In this way they performatively legitimate the experience of the individual, thereby countermanding the strong forces of the collective ideal of marriage.

Significantly, like Strathern's notion of the 'dividual being' in Melanesian society, the Hmub indigenous conceptualization of individuality is the 'paired individual'. There are recurrent pervasive linguistic references to people in pairs throughout the more than four hundred lines of this Hmub love-song. Consider lines 224 to 228:

Dat Deik	**Male Singers**
224 *Meb dlab let lil rak renf.*	You two are good at talking.
225 *Lab qet juf wak wek.*	Your hearts are distant.
226 *Ment ghad ghuf dek deif.*	Girls touch the boys with their bodies.
227 *Dlek xongx dangf dlek dok.*	You desire to be close to the boys, as you desire to be near the fire in the winter cold.
228 *Diuf xongx nongf wek yef.*	We two boys are all alone.

Chapter 2   Tensions between Romantic Love and Marriage:
            Performing Hmub Cultural Individuality in an Upland Hmub Love-Song

The thematic emphases here are individual personal desire, strong longing and loneliness. In every line, however, the singing voice and the addressee are in fact not 'one person', but 'two persons'. I argue that this is a performative device which demonstrates that the individual is essentially a social being, and further, that individuals identify themselves that way, happily. In brief, Fangf Bil Hmub villagers performatively express their unique indigenous individuality using this text.

Individualism has long been considered a definitive aspect of modern, Western ideology. Consequently debate on individuality has also involved the concept of modernity (Dumont 1986: 4). This chapter has argued that the Hmub view of individuality also demonstrates a sense of the modern. It has presented observations of the collective social ideal of affinal alliance, the Hmub awareness of individual personal identity and the tensions between individual sentiments and affinal alliance in various institutionalized contexts, all performatively instantiated in the love-songs. The sense of the modern present in Hmub individuality as indicated in the love-song lyrics is, however, not a development in the direction of an extreme, strictly Western individualism. Hmub individuality is characterized by an ongoing negotiated competition between a collective ideal —— cross-cousin marriage within the village —— and individual sentiment, including the playfulness and thinly veiled erotic nature of extra-marital flirtation in the local Hmub flirtation and feelings of personal solitude expressed by the local love-song lyrics. The complex but essentially resolved relationship between Hmub society and the Hmub individual is performatively legitimated. And it is important to note that the audience consists of precisely those 'young people' who will give birth, literally and figuratively, to the next Hmub generation.

This can be linked to Dumont's rethinking of Western individualism. Dumont saw totalitarianism as an attempt to 'turn the clock back' and restore the collectivism that Western individualism had undermined:

> Indeed, totalitarianism expresses in a dramatic way something we keep running into in the contemporary world: individualism is all powerful on the one hand and, on the other is perpetually and irremediably haunted by its opposite. ... This coexistence in the contemporary ideology of individualism and its opposite comes forth more forcefully than ever at the present stage of research. In this sense, the individualistic configuration of ideas and values characterizes modernity, but it is by no means coextensive with it. (Dumont 1986: 17)

Examining how individualism relates to a local, historical and cultural view of the person or self, I conclude that 'Hmub individuality' has a substantial aesthetic dimension in the performance and social dynamics of this Hmub love-song in the form in which it has been conventionally transmitted, both before and after 1949; moreover, 'Hmub individuality' is essentially modern.[19]

In response to the general approach of the classical debates and theories on Western individualism and modern development in the field of anthropology, and in line with Dumont's reflective aspect and with the linguistic, aesthetic dimension articulated by Marilyn Strathern, this chapter further suggests

附錄

Chapter 2　Tensions between Romantic Love and Marriage:
　　　　　　Performing Hmub Cultural Individuality in an Upland Hmub Love-Song

that the performance is an imaginative outlet whereby these contemporary Hmub villagers in eastern Guizhou can release emotional and ideological tensions between the ideal of marriage and their individually lived experiences embodying personal feelings, eroticism and various freedoms.

Secondly, the lyrics and performance of the love-song clearly demonstrate that Hmub villagers construct 'individuality' and 'modernity' in their own terms, both in their lives and performatively. Hmub individuality challenges the whole evolutionist positioning of 'individuality' and 'individualism' in the historical Western anthropology tradition, outlined with its thinly veiled implied heirarchy predicated on Western individualism occupying a superior and more advanced position. There is an irony to this: contemporary Hmub villagers' vibrant maintainence of their own particular individuality is itself an expression of cultural individuality in international society. In this sense, it constitutes a modern-day 'morally autonomous individualism'.

Chapter 4
Cultivating the Ethnographer's Ear

Would I be able to relive those feverish moments when, notebook in hand, I jotted down second by second the expressions which would perhaps enable me to fix those evanescent and ever-renewed forms? I am still fascinated by the attempt and often find myself risking my hand at it.

[Lévi-Strauss 1992 [1955]: 62]

But what of the ethnographic ear?

[James Clifford 1986: 12][1]

In *Tristes Tropiques* (1955), Lévi-Strauss more than once mentions his field experiences with Indians in Brazil, experiences that linked him emotionally and intellectually to his identity as an anthropologist. Those fieldwork descriptions have not always earned accolades from peers and colleagues, but as an ethnographer who has also experienced cultural learning during fieldwork, I can attest that I am still touched by Lévi-Strauss' vivid accounts of trying to find a place in his mind to explore human knowledge in the context of changing indigenous cultures. We are still witnesses to the enormity of his effort: 6,000-plus drawings and copious field notes from multiple Brazilian field trips, all in support of the data, observations, and hypotheses he offered.

This chapter will consider my own ethnographic apprenticeship while studying Hmub[2] courtship in a village in China's Guizhou Province. I will explore how the interaction (or lack thereof) between what I heard and wrote during my observations transformed my internal understanding of both this specific culture and my self. I will also examine the issue of whether the record that flowed from my pen truly reflected the reality captured by my eyes and ears, and if not, what I missed.

Many times during my fieldwork I asked myself *what* to listen for and *how* to hear it. Like many anthropology graduate students, I had little training in listening and hearing beyond learning the importance of transcribing interviews. Most graduate training focuses on a combination of watching and speaking with study participants. Despite the lack of formal training in listening, I had no choice but to practice hearing/listening techniques, especially when my study focus shifted to nighttime courtship practices. While analyzing my field notes, I unexpectedly discovered that they conveyed a mix of detailed visual and aural descriptions, which sparked my realization of the importance of auditory cues in Hmub courtship, as well as the methodological challenges and epistemology of cultural fieldwork. That recognition has led me to examine how my Hmub experiences might fit into current discussions of the senses in anthropology, the technology of self, and ethnographic apprenticeships.

Senses

According to Paul Stoller (1989), it was through his long-term apprenticeship learning Songhay spirit possession rituals that he discovered the centrality of sound in understanding cultural sentiment:

> One afternoon in 1970 in Tillaberi, the haunting cries of the monochord violin drew me over a dune to witness my first ceremony of Songhay spirit possession ... The sounds of these instruments so impressed me that I continued to attend possession ceremonies in 1971 ... In 1977 I began to learn about the sounds of spirit poetry in the village of Mehanna. Two years later I was invited to join in the Tillaberi possession troops as a "servant to the spirits" ... *Throughout this myriad of experiences, my teachers continually focused my attention on the sounds of possession.* [Stoller 1989:101, emphasis added]

However, Stoller also noted that sound dimensions are more often than not ignored in current Western anthropological sensory training. We learn how to interview and observe, but focusing on sounds or voices associated with events and determining how they fit into the ethnographer's observations and interpretations of a local culture are overlooked as teachable skills. Still, Stoller and others remind us that the senses employed in anthropology or ethnography should be more diverse, that tone and sound are invaluable for describing and interpreting local cultures. If we are fortunate, we learn through our own apprenticeships the lesson Stoller learned in his work: that paying attention to sound helps ethnographers make sense of local meanings by engaging the communication and interaction of bodily senses.

The Technology of the Self

Foucault (1988: 18) uses the term "technology" to address the means through which individuals are "trained and modified." He lists the four major kinds of technology as production, sign systems, power, and the self (ibid.). After "insist[ing] too much on the technology of domination and power," he expressed new interest in the technology of the self, and used the historically contiguous relations between the expressions "know yourself" and "take care of yourself" as a departure point to show how relations between care and self-knowledge were constituted in Greco-Roman and Christian traditions (ibid.: 19-20). Foucault argued that it was due to different forms of "care" in relation to the self that different forms of self exist (ibid.: 22). According to his analysis, writing in the Greco-Roman tradition was an important device in the invention of the concept of "taking care of the self" (ibid.: 27). Examples include taking notes for re-reading, writing treatises and letters to help friends, and keeping notebooks for reflective study (ibid.). Thus, the practice of writing is now intimately linked with taking care of oneself. In the same work he uses Marcus Aurelius's letter to Fronto in 144 or 145 A.D. to illustrate interrelations between self and body through the constant practice of writing "unimportant" daily details (ibid.: 28-30).

Cultivation and Apprenticeship:
The Legacy of Foucault, Stoller, and Castaneda

In line with Foucault's and Stoller's positions, I will focus on my attempts to account for what I heard through the act of writing. Just as "taking care of one's self" emerges from the activity of writing about "unimportant" everyday details in a letter or journal, my experiences in cultivating my ear and adjusting my perceptions occurred through the process of writing about field experiences in my notes and in a diary.[3] I use the term *cultivation*[4] because it expresses the idea of conscious and continuous pursuit and of something internal being trained and modified, which I view as analogous to Foucault's "technology of self." In the context of field ethnography, I examine how the technique or ongoing practice of writing affects bodily cultivation, and how it opens a door to self-disclosure and to learning how the sense of hearing is used in other cultures.

An analogous concept, that of *apprenticeship*, is discussed by Stoller (1987) and Carlos Castaneda (1998[1969]). Ethnographers generally consider themselves students or like children——learning other cultures through their fieldwork. Few make explicit use of the term "apprenticeship" in ethnographic practice. Stoller (1987) describes his two apprentice experiences as learning the perspective of a Songhay individual and the perspective of a ritual specialist. The first experience occurred during the early stages of his fieldwork, when he encountered frustration from what he felt were misleading responses from Songhay villagers to survey questions. He then received advice from a village friend: "You must learn to sit with people, Monsieur Paul. You must learn to sit and listen" (ibid.: 11). Stoller acknowledged feeling ambivalent about his professional identity as a fieldworker and taking a passive approach to learning Songhay ways. However, the practice of sitting and listening proved key to his acceptance as a qualified Songhay person, to "have acted and have become a person in the village" (ibid.: 17).

Stoller's (1987: 21-41) second fieldwork apprenticeship benefited from Songhay sorcerers. Following an intensive period of memorizing ritual texts and praise poems and of procuring folk medicines, he experienced intense internal conflict between his roles as a sorcerer's apprentice and anthropologist:

Djibo immersed me in memorization. So busy was I with the memorization of texts that I did not have time to figure out what they meant, let alone how they corresponded to the vagaries of Songhay culture. I worried that I was failing in my mission as an anthropologist. [Stoller 1987: 38]

Another example is Castaneda's (1998[1969]) description of his apprenticeship under the guidance of a Yaqui Indian sorcerer named don Juan, who forced him to give up his Western way of thinking and adopt certain practices in order to learn and understand the reality of the Yaqui world. According to Castaneda,

In don Juan's system of beliefs, the acquisition of an ally meant exclusively the exploitation of the states of non-ordinary reality he produced in me through the use of hallucinogenic plants. He believed that by focusing on these states and omitting other aspects of knowledge he taught, I would arrive at a coherent view of the phenomena I had experienced. [Castaneda 1998[1969]: 10]

Castaneda encounters considerable challenges in his efforts to refrain from professional methods that his Indian mentor forbids, including interviews, observations, and systematic note taking. Still, field notes played a significant part in his internalizing the sensual experiences of the Yaqui Indian and understanding their worldview, disclosing his subjective perception of the experience and revealing the content of don Juan's belief system. Although Castaneda never extends his discussion to the link between writing and his Yaqui cultural apprenticeship, several times he states that writing notes after calming down from extreme sensual experiences allowed him to examine those experiences more closely.

Before discussing the importance of careful listening as a primary field technique, I will describe my training in cultural anthropology research methods at Taiwan's Tsing Hua University and present a brief analysis of how sounds and/or voices play an important role in the daily and ritual lives of upland Hmub villages, especially their central position in ritual courtship behavior. In this chapter, "sound" (non-linguistic construction) means a system of symbols for communication (Feld 1982)——for instance, the sound of a person knocking on a door or window. "Voice" will refer to a linguistic construction by social persons, such as human conversation or other forms of dialogue (Keane 2000).

Learning and Experiencing Anthropological Methods

I began my ethnographic training in the early 1990s. Through course work, reading, and seminar discussions, I built an understanding of what was required for fieldwork: learning new languages, drawing maps, performing censuses and/or genealogies, doing interviews, participating, observing, writing notes, and perhaps also keeping a diary. At that time, H. Russell Bernard's *Research Methods in Cultural Anthropology* (1988) was one of the most popular titles on this subject. My copy was never far away, either during my course work or at a field site where I did ethno-medical research involving the Ami indigenous group living in Hualien County on Taiwan's east coast (1992-93). In chapters 7-13, Bernard discusses data collection—participant observation; taking and managing field notes; structured, unstructured, and semi-structured interviews; questionnaires and surveys; and direct, reactive, and unobtrusive observation. All these methods of obtaining information emphasize visual perceptions. The terms *hearing* and *listening to* rarely appear in Bernard's text. Specific listening techniques are rarely, if ever, discussed in anthropology classes, but I believe it is possible to teach accurate listening techniques when addressing such processes as transcribing, translating, categorizing, describing, and interpreting both verbal and nonverbal auditory messages or signals.

Under the influence of my professors and Bernard's text, standard observation, interviewing, and participation procedures were my primary tools during my Ph.D. fieldwork on Hmub kinship in eastern Guizhou (1998-2000). My initial focus was on village social structure; I conducted a census of more than 300 households and created pedigree and genealogical records for each family using information gathered in semi-structured interviews.[5] I also collected kinship terms used by native Hmub speakers and recorded the actual use of those terms in everyday and ritualized settings. In addition to supporting my understanding of personal relationships in the village, these data helped me learn marital concepts described by my informants, observe marital realities, and determine where the two converged and diverged. My explorations of the interplay between personal emotions and social institutions (marriage, courtship etc.) gave me abundant opportunities to try new ethnographic procedures and techniques.

During my fieldwork I lived in the home of a girl named Ghaif Wangk, a 20-year-old who was unmarried. At first, her family made arrangements for me to sleep on the second floor, but since the second floor room was next to the granary, I asked to sleep in their daughter's room. We spent a great deal of time together, and we eventually started to call each other Sister. She taught me the Hmub language, assisted me with translations, sang and dictated Hmub songs and stories, and helped me with my interview data. The amount of time I spent with her over fifteen months allowed me to understand her experiences and moods, her views on marriage and emotions, and occasionally her views on local gossip. Through her I gained acceptance as a young girl according to local tradition.

Listening to the Sounds of Late-Night Rituals

While working in my village, I discovered that I needed to take a different approach to my research. In a growing number of situations I realized that if I did not make an exceptional effort to listen to the sounds and voices that one could hear in the dark of night, I was in danger of missing out on critical aspects of Hmub social life and misinterpreting Hmub courtship and marriage customs. The following example is from my field notes at the beginning of 1999:

I heard the cocks crowing two or three times in the darkness. I still struggled to get up at 5 o'clock in the cold early morning. At 6 o'clock, I decided to observe the calling of ghosts for a new house. I woke up Ghaif. Ghaif's mother said that a person with a new house had called the ghosts a few days before. She also said there were some households in Si-Zu (the fourth hamlet in the village) calling ghosts, but she did not know which ones. Ghaif suggested that we go outside to take a look. We didn't wash our faces before leaving, simply took flashlights to go out at dawn. Ghaif said there was noise somewhere there on the slope, but I heard nothing. I followed her to Si-Zu on the slope. As we approached, another person came toward us. After listening to Ghaif's statement, he told Ghaif which household was holding the ceremony. I sensed that he was laughing. Later we found out that he was the *ghet xangt* (the ghost master, or shaman and ritual specialist) who had just finished calling the ghosts and was on his way home.

My field notes, whose contents record my nervousness and anxiety as a fieldworker, especially my fear of losing an opportunity to observe ritual activity, point to the importance of *hearing*. My nervousness can also be explained by my unfamiliarity with hearing the unique sounds and auditory patterns of Hmub rituals. I could not predict the duration of a ritual and had

Chapter 4 Cultivating the Ethnographer's Ear

no idea what was being signaled by the sounds I heard.[6] Many of the ritual activities in the village (e.g., rituals for protecting households, for healing, even wedding ceremonies) took place without obvious signs being given by villagers other than the members of the household experiencing the ritual. I remembered thinking upon my arrival in November of 1998 that "I"——the only outsider living in the village——was excluded from the circle in which news was shared regarding ritual activities. Later I learned that I wasn't so special in this regard: villagers themselves were not necessarily aware of the scheduling of rituals in their own neighborhoods, let alone households in other hamlets. Still, many villagers told me, "If you want to know where a ritual is being performed, just carefully *listen to* the sounds [chanting by the ritual specialists]." However, sorting out the abundance and diversity of auditory signals pointing to ritual activities was a challenge for me, the new apprentice. I needed contextual information from the type of hearing that I was accustomed to in my everyday life.

During my fifteen months of fieldwork I learned the social meanings of specific sounds and voices: the chanting of shamans indicated healing or household rituals; the sound of fireworks meant celebrations for a new year or a wedding ceremony, but sometimes also signaled someone's death; and the enthusiastic rapping on doors or windows by parallel cousins at midnight indicated that a wedding was to take place early that morning. But it wasn't until late in my fieldwork that I recognized I had been living in the midst of these sounds and voices since my arrival in the village. Only at that point could I commit myself to exploring the late-night auditory dimensions of Hmub courtship.

To understand the relationship between marriage and courtship outside the kinship structure and village marital system, my second fieldwork focus was eroticism and its emotional contexts. By examining institutionalized courting activities I arrived at an understanding of the emotional world of the *vangt* (young people), as defined locally.[7] While researching courting activities, however, I experienced methodological and ethical conflicts, which increased my sense of how the sounds and voices I heard were significant to my interpretations of Hmub courtship culture.

I was already the mother of two sons when I conducted this research, making me *lok* (old) in the village, and therefore excluded from courting activities. But despite my status as a married mother, the villagers still regarded me as a young girl, perhaps due to my status as a graduate student and the clothes I wore, which were similar to those worn by local girls[8] who accompanied me during my fieldwork. For this reason I had greater freedom to participate in and observe courting activities, which take the form of gatherings by groups of young males and females or one-to-one courtship at night outside the windows of young women's rooms. I was a direct participant in the group gatherings, but an indirect *listener* to the late-night conversations, filling in the details in later interviews with the girls being courted. I learned that courting activities could be very open——having some features of ritualized performance——but at times they could be very private and personal. Without the assistance of the girls who accompanied me and their willingness to share their romantic emotions and experiences, I never could have understood the content and value of institutionalized courtship in the minds of individual participants.

An Experience of Listening in the Field

As I noted in an earlier excerpt from my field notes, sound is related to calling ghosts. Sound is also a central index pointing to occurrences of courtship. In fifteen notebooks I wrote voluminously on what I had *heard* about Hmub courtship activities. Those notebooks contain evidence of my learning to recognize the importance of knocking on a window late at night. The following entry was written in January 1999, during the early stages of my fieldwork.

I hurriedly returned to my fieldwork today, knowing that there will be a "building of a new house" and ghost-calling ritual tomorrow. By the time I finished discussing expenses with Ghaif's father, it was 9:30 in the evening. In order to get up early (the calling was to begin after second cock's crow), and feeling tired anyway, I went to sleep early. Both Ghaif and I fell asleep quickly. . . . I was awakened by knocking sounds. I thought it was dawn, but discovered it was only about eleven o'clock after looking at my watch. The knocking came at different tempos and had different beats. (It occurs to me that if I have the chance, I should record these.) I was awake by that time, but wanted to sleep. The knocking sounds continued. Ghaif woke up as well and said to the boys outside, "*Nat youl. Det dak youl!*" (I hear you, but I do not want to come [to the window]). She said these sentences two or three times, sounding a little bit angry. Later she told me that it was because they knocked too loudly. The knocking sounds did not stop immediately, but ceased after a while. We gradually fell asleep.

This excerpt conveys my initial feelings about and experience of the late-night knocking. These sounds usually woke me up unexpectedly; sometimes the knocking was so loud that it frightened me, and sometimes it occurred too many times in the same evening. It was a long time before I stopped feeling ambivalent about the knocking, which struck me as impolite since the noise interrupted my sleep. At the same time, my very reason for living in this village was to *study Hmub courtship*, and I came to recognize that these unwelcome signals were a part of my subject, and that they carried cultural and symbolic significance.

Every time a girl hears knocking, she recognizes the knocker by the tempo, speed or volume of the rapping. To an outsider like me, such knocking all sounded similar, but to the girls of the village it conveyed subtle or minor variations. Special knocking strategies can be identified. For example, using a special pattern, such as knocking the first three times softly at normal speed, then a pause, and knocking three times again, much louder or quicker, etc., may be arranged by the girl and boy who are courting each other regularly. Girls especially look forward to the knocking of their sweethearts (*ghat mal ghob*), but sweethearts are not the only knockers. In fact, knocking is mostly done by affines. Thus, what girls usually do is to differentiate between the knocking of a common affine of the same village and that of a stranger from the outside.

I began to categorize non-verbal sounds by linking them with specific personal relations——boyfriends, affinal cousins, friends, and strangers. At first, the rhythm and frequency of the knocking all seemed alike, and I assumed that it was all by the same boy who was interested in Ghaif. I later understood that the sounds were in fact made by several different courting boys.

I started to pay much closer attention to these late-night events. Almost every morning I would talk with Ghaif about the previous night's visitors and write about our discussions in as much detail as possible before planning my schedule for the day. Most of my questions concerned the identities of the visitors, their consanguineal or affinal relations, and the content of their conversations. The knocking eventually became an index for understanding late-night courting practices, and I learned that where I had perceived no differences between knocks, local village girls recognized a diverse range. This gave me an important opportunity to *feel* institutional courtship through listening as opposed to seeing or gaining knowledge from the explanations of informants. Ultimately, and with Ghaif's help, I was able to not only establish a musical and social view of late-night knocking, but also to complement it with values associated with interpreting what I was hearing. For example, I learned from Ghaif that if more than a couple of nights passed without someone knocking on her window, she experienced feelings of loneliness and sadness. She therefore generally looked forward to the late-night knocking, even though she never knew who the visitor would be on any given evening.

While I never analyzed the knocking in terms of pattern, frequency, volume, etc., hearing the sound assumed a position of value in my fieldwork. Experiencing the knocking first-hand created a link between emotions and knowledge of Hmub courtship. For Hmub girls, the sound of knocking is a clear indication of courtship. Parents and other family members usually ignore the sound (or pretend to), regardless of its volume, frequency, or timing. However, girls feel a need to respond and must deal with the emotions tied to it. Most girls feel excitement when they hear knocking. In its absence, they may recite "*Sent feb lel, bib lek yaf*" (So quiet and cold like winter, how lonely we old ladies are), revealing a sense of desolation and perhaps concern that they will not find partners. This sensitivity explains the facility of Hmub girls to recognize their visitors by their knocks. Girls feel emotionally safe and confident about opening their windows at the familiar knocking of an affine, but may feel uncertain or even frightened at an unfamiliar sound and therefore refrain from opening their windows.

It was not the specific content or patterns of late-night knocking that produced meaning for me, but the aural experience that created links among various kinds of emotions. The transformation in my personal emotions from culture shock, fear, and strangeness to a familiar and regular daily experience was dramatic. Toward the end of my fieldwork, it wasn't unusual for me to not notice these late-night sounds and to sleep through even vigorous knocking. I learned that the sound was for the most part considered friendly and a practical symbol relevant to a collective core value of the village: maintaining its kinship system. This transformation of my emotions made it possible to understand and sympathize with the emotional world of the village girls, and to recognize how the experience of being awoken in the middle of the night enriched their lives. By focusing on auditory cues, I was able to rethink the relevance of such events to my understanding of Hmub courtship culture. I also was able to consider my own subjective experiences of hearing and feeling the emotions of Hmub girls during courtship, as well as my growth from an ethnographer experiencing culture shock to one feeling at ease in my fieldwork.

Being an Apprentice Fieldworker Once Again

I was not a complete novice in fieldwork when I started my Hmub research, but the need to hone a new skill——listening——to collect ethnographic data resurrected feelings of unease and uncertainty I had felt during my first project in Taiwan. I lost some of my confidence and the ability to feel at home as a trained fieldworker. Outside the standards of observation I was familiar with, the need to understand the meaning of unrecognized sounds and voices in the context of Hmub courtship created a level of anxiety and uncertainty that threatened my identity. Culture shock clearly played a role in generating these feelings, but more importantly for this discussion was the immediacy and the impact of hearing verbal and nonverbal sounds without confirming or supporting visual information about my perceptions of self and my sense of place. The following quote from Bull and Back (2003: 7) underscores the difference I felt between knowing the world and self through seeing and through hearing:

> In vision, subject and object "appear" as transparent. Implied in the objectification of the world through sight is the control of that world. Yet if, as Bishop Berkeley notes, "Sounds are close to us as our thoughts," then by listening we may be able to perceive the relationship between subject and object.

In other words, if I (as subject) merely perceived the phenomenon of Hmub courtship (the object) through visual observation, then relations among the data, methods, and my identity as a fieldworker became transparent, thus removing any space for rethinking the process and fully experiencing my Hmub courtship fieldwork. However, my hearing previously unrecognized late-night knocking sounds and courtship conversations in the absence of familiar standards of observation created anxiety and uncertainty while simultaneously providing an immediate channel for *feeling* where I was, who I was, and what I was encountering in the village.

Cultivating My Ear

Even though I convinced myself to depend on hearing as an additional data collection method, the contents of my field notes still reflect uncertainty in my ability to make full use of auditory sources of information. Part of the reason was my belief that "seeing is believing," which echoes Erlmann's (2004: 20) observation in *Hearing Cultures*: "Audio-centered forms of social practice cannot in themselves be construed as alternatives to relations of power thought to be anchored in vision, surveillance, and mass-mediated forms of visual production and consumption."[9] Still, I had to write down my observations to achieve the goals of preserving and intellectually integrating what I had experienced. In addition to recognizing the semantic messages produced by writing, it was by exploring the material level of writing in the field that I learned how writing also helped me make sense of what I had heard. As ethnographers we are trained to record data and write them down as notes. During my Hmub courtship project I did not use a tape recorder to capture the late-night knocking, in large part because the voices and conversations were frequently subdued, and (except for the knocks on Ghaif's window) advanced recording techniques would have been required to record knocking at other houses. Another problem was ethical: courtship activity, especially at night, is more private and personal than almost all other public activities in Hmub society. Using a tape recorder (or camera) would have introduced a degree of intrusion and threat into the private zone of nighttime courtship activity. I therefore reverted to recording what I heard with pen and paper.

Most ethnographers recognize the need to write extensively in the field, and believe that their work benefits from meanings and information that is written down and submitted to later analysis. However, the act of writing——that is, the writing process and its materiality——has not been scrutinized to the same degree as the process of collecting data and recording it. As my experience in Guizhou shows, writing in the field is multi-functional——in other words, it is also associated with bodily experiences. Christina Haas (1996: 24) is one of the few scholars to specifically comment on the materiality of writing from the aspect of its technology and transformation——"from the heft of the manuscript and the feel of a new Blackfeet pencil, to the bright, wired-up, whirring box and clicking keyboard on the desk." Hass has also found that there is a sense problem with text for writers making the transition from pen-and-paper to computer. For example, "I have to print it to get *a perspective* on it," or "I don't have the *intimacy* I need with my text on the computer" (ibid.: 120, original emphasis). The text senses are described as spatial, living, or moving objects (ibid.).

I believe there are two types of writing materiality: technological and time consumption, and both create certain resonances in my body. Hass (1966: 24) notes that "writing is made material through the use of technologies, and

writing is technological in the sense and to the extent that it is material."
During my Hmub fieldwork, writing was very material in the technological
sense: I used my old Mont Blanc pen to write down everything I observed and
heard in hardcover notebooks, page by page, volume by volume. Since there
was no bookstore in the village, I tried my best to conserve paper by writing
field notes in small versions of Chinese characters and English letters, and
made attempts to romanize my transcriptions of oral Hmub speech. Second,
although I had a laptop computer, electricity was intermittent and I mostly
wrote my field notes or diary entries in a labor-intensive and time-consuming
manner with pen and paper. Sitting and writing for long periods of time usually
brought some physical discomfort, but once a regular routine was established,
my writing——like meditation or exercise——helped me to deal with my
emotions of anxiety, uncertainty, and/or confusion that came from being in
another culture. I felt safe in the visible accumulation of notes. The repetitive
act of writing contributed a great deal to my practice in focusing on sounds and
voices and the social meanings they have for the Hmub.

Verbal and non-verbal sounds may be perceived, encoded, and decoded
by different cognitive processes, but both convey social meaning and emotions
among Hmub youth. I therefore consider them sound/voice units similar to the
Chinese concept of *shengyin* (聲音 , "voice and sound") for descriptive and
analytical purposes. It was important to record aural tones and to transform
them into words and sentences——concrete data for safe storage in my
notebooks.

The literary theorist Walter Ong's idea on the movement from orality to
literacy provides a basis for extending our understanding of the relationship

between ear work and hand work. According to Ong, writing is "the most monumentous of all human technological inventions" (Ong 1982: 72), translating sound into space and "transform[ing] the human life world" (ibid.: 85). In other words, Ong believes the interdependence between hearing and writing is exposed as a return to the superiority of the visual sense. More or less parallel to Ong's theory, ethnographic training entails a hierarchy of bodily experiences and resonances. Sight is usually at the top of that hierarchy, while hearing holds a much lower position.

In this chapter I have tried to express how transposing heard experiences and felt resonances into writing allowed me to use multiple senses to understand how the Hmub invent and perceive their courtship culture. Two additional layers of experience can be pursued further. First, parallel to Foucault's technology of self, I experienced the cultivation of self via the specific technique of writing. In addition to feeling safe in the visible accumulation of my field notes, I trained and grew through my regular and extensive writing practice. This bodily cultivation experience became evident in the transformation of my emotional world of self and identity as I increasingly internalized my field experience as an ethnographer. This process is partly in line with Vygotsky's notion of "mediational means," the theory that writing's transformative efficacy is both material and symbolic at the same time (Hass 1996: 225).[10]

The second layer concerns verification of the meanings of non-verbal sounds. Like Stoller's (1987, 1989) insights, my point is that learning how to hear, understand, and interpret non-verbal sound is an important skill that has been neglected in our field. Stoller is one of several anthropologists who have demonstrated that recognition of the force of auditory cultures is largely absent in Western traditions, and perhaps the sound of knocking in a Hmub village is not sufficiently exotic an example. Still, those night-time sounds might carry different meanings in my own culture, so I had to learn anew and consciously practice listening skills crucial to carry out the research. The experience of hearing linked various emotions (e.g., disclosing the emotions of Hmub girls being courted), while the act of writing allowed me to reflect on and make sense of the knocking and its associated conversations, events, and participants. Through writing I was able to attach social and emotive value to the sounds I heard and to understand the social and emotional lives of Hmub youth.

Concluding Remarks

The processes of emergence and transformation of self identity and the bodily experiences of ethnographers in the field are rarely noted beyond textbook references to culture shock and its accompanying symptoms of loneliness, homesickness, and depression. Its symptoms may have far-reaching implications regarding the quality of data and its value within the larger social settings perceived by ethnographers. How I cultivated my ear through the practice of listening and writing and how I navigated the transformation of senses, emotions, identity, and professional self during my fieldwork bring into sharper focus how the bodily experiences may combine to make the ethnographer a keener perceiver of events. Those experiences all contributed to my transformation as an ethnographer and a self, as well as my knowledge of Hmub courtship, a phenomenon that complements Foucault's (1988: 18) ideas about the technologies of self:

> ...which permit individuals to effect by their own means or with the help of others a certain number of operations on their own bodies and souls, thoughts, conduct, and way of being, so as to transform themselves in order to attain a certain state of happiness, purity, wisdom, perfection, or immortality.

Listening carefully allowed me to also experience my knowledge of Hmub courtship. The late-night knocking on windows, an "audio-centered form of social practice" (Erlmann 2004: 20), revealed to me the institutional, formal, and collective features of Hmub courtship by its "sense of aural immediacy" (ibid.), which led me to then categorize the sounds I heard. In analysis elsewhere (Chien 2009a, see also Chapter 1) the long- and short-term effects of premarital and extra-marital flirtation, I interpreted Hmub courtship as an emotional zone of great value to young villagers. Here I emphasize how that courtship can be better understood by adding data gathered by careful listening. But as Erlmann (2004: 18) observes, this raises the question of what kind of ears are needed to gather and sift through the sounds of everyday life, to "pick up all these sounds adrift, these echoes, reverberations, hums, and murmurs outside or in between the carefully bounded precincts of orderly verbal communication and music"? This aspect of ethnographic methodology deserves further attention so it may be better integrated into our repertoire of skills for understanding the communities we study.

Chapter 7
Anonymous Voices and Authorship Politics in Printed Genealogies in Eastern Guizhou

An Encounter in Eastern Guizhou

In 2003, I did fieldwork in a Fangzhai Hmub[1] village near Shidong, a township on the Qingshuijang River in Eastern Guizhou that has been considered a major port since the Qing dynasty. This area is called the Shidong Entrance (*Shidong Kou* 施洞口) and has been known for its floods (*xun* 汛) dating to the Qing dynasty. A ferry (*du* 渡) was established in the fourth year of the Guangxu period (1878). The Qingshuijang River is the main waterway for the area, and the road from Zhenyuan to Taigong is its main trade artery. A regular market developed here beginning in the third year of the Qianlong period (1738), attracting merchants from foreign provinces. During the revolt by the Miao/Hmub people during the Xianfeng and Tongzhi periods, Xu Jia-Qian was the secretary of the Xiang army and entered the provinces of Xiang and Qian, with the army stationing in Shidong. In *Miaojiang wenjianlu (What I have Seen and Heard in Frontier Miao)*, which was completed in the fourth year of the Guangxu period, Xu describes the Miao/Hmub market as already prosperous, 'situated 60 lis (about a half kilometer) south from the Zhenyuan government, and in the territory of Taigong County. There are mountains in the back and the Qingshuijang River flows in the front. It is a fertile land, and the whole district extends for several kilometers. Bageng Village stands in the west, and villages assemble in the east. In the front lie the places of Shawan, Yanjiaowan, Batuan, and Pingdiying; in the back flows the Jiugu River. It has been a big market in the Miao/Hmub frontier, and many different kinds of people live there' (Xu 1997).

In the summer of 2003 it had 193 households, making it a large village in the area. Except for a few families surnamed Zhang and Wu who emigrated to the village of Fangzhai in the 1960s, the majority of residents have the surname Liu. For the most part, village residents converse in an eastern Hmub dialect. During my fieldwork I found a wooden box containing a genealogy written in Chinese that had been printed in 1985. I was immediately struck by its detailed content and advanced features, which included prefaces, ancestral biographies, and a genealogical tree (Taga Akigorô 1982).[2] Nearly 2 years after this encounter, I went back to Guizhou again for further research. When I went to do fieldwork in Tianzhu, the senior headman of the Kam[3] village kindly let me read closely the previous version of the 1985 edition of the Genealogy of Liu, which is dated Guangxu 34 (1908) of the Qing dynasty.

Even more interesting was the fact that the genealogy was compiled, edited, and circulated by and among heterogeneous Liu descent groups——Hmub in Taijang and Kam in Tianzhu. Not only are the two counties separated by a full day's travel by bus[4] but also have significant differences in terms of language, ethnicity, and cultural practices.

To understand these phenomena, one must look back at history. There are differences in the historical contexts of the genealogy compiled in the late Qing period and that of the 1980s in which the latest version of the genealogy was compiled. The Chinese state's imperial expansion to the southwest in the Ming——and particularly the Qing——period placed Eastern Guizhou under state administration. After 1949, the state established the minority administrative institution and state projects of ethnic classification, as well as the official Miao (Hmub) and Dong (Kam) writing systems. The native textual strategies and the state's influences on the cultural practices of genealogy production in the imperial state system are different from those in the modern Chinese state. Both the Hmub and the Kam were put under the same umbrella category of 'Miao' in the imperial scheme of classifying non-Han natives, whereas they belong to two different ethnic minorities under the contemporary official ethnic classification system established after 1949. *Zongpu* (宗 譜 genealogy)[5] is a long-established and widely used style of writing in Asia, especially among countries that in the past used Chinese characters for written communication. Characteristics and limitations of this type of writing determine the exceptionally strong normative power of its system (Taga Akigorô 1982). The compilation of genealogies among non-Han aristocratic families in the south of China relates to the history of the native chieftaincy (*tusi*) system. Compiling a genealogy and presenting it to the imperial court became a requirement for succession to chiefly office during the Ming dynasty. Genealogies were 'naturally' written in Chinese (they had to be), and they needed to show that the candidate for succession stood in an orthodox line of descent within the chiefly lineage. Pressure to conform to Chinese orthodox family law became intense at this time. Apart from chiefly lineages, many other aristocratic clans found it expedient to compile Chinese-style family registers and claim Chinese ancestry. This process was widespread in Guizhou as well as in other southern provinces. Many of the Hmub and Kam in Guizhou also claimed that their Han ancestors came from Jiangxi (Herman 2007).

In light of this background, genealogies were not a 'knowledge index' of 'the nature or properties of those societies' (certainly not the societies as a whole), nor, following Pieke (2003: 120), were they necessarily a representation of 'a specific mentality that marks a strong association with the modern Chinese state.' For chiefly families, they had nothing to do with mentality; they were a bureaucratic requirement. For others, they served as a form of protection.

Based on the review of the literature noted above and the debate among scholars, I want to understand how local peripheral societies interact with the strong normative power of written genealogies. I will employ a discursive approach to analyze the meaning of genealogy in peripheral regions of the Chinese state.

Specifically, I will first highlight how local elites from the Hmub and Kam speech communities of Eastern Guizhou work together to claim their textual authority through acts of writing and editing.[6] Second, I will examine the authorship of the two versions of Liu genealogy in terms of relations between texts and social contexts. Working from the premise that social power or relations can be invented through genealogical compilation, I will focus on aspects of genealogical recording and inter-textual relations. Specifically, I will examine the processes involved in inventing interethnic differences and consanguine or genealogical relations, such as those asserted by the Hmub and the Kam in Eastern Guizhou.

Having studied the upland Fangf Bil Hmub village in Taijang since 1997, I was aware of the conventional structure of Hmub social networks and the means through which they are maintained. The village is composed of over 330 households and has a population of almost 1,500 persons. It is divided into 11 hamlets (*vangf*), whose respective names refer to nearby geographic features. The 11 hamlets of Fangf Bil Hmub are organized into five patrilineal marriage groups. Marriage within a marriage group is forbidden. The proportion of intermarriages between these marriage groups within the village far exceeds the proportion of marriages outside the village. Based on the family genealogies of some hamlets, it is furthermore clear that women marry in both directions. The affinal classifications of this village seem to constitute something approaching a binary structure. Therefore, it is clear that the social network of the Hmub society in early times was more or less limited. My concern in the present chapter is in determining how this cooperation came about. What was the process? How did the directions on the recording standards factor in; was it a joint agreement between the parties involved? Moreover, from the individual Hmub and Kam speakers' points of view, what was the relation between the genealogy compilation and their ethnic identities?

Genealogy as Act

Ever since the Communist takeover of China in 1949, classic texts and written genealogies have been viewed as symbols of a repressive age in which the circulation of printed works was restricted to elites at all levels of society. A large number of genealogies were burned during the Cultural Revolution (1966–1976)——acts made irrelevant by that country's rapid cultural transformation and economic development beginning in the 1980s. With the cultural and religious revival——by way of traditional family and community rituals, as well as religious activities, gradually appearing again——local practices of writing Chinese-language genealogies have been restored by the Hmub and Kam elites in an effort to assert past kinship relationships with the so-called *Hanzu laodage* (Han Chinese Elder Brother——majority Han Chinese). In Fangzhai, a village in Taijang County, and in Lantian, a village in Tianzhu County, local elites (now in their 60s and 70s) claim to have inherited the Chinese surname Liu from a locally recognized Hanren/Hanzu (Han Chinese people or ethnic group) ancestor from many generations ago. This belief is reflected in their written genealogies. These elites also argue that their shared Hanren/Hanzu ancestry is evidence of past histories of interethnic brotherhood.

Literacy is repeatedly asserted as one of the criteria that determines who is selected to join in the genealogical practice. Another important criterion is seniority. Born between 1920 and 1940, these local elites are the recipients of both traditional and modern Chinese educations. Liu Yongheng (1924–), a Hmub speaker and Fangzhai resident, is a prime example of someone who was raised in an era dominated by Confucian ideology and who survived the ensuing decades by adapting to the official ideologies of various state regimes. The educational process experienced by Liu Yongheng is typical of these local senior elites. Some even obtained higher education. Liu Yaobi (1940–), after graduating from high school in 1963, entered Guiyang First Public Institute, the training institution for cadre members of the government. Besides reading the traditional Chinese canons and studying math, language, geography, and so on, writing in Chinese characters was also asserted as part of their educational experience. Among these local elites, others have more extensive experience writing in Chinese characters. Liu Kaixuan (1926–), a Kam elite from Tianzhu, has spent every day for over a year single-handedly drafting another version of the Liu family genealogy in Chinese characters. I witnessed the magnitude of his written work at his house during my fieldwork. Liu Kaixuan's laborious effort at writing up this genealogy offers a look into the extremely complicated interaction between Han and non-Han Chinese ethnic groups.

Genealogical Compilation

The following editorial note from the genealogy in question sheds light on how my informants viewed their task. It was written by a Kam elite, Nanchong Guangkuei.

The continual revision of the genealogy is a great task of reorganizing lineal relations among descent groups. We had a fortunate start and successfully proceeded in extending our meetings for revising the genealogy, the first held at Lantian on June 29, 1985. After this meeting, we sent people to different counties to establish contact by going door to door, collecting information and arranging financing [perhaps including asking for donations]. The filial offspring of the male ancestor Xionggong who live throughout the area gave us warm and sincere support by offering information and money. Within two months, information and money for revising the genealogy was pouring in. On September 11 of the lunar calendar the cultural men [that is, men who were literate] from our clan started to compile the data as a first draft. After forty days they started to draft a manuscript.... (*Liu shi zupu* 1985: 115)

Besides the expressed need to carefully guard the genealogy to preserve the goodwill of the ancestors, another focus here is the relationship between the act of recording and the factual value of the written word. The autobiographical accounts of these Hmub and Kam elites further support how their education both qualified them for the task and contributed to a fluidity of ethnic identity that broke down and rebuilt boundaries during the process of documentation.

Distant ancestors were recorded based on scattered pedigrees. Similar to the cultural person mentioned in the editorial note, literate elites have been key to genealogical editing. Upon his retirement in 1981, Liu Yongheng, one of the editors of the 1985 Liu genealogy, spent 2 months collecting information household-by-household on distant ancestors. He told me that editors were selected 'according to our social rank among the villagers.... The key elements were our knowledge, cultural background, and available time.'

Liu Guangde passed away several years before I went to Guizhou in 2003–2004 for this study. All my interviewees expressed to me their deep respect and strong admiration for an editor named Liu Guangde, a former vice head of rural Jianhe County. He was consistently described as the best educated elite and was perceived as having a large amount of local knowledge and of playing an important role in arranging the project. In fact, all genealogy content had to be revised by him before being accepted for publication. His Chinese-language editing status might be explained by his education and cultural background, as he communicated exclusively in Mandarin. But he did not understand the Hmub language at all.

Evident from the above editorial note, literacy is a required ability for genealogical production. The portrait of Liu Guangde also exemplified the importance of literacy among local elites. However, here the crucial figure in editing the genealogical record of the Hmub and Kam ethnic groups neither spoke nor understood the Hmub and Kam languages. This means that being well educated is defined as someone who speaks and writes Chinese written characters. How then could a person like Liu Guangde decide ethnicity in recording material about Hmub or Kam ancestors?

Another factor in the compilation of genealogical records is the importance of money, which has played a role in determining who are and are not included in the process. The money that served as funding for genealogy-repair was collected according to the number of persons in the genealogy. For each individual recorded within it, a family must pay 5 yuan. A couple of families in Huangpao didn't give money; therefore, the editors didn't want them as part of the project and excluded them. If they wanted to be included after the fact, it would then require the agreement of all of the individual families. In other words, those chosen to organize the project had been given the authority to exclude from the genealogy those members who did not contribute money. Descent group membership was in this way determined by money and editorial decisions, not exclusively by patrilineal relations.

Genealogical Circulation

According to the informants, compilation rules and circulation determine the power of genealogies. For members of descent groups with the surname Liu, the yearly custom of 'basking' (displaying) their genealogy (shaipu 曬 譜) ensured circulation. The old genealogy was kept in Fangzhai and was placed on display on 6 June of the lunar calendar each year. Every member in the Liu family would come to view it. They would pool their money and have a shared feast that day. Both men and women were allowed to participate. This activity was held up until fifty years ago, but it was stopped around Liberation. Now, the genealogy can only be displayed during the Qingming Festival. One copy is permanently held in Fangzhai, and the other is rotated among neighboring villages.

Unlike in Fangzhai, the yearly genealogy basking ritual is still performed and well attended in Tianzhu County. Liu Guangsong recalled that during one recent basking event, the senior village-head was invited to explain the roots and origins of the Liu family according to the compiled genealogy——an example of the combined power of literacy and seniority.

The custom of genealogy-basking provides opportunities to ritually and publicly circulate a genealogy in front of the descent group that is the focus of the work. Genealogical circulations can also give or confirm text-related authority——a phenomenon that was obvious in Shidong but not in Lantian. Having inherited the position from his great-grandfather, Liu Yongyue is now the keeper of the Liu family genealogy circulated in the Shidong area. The keeper of the genealogy is selected according to his rank in the family, educational background, and authority, for he is the person acting on behalf [responsible for the genealogy] of the entire family. Other family members are not allowed to look at the genealogy. In contrast to this authoritative tone and serious attitude toward genealogical keeping and circulation, the Kam elites in Tianzhu take a flexible and relatively relaxed attitude toward genealogical circulation. These differences can be explained by variations in literacy level among ethnic groups in areas considered to be on the periphery of the Chinese state. A comparison of these two approaches to displaying a genealogy indicates that the number of printed copies released and circulated influences the value of the genealogy and degree of authority in its production.

Inventing Consanguinity: Exclusiveness and Inclusiveness

In his work *Kinship*, Robert Parkin addresses the difficulties associated with the use of the term *descent*:

> As a professional academic notion, descent has certainly suffered a degree of reification in the past, to the extent that anthropologists have sometimes imagined it rather than identified it in the field. This does not render it useless, for there are still many societies which give it importance. (Parkin 1997: 26)

My analysis of the Liu genealogies may be examined in terms of local conceptualization of the concept. Whereas biologists might consider ties of descent and consanguinity as ongoing and incapable of disruption, kinship researchers view societies and descent according to specific and narrow limitations. Regarding descent group membership, Parkin describes recruitment as a central principle, and accounts of textual power or authority are viewed as constituting a special social relationship: *consanguinity*, achieved by both exclusiveness and inclusiveness. The distinguishing characteristic of the written genealogy for the Liu descent group is exclusivity. Despite Pieke's demonstration that the new genealogical form in modern China provides flexible boundaries for determining unity and diversity within ethnic groups (Pieke 2003: 120), the feature of exclusiveness is still common to most genealogical practices. This feature is especially clear in terms of participants in genealogical compilation and circulation activities. As Liu Guangsong pointed out to me, 'Families with different surnames don't display their genealogies together. Families of different clans do, but only by invitation.' This explains the motivation behind the editorial note presented in the above 'Genealogy as Act' section.

In contrast, *inclusiveness* in the form of genealogy coauthorship using the Chinese written language allows for the blurring of multiethnic identities and boundaries among local Hmub, Kam, and Hanren/Hanzu concepts. A clear example is the adoption of the brotherhood metaphor. The following are two examples of many statements regarding Liu ties across ethnic boundaries:

> If one of two brothers suffers from some hardness and runs away to the Hmub area, then he becomes a Hmub. It is just a difference of language, not of lineage. (Liu Yongyue, Taijang County)

There are two villages in Lanchong that are inhabited by Liu people. They are from the Kam clan. The Kam language as well as Mandarin is spoken there. Mandarin was used during the process of reediting the genealogy. The genealogy belongs to all Liu people. It makes no difference whether some speak Han and some speak Kam. All the people are kin brothers. The ethnicity issue is not important to everyone. (Liu Yongheng, Taijang County)

I heard many assertions of flexible attitudes toward linguistic diversity, thus establishing a sense of multiple ethnic roots and blurred boundaries. Written records occasionally confirmed the glossing over of boundaries that I heard during conversations with informants. In some cases the texts spoke of cultural hegemony on the part of Han Chinese, while in others they mention unified Hanren/Hanzu ancestral roots tied to the Liu surname. The attitudes of local elites such as Liu Taian reveal the emphasis on geographic location and generation over ethnicity:

There are some people speaking Hmub, some speaking Kam, and some speaking Mandarin, but they all belong to the same genealogy, and it doesn't matter. The coincidence of ethnicity and language are not imposed. It depends on the area one lives in. He belongs to a specific ethnic group as long as he thinks he does. The rank by generation, instead of ethnicity, is important in the genealogy. The people who are of the same generation belong to the same rank, no matter where you live.

According to these statements, generation supersedes locality and locality supersedes ethnicity among those having the Liu surname. In other words, local elites recognize shared Hanren/Hanzu ancestry as evidence of a Hmub-Han and Kam-Han interethnic history as well as the importance of individual choice in ethnic identification. The result is multiple identities and blurred boundaries expressed through personal accounts and interpretations of a co-authored genealogy. Combined, the two versions of the Liu genealogy lend authority to claims of consanguine bonds between Hmub and Kam speech communities.

Genealogy as Text

The genealogy texts and information from interviews with their editors or keepers contain evidence of the influence of the creators, a center of authority reflected in the oral and written language of the genealogy. Further examination of relationships between different textual practices reveals another kind of authorship, thereby challenging the notion of a single type of power achieved through authorship. Local elites emphasized basking and holding genealogies, and the editor's note invoked the power of ancestors——two indications of multiple textual authorities and a complex relationship between text and ritual that indicates a distribution as opposed to centralization of influence.

Alessandro Duranti is one of several researchers of conversation emphasizing a need to distinguish between *speaker* and *hearer*, which also suggest a need for reassessing the ideas of *textual authority* and *authorship* (Duranti 1994). In scenarios where multiple actual and latent authors use either language or purely symbolic acts of communication, the designation of authorship depends on community perceptions of authority (ibid.). However, in the same manner as speech act theory or the relationship between intention and language, textual authority lies within the confines of person-centric theory. In speech or language activities, authority may shift to what Du Bois refers to as a *nonpersonal* agent, meaning that authorship belongs not to a first or second person, but a third (Du Bois 1992). In this section, I will give three examples of the nonpersonal agent from the Liu genealogy in order to discuss anonymous voices and authorship politics in printed genealogies in Eastern Guizhou.

Example One: Individual Name

The anonymous voices emerge in the form of the patronymic practice of referring to parents via the names of their children. The first volume of the new version of the Liu genealogy presents the story of the Liu ancestry plus the prefaces and family injunctions for each subsequent volume. Volumes 1 through 4 contain records of the patrilineal descendants of four male ancestors—Tengshangong (滕山公), Fengshangong (鳳山公), Meishangong (梅山公), and Zhengbogong (正伯公). In other words, the detailed records for each line of patrilineal offspring constitute the main content of this genealogy. Age at death and burial locations are recorded, and official occupations are occasionally given.

All of this information is written in Chinese characters, with the name of each male preceded by information as required by an elegant and complex traditional Hanren/Hanzu naming system: rank (generational name), official name (*hao* 號), and given name (*ming* 名). The following is an example from the record of descendants of Meishangong:

Wenlu's（文陸）eldest son Changhai（昌海）, hao Baoliu（寶六）, born in 1908, year of death unknown, buried in Baoyinmei. Married Zhang Shi, year of death and burial site unknown. Remarried Zhang Shi, born in 1930, bore two sons: Qiao（橋）and San（三）. Changhai's eldest son Yongde（永德）, ming Qiaobao（橋寶）, born in 1954. Married Zhang Shi, people of Pangba. Bore two sons: Heping（和平）and Zhengqiao（正橋）.

Yongde's（永德）eldest son Yaohe（耀和）, ming Heping（和平）, born in 1980. Yongde's second son Yaozheng（耀政）, ming Zhengqiao（正橋）, born in 1982. Changhai's（昌海）second son Yongqing（永清）, ming Sanbao（三寶）, born in 1950, an elementary school teacher. Married Yao Shi, ming Moying, bore a son Linsan（林三）.

Yongqing's（永清）son Yaolin（耀林）, hao Linsan（林三）, born in 1982.

In this excerpt the individual names constitute a system that represents inheritance relationships between three generations of patrilineal descendants. Two naming systems are used, one written in Chinese and the other in Hmub. The most obvious feature of the Hanren/Hanzu system is the succession of name cliques——for instance, 'Wenlu（文陸）bore Changhai（昌海）, Changhai bore Yongde（永德）,' etc. The dual names mark the inheritance relationship between different generations: *wen*（文）, *chang*（昌）, *yong*（永）, *yao*（耀）, *zong*（宗）. All of these are on the list of 60 generational names presented in the genealogy.

However, another regular pattern among names between generations emerges. Each name is followed by a second name, designated by *hao* or *ming*:

Changhai (昌海), *hao* Baoliu (寶六); Yongde (永德), *ming* Qiaobao (橋寶), etc. These *haos* and *mings* formally resemble the double names used among the society of Han Chinese. Using as an example the relationships in 'Baoliu (寶六) bore Qiaobao (橋寶) and Sanbao (三寶), Qiaobao (橋寶) bore Heping (和平) and Zhengqiao (正橋); Sanbao (三寶) bore Linsan (林三),' note that the first character of the father's name moves to the second position for his descendants (the only exception being Qiaobao's eldest son, Heping). This movement is a clear example of the patronymic custom followed by the Hmub of Eastern Guizhou province—that is, the individual Hmub name is used with a single Chinese name (e.g., Liu [六], Bao [寶], Qiao [橋]). The complete name consists of a son's own name followed by his father's name——a system that is still followed among Hmub Liu families in the Shidong area. Furthermore, complete Hmub names in upland Hmub villages of Taijang County include the grandfather's name.

Note that in the genealogy the normative naming systems are still recorded. Names are written with Chinese characters, and the *ming* or *hao* name is added in a Hanren/Hanzu style of *shu ming* (書名), which the Hmub of Guizhou generally interpret to mean 'the name of the educated person'; this is used when children start attending school. According to this multi-layered naming system, Chinese written characters are used to represent both the Hmub language and Hmub patronymy practices. This mix of Chinese written characters and Hmub language patterns transforms the property or voice of individual names from the personal to the nonpersonal, or anonymous. In other words, the Chinese written characters represent non-personal phonetic symbols of the Hmub language——the 'third voice' embedded in written accounts of the Liu genealogy. I suggest that the Hmub and Kam minority writing systems invented in the 1950s played a role in the compilation of the native genealogy in the 1980s. Also, comparing to the use of Chinese characters to represent the Hmub phonetic system, logical alternatives to this writing system can be found in Zhuang's cosmological and ritual contexts, such as in *Hanvueng: The Goose King and Ancestral King* (2015), which is an epic and one of the Zhuang traditional texts widely circulated from Guanhgxi in Southern China.

Example Two: Basking the Genealogy

My senior informants told me that in Taijang and Tianzhu, the family genealogy was only open to community inspection at a yearly event. I view this event as an extension of textual authority: since the Liu genealogy cannot be displayed in tandem with other genealogies, it serves as a confirmation of boundaries between families. The annual genealogy basking event also conveys the message that the document's power resides within the Liu family. Informants in both villages talked about the sharing of money for food and wine—— a participatory event of celebration suggesting that genealogical content and textual authority are not viewed as the central reasons for the gathering. When examining the annual gathering from linguistic or ritualistic perspectives, it is difficult to determine whether the event celebrates the text, its authors, or event participants.

Although I have not come across the mentioning of basking genealogies in Guizhou chronicles published since the Qing dynasty, the terms *basking books* and *basking clothes* do appear in chronicles of Guiyang city and other sectors in Guizhou province. Such occasions are meant to take place on the sixth day of the sixth lunar month (Ding & Zhao 1991). For instance, in an edition of the *Puan Prefectural Gazetteer* (普安直隸廳志) the following tasks are associated with that date: 'planting reeds and beans, basking books and drying clothes, worshiping new shoots and grain gods, cutting wild grass, and stocking manure' (ibid.: 473). According to some documents, only local gentry families practiced the custom of basking books. An edition of the *Anshun Prefectural Gazetteer* (安 順 府 志) states that 'on the sixth day of the sixth moon, worship earth god, dry clothes, scholars bask books, farmers worship ancestors with wine and rice and plant paper money in the field to pray for an abundant harvest' (ibid.: 507). In other words, the basking genealogy ceremony still practiced by Taijang Hmub and Tianzhu Kam members of the Liu family may represent interactions between text and culture within a complex peripheral society. Further investigation is needed to determine whether the chronicle records were incorrectly copied from other sources, but what they reference illustrates broader connections regarding the basking of genealogies. The first and second examples also share in common a detachment from human authorship.

Example Three: Receive Genealogy

The following excerpt is from the older version of the Liu genealogy, compiled and printed during the Guangxu 34 period of the Qing dynasty (*Liu shi zupu* 1908, *my emphasis*).

We are the offspring of the Great Han Ancestor, Liu Bang (劉邦). From then on until the establishment of the ancestry by the six brothers of the Xionggong, all of our ancestors were well-known officials....

Twenty volumes of the common genealogy were completed. Each volume was given a distinguished name.... Anyone who respected Xionggong as his ancestor is the kin of bone and flesh and should not be thought of as distant, as is the case between the Qin and Yue people.[7] So, *compiling a genealogy* is a way to bring distant people together, which is the way it should be. This is to serve as an introduction.

Praise: The genealogy has been completed, and the virtuous acts of the ancestors will be spread for hundreds of years. Their offspring will develop many branches, with descendants continuing to compile and amend our genealogy....

What the genealogy has recorded are the names or titles of our patrilineal ancestors and whereabouts of their tombs. *We hope each keeper will treasure and take good care of it.*

The concept of *intertextuality*——relations between texts——can be used to examine the dialogical relations within the paragraphs of the above excerpt and between this account and other excerpts from the same genealogy. At the beginning of the first paragraph of the latest excerpt, the story of the ancestors establishes the type of authorship as personal. However, the non-personal language used throughout these paragraphs ('the loss of the old genealogy' and 'the recompiling of the common genealogy''') conveys a certain detachment from a person-centric authorship or viewpoint. The second and third paragraphs also contain examples of non-personal or anonymous concepts: praising the genealogy, naming the 22 volumes, and asking keepers to carefully protect the genealogical works. In other words, both inter-textual relations and dual authorship exist within this single excerpt.

Concluding Remarks

The practice of writing genealogies and the circumstances of their circulation is generally analyzed in terms of the literacy capabilities of local elites. Taking a theoretical approach based on recent discussions of intertextuality, or interdiscursivity, this chapter first examines the nature of genealogical nonresponsibility——that is, anonymous voices in the genealogies are imparted differently than those in the main text; the accounts of ancestors or descent groups invent a strong ideology of consanguinity that directly contributes to the textual authority. But anonymous voices in the other texts carry a nonpersonal tone, a nonresponse to textual authority (Du Bois 1992; Irvine 1996; Keane 1995). As Silverstein describes, text or discourse is a 'processual, real-time, and event-bound social action.... Communicational interdiscursivity is a relationship of event to event and is projected from the position of the personal——authorial and/or animating senders, responsible receivers, [and] non-responsible monitors" (Silverstein 2005). Du Bois also challenges the 'personalist ideology of language use' when discussing how Azande, an ethic group of Central Africa's Triangle, was reluctant 'to seek a personal or personified source for the meanings derived from divination' (Du Bois 1992). Analogous to discussing the problem of the non-personal and the lack of intention in spoken acts (Du Bois 1992: 57), this chapter uses native genealogies to explore the intent of emphasizing an imagined interethnic brotherhood or consanguine relationships among members of the Liu family via local notions of exclusiveness and relatedness invented through the concepts of intentionlessness, or no responsibility as expressed in the printed genealogies.

Secondly, this chapter describes how the Hmub and Kam elites have created genealogies using the written Chinese language, resulting in both the bridging of interethnic differences and the opening of a gap between these two ethnic groups and the Chinese state. It specifically examines the two versions of a printed Chinese language genealogy collated (jointly created) by the Hmub and Kam living in the eastern part of China's Guizhou province.[8] Combined, the two versions lend authority to claims of consanguine bonds between the Hmub and Kam speech communities. However, despite the collaborating editors' invocation of the spirit of 'our' ancestors and their request that readers resist profaning the name of their ancestors, neither one claims responsibility for the content. This chapter argues that the textual authority of genealogies is not always located within the confines of its narrowly defined authors. It instead focuses the attention on the broader social processes of authorship when describing how inter-ethnic assertions of a shared consanguinity are present in genealogies written in Chinese, as well as when showing how these interethnic assertions alternately emphasize exclusiveness and relatedness. As a collective writing strategy, authorship in genealogies written in Chinese becomes diffuse and anonymous, while simultaneously asserting a sense of Hmub and Kam from the Chinese state.

Thirdly, drawing from the above examples, anonymous utterances in the other texts need to be considered carefully due to deictic phenomena invented by a pair of anonymous dispositions between the main text and other texts. The anonymous voices in the above three examples are verbalized differently than those in the main text: the accounts of ancestors or patrilineal descent groups invent a strong ideology of patrilineal consanguinity that directly contributes to the textual authority. This ideology is intentional and personalist. Yet, distinctive expressions in the other texts (as well as in the above three examples), carry a nonpersonal, anonymous tone, a nonresponse to authority. Moreover, the anonymous voices in the Liu genealogies possess distinctly different dispositions. The basking genealogy ritual and receiving genealogy text contribute to the authority of the genealogy. But the use of Chinese characters to represent the Hmub phonetic system coexists with the Hmub system of patronymy within the assemblage of the individual Liu descendant names——indications of compromised authority. The result is a shift in the nature of authorship from an overtly collective authority to a covertly diffused anonymity. In other words, the anonymous voices struggle with two dispositions deictically related to the genealogical texts.

The presence of a nonpersonal, anonymous voice in native genealogies is reflected in Du Bois' divination study (Du Bois 1992: 57). Du Bois uses his observations of Azande divination ceremonies to explain the concept of the nonpersonal in language use. Here is the quote originally collected in Azande by Evans-Pritchard:

Poison oracle, that woman, since I intend to marry her, she is my wife? Poison oracle, listen, kill the fowl. It is not so, mine is the weariness of piercing boils.... I must do without her and may not marry her, poison oracle, listen and spare the fowl. (Evans-Pritchard 1976)

He reconsiders the personalist ideology of language use (Austin 1962; Searle 1969) by the reluctance of Azande to seek personal or personified sources for meanings derived from divination.

If all linguistic actions are always meaningful, how can we explain the nonpersonal, or anonymous voices, in genealogical construction and texts? Are they products of the imaginations of the Eastern Guizhou Hmub or Kam communities, or their responses to state influences on rituals, mannerisms, and literacy? Once again looking at the use of Chinese written characters with Hmub language patterns in the genealogies, the detachment noted in the original Chinese lexicon and the transformation to Hmub phonetic symbols may be analyzed as processes of detached individuality for communities with collective consanguine values or purposes, especially in terms of Hmub patronymy in the oral narrations of their genealogies. Such characteristics are especially insightful upon discovering that the Hmub naming system is embedded in or juxtaposed with Hanren/Hanzu generational names and the *ming-hao* double-naming system.

Finally, in light of the discussion on the importance of the Chinese surname as a means for non-Han native groups' Sinicization throughout the imperial history of China (Wang 2000), the practice of mimicry does not necessarily lead to assimilation and transformation of the natives into Han; it could be, rather, a significant native practice of appropriating otherness to assert the native self and identity (Cheung 2012). In this chapter, the use of

Chinese language in the genealogy as well as the intertextuality as the mimetic process of the native and their assertion of self through alterity (Taussig 1993) suggests that the imagined consanguine community of peripheral Hmub and Kam have found ways to express its local identity, even under the influences of state language use in rituals, mannerisms, and literacy.

註釋

序

1 "イタリアでの受賞と "洞窟感覚" 村上春樹をぬぐるメモらんだむ --- 村上さんは授賞式の行われたイタリア北西部のアルバで「洞窟の中の小さなかがり火」と題して講演した。共同通信によると、「小説──すなわち物語を語ること──の起源ははるか昔、人間が洞窟に住んでいた古代までさかのぼります」と述べ、「物語」の根源的な普遍性について語っている。"（《每日新聞》，2019 年 10 月 19 日）。

導言

1 Chien, Mei-ling. "Extramarital Court and Flirt of Guizhou Miao," *European Journal of East Asian Studies*, Vol. 8, No. 1 (2009), pp. 135-159.

2 Chien, Mei-ling. "Tensions between Romantic Love and Marriage: Performing 'Miao Cultural Individuality' in an Upland Miao Love Song," *Modalities of Change: The Interface of Tradition and Modernity in East Asia*, Eds. James Wilkerson and Robert Parkin, (2012), pp. 93-116.

3 簡美玲，〈「你倆是我倆一輩子的丈夫」：Hmub 人情歌語言的兩性意象與結伴理想〉，《歷史人類學》，第 5 卷，第 2 期（2007），頁 115-149。

4 英年辭世的清華大學人類學教授林淑蓉老師，與臺灣大學人類學教授顏學誠兄，生前也是身體經驗研究群重要的學術夥伴。

5 Zajonic, R. B. "Feeling and Thinking: Preferences Need No Inferences," *American Psychologist*, Vol. 35, No.1 (1980), pp. 151-175。

6 Chien, Mei-ling. "Cultivating the Ethnographer's Ear," *Taiwan Journal of Anthropology* Vol. 7, No. 2 (2009), pp. 87-106. Special Issue: Bodily Cultivation as a Mode of Learning.

7   簡美玲，〈煩悶、日常與黔東南高地村寨 Hmub 人的遊方〉，《考古人類學刊》，第 74
     期（2011），頁 53-88。專號「感同身受：日常生活的身體感」。

8   2013 年夏季在「歌師 Sangt Jingb 的手稿、知識與空間」一文首刊之前的最後修改階段，
     我很幸運地，在一場學術會議結識武漢大學朱炳祥教授。朱老師擔任這篇文章的評論人。
     朱老師提到此文與他當時正構思的主體民族誌的理論觀點，不謀而合。其後通過持續交
     流與閱讀朱老師的相關著述，讓我對於民族誌主體書寫的想法與作法，更感到創作上的
     深刻與清晰。

9   簡美玲，〈阿美族起源神話與發祥傳說初探——兼論阿美族亞群的類緣關係〉，《臺灣
     史研究》第 1:2 期（1994），頁 85- 108。

10 簡美玲，〈Hmub 人古歌的記音與翻譯：歌師 Sangt Jingb 的手稿、知識與空間〉，《民
     俗曲藝》，第 183 期（2014），頁 191-252。

11 Chien, Mei-ling. "Anonymous Voices and Authorship Politics in Printed Genealogies in
     Eastern Guizhou," *Asian Ethnicity*, Vol. 18, No. 3 (2017), pp. 204-217. Special Issue: Religion
     and Ethnicity in Southern China. 2017.

第一章
婚姻外的談情與調情

1   Jankowiak, W., M. D. Nell and A. Buckmaster,"Managing Infidelity: A Cross-Cultural
     Perspective," *Ethnology*, Vol. 41, No. 1 (2001), pp. 85-101.

2   Shackelford, T. K., M. Voracek, D. P. Schmit, D.M. Buss, V. A. Weekes-Shackelford, and R.
     L. Michalski, "Romantic Jealousy in Early Adulthood and in Later Life," *Human Nature*, Vol.
     15, No. 3 (2004), pp.283-300.

3   Buss, D. M., *The Evolution of Desire: Strategies of Human Mating* (New York: Basic Books,
     1994).

4   楊庭碩，《人群代碼的歷時過程：以苗族族名為例》，貴陽：貴州人民出版社，1998，
     頁 99。

5   Du, S. S., *Chopsticks Only Work in Pairs: Gender Unity and Gender Equality among the Lahu
     of Southwest China* (New York: Columbia University Press, 2003).

6　Malinowski, B., *The Sexual Life of Savages in North Western Melanesia: An Ethnographic Account of Courtship, Marriage, and Family Life among the Natives of the Trobriand Islands, British New Guinea* (London: Routledge & Kegan Paul, 1982[1932]), p.xx.

7　Malinowski, B., *The Sexual Life of Savages in North Western Melanesia*, p.xx.

8　Cate, R. M., and S. A. Lloyd , Courtship. *Sage Series on Close Relationships* (London: Sage Publications, 1992), p. 32. Robins, E. and T. L. Huston, 'Testing Compatibility Testing. Paper presented at the National Council on Family Relations Annual Meeting,' St. Paul, MN, 1983.

9　Rothman, E., *Hands and Hearts: A History of Courtship in America* (New York: Basic Books, Inc., Publishers, 1984). Bates, C., *The Rhetoric of Courtship: In Elizabethan Language and Literature* (Cambridge: Cambridge University Press, 1992). Mainardi, P., *Husbands, Wives, and Lovers: Marriage and Its Discontents in Nineteenth-Century France* (New Haven: Yale University Press, 2003).

10　Rothman, E., *Hands and Hearts*, p.5.

11　Bates, C., *The Rhetoric of Courtship*, p.2.

12　Bates, C., *The Rhetoric of Courtship*, p.2.

13　Bates, C., *The Rhetoric of Courtship*, p.2.

14　Bates, C., *The Rhetoric of Courtship*, p.19.

15　Mainardi, P. ,*Husbands, Wives, and Lovers*, p.213.

16　Mainardi, P., *Husbands, Wives, and Lovers*, p.213.

17　Mainardi, P., *Husbands, Wives, and Lovers*.

18　Malinowski, B., *The Sexual Life of Savages in North Western Melanesia*. Cate, R. M., and S. A. Lloyd, Courtship.

19　Rothman, E., *Hands and Hearts*.

20　Bates, C., *The Rhetoric of Courtship*. Mainardi, P., *Husbands, Wives, and Lovers*.

21　Chien, M. L., Relationship Terms, Cross-Cousin Marriage, and Gender Identity: The Fanpaizai Miao of Eastern Guizhou. The Workshop on Kinship and Economy on the Yun-Gui Plateau. Institute of Ethnology, Academia Sinia, Taipei. May 19, 1999.

22　親屬稱謂代碼請參本書頁 13。

23 她們相互爲遠房的堂姊妹。

24 Donnelly, N. D., *Changing Lives of Refugee Hmong Women* (Seattle: University of Washington Press, 1994).

25 Collier, J., *From Duty to Desire: Remaking Families in a Spanish Village* (Princeton: Princeton University Press, 1997), pp. 67-112.

26 Malinowski, B., *The Sexual Life of Savages in North Western*. Cate, R. M., and S. A. Lloyd, *Sage Series on Close Relationships*. Collier, J., *From Duty to Desire: Remaking Families in a Spanish Village*. Yan, Y. X., *Private Life under Socialism: Love, Intimacy, and Family Change in a Chinese Village 1949-1999* (Stanford: Standford University Press, 2003).

27 Rothman, E., *Hands and Hearts: A History of Courtship in America* (New York: Basic Books, Inc., Publishers, 1984) Donnelly, N. D., *Changing Lives of Refugee Hmong Women* (Seattle: University of Washington Press, 1994)

28 Bates, C., *The Rhetoric of Courtship.*

29 Jankowiak, W., M. D. Nell and A. Buckmaster, 'Managing Infidelity: A Cross-Cultural Perspective', pp. 85-101.

30 Phillips, A., *On Flirtation* (Cambridge, Mass.: Harvard University Press, 1994).

第三章
「你倆是我倆一輩子的丈夫」：情歌語言的兩性意象與結伴理想

1 吳澤霖先生於 1950 年代，在清水江流域進行 Humb 人公開談愛研究時，將原本漢語所稱的搖馬郎，轉譯爲游方一詞。吳澤霖先生係接納台江 Humb 人青年的建議，而採用游方。他們認爲搖馬郎有其他含意。而游方「這二字的聲音，接近台江的方言，意義也近似」參見吳澤霖，〈清水江流域部分地區苗族的婚姻〉，《苗族社會歷史調查》，（貴陽：貴州出版社， 1987〔1956〕），頁 107。接下來針對游方二字的漢語書寫進行考證。在漢語典籍的用字傳統，遊、游二字可相通。但早期的典籍裡只查到「遊方」二字的記載。此二字並用最早見於莊子的「大宗師」（孔子曰：「彼，遊方之外者也；而丘，遊方之內者也」）。「方」字有天下四方的意義。此外如「遊方弘化遍歷諸國」與佛教有關，意義上也與孔子所說的大同小異。而從現代的用法上來看：已將遊與游二字分開使用，遊字用於行動上，例如旅遊、遊蕩、遊子。游字則是流動的或是與水有關的解釋較多，例如游牧、游泳、游言（流言）、游日（閒暇之日）。字典上至多只在解釋欄加上註明：遊與游同。《辭海》上解釋遊方爲：僧道雲遊四方，無游方的詞條。《國語大辭典》上的記載亦然。因此，我們可推論，吳澤霖當年可能借用古漢語的遊方。游方則是中國大陸的簡體字系統下的結果，故遊字均寫為游。

2　Marcel Mauss，Michelle Rosaldo 以來的人類學對「人觀的研究，主要探討不同的族群如何以其特定的文化方式表達個體、自我、社會人的內容。本章指出 Humb 人對歌語言展現的性別意象裡，蘊含以姻親為核心價值，以及個人與集體之流動的人之屬性。

3　Hmong 相對於本書的貴州東部 Hmub 人是另一個苗族支系。

4　此語言學術語的中譯係參考 David Crystal 編，沈家煊譯，《現代語言學辭典》（北京：商務印書館出版，2004 年）。

5　參　見 R. Jakobson, "Shifters, Verbal Categories, and the Russian Verb," *Selected Writing* (1957[1971]), 132。

6　B. Mannheim, "Iconicity," *Journal of Linguistic Anthropology* 9:1-2(2000):107-110.

7　C. S. Peirce, *Logic Semiotic: Philosophical Writings of Peirce,* Justus Buchler, ed., (New York: Dover, 1955[1902], 98-115).

8　參見 B. Mannheim，"Iconicity," *Journal of Linguistic Anthropology* 9:1-2(2000)。

9　參見 B. Mannheim，"Iconicity," *Journal of Linguistic Anthropology* 9:1-2(2000)。

10　高地 Hmub 人婦女婚後生子之前多半住在娘家，對此居制，英文書寫的人類學文獻稱之為 natolocal residence 婚後原居制（或兩可居制）。在中文的文獻裡，以福建省惠東地區為主的 婦女婚後居研究，學者多以佳住娘家或不落夫家描述此居制。我將此二用語改為緩落夫家，理由在於施行此類婚後居的婦女於生子之後，即需改行從夫居。換言之，婚後住娘家即使可能長達數年，仍屬暫時。這是我以緩落夫家取代不落夫家的用意。村寨 Hmub 人對女性婚後居制的用語為 *niangt zix*（坐在女家）。

11　針對黔東南地區苗情歌的音樂形式與歌詞結構，民族音樂學者指出前者包含二聲部重唱，男聲用假嗓，女聲用窄嗓；後者為慣用五言句式或長短句式，不押韻，諧聲調，長篇歌的不同段落可換調，出現對歌的結構（參見李惟白，《苗嶺樂論》（貴陽：貴州民族出版社，1996），頁 68、124、130。由音樂到語言的結構，黔東南 Hmub 人的情歌對唱，在形式上都形成顯著的焦點。

12　本章的基礎資料為我對這部即興對歌聽所完成約 450 句對歌的聽寫稿。（簡美玲 2002、2009a）。

13　第 10 句與第 11 句歌，當地人也聽不出精確的語意，他們認為可能是類似只有音，沒有「話」的歌頭。

14 首先，在 Hmub 人遊方對話互動時的開頭、中段與結尾，都有明顯的輪流及順序的設計。輪流的現象，不僅出現在會話的開頭，也呈現在整個會話活動。輪流的原則，似主導整個會話活動的推進（簡美玲 2005b）。

15 本文以包含實質語意內涵的人稱名詞為主，暫不討論人稱代名詞（如第 65、66 句的 *meb*）的部分。

16 *Deif* 為村寨常用的親屬稱謂，作為女性說話者稱呼其弟兄，男、女長輩稱呼兒子或姪兒時所用。

17 歌中表述性別化個人的話，在性別指向上固定、絕對的，還包括 *but*（FZS/MBS〔表兄〕；eZH〔姊夫〕），*maib yut*（yBW〔叔媽，弟之妻〕）等親屬稱謂。

18 雖然指定型婚配的親屬稱謂體系，與指定形的婚姻組織之間不是絕對必然的關聯。

19 親屬稱謂代碼請參本書頁 13。

20 未清楚記錄的部分用語，以？標出。

21 參見 L. Schein, *Minority Rules: The Miao and the Feminine in China's Cultural Politics* (North Carolina: Duke University Press, 2000); N. D. Donnelly, *Changing Lives of Refugee Hmong Women* (Seattle: University of Washington Press, 1994)。

第四章
田野裡的「聽」

1 「民族誌的耳朵」（ethnographic ear）這一詞語，最初由納撒尼爾 · 塔恩（Nathaniel Tarn 1975）開始使用。他描述自己於一個多語社群進行田野工作的經驗時，寫道：「這或許是民族誌學者或人類學家再次對於他認為是異文化，而非熟悉的事物敞開耳朵。但是我仍然感覺，幾乎是在這裡的每一天，我都能在使用語言時發現新意。幾乎每一天，我都獲得新的詞語，彷彿語言是從每一個可能的幼芽中生長出來」（ibid.：9）。

2 本章的目的與寫作技術的歷史發展無關，也與特定歷史及空間背景下對自我的實踐與態度的轉變無關，但我仍有兩個理由來思考和遵循傅柯對於技術與自我關係的見解。首先，兩者都與口頭到書寫的轉變相關；其次，兩者都考察了某些心理經驗和身體經驗是如何從特定的技術（寫作）中產生的。

3 戈夫（Gove）等人（1986：552）認為，"to cultivate" 指「通過勞動、關懷或學習，來獲得提升，通過重視或通過學習、推進、發展、實踐、發表從而使文化、文明、修養得以成長。」梅裡亞姆－韋伯斯特（Merriam-Webster）（1984：203）指出，「cultivation 通常與文化有所關聯，因為它表明了對文化的持續追求和伴隨著這種追求的自律，而非強調其成果。因此，這個用語是比較中性與恰當」。

4　根據巴納德（Barnard）和古德（Good）（1984）的研究，家譜（pedigree）是指對家庭成員的基本人口統計學資料的記錄（姓名、年齡、婚姻狀況、出生日期等）。族譜或宗譜紀錄（genealogical records）是指家戶、家族和宗族之間的血緣和姻親關係。

5　本章不使用不同術語來區分噪音、雜訊（noise）或聲音（sound）的現象。這裡的聲音一詞用於傳達任何非言語的語言符號，這些符號可以被聽到，並可以作為索引符號被識別為 Fangf Bil 當地語境中的指示符號。例如家庭儀式的發生，婚禮儀式的開始，以及關乎遊方（調情與求愛）活動的開始及實踐。

6　*Vangt* 和 *lok* 是一對反義詞，可以翻譯成年輕人和年長者的意思。定義這兩個名詞的社會標注是婚姻和為人父母。未婚，或未當父母的男女成年人都被視為 *vangt*。一般而言，參與日常的遊方活動的人都是年輕人，但在節慶遊方活動進行對唱的場合裡，許多年長者也會參加。

7　已婚婦女通常穿著傳統服飾，年輕未婚女子或未生小孩的已婚婦女，都穿著外面買來的褲子和上衣，例如夏季的襯衫、運動服和冬季的毛衣。

8　我誠摯感謝匿名審查人之一，提醒我留意莫里斯·布洛克（Maurice Bloch）的一篇文章〈真相與視界：非普遍性概括〉（"Truth and Sight: Generalizing without Universalizing"〔2008〕）。

9　受馬克思主義和恩格斯歷史唯物論的影響，俄羅斯理論家利維維果茨基的中介理論將工具、符號和技術，視為增強人類心理機能的空間性和文化性分佈的系統（Haas 1996：17）。哈澤認為，「從這種觀點出發，那麼技術——特別是書寫技術——本身就是複雜的系統。從維果茨基的理論意義來說，探索這類系統的源頭或歷史，將可望有豐碩的成果」（ibid.）。

第五章
煩悶、日常與村寨 Hmub 人的遊方

1　Hmub 是中國境內「苗族」的一個支系。貴州民族史學者楊庭碩（1998）根據語言、地理環境、生業型態、風俗等，探討五個不同自稱的苗族支系及其與宋代之後諸多史料所載之不同族稱的比較對應。相對於 Hmong，Hmao，或 Gho Xiong（GhaoXong），Hmub 是群聚於黔東南苗支系的自稱。就歷史與民族誌的材料 Hmub 的群聚特性較 Hmong 明顯。

後者的社會特性突出於離散與因應不同環境展現矛盾與折衝的文化實踐（Tapp 2001）。我同意王富文（Nicholas Tapp）的看法，雖然同樣是 Hmong，可是在中國與在泰北的 Hmong，並不能單純視為相同的文化結群。對於遷移路徑迥遠的 Hmong，不能單就文化本質來解讀，而需正視其處於不同地區與環境的脈絡化結果。何為 Hmong 與何為 Hmub，兩者皆需要更多民族誌與歷史文獻的細節才得以建立描述與解釋的基礎。

2　本章採用黔東苗語的羅馬拼音體系，每個苗文最後一個英文字母為聲調的標示。

3　人類學自 1980 年代以來因關注情緒與身體經驗的研究得以反省過去偏重理性、心智、知識與社會結構描述與瞭解社群或個人的研究取徑（Lutz and White 1986）。我由一個 Hmub 人村寨的民族誌資料，來書寫煩悶——這樣一個乍看無關緊要的尋常經驗，與情感人類學的知識史發展有所關聯。

4　Fangf Bil 村寨 Hmub 的語彙 *iut fub*，字面上譯為遊方，指到處去走村寨與隨處遊蕩。不過遊方所衍生的語意有性的暗示，所以通常這個語彙，是不會出現在 Hmub 人日常對話中。遊方是 Hmub 人社會生活中不可避免的部分，具有特別安排的時間與空間，和特殊分類與識別的個體（以異性的姑舅交表親為遊方的對象）。遊方的社會性展現在時間、空間與人有序的組成及可變通的規律。在時間與空間的組合上，平常有村寨內家屋旁的隔窗夜談與夜間聚會，節慶時有村寨邊緣及寨外的坡上遊方及春暖花開時的姊妹飯。在空間上，姊妹飯通過寨邊同炊共食，突顯其專屬與邊緣性。而在人的組成上，突顯異性交表親互為遊方參與者的結構，且有男女年齡與婚姻身分的錯置。例如在姑娘集聚一起的遊方，可以聽到女孩叫男孩姊夫（*but*）、舅（*daid nenk*）、伯（仿如面稱丈夫的兄 *bad liut*），或者是叔（仿如面稱丈夫的弟 *bad yut*）（簡美玲 2009a：31-77；亦參本書第一章）。

5　例如，在婚禮儀式以米、飯、肉、酒、布等儀禮物交換，建立男家與女家世代締結的婚姻關係；以及通過親屬稱謂的語意結構與呼喊體系，展現交表聯姻的指定特性（prescription）（簡美玲 2005c：23-67；簡美玲 2009a：119-160, 161-192）。

6　Fangf Bil 村寨的 Hmub 同時具有短程的婚前遊方，與長程、無關乎婚姻，而是通過花帶、苗衣、身體、語言等交換，建立富有浪漫想像的婚後或婚姻外的遊方。以多元的溝通型式－言語、身體、社會習俗與制度化行為，貴州 Hmub 人遊方習俗不只為年輕人的情感創造出一個獨一無二的表達場域，亦為已婚的成年人展現出一個制度化婚姻外遊方調情的場域，在此同時也瓦解了遊方談情或調情與一夫一妻專偶制婚姻間的線性結構（Chien 2009a：135-159；亦參本書第一章）。

7　親屬稱謂代碼請參本書頁 13。

8　〈說文〉裡指出「煩，熱頭痛也」，相關字詞如煩歊、煩熱，即因暑熱而悶熱所產生的天熱心煩之感。如〈夜坐詩〉「沖襟謝煩歊，廣篲生離索」、〈過張邯鄲莊詩〉「客行煩似病，煩熱束四肢」（三民書局大辭典編撰委員會 1985：2878-2879）。

9　例如，〈孔雀東南飛〉「阿兄得聞之，恨恨心中煩」，相關字詞有煩惱、煩悶、煩憂、煩懵、煩躁，皆為情緒不愉快、抑鬱或急躁之意（三民書局大辭典編撰委員會 1985：2878-2879）。

10　如〈說文〉「悶，懣也」（三民書局大辭典編撰委員會 1985：2878-2879）。

11　雖然我不在本章探索民族誌研究方法論的問題，但在此所流露的資料特性與產出過程，都具有面對田野工作與書寫的可能性。

12　1990 年代起多數的男子，無論已婚或未婚都有出外打工的經驗（近則如貴陽，遠則如廣東、上海、北京等地）。短則一兩年，長則十餘年。2000 年以前，女子必需是已婚才隨丈夫出外打工。2000 年以後打工的潮流更為盛行，未婚女子也一個拉一個，出外打工去了。

13　過去此村寨未婚的女人隻身赴外省打工，是會引發村人閒言閒語，帶來不好的名聲。但 2009 年夏天我到 Fangf Bil 村寨進行遊方變遷的田野研究，才知近幾年所有未在學的青年男女，無論婚嫁與否，幾乎全數出外地打工了。

14　括弧內為農曆。在村寨裡，他們稱農曆為 Hmub 家的曆。

15　在這日誌裡的「交向」或「養機」等皆為此村寨鄰近周邊的山、坡、田、土等地名。這些漢字在此語境，僅被用作 Humb 語讀音，無關漢字原有的語意（相同的原則下，一些沒有到外面唸書的女性名字，亦用此法將 Humb 語的名字以漢字書寫。如唐偉九，唐為漢姓，偉九的漢字則僅是苗語的讀音）。依據 1930 到 1940 年代石啓貴先生所蒐集的湘苗文書，即是大量以漢字苗讀為記音系統，記錄湘西苗族地區的各種儀式的祭辭、唸誦、古歌、情歌等（石啓貴編著 2009）。由此可知包括湖南西部、貴州東部、廣西西北部等相接壤的東部苗族地區，都有漢字苗讀的書寫與記音系統在流通。有關於西南中國廣西、貴州與四川等部分地區周邊族群如壯族或苗族的儀式專家或一般（讀書）人如何在形、音、義借用漢字的系統以及流通的區域，David Holm（賀大衛）教授及其研究團隊的研究與成果，值得關注（Holm 2010）。

16　在 1950 年代起的集體生產時期 Fanngf Bil 村寨被分為十個生產組。組與小寨（vangf）以及父系繼嗣群體大抵可以一一對應。僅較大的小寨 Vangf Dof 分為兩個組。一直到現今，村人仍延用之。尤其在使用普通話或以漢字書寫時，更是以組來取代小寨。

17　此村寨的親屬稱謂體系與南亞 Dravidian 類型相同（簡美玲 2009a，2009b：89-116）。

18 在農忙期間，Fangf Bil 村人之間，尤其是關係較近的親屬與姻親，會輪流到彼此家幫忙。
    這種行爲普見於亞洲南方稻作文明的諸族群社會。例如臺灣東部說南島語的南勢阿美族
    （Amis）自日治時期起配合水稻的種植與收割，就有制度化輪流幫工的現象（王智珉
    2005）；或臺灣南北客家也有類似幫工或交工的行爲。

19 有關遊方的描述與討論另參簡美玲（2005b：347-380；2009a：31-77）。

20 吃鼓藏（*nenk jet niuf*）是黔東南 Hmub 社群盛行的大型砍牛祭祖儀式，傳統上十三年進
    行一次（吳澤霖等 1986〔1956〕：247-270）。1950 年起中斷多年，2000 年起許多經濟
    條件還可以的村寨，又開始做起吃鼓藏（簡美玲 2007a：157-203，2009b：153-187）。

21 未當家姑娘的身分是未婚且未生養孩子的女性。這樣身分的女性是尚未獨立持家的女性，
    她們是遊方裡的主要成員（簡美玲 2009a：31-77）。

第六章
Hmub 人古歌的記音與翻譯：歌師 Sangt Jingb 的手稿、知識與空間

1 田野報導人歌師與我在本文均採用黔東方言的苗文聲韻調系統。每個苗文最後一個英文
   字母爲聲調的標示（王輔世 1985：145-158；張永祥 1990），相對應的聲調符號請見本
   書頁 12。建立黔東方言的苗文聲韻調系統的語言材料，是在 1950 年代由中國科學院少數
   民族語言調查第二工作隊，在貴州省凱里市掛丁鄉養蒿寨所蒐集的，他們以此地的語音
   材料，作爲苗語黔東方言北部土語的代表（王輔世 1985：107；李雲兵 2003）。

2 在語言人類學的研究領域裡，"transcription" 除了紀錄語音、聲音，也包含記錄人在
   說話或對話時的手勢，站的位置，眼睛看的方向等肢體語言。Alessandro Duranti 給
   "transcription" 如下的定義："I will hereafter use the term transcription for the process of
   inscribing social action and transcript for the finished, although by no means of definitive,
   product of such a process."（Duranti 1997b：137）。

3 此部分引文之斷句爲筆者所加。

4 以中央研究院史語所傅斯年圖書館所藏的善本書湘苗文書爲例，由石啓貴編的《吃牛秘
   訣》，就是以漢字苗讀的書寫方式，將祭牛的儀式唸詞以及湘西苗歌或情歌進行記音（湘
   西苗族考察紀錄 第三本，抄本，34 葉；28 公分，末附：楊家吃牛之擺法）。

5 如貴州省黃平縣民族事務委員會編，出版年未敘明的《苗族古歌古詞》；1979 年由田兵
   編選、貴州省民間文學組整理的《苗族古歌》；1984 年由中國民間文藝研究會貴州分會
   重新編印的《民間文學資料》裡的苗族古歌部分作品；1991 年由貴州民族出版社發行的
   《開親歌》。

6 本章所提及的相關田野地點，歌師習歌地點，古歌傳唱地區，參圖一。

7 遊方（*iut fub*），黔東南苗族地區普遍的，有制度性與儀式化傾向的年輕人的談情說愛的習俗，並也與日常生活、村寨年輕人的社會化有關，與婚姻之間並置著因果關係與非一對一對應的兩重關係，後者指的是在該社會重要的婚姻外的遊方談情。

8 吃鼓藏（*nenk jet niuf*）是黔東南地區苗族最盛大的砍牛祭祖儀式，通常會形成跨村寨的饗宴、交換與結盟。由父系氏族、村寨的鼓社組織與儀式頭人共同來舉辦。傳統上是十三年才舉行一次，但鼓藏儀式由開始到完成，前後歷時四年，是一極為繁複的大型儀式，過程中由歌師唱連續數日的苗族古歌，一般稱為鼓藏歌。

9 Fangf Bil 村寨位於台江縣方召鄉。相對於台江地區鄰清水江較近地勢較低的村寨，緯度較高的方召片區的村寨，藏於層層大山內，在當地稱為高坡村寨。

10 棉花坪（Zangx Bangx Hsenb）位於台江縣台盤鄉的一個自然村。地名源自此片平地種植許多棉花（*bangx hsenb*）。

11 凱棠（Ghab Dangx Gix，意思為蘆笙場，在過去是一個較大的地方可以跳蘆笙〔吳一文 1995〕）位於黔東南州政府所在的凱里市東北面，東與台江縣的台盤、革一相鄰，西與旁海鎮相連。

12 此部分對 Sangt Jingb 生命史的描述，主要是我 2007 年一月在台江與 Sangt Jingb 的訪談。2002 年台江文聯的地方文人刊物《新世紀金秋筆會專集》，2003 年由華夏文化藝術出版社發行的《方妮乃—台江人物錄》，2006 年 11 月 1 日的《西部開發報》，都有專文報導 Sangt Jingb 與古歌書寫的事。《新世紀金秋筆會專集》述及 Sangt Jingb 收集古歌的範圍（貴州、雲南、廣西、湖南）、整理的內容，以及進行工作的方式（查證、對應、研究，力求真實的古歌翻譯）。《西部開發報》中的報導，則以感性與微帶誇飾的文字描述 Sangt Jingb 所扮演的古歌傳承角色，並陳述他在遭遇困境、病危時仍心繫古歌。終於受到唐春芳、燕寶等人引薦，獲得縣裡的重視，願意協助他完成古歌的整理出版並曾先後在貴州地方刊物《苗嶺》發表。2007 年我訪問了前述兩篇文章的作者張少華（作家、台江縣文藝作家聯合委員會主席）。張少華跳脫他在前兩篇報導中所採用的客觀角度，而以自己本身與 Sangt Jingb 共事、相處的經驗，以及其他台江學者對 Sangt Jingb 的評論，來表達自己的看法。

13 1961 年中國為了應對嚴重的自然災害，對公職人員實施有計畫的下放回家務農政策。Sangt Jingb 被列入下放對象，自此回到家鄉務農，其後再也沒有出任過公職。原因具有多重性，一是中國經濟恢復後，對下放公職人員恢復公職具有很強的競爭性，Sangt Jingb 老家距縣城較遠，可能信息不易傳達，就此錯過了復職的機會。二是 Sangt Jingb 與妻子結婚後，九年尚未有生育，他和妻子在家族內受到很大的輿論壓力，遂不再外出任職。但更重要的原因還是 Sangt Jingb 的父親在 1949 年以前加入過國民黨，這在當時是嚴重的政治問題，Sangt Jingb 因此在政治上受到影響，致使主管公職人員任用的幹部（官員）認定他達不到繼續擔任教師的資格，包括擔任代課教師的資格也不符合。因此，他只能留在家中繼續務農為生。不過這樣卻給了他繼續學習記錄和翻譯苗族古歌的機會。

14　如本章第二節所述，《運金運銀》（Qab Nix Qab Jenb）在十二部古歌當中，是婚禮等重要生命儀禮，最常被演唱的古歌。其內容也和祖先遷徙有關，並包含運送金銀等生財致富的文化母題。此部古歌的長度達千行，可分為數百段短歌。因其傳唱的普及，以及生財致富的主題，應該是此理由，歌師 Sangt Jingb 由此部古歌開始學起。

15　歌師在述說時，指因「大躍進」（1958-1960）而停班。但依其所述的時代背景與年代，應是指「文化大革命」（1966-1976）時期。

16　參本章註釋 14。

17　指黃平地方政府出版的《苗族古歌古詞》，未註明出版年。

18　燕寶（苗名），學名王維寧、漢名顧維君。出生於 1927 年，貴州省凱里市凱棠鄉龍塘村人。1950 年貴州大學外文系英語文學專業畢業；1957 年中央民族大學語文系語言學專業畢業。曾任貴州民族出版社苗文總編輯。代表作《苗族古歌》、《苗族民間故事選》、《張秀眉歌》、《貴州情歌選》第二集、中國民間文學集成《貴州苗族民間故事選》、《貴州苗族歌謠選》，主編《中國民間故事集成貴州省卷》、《紅軍在貴州的故事》、《貴州神話傳說》、《貴州民間故事》、《崎嶇的路：貴州民間文學三十年》、《楊大陸之歌》，以及單篇作品〈苗族宗教神話〉、〈苗族飲食之花〉、〈水族文學概況〉、〈雙歌百則〉。（取自三苗網，2012 年 9 月 11 日：http://www.3miao.net/viewthread-9777.html）

19　今旦，苗名 Jenb Dangk，漢名吳滌平。出生於 1930 年 10 月，台江縣革東鎮搞午寨人。1954 年至 1956 年擔任中央民族學院語文系教員；1956 年至 1959 年在貴州民族學院協助開辦民族語文班，任教研室副主任，教研組組長；1959 年至 1981 年因被錯劃「右」派，在貴州省扎佐林場監督勞動。1981 年至 1985 年任貴州省民族研究所助理研究員、副所長；1985 年後在貴州民族出版社擔任副社長、副總編輯、總編輯、研究員。歷任六屆全國政協委員，六屆貴州省人大代表，六、七屆貴州省政協常委，以及中國少數民族漢語教學研究會副理事長，中國民族語言學會理事，貴州省苗學研究會副會長，貴州省宗教學會理事等。代表作有《苗族史詩》、《苗語的情狀量詞初探》、《苗族史詩詞彙探古》、《苗語革東 話音系》、《民族文字在教學中的幾個問題》、《牧鵝姑娘梅朵》等（引自政協台江縣第五屆委員會、學習文史委員會編《方妮乃—台江人物錄》，第 30 頁）。

20　唐春芳，苗名 Dangk Jux，出生於 1919 年 9 月，台拱鎮養旎寨（Vangx Nix）人。自幼貧苦靠著親友接濟才有讀書的機會，再加上父親通曉苗族歷史、母親是位歌手，因而培養了從事苗族文藝工作和歷史研究的背景。曾任邊胞文化研究會會長、行行學術研究社社長、貴州省參議會《民意月刊》執行編委、貴定中學教務主任、貴陽市民族事務委員會宣傳秘書、貴州少數民族文藝工作隊隊長、貴陽市民政局科員、貴州民族學院文工團創作員、中央民族學院文工團創作員、貴州省文聯《山花》文藝月刊編輯、中國民間文藝家協會會員、貴州民間文學工作組組員、貴州民間文藝家協會副主席、中國人民政治協商會議貴州省第五屆委員會會長。唐春芳的作品有《苗族古歌》、《爲媽媽報仇》、《阿嬌與金丹》、《仰阿莎》、《山花》、《中國民間長詩》，以及《嘎百福歌》。1946 年在貴州大學讀書時，創辦《行行月刊》。用苗語、苗文進行苗族詩歌創作：《苗家优儸情》；用苗語、苗文、苗調進行苗族新歌曲創作，例如：《歌唱民族區域自治》、《花開滿樹枝》與《盼紅軍、新翻身》等。另有關苗族古代史著述：〈論苗族族稱的含意及其來源〉、〈論苗族的原始居地〉、〈論東夷族就是苗族〉、〈論苗族祖先蚩尤在中國歷史上的功績與地位〉等（引自政協台江縣第五屆委員會學習文史委員會、學習文史委員會編《方妮乃—台江人物錄》，第 261-266 頁）。

21　潘定發，凱里市人。曾任雷山縣苗學會副會長，中國民族博物館苗族文化雷山研究中心特約研究員（引自中國苗族網，2012 年 9 月 11 日：http://www.chinamzw.com/wlgz_readnews. asp?newsid=999）。

22　Sangt Jingb 所記音、翻譯與書寫的苗族古歌，最後是由貴州大學出版社於 2008 年出版。

23　作者未將封面標上頁數，之後包括內容提要、序文，總共到第 7 頁，但在第一首 ot hxak 部分作者又將其頁數標爲 1，因此，此部分所算總頁數，是將所有頁數加總，而非文本最後一頁的頁數。

24　作者在標示第幾首 ot hxak（短歌）時，部分標示錯誤，或是中間有許多首短歌未標上數字。因此，此部古歌被記音與翻譯共 141 首，是經過我與研究助理整理古歌手稿所得的結果，而非 Sangt Jingb 原有的編號與短歌的總數。

25　在目前已出版的苗族古歌，多半傳達以語意爲主的故事（如：1979 年由田兵編選、貴州省民間文學組整理的《苗族古歌》），少數爲苗文與漢文雙語對照（如：1984 年由中國民間文藝研究會貴州分會編印的《民間文學資料》的部分作品、1991 年由貴州民族出版社發行的《開親歌》，以及由貴州省黃平縣民族事務委員會編的《苗族古歌古詞》）。

26　台江地區普遍以山沖來表述山區裡的平地。如在貴州東部高地 Fangf Bil 村寨外有一自老祖公以來，逢大型儀式慶典跨村寨放牛打架時的小坪壩，就位在四周都有緩山坡的山沖裡。

27　在台江、凱棠片區各類儀式場合所唱的古歌，常見以誇（讚美）人、地、空間乃至日常物（如桌、椅、碗等等）來開頭。

28　不確定是否爲「面」。手稿此處漢字有塗抹的痕跡。就苗文的原意此句應該翻譯爲「見江河往東流」。

29　碓杆是一根架於支撐點上的長木，以短臂爲用力端，而長臂爲作業端。苗族村寨家戶內的碓杆用作舂米。此句是說「仿佛看見一根碩大的碓桿在波濤中翻滾」。

30　青魚是苗族經常食用的魚類，但體長最多不超過兩三尺，因而古歌描述的青魚很可能不是青魚，而是其他大型魚類（如長江中的白鱀豚或江鱘）。本句是說「仔細一看發現是一條碩大的青魚，它的身軀大得像一匹馬」。此句苗文原文當中的「大」字非形容詞，其句法功能不是用來修飾馬匹，而是作句子的謂語使用。

31　本句苗文單詞 bongf，因爲是指感知聲音，所以應該翻譯爲聽見。原文中都翻譯爲見和看見，屬於誤譯。

32　轉寫爲散文體的過程裡，已無可免地加入我對這些五言詩句中文翻譯的解釋與文字的增添。

33　本節有關古歌手稿資料的分析與理解，主要得自吳宓蓉由空間切入，潘怡潔由人觀切入進行分析的協助，以及我們之間在分析古歌手稿過程中，密切而持續的對話與嘗試。本章的書寫尤其著重以空間爲主的分析。

34　人群的繁衍也是這部古歌的主題。如，短歌第七十餘首至第八十餘首，樹木與船舶都作爲傳宗接代的比喻。如短歌第 79+1 首：「砍樹多少節、得來多少節、砍樹九段長、余砍七節短」。根據 Sangt Jingb 的註解，此可引申爲九男七女，並與男女之生育有關。另外，與船舶相關的，如短歌第 84+1 首：「伯媽多少船、多少船叔媽、九十船的叔媽、叔媽七十船」。當眾多女性都身處具有重要意涵的船舶中時，兩者結合或許可顯示對於傳宗接代的重視。若只有遷移卻無法持續繁衍，就無法延續族人的香火。此主題亦表現於古歌在演述樹木、船舶或者其他如田地等物時，皆將部分細節提出。短歌第 77+1 首：「樹腳成什麼、樹根成什麼、碎屑成什麼、樹葉成什麼、樹腳成小孩、長小孩管家、樹根成黃鱔、田裡長泥鰍、碎屑成魚秧、成鯽魚群群」，以及短歌第 80+1 首：「船頭要啥比、船角什麼比、船內什麼比、船尾要啥比、船頭螳螂比、角船角尺比、船里竹蓆比」。樹腳最後會變成小孩，長大後能夠管家；而碎屑會變成魚秧，也會生成許多魚群。從中可看出對傳承的期待。等小孩長大以後，就能夠做許多事情。成群的魚群，也可聯想成 Hmub 人不僅希冀遷移到一個土地肥沃的好地，也期待能多子多孫。

35　苗族古歌中所指的可能爲薏苡或薏仁米，參本章註釋 42。

36　植物的根或近根之莖稱苑，如禾苑。此句意指：「一根苑粗得像腳　　。」

37　此句意指：「一根稻梗粗得像手指。」

38　田萍，浮水類型的植物。葉體四片并出浮於水面，外形酷似盛滿米飯的大碗。此句意指：「水面漂浮的田萍，大得像盛滿米飯的大碗。」

39   此句意指：「水裡的鱔魚大如碓杆。」

40   此句意指：「購買一斗小米只需五個銅錢」，意思是說：小米價格非常低廉。

41   此句意指：「只需支付一分（十分之一錢，百分之一兩，約合 0.36 克）重量的白銀，就可以購買到一匹馬」。此句意在誇耀價格低廉。

42   原句中的「剩」字可能為 Sangt Jingb 翻譯時誤用的漢字，按上下文意，當正作「盛」。此句「玉米」亦可能屬 Sangt Jingb 誤譯，苗文原意應是指「薏苡」（或稱薏仁、薏仁米）。這是中國南方的一種糧食作物。是一種喜溫暖耐澇的禾本科植物，原產於中國南方和中南半島，也是古代苗族的主要糧食之一。此句意指：「一旦和當地人相逢，當地人就端出薏仁米飯來招待我們」，銜接此，下兩句意指：「當地薏仁米的谷苞比腳腕還大，一顆薏仁米粒大得像一個拳頭」。

43   參本章註釋 42。

44   參本章註釋 42。

45   原文為："Sho, hey! Your Ancestors will say 'Who showed you the way here?' You will answer: 'It was a fellow with a face as big as fan and eyes like saucers…' Your Ancestors will say next: 'How can we follow his tracks? …' "（Lemoine 1983：38-39）。

46   原文為："The language of the death songs is not only replete with flowery metaphor and analogies but also contains abundant references to the material culture and the agricultural rhythms of life of the Hmong in their traditional geographic setting: that is, the high mountain ridges of mainland Southeast Asia. References abound in the texts to specific flora and fauna, to specific relationships to and between topographical features—the rivers, the streams, valleys and mountain passes, to agricultural implements and tools and methods of food preparation, to heroes and heroines of legend and myth located in their specific geographical settings, and to specific aspects of domestic architecture."（Falk 1996：220）。

47   歌師 Sangt Jinb 在手稿裡對於古歌地名的翻譯包含：音譯、意譯，以及音譯與意譯混成。與此相關的討論參見本文下一小節。

48   根據歌師 Sangt Jingb 的解釋，此指「河水邊，淺淺的沙灘，有時水會蓋上，有時又退出」。

49   瞄：以目注視。（瞄準）發射槍砲時，為命中目標，以眼注視（引自三民書局《大辭典》，第 3303 頁）。

50   （1）市：作買賣的場所。 說文 「市，買賣所之也。」 戰國策 · 秦策一 「臣聞：爭名者於朝，爭利者於市。」（2）聚集貨物，從事買賣。 爾雅 · 釋言 「貿、賈、市也。」（引自三民書局《大辭典》，第 1394 頁）。

51 「烏狂」一詞,在《元史·地理志》中,就已經明確地提到過。此部分值得將來另文探討。

52 九江:縣名,古稱潯陽,清稱德化,爲江西省九江府附郭首縣,民國裁府留縣,並改今名。

53 黃石:港名,在湖北省大冶縣之東北。

54 鄂州:此地名最早出現在唐代,指湖北省的武昌〔縣名〕。鄂州市也是現今湖北省的地級市,位於長江南岸。

55 黃岡:縣名,在湖北省。城瀕長江,負險臨深,與武漢、九江相爲首尾。

56 武漢:長江、漢水將武漢一分爲三,形成武昌、漢口、漢陽隔江鼎立。現爲湖北省會,也是華中地區最大的都市。

57 嘉魚:縣名,在湖北省。縣城位於長江之東岸,交通便利,居民稠密,城內商務以西門正街爲最盛。

58 洪湖:湖名,在湖北省沔楊縣南部,當長江之北,西爲監利縣,爲雲夢澤諸湖之一。有支流西北貫通長湖、白鷺等湖而入長江。

59 岳陽:縣名,在湖南省。城介長江與洞庭湖之間,爲湖南省門戶。

60 烏狂,在《元史·地理志》中就已經明確地提到過。

61 歌詞內容見《跋山涉水》古歌手稿,第 97、98 與 99 首短歌。

62 歌詞內容見《跋山涉水》古歌手稿,第 99、100 與 101 首。

63 黔東南苗族最重要也最普遍的傳統竹製樂器。此樂器型制由小到大十分多元,大型者比一個成年男性還高。

64 歌詞內容見《跋山涉水》古歌手稿,第 101、102 與 103 首。

65 原文爲:"No poem is intended for the reader, no picture for the beholder, no symphony for the listener." Walter Benjamin(2004〔1923〕:75)。

66 中譯:「一個譯本不論多麼的好,都永遠無法到達原著的境界」(ibid.:76)。

67 學徒(apprenticeship)與民族誌田野研究的探討(Stoller 1987; Castaneda 1998[1969]),參本書第四章。

68 唐春芳,知名的苗歌學者與創作表演家,台江 Hmub 人。2007 年初我在春芳爺爺家與他再次見面談古歌。90 多歲的他,耳力已不佳,唱起自己創作且流行黔東南的苗歌,《花開滿樹枝》等,歌聲依舊宏亮。我從貴州回臺灣後,寄照片給春芳爺爺。不久收到春芳爺爺長子來信說,我所拍攝的是爺爺生前最後的留影。

69　台盤平水的歌師張啓庭，也提到古歌一層一層唱上去的意象。

附錄 英文原版

Chapter 1
Extramarital Court and Flirt of Guizhou Hmub

1　　Jankowiak, W., M. D. Nell and A. Buckmaster, "Managing Infidelity: A Cross-Cultural Perspective," *Ethnology*, Vol. 41, No. 1 (2001), pp. 85-101.

2　　Shackelford, T. K., M. Voracek, D. P. Schmit, D.M. Buss, V. A. Weekes-Shackelford, and R. L. Michalski, "Romantic Jealousy in Early Adulthood and in Later Life," *Human Nature*, Vol. 15, No. 3 (2004), pp. 283-300.

3　　Buss, D. M., *The Evolution of Desire: Strategies of Human Mating* (New York: Basic Books, 1994).

4　　Du, S.S., *Chopsticks Only Work in Pairs: Gender Unity and Gender Equality among the Lahu of Southwest China* (New York: Columbia University Press, 2003).

5　　Such distinction is important because that can be related to the debates over the link between individual feelings, emotions, and collective representations. For example in his work on Robert Hertz and the study of "sin," Robert Parkin points that "in a more general sense, one can say that much of Durkheim and Mauss's work concerned the nature and maintenance of social control; Hertz's magnum opus would have been concerned with the contrasting but related theme of what happens when the individual goes against society's injunctions." Parkin, R., *The Dark Side of Humanity: The Work of Robert Hertz and its Legacy* (Amsterdam: Harwood Academic Publishers, 1996), p. 124.

6　　Malinowski, B., *The Sexual Life of Savages in North Western Melanesia: An Ethnographic Account of Courtship, Marriage, and Family Life among the Natives of the Trobriand Islands, British New Guinea.* (London: Routledge & Kegan Paul, 1982[1932]), p. xx.

7　　Malinowski, B., *The Sexual Life of Savages in North Western Melanesia*, p. xx.

8　　Cate, R. M., and S. A. Lloyd, Courtship. *Sage Series on Close Relationships* (London: Sage Publications, 1992), p. 32. Robins, E. and T. L. Huston, "Testing Compatibility Testing." Paper presented at the National Council on Family Relations Annual Meeting,' St. Paul, MN, 1983.

9   Rothman, E., *Hands and Hearts: A History of Courtship in America* (New York: Basic Books, Inc., Publishers, 1984). Bates, C., T*he Rhetoric of Courtship: In Elizabethan Language and Literature* (Cambridge: Cambridge University Press, 1992). Mainardi, P., *Husbands, Wives, and Lovers: Marriage and Its Discontents in Nineteenth-Century France* (New Haven: Yale University Press, 2003).

10   Rothman, E., *Hands and Hearts,* p.5.

11   Bates, C., *The Rhetoric of Courtship*, p.2.

12   Bates, C., *The Rhetoric of Courtship*, p.2.

13   Bates, C., *The Rhetoric of Courtship*, p.2.

14   Bates, C., *The Rhetoric of Courtship*, p.19.

15   Mainardi, P., *Husbands, Wives, and Lovers,* p.213.

16   Mainardi, P., *Husbands, Wives, and Lovers*, p.213.

17   Mainardi, P., *Husbands, Wives, and Lovers*.

18   Yang, T. S., *Renqun Daima de Lishi Ghocheng--Yi Miaozu Zuming Wei Li* (The Historical Process of Signs in Human Groups: the Case of Miao〔Hmub/Hmong〕Nationality Names) (Guiyang: Guizhou Renmin Chuban She, 1998), p. 99.

19   Pedigree is recording basic demographic data (such as name, age, marriage, birth) of the members of each household. Genealogical records express consanguine and affine relations among households, family, and lineages.

20   The "young people" with quotation mark in this chapter indicates that the people involved in courtship are not always young people in its strict sense; especially on the occasions of festival courtship activities and singing antiphonal songs, there are lots of old people participating in them.

21   The unmarried young women wear trousers and coats bought from the outside, usually blouses or sportswear in summer and woolen sweaters in winter.

22   FZD means father's sister's daughter; MBS, mother's brother's son; MBD, mother's brother's daughter; FZS, father's sister's son. Hereafter, I follow the kin abbreviations: F=father, M=mother, B=brother, Z=sister, G=sibling, E=spouse, S=son, D=daughter, P=parent, C=child, e=elder, y=younger, ms=man speaker, ws=woman speaker, etc. Barnard, A. and A. Good, *Research Practices in the Study of Kinship.* (London: Academia Press, 1984), p. 4.

23 They consider themselves classificatory sisters.

24 This is a Hmub idiom which means a couple of years.

25 The two kinds of marriages show their differences in certain ways. Almost all the public marriages are arranged marriages that take the form of prescriptive cross-cousin marriage with village endogamy, and they have a more complicated wedding ceremony. Other rituals are involved in public marriages. First, the bride's family will approve of her leaving by undertaking a ceremony involving the slaughter of a chicken. She may leave if the eyes of a chicken killed by the groom or the bride's brothers are open. Another ritual involves a ceremonial farewell in which the bride shares a cup of wine with her brothers to express farewell. After these rituals are performed, the bride leaves her family's house. Wearing formal Hmub clothes and silver ornaments, the bride in a public marriage departs for her groom's house with her "parallel" sisters in the daytime. Elopements, on the other hand, are much simpler, and lack the rituals of the public marriages. Elopements violate village endogamy and are finalized when the bride, wearing a dress bought from the market (*ux diuf*, literally "the Han dress"), cross the threshold of the house alone with her groom in the middle of the night. Such marriages occur without her family's consent or knowledge. Elopements of the Hmub are not necessarily related to romantic love. However, we may consider "elopement from the perspective of a bride's weighing the uncertainties and special ambivalence of an alternative cognatic marriage against the certainties and general ambivalence of a restricted marriage. Moreover, elopements make intelligible Hmub ambivalence about the collective marital ideal and individuality (Chien 2005a). Chien, M., "Hmub Elopement in Eastern Guizhou: Ambivalent Collective and Individual," *Taiwan Journal of Anthropology*, Vol. 3, No. 1 (2005), pp. 49-86.

26 Parkin, R. "The Joking Relationship and Kinship: Charting a Theoretical Dependency," *Journal of the Anthropological Society for Oxford*, Vol. 24, No. 3 (1993), pp. 251-263.

27 They did not actually have an actual blood relationship.

28 Most of the women with the status of "the old", from those who have just given birth to her first baby to the old women, wear Hmub clothes and a black cloth over their heads rather than colorful jewelry.

29 Chindarsi, N. *The Religion of the Hmong Njua*. (Bangkok: The Siam Society, 1976).

30 Collier, J., *From Duty to Desire: Remaking Families in a Spanish Village* (Princeton: Princeton University Press, 1997), pp. 67-112.

31 Simpson, J. A. and E. S. C. Weiner, *The Oxford English Dictionary*, Volume III. (Oxford: Clarendon Press, 1989b), p. 1064.

32 Simpson, J. A. and E. S. C. Weiner, *The Oxford English Dictionary,* Volume V. (Oxford: Clarendon Press, 1989c), p. 1064.

33 Collier, J., *From Duty to Desire*.

34 Collier, J., *From Duty to Desire*, p.81.

35 Ideally, sexual relations are not included in the permitted extra-marital long term flirting of the Hmub society.

36 "Hmong people refer to an Asian ethnic group in the mountainous regions of southern China. There, they remain one of the largest sub-groups in the Miao *minzu*. Beginning in the 18th century, Hmong groups began a gradual southward migration due to political unrest and to find more arable land. As a result Hmong currently also live in several countries in Southeast Asia, including northern Vietnam, Laos, Thailand, and Myanmar-Burma. In Laos, a significant number of Hmong/Mong people fought against the communist-nationalist Pathet Lao during the Secret War, When the Pathet Lao took over the government in 1975, Hmong/Mong people were singled out for retribution, and tens of thousands fled to Thailand for political asylum. Since the late 1970s, thousands of these refugees have resettled in Western countries, including the United States, Australia, France, French Guiana, and Canada. Others have been returned to Laos under United Nations-sponsored repatriation programs. Around 8,000 Hmong/Mong refugees remain in Thailand" (Retrieved October 26, 2008, from http://en.wikipedia.org/wiki/Hmong_people).

37 Donnelly, N. D., *Changing Lives of Refugee Hmong Women* (Seattle: University of Washington Press, 1994).

38 Donnelly, N. D., *Changing Lives of Refugee Hmong Women*, p. 120.

39 Donnelly, N. D., *Changing Lives of Refugee Hmong Women* , pp. 120-121.

40 Yan, Y. X., *Private Life under Socialism: Love, Intimacy, and Family Change in a Chinese Village 1949-1999* (Stanford: Stanford University Press, 2003).

41 Jankowiak, W., M. D. Nell and A. Buckmaster, "Managing Infidelity: A Cross-Cultural Perspective," *Ethnology*, pp. 85-101.

42 Phillips, A., *On Flirtation* (Cambridge, Mass.: Harvard University Press, 1994).

43   Given that the Hmong and the Hmub in this chapter are branches of Miao, it is necessary
      to examine if extra-marital flirting exists among the former before undertaking a systematic
      comparative analysis on the courting and flirting customs of these two subgroups. There are
      Hmong courtship and marriage literatures, e,g, Chindarsi 1976: 67-80, Cooper 1984: 143-145,
      Cooper 1995, Lee 1998, Lee 2005, and Tapp 2001. Chindarsi, N., *The Religion of the Hmong
      Njua*, pp. 67-80. Cooper, R., *Resource Scarcity and the Hmong Response* (Singapore: National
      Singapore University Press, 1984). Cooper, R. *The Hmong* (1995). Lee, G. Y., "Marriage and
      Reidence in a Thai Highland Society," *Journal of Siam Society*. (1988). Lee, G. Y. "The Shaping
      of Tradition." *Hmong Studies Journal*. (2008). Tapp, N., *The Hmong of China: Context, Agency
      and the Imaginary* (Leiden: BRILL, 2001).

Chapter 2

Tensions between Romantic Love and Marriage: Performing 'Hmub Cultural Individuality' in an Upland Hmub Love-Song

1   I collected this material at an institutionalized flirting event that took place in conjunction with a
      bullfight during my village-based fieldwork related to marriage and flirting conducted for more
      than fifteen months between November 1998 and February 2000.

2   This is clear from Dumont's own words (1986: 9, 16, original emphasis): 'A system of ideas
      and values current in a given social milieu I call an ideology. I am calling the system of ideas
      and values that characterizes modern societies modern ideology…. Certainly, Durkheim saw
      individualism quite clearly as a value, but he did not work it indelibly into his vocabulary: he did
      not adequately emphasize the distance created by this value between modern man and all others;
      only by failing to do so could he come, in the passage from *The Elementary Forms* that Descombes
      pinpoints, to imagine that modern societies might go through a communal "effervescence" similar
      to that of Australian tribes.'

3   According to Marriott, the South Asian theory of a person was as 'dividual' or 'divisible'. Each
      person absorbs different material influences (1976: 11).

4   The five groups are the southern, central, western, eastern and northern Miao (Yang 1998).

5   I am using the dialect pronunciation of Miao in eastern Guizhou for Hmub terms, in which the
      final consonants are not pronounced but indicate tones. For example, I refer to the village of Fang[31]
      Bi[11] as 'Fangf Bil' in the discussion and the song extracts, following village pronunciation as
      closely as possible.

6   The central group comprises the northern subgroup in the Wuyang and Qingshuijiang river basins, a southern subgroup living in the mountain region of the Duliujiang River and an eastern subgroup in the transitional region between the Yun-Gui Plateau proper and adjacent uplands.

7   The case was identified as a 'real' sibling marriage, which should have been avoided.

8   FZD stands for father's sister's daughter; MBS, mother's brother's son; MBD, mother's brother's daughter; FZS, father's sister's son. Hereafter, I follow the kin abbreviations: F=father, M=mother, B=brother, Z=sister, G=sibling, E=spouse, S=son, D=daughter, P=parent, C=child, e=elder, y=younger, ms=man speaker, ws=woman speaker, etc. (Barnard and Good 1984: 4).

9   *Gad ghat*, agnates, 'hosts', refers to the in-group, and khait, affines, 'guests', is used to refer globally to non-in-group members and other outsiders.

10   Flower belts or clothes are exchanged as gifts.

11   The four subcategories of the 'young' songs are *diut hxad vangx*, *qint hxad*, *et hed* and *iof het*. The love-song discussed below belongs to *diut hxad vangx*.

12   The Hmub phonetic system is composed of 31 consonants, 26 vowels and 8 tones.

13   Wearing the same style of Hmub clothes is in fact a strict requirement for marriageability (Chien 2005a, 2009b).

14   Unlike Western 'duet' performances, the four never all sang together.

15   Reputation is extremely important in Hmub society (Chien 2005a, 2009b).

16   The meanings of lines 75 and 76 are the same.

17   Joyful emotions are linked in some lines with joking and teasing, but it is difficult to convey the jokes across languages.

18   Though this is different from Mauss (see above).

19   That is, both before and after 1949.

Chapter 4

Cultivating the Ethnographer's Ear

1   The term "ethnographic ear" was first used by Nathaniel Tarn (1975). In describing his experience of doing fieldwork in a multi-lingual community he wrote: "It may be the ethnographer or the anthropologist again having his ears wide open to what he considers the exotic as opposed to the familiar, but I still feel I'm discovering something new in the use of language here almost every day. I'm getting new expressions almost every day, as if the language were growing from every conceivable shoot" (ibid.: 9).

2   I am using the Eastern Miao romanization for Hmub terms, in which the final consonants are not pronounced but indicate tones.

3   Although the purpose of this chapter is not related to the historical development of writing technologies and the change of the practices and attitudes toward self in a specific historical and spatial context, there are two reasons for me to consider and follow the Foucaultian notion on the relations between techniques and self. First, both are related to the transformation from orality to literacy; second, both examine how certain psychological experiences as well as bodily ones emerge from a specific technique (writing).

4   According to Gove et al. (1986: 552), to cultivate means "to improve by labor, care, or study, bring to culture, civilization, refinement … to cause to grow by special attention or by studying, advancing, developing, practicing, publishing." Merriam-Webster (1984: 203) states that cultivation is "often preferred to culture because it suggests the continuous pursuit of culture and self-discipline which accompanies such pursuit, rather than its achievement, and therefore more modest and often more appropriate."

5   According to Barnard and Good (1984), pedigree means the recording of basic demographic data on household members (name, age, marital status, births, etc.). The term of genealogical records refers to consanguineal and affinal relations among households, families, and lineages.

6   In this chapter I do not use different terms to distinguish the phenomena of noise or sound. The term "sound" is used here for conveying any non-verbal linguistic signs, which can be heard and can be identified as the indexical signs to "meaningfully" local context of the Fangf Bil Hmub village: e.g., the occurrences of household rituals, the start of wedding ceremonies, or the initiation and practice of institutionalized flirting and courting activities.

7   *Vangt* and *lok* are the opposite terms, which could be translated as the meaning of young and old people. The social markers in defining these two terms are marriage as well as being a parent. Any male or female adult without the marital and parental status will be considered as *vangt*. Generally, the people involved in daily courtship are the vangt, but on the occasions of festival courtship activities and singing antiphonal songs, there are lots of old people participating in them.

8   Married Hmub mothers usually wear traditional clothes; most young unmarried women or married women without children wear pants and coats bought from "the outside"—e.g., summer blouses or sportswear and winter woolen sweaters.

9   I am grateful to one anonymous reviewer for drawing my attention to Maurice Bloch's recent work, "Truth and Sight: Generalizing without Universalizing" (Bloch 2008).

10 Influenced by the Marxist principles and Engle's historical materialism, "(Russian theorist Levy) Vygotsky's theory of mediation helps us to see tools, signs, and technologies as spatially and culturally distributed systems that function to augment human psychological processing"(Hass 1996: 17). According to Hass, "Viewed in this way, then, technologies—in particular, literacy technologies—are themselves complex systems that might fruitfully be studies genetically, in the Vygotskian sense" (ibid.).

Chapter 7
Anonymous Voices and Authorship Politics in Printed Genealogies in Eastern Guizhour

1   Hmub society is cognate with Hmong, both acting as patrilineal descent groups, including cross cousin marriage and duolocal post-marital residence. Hmub and Hmong have been called Miao in Chinese since the Qing dynasty.

2   According to Taga, these regular items are very common among Chinese written genealogy by different surnames. Taga, *Zhongguo zongpu de yanjiu* (A *Study of Chinese Genealogical Books*), 1.

3   Kam and Hmub have been considered two distinct ethnic groups in East Guizhou since the 1950s. Dou, ji, gong and the household are main structures for the Kam society. Similar to the Hmub, Kam society acts as a patrilineal descent group, including cross cousin marriage and duolocal post-marital residence. Kam has been called Dong in Chinese since the Qing dynasty.

4   The earlier version of the genealogy mentioned that the Liu descent groups lived along the Qingshuijang River. They would commute by boat along the river during early times.

5   Other commonly used terms are *jiapu* 家譜 (family pedigree), *zupu* 族譜 (clan pedigree), and *pudie* 譜牒 (genealogical tree).

6   Related works are Blommaert, "Grassroots Historiography and the Problem of Voice: Tshibumba's *Histoire du Zaire*"; Faure, "The Lineage as an Invention: The Case of the Pearl River Delta"; Konkle, *Writing Indian Nations: Native Intellectuals and the Politics of Historiography, 1827-1863*; Shryock, *Nationalism and the Genealogical Imagination: Oral History and Textual Authority in Tribal Jordan*; Wilkerson, "Late Imperial Education and Control: Rural Villages in the Penghu Islands"; Wilkerson, "A New Page: Literacy and Learning as a Form of Power in Local Society."

7   During the Qin empire, the two countries of Qin and Yue were far apart, with one in the northwest, the other in the southeast. The proverb, "perceived as Qin Yue," was used to describe a distant relation with no contact.

8   As topics for future research I will provide more detail on differences between the late Qing and the 1980s versions of the genealogy. Does the counting of descent in the two versions have the same geographical spread and cross-linguistic/ethnic dimension? Are the anonymous voices and authorship politics in the two versions similar? How do these issues correspond to the historical contexts of the compilation of these genealogies in the late Qing dynasty and the 1980s? These issues seem to be directly related to questions about the non-personal plus anonymous voices in these genealogical texts.

參考書目

丁世良、趙放編

    1991 中國地方誌民俗資料彙編：西南卷（下卷）。北京：書目文獻出版社。

三民書局大辭典編撰委員會

    1985 大辭典。臺北：三民書局。

大衛 · 克里斯托（David Crystal）編，沈家譯

    2004 現代語言學辭典。北京：商務印書館出版。

王安江

    2008 王安江版苗族古歌。貴陽：貴州大學出版社。

王智珉

    2005 性別、差異與社會理想的承轉與維繫—南勢阿美的女性結拜。花蓮：慈濟大學人
           類學研究所碩士論文。

王輔世

    1985 苗語簡志。北京：民族出版社。

未刊作者名 *

    1984 仰阿莎。民間文學資料（第六十二集）。貴陽：中國民間文藝研究會貴州分會編
           印。

未刊作者名

    1983 （清雍正十年敕編；乾隆三年告成）世宗憲皇帝硃批諭旨（360卷），卷
           一百二十五之五，頁 420：409-410。臺北：臺灣商務印書館。

田兵編選、貴州省民間文學組整理

    1979 苗族古歌。貴陽：貴州人民出版社。

---

* 書中提及歌師王安江爲此部苗族古歌《仰阿莎》的苗文記音者與中文譯者。

石啓貴編

2009　民國時期湘西苗族調查實錄。麻樹蘭、石建中譯注，王明珂協編。北京：民族出版社。

李惟白

1996　苗嶺樂論。貴陽：貴州民族出版社。

李雲兵

2003　苗瑤聲調問題。Language and Linguistics 4.4：683-712。

呂左

1998　貴州省清水江幹流沿岸人口經濟環境協調發展研究。刊於中國學術期刊文摘（科技快報）4（9）：1024-1496。

吳一文

1995　黔東南苗語地名與苗族歷史文化研究。刊於貴州民族學院學報（哲學社會科學版）3：48-52。

吳德坤

1986　苗族詩歌格律。刊於少數民族詩歌格律，中央民族學院少數民族文學藝術研究所研究室編，頁204-222。拉薩市：西藏人民出版社。

吳澤霖

1986〔1956〕　台江縣巫腳鄉苗族的吃鼓藏。刊於苗族社會歷史調查（一）。貴州省編輯組編，頁247-70。貴陽：貴州民族出版社。

1987〔1956〕　清水江流域部分地區苗族的婚姻。刊於苗族社會歷史調查（三）。貴州省編輯組編，頁88-174。貴陽：貴州民族出版社。

陸景宇編著

1977　新編中國地名辭典。臺北：維新書局。

南山人（張少華）

2002　苗族歌師王安江。刊於新世紀金秋筆會專集，頁45-54。台江：台江縣文聯編印。

政協台江縣第五屆委員會、學習文史委員會編

2003　方妮乃—台江人物錄。深圳：華夏文化藝術出版社。

〔清〕徐家乾著，吳一文校注

1997　苗疆聞見錄。貴陽：貴州民族出版社。

唐春芳

1985　苗族古歌：運金運銀。民間文學資料（第七十二集）。貴陽：中國民間文藝研究會貴州分會編印。

張少華

　2006　前人不擺古，後人失落譜—苗族老人王安江歷盡艱辛守護古歌 38 年。刊於西部開發報，頁 3。2006 年 11 月 1 日。

張永祥

　1990　苗漢辭典：黔東方言（Hmub diel cif dieex: hveb qeef dongb）。貴陽：貴州民族出版社。

曹維祺

　1974　〔清光緒十五年〕　貴州省普安直隸廳志卷之四，頁 194。臺北：成文出版社有限公司。

貴州省黃平縣民族事務委員會編

　　　出版年未知　苗族古歌古詞。貴州：貴州省國營天柱縣印刷廠印刷。

貴州省地圖集編輯辦公室

　1985　貴州省地圖集。貴陽：貴州省測繪局。

貴州省少數民族古籍整理出版規劃小組辦公室主編。

　1991　開親歌。貴陽：貴州民族出版社。

過竹

　1988　苗族神話研究。南寧：廣西人民出版社。

臺灣中華書局辭海編輯委員會編、熊鈍生主編

　1982　辭海。臺北市：臺灣中華書局印行。

楊鵾國

　1997　苗族服飾—符號與象徵。貴陽：貴州人民出版社。

楊庭碩

　1998　人群代碼的歷時過程：以苗族族名為例。貴陽：貴州人民出版社。

簡美玲

　1994　阿美族起源神話與發祥傳說初探——兼論阿美族亞群的類緣關係。刊於臺灣史研究 1:2：85- 108。

　1999　關係稱謂、交表婚與性別身分的認同：黔東南反排苗族的例子。刊於雲貴高原的親屬與經濟計畫第一年度期末報告會議論文集。魏捷茲編（會議地點：昆明澄江），頁 202-233。

　2002　貴州東部高地苗人的情感與婚姻。國立清華大學人類學研究所博士論文。

　2005a　貴州苗人的私奔婚：集體與個人的曖昧。刊於臺灣人類學刊 3（1）：49-86。

2005b 語言、戲謔與聯姻：貴州苗人平日游方說話的分析。刊於臺大文史哲學報 62：347-380。

2005c 貴州東部苗人的米飯禮物與親屬關係：以新生兒命名儀式爲例。刊於民俗曲藝 149：23-67。

2007a 讓吃鼓藏及我們的村子走向世界：地方菁英的敘述與苗的現代性。刊於民俗曲藝 156：157-203。

2007b 「你倆是我倆一輩子的丈夫」：苗人情歌語言的兩性意象與結伴理想。刊於歷史人類學 5（2）：115-149。

2009a 貴州東部高地苗族的情感與婚姻。貴陽：貴州大學出版社。

2009b 清水江邊與小村寨的非常對話。新竹：交通大學出版社。

2012 煩悶、日常與黔東南高地村寨 Hmub 人的遊方。刊於考古人類學刊 74：53-88。專號「感同身受：日常生活的身體感」。

2014 Hmub 人古歌的記音與翻譯：歌師 Sangt Jingb 的手稿、知識與空間。刊於民俗曲藝 183：191-252。

2015 人類學與民族誌書寫裡的情緒、情感與身體感。刊於《身體感的轉向》（身體與自然叢書）。余舜德編，頁 129-163。臺北：臺大出版中心。

2016 主體民族誌研究：布與貴州苗寨的當家女人。刊於廣西民族大學學報38（4）：27-38。

顏華、羅時濟
1986〔1957〕 台江縣苗族的家族：巫腳鄉反排村苗族的家族。刊於苗族社會歷史調查（一）。貴州省編輯組編，頁 353-409。

羅繞典
1987〔清道光27年〕 黔南職方紀略。（與《黔南識略》合刊）。貴陽：貴州人民出版社。

Abu-Lughod, Lila
1985 Honor and the Sentiments of Loss in a Bedouin Society. American Ethnology 24：245-61.

1986 Veiled Sentiments: Honor and Poetry in a Bedouin Society. Berkeley: University of California Press.

Austin, J. L.
1962 How to Do Things with Words. New York: Oxford University.

Barnard, Alan, and Anthony Good
1984 Research Practices in the Study of Kinship. London: Academia Press.

Bates, Catherine

    1992   The Rhetoric of Courtship: *In* Elizabethan Language and Literature. Cambridge: Cambridge University Press.

Bauman, Richard

    1977   Verbal Art as Performance. Rowley: Newbury House Publishers.

Bauman, Richard, and Charles L. Briggs

    1990   Poetics and Performance as Critical Perspectives on Language and Social Life. Annual Review of Anthropology 19: 59-88.

Beauclair, Inez de

    1960   A Miao Tribe of Southeast Kweichow and Its Cultural Configuration. Bulletin of the Institute of Ethnology 10: 127-205.

    1970   Tribal Cultures of Southwest China. Taipei: Orient Cultural Service.

Ben-Amos, Dan

    1971   Toward a Definition of Folklore in Context. Journal of American Folklore, 84: 3-15.

    1972   The Elusive Audience of Benin Narrators. Journal of the Folklore Institute 9 (2-3): 177-184.

    1998   A Performer-Centered Study of Narration: A Review Article. Anthropos 93 (4-6): 556-558.

Benjamin, Walter

    2004 [1923]   The Task of Translator: An Introduction to the Translation of Baudelaire's Tableaux Parisiens. Trans. Harry Zohn. *In* The Translation Studies Reader. Lawrence Venuti, ed. Pp. 75-85. New York: Routledge. （法文版初次發表 1923 年；英譯版初次發表於 1968 年）

Benveniste, E.

    1971a   The Nature of Pronouns: Problems in General Linguistics. Mary Elizabeth Meek, trans. Pp. 217-222. Coral Gables (Florida): University of Miami Press.

    1971b   Subjectivity in Language: Problems in General Linguistics. Mary Elizabeth Meek, trans. Pp. 223-230. Coral Gables (Florida): University of Miami Press.

Bernatzik, Hugo Adolpph

    1970 [1947]   Akha and Miao: Problems of Applied Ethnography in Farther India. Alois Nagler, trans. New Heaven: Human Relations Area Files.

Bernard, H. Russell

    1988   Research Methods in Cultural Anthropology. London: Sage.

Bloch, Maurice
      2008   Truth and Sight: Generalizing without Universalizing. Journal of the Royal
                 Anthropological Institute (N.S.), 14(1): S22-S32.

Blommaert, Jan
      2004   Grassroots Historiography and the Problem of Voice: Tshibumba's Histoire du Zaire.
                 Journal of Linguistic Anthropology 14 : 6-21.

Bourdieu, Pierre
      1977   Outline of a Theory of Practice. R. Nice, trans. Cambridge: Cambridge University
                 Press.

Bull, Michael, and Les Back, eds.
      2003   Introduction: Into Sound. In The Auditory Cultural Reader. Pp. 1-18. Oxford: Berg.

Buss, D. M.
      1994   The Evolution of Desire: Strategies of Human Mating. New York: Basic Books.

Cate, R. M., and S. A. Lloyd
      1992   Courtship. Sage Series on Close Relationships. London: Sage Publications.

Caton, S. C.
      1987   Contributions of Roman Jakobson. Annual Review of Anthropology 16: 223-260.

Castaneda, Carlos
      1998 [1969]   The Teachings of Don Juan: A Yaqui Way of Knowledge. Berkeley: University
                 of California Press.

Cheung, Siu-woo
      1995   Millenarianism, Christian Movements, and Ethnic Change among the Miao in
                 Southwest China. In Cultural Encounters on China's Ethnic Frontiers, Stevan Harrell,
                 ed. Pp. 217-247. Seattle: University of Washington Press.

      2012   Appropriating Otherness and the Contention of Miao Identity in Southwest China.
                 The Asia Pacific Journal of Anthropology 13(2) : 142-169.

Chien, Mei-ling
      1999   Relationship Terms, Cross-Cousin Marriage, and Gender Identity: The Fanpaizai
                 Miao of Eastern Guizhou'. Paper presented at the Workshop on Kinship and
                 Economy on the Yun-Gui Plateau, Institute of Ethnology, Academia Sinica,Taipei, 19
                 May.

2005a Guizhou miaoren de sibenhun: jiti yu geren de aimei [Hmub Elopement in Eastern Guizhou: Ambivalent Collective and Individual]. Taiwan renleixue kan [Taiwan Journal of Anthropology] 3(1): 49–86.

2005b Yuyan, xinüe yu lianyin: guizhou miaoren pingri youfang shuohua de fenxi [Conversation, Joke and Alliance: An Analysis of the Hmub Daily Talk of Courting]. Taida wenshizhe xuebao [NTU Studies in Language and Literature] 62: 247–380.

2007 Niliang shi woliang yibeizi de zhangfu': miaoren qingge yuyan de liangxing yixiang yu jieban lixiang ['You two and we two are life-long mates': Gender Images and Pairing Ideals in Miao Songs from Southeastern Guizhou]. Lishi renleixue [Journal of History and Anthropology] 5(2): 115–149.

2009a Extramarital Court and Flirt of Guizhou Miao. European Journal of East Asian Studies 8(1): 135–159.

2009b Guizhou dongbu gaodi miaozu de qinggan yu hunyin [Sentiment and Marriage among the Hmubo in Eastern Guizhou]. Guiyang: Guizhou University Press.

2009c Cultivating the Ethnographer's Ear. Special Issue: Bodily Cultivation as a Mode of Learning. Taiwan Journal of Anthropology 7(2): 87-106.

2012 Tensions between Romantic Love and Marriage: Performing 'Miao Cultural Individuality' in an Upland Miao Love Song. *In* Modalities of Change: The Interface of Tradition and Modernity in East Asia. James Wilkerson and Robert Parkin, eds. Pp. 93-116. Oxford: Berghahn Books.

2017 Anonymous Voices and Authorship Politics in Printed Genealogies in Eastern Guizhou. *In* Asian Ethnicity 18 (3): 204-217. Special Issue: Religion and Ethnicity in Southern China.

Chindarsi, N.
1976 The Religion of the Hmong Njua. Bangkok: The Siam Society.

Clastres, Pierre
1987 Society against the State: Essays in Political Anthropology. New York: Zone Books.

Clifford, James
1986 Introduction: Partial Truths. *In* Writing Culture: The Poetics and Politics of Ethnography. James Clifford and George E. Marcus, eds. Pp. 1-26. Berkeley: University of California Press.

1997 Travel and Translation in the Late Twentieth Century. Cambridge: Harvar University Press.

Collier, J.

    1997   From Duty to Desire: Remaking Families in a Spanish Village. Princeton: Princeton University Press.

de Certeau, Michel

    1984   The Practice of Everyday Life. Steven Rendall, trans. Berkeley: University of California Press.

De Munk, Victor

    1996   Love and Marriage in a Sri Lankan Muslim Community: Toward a Reevaluation of Dravidian Marriage Practices. American Ethnologist 23 (4): 698-716.

Ding Shihliang and Zhao Fang

    1991   Zhongguo difangzhi minsu ziliao huibian – Xinanjuan.Compilation of Folklore and Custom from Chinese Chronicles, the Volume of Southwest China. Beijing: Shumu wenxian chubanshe.

Don Siam Society

    1982   Let's Go around Heaven and Earth, Hmong Shamanism Seen from the Texts. Bangkok: Don Bosco Press.

Donnelly, Nancy D.

    1994   Change Lives of Refugee Hmong Women. Seattle: University of Washington Press.

Douglas, Mary

    1966   Purity and Danger. London: Routledge and Kegan Paul.

Dumont, Louis

    1986   Essays on Individualism: Modern Ideology in Anthropological Perspective. Chicago: University of Chicago Press.

Du Bois, John W.

    1992   Meaning without Intention: Lessons from Divination. In Responsibility and Evidence in Oral Discourse. Jane H.Hill and Judith T. Irvine, eds. Pp. 48-71. New York: Cambridge University Press.

Du, S.S.

    2003   Chopsticks Only Work in Pairs: Gender Unity and Gender Equality among the Lahu of Southwest China. New York: Columbia University Press.

Duranti, Alessandro

    1994   Units of Participation. *In* Linguistic Anthropology. Pp. 280-330. New York: Cambridge University.

    1997a Meaning in Linguistic Forms. Linguistic Anthropology. Pp. 162-213. Cambridge: Cambridge University Press.

    1997b Transcription: from Writing to Digitized Images. *In* Linguistic Anthropology. Pp.122-161. Cambridge: Cambridge University Press.

Durkheim, Émile

    1976 [1915]   The Elementary Forms of Religious Life. Trans J. W. Swain, 2nd edn. London: Allen and Unwin.

    1992 [1915]   宗教生活的基本形式。芮傳明、趙學元譯。臺北：桂冠圖書。

Erlmann, Veit

    2004   But What of the Ethnographic Ear? Anthropology, Sound, and the Senses. *In* Hearing Cultures: Essays on Sound, Listening and Modernity. Veit Erlmann, ed. Pp. 1-20. Oxford: Berg.

Errington, Joseph J.

    1998   Shifting Languages: Interaction and Identity in Javanese Indonesia. Cambridge: Cambridge University Press, 1998.

Evans-Pritchard, E. E.

    1976 [1937]   Witchcraft, Oracles, and Magic among the Azande. New York: Oxford University.

Falk, Cathy

    1996   Riddles and Lies: Instructions to the Dead in the Hmong Funeral Ritual. *In* Aflame with Music: 100 Years of Music at the University of Melbourne. B. Broadstock et al., (eds). Pp. 215-222. Melbourne: Centre for Studies in Australian Music.

    2004a Hmong Instructions to the Dead: What the Qeej Says in the Qeej Tu Siav. Part 1. Asian Folklore Studies 63 (1): 1-29.

    2004b Hmong Instructions to the Dead: What the Qeej Says in the Qeej Tu Siav. Part 2. Asian Folklore Studies 63 (2): 167-220.

Faure, David

    1989   The Lineage as an Invention: The Case of the Pearl River Delta. Modern China 15 (1): 4-36.

Feld, Steven

    1982   Sound and Sentiment: Birds, Weeping, Poetics, and Song in Kaluli Expression. Philadelphia: University of Pennsylvania Press.

Foucault, Michel

    1984   Of Other Spaces, Heterotopias. Architecture, Mouvement, Continuité 5 (1984)：46-49. http://www.foucault.info/documents/heterotopia/foucault.heterotopia.en. html. Accesssed October 14, 2013.

    1988   Technologies of the Self. *In* Technologies of the Self: A Seminar with Michel Foucault. Luther H. Martin, Huck Gutman, and Patrick H. Hutton, eds. Pp. 16-49. Amherst: The University of Massachusetts Press.

Friedrich, P.

    1979   The Symbol and Its Relative Non-Arbitrariness: Language, Context, and the Imagination, P. Alto, eds. Pp. 1-61. Stanford: Stanford University Press.

Gal, Suzan

    1989   Language and Political Economy. Annual Review of Anthropology 18: 345-367.

    1998   Multiplicity and Contestation among Linguistic Ideologies. *In* Language Ideologies: Practice and Theory. K. Woolard & B. Schieffelin, eds. Pp.317-331. Oxford University Press.

Geertz, Clifford

    1973   The Interpretation of Culture. New York: Basic Books.

Giddens, Anthony

    1992   The Transformation of Intimacy: Sexuality, Love and Eroticism in Modern Societies. Stanford: Stanford University Press.

Goody, Jack

    1971   Marriage Transactions. *In* Kinship: Selected Readings. Pp.117-148. Harmondsworth: Penguin Books.

Gove, Philip Babcock, et al.

    1986   Cultivate. *In* Webster's Third New International Dictionary of the English Language, Unabridged. Gove, Philip Babcock, et al., eds. Pp.552. Springfield: Merriam-Webster, INC., Publishers.

Graham, David Crockett

    1923   A Ch'uan Miao Tribe of Southern Szechuen. Journal of the West China Border Research Society 1: 1-56.

1954   Songs and Stories of the Ch'uan Miao. Washington: Smithsonian Institution Miscellaneous Collection Vol. 123, No.1.

Haas, Christina

1996   Writing Technology: Studies on the Materiality of Literacy. Mahwah: Lawrence Erlbaum Associates, Publishers.

Hammer, Espen

2004   Being Bored: Heidegger on Patience and Melancholy. British Journal for the History of Philosophy 12(2): 277-295.

Heidegger, Martin

1995[1929]   The Fundamental Concepts of Metaphysics: World, Finitude, Solitude. William McNeill and Nicholas Walker, trans. Pp. 78-164. Indianapolis: Indiana University Press.

Herman, John E.

2007   Amid the Clouds and Mist: China's Colonization of Guizhou, Pp. 1200-1700. Cambridge (Massachusetts): Harvard University Asia Center.

Highmore, Ben

2001   The Everyday Life Reader. London: Routledge.

2002   Everyday Life and Cultural Theory: An Introduction. London: Routledge.

2005 [2002]   分析日常生活與文化理論。周群英譯。臺北：韋伯文化。

Holm, David

2010   Mogong and Chieftaincy in Western Guangxi. Presented at the Work-shop of Language, Trade, and the State in Southwest China and Upland Southeast Asia. Institute of Ethnology, Academia Sinica, Taipei, December 17.

Holm, David and Meng Yuan-Yao

2015   Hanvueng: The Goose King and Ancestral King. Leiden: Brill.

Holquist, Michael

1986   Introduction. In Speech Genres and Other Late Essays: M.M. Bakhtin, Cary Emerson and Michael Holquist, eds. Pp. ix–xxiii. Austin: University of Texas Press.

Homans, George C., and David Schneider

1955   Marriage, Authority, and Final Causes: A Study of Unilateral Cross-Cousin Marriage. Glencoe, Ill.: The Free Press.

Humphrey, Caroline
  1995   Chiefly and Shamanist Landscapes in Mongolia. *In* The Anthropology of Landscape: Perspective on Place and Space. E. Hirsch and M. O'Hanlon, eds. Pp. 135-162. Oxford: Clarendon Press.

Hymes, Dell
  1964   Language in Culture and Society: A Reader in Linguistics and Anthropology. New York: Harper & Row.

Ingold, Tim
  2000   The Perception of the Environment: Essays on Livelihood, Dwelling and Skill. London: Routledge.

Irvine, Judith
  1996   Shadow Conversations: The Indeterminacy of Participant Roles. *In* Natural Histories of Discourse, Michael Silverstein and Greg Urban, eds. Pp. 131-159. Chicago: the University of Chicago Press.

Irvine, J. and Gal, S.
  1999   Language Ideology and Linguistic Differentiation. *In* Regimes of Language: Language Ideologies and the Discursive Construction of Power and Identity, Paul Kroskrity, ed. Pp. 35-83. Santa Fe: School of American Research Press.

Jakobson, R.
  1957 [1971]   Shifters, Verbal Categories, and the Russian Verb. Pp. 130-147. Netherlands: Mouton & Co., Printers, the Hague.

Jankowiak, W., M. D. Nell and A. Buckmaster
  2001   Managing Infidelity: A Cross-Cultural Perspective. Ethnology 41 (1):85-101.

Keane, Webb
  1995   The Spoken House: Text, Act, and Object in Eastern Indonesia. American Ethnologist 22(1): 102-124.

  2000   Voice. Journal of Linguistic Anthropology 9(1-2): 271-273.

Konkle, Maureen
  2004   Writing Indian Nations: Native Intellectuals and the Politics of Historiography, Pp. 1827-1863. Chapel Hill:The University of North Carolina Press.

Langbauer, Laurie
  1993   The City, the Everyday, and Boredom: The Case of Sherlock Holmes Difference 5(3): 80-120.

Lakoff, George and Mark Johnson

    1980   Metaphors We Live By. Chicago: University of Chicago Press.

Leach, Edmond

    1971   The Structural Implications of Matrilateral Cross-Cousin Marriage. *In* Rethinking Anthropology. Pp. 54-104. London: The Athlone Press.

Lee, Garry Yia

    1981   The Effects of Development Measures on the Socio-Economy of the White Hmong. Ph.D. dissertation,Department of Anthropology, University of Sydney, Australia.

Lefebvre, Henri

    1991 [1958]   Critique of Everyday Life: Volume One. John Moore, trans. London: Verson.

Lemoine, Jacques

    1972   Un Village Hmong Vert du Haut Laos: Milieu, Technique et Organisation Sociale,(A Village Green Hmong of High Laos: Place, Technique and Social Organization). Paris: Centre National de la Recherche Scientifique, (National Center of Scientific Research).

    1983   Kr'ua Ke: Showing the Way, Kenneth White, trans. Bangkok: Pandora.

    1987   Myths of the Origins, Myths of Identification. L'Homme 101: 58-85.

Lévi-Strauss, Claude

    1969 [1949]   The Elementary Structure of Kinship. Boston: Beacon Press.

    1992 [1955]   Tristes Tropiques. John and Doreen Weightman, trans. New York: Penguin Books.

Lewis, Gilbert

    1980   Day of Shining Red: An Essay on Understanding Ritual. Cambridge Studies in Social Anthropology, 27. Cambridge: Cambridge University Press.

Liu shi zupu [The Genealogy of Liu Family]

    1908   Liu shi zupu. Dated Guangxu 34 of the Qing dynasty. Guizhou: Tianzhu County.

Liu shi zupu [The Genealogy of Liu Family]

    1985   Liu shi zupu. Guizhou: Tianzhu County.

Lukes, Steven

    1973   Émile Durkheim. New York: Penguin Books.

Lutz, Catherine

    1988   Unnatural Emotions: Everyday Sentiments on a Micronesian Atoll and Their Challenge to Western Theory. Chicago: The University of Chicago Press.

1997　Comments to William M. Reddy's "Against Constructionism." Current Anthropology 38(3): 345-346.

Lutz, Catherine and Lila Abu-Lughod

1988　Language and the Politics of Emotion. New York: Cambridge University Press.

Lutz, Catherine and Geoffrey M. White

1986　The Anthropology of Emotions. Annual Review of Anthropology 15：405-436.

Mainardi, P.

2003　Husbands, Wives, and Lovers: Marriage and Its Discontents in Nineteenth-Century France. New Haven: Yale University Press.

Malinowski, Bronislaw

1982 [1932]　The Sexual Life of Savages in North Western Melanesia: An Ethnographic Account of Courtship, Marriage, and Family Life among the Natives of the Trobriand Islands, British New Guinea. London: Routledge & Kegan Paul.

Mannheim, B.

2000　Iconicity. Journal of Linguistic Anthropology 9: 1-2.

Marriott, McKim

1976　Hindu Transactions: Diversity without Dualism. *In* Transactions and Meanings, B. Kapferer, ed. Philadelphia: ISHI Publications.

Mauss, Marcel

1979　A Category of the Human Mind: The Notion of Person, the Notion of 'Self'. *In* Sociology and Psychology: Essays. Boston: Routledge & Kegan Paul.

Merriam-Webster, ed.

1984　Cultivation. *In* Merriam-Webster's Dictionary of Synonyms, P. 203. Springfield: Merriam-Webster, Incorporated.

Mickey, Margaret Portia

1947　The Crowie Shell Miao of Kweichow. Papers of the Peabody Museum of American Archeology and Ethnography 32(1): 1-94.

Mines, Diane P. and Sarah Lamb, eds.

2002　Everyday Life in South Asia. Bloomington: Indiana University Press.

Moore, H. L.

1993　The Differences Within and the Differences Between. *In* Gendered Anthropology, Teresa del Valle, ed. Pp.193-204. New York: Routledge.

1994   A Passion for Difference: Essays in Anthropology and Gender. Cambridge: Polity Press.

Morgan, Henry Lewis

1871   Systems of Consanguinity and Affinity of the Human Family. Washington: Smithsonian Institution.

Mottin, Jean

1980   55 Chants D'amour Hmong Blanc (55 zaj txhiaj hmoob clawb). Bangkok: Don Siam Socity.

1982   Let's Go around Heaven and Earth, Hmong Shamanism Seen from the Texts. Bangkok: Don Bosco Press.

Mucha, Janusz

1996   Everyday Life and Festivity in a Local Ethnic Community: Polish-Americans in South Bend, Indiana. New York: Columbia University Press.

Needham, Rodney

1960   Alliance and Classification among the Lamet. Sociologus 10 (2): 97-119.

Ong, Walter J.

1982   Orality and Literacy: The Technologizing of the Word. London: Methuen.

Parkin, Robert

1993   The Joking Relationship and Kinship: Charting a Theoretical Dependency. Journal of the Anthropological Society for Oxford 24 (3): 251-263.

1996   The Dark Side of Humanity: The Work of Robert Hertz and its Legacy. Amsterdam: Harwood Academic Publishers.

1997   Descent. *In* Kinship: An Introduction to the Basic Concepts. Pp. 14-27. Oxford: Blackwell Publishers Ltd.

Parkin, David

1991   Sacred Void: Spatial Images of Work and Ritual among the Giriama. Cambridge: Cambridge University Press.

Peirce, C. S.

1932   Divisions of Signs. Collected Papers of Charles Sanders Peirce 2(2). Cambridge, Mass: Harvard Univ. Press.

1955 [1902]   Logic Semiotic: Philosophical Writings of Peirce, edited by Justus Buchler. Pp. 98-115. New York: Dover.

Phillips, Adam

    1994   On Kissing, Tickling, and Being Bored: Psychoanalytic Essays on the Unexamined Life. Cambridge, Mas.: Harvard University Press.

    2000 [1994]   吻、搔癢與煩悶：亞當 · 菲立普論隱藏的人性。陳信宏譯。臺北：究竟出版社。

Pieke, Frank N.

    2003   The Genealogical Mentality in Modern China. The Journal of Asian Studies 62 (1): 101-128.

Radcliffe-Brown, A. R.

    1922   The Andaman Islanders. Cambridge: Cambridge University Press.

    1924   The Mother's Brother in South Africa. South Africa Journal of Science 21：542-555.

    1952 [1924]   The Mother's Brother in South Africa. South Africa Journal of Science 21: 542–55.

Rapport, Nigel, and Joanna Overing

    2000   Social and Cultural Anthropology: The Key Concepts. New York: Routledge.

Riley, D.

    1988   Am I That Name? : Feminism and the Category of 'Women' in History. London: Macmillan.

Robins, E. and T. L. Huston

    1983   Testing Compatibility Testing. Paper presented at the National Council on Family Relations Annual Meeting, St. Paul, MN.

Rosaldo, Michelle

    1980   Knowledge and Passion: Ilongot Notions of Self and Social Life. New York: Cambridge University Press.

    1984   Toward an Anthropology of Self and Feeling. In Culture Theory: Essays on Mind, Self, and Emotion. R. A. Shweder and R. A. LeVine, eds. Pp. 137–157. Cambridge: Cambridge University Press.

Rothman, Ellen

    1984   Hands, and Hearts: A History of Courtship in America. New York: Basic Books.

Rubel, Paula and Rosman, Abraham

    2003   Introduction. In Translating Cultures: Perspectives on Translation and Anthropology. Pp. 1-22. Oxford: Berg.

Savina, Francoise

    1924   Histoire de Miao [History of Miao]. Hong Kong: Imprimerie de las Societe des Missions-Etrangeres (Publication of the Company of Foreigners-Missions).

Schein, L.

    2000   Minority Rules: The Miao and the Feminine in China's Cultural Politics. North Carolina: Duke University Press.

Searle, John

    1969   Speech Acts: An Essay in the Philosophy of Language. New York: Cambridge University Press.

Shackelford, T. K., M. Voracek, D. P. Schmit, D.M. Buss, V. A. Weekes-Shackelford, and R. L. Michalski

    2004   Romantic Jealousy in Early Adulthood and in Later Life. Human Nature 15 (3): 283-300.

Shryock, Andrew

    1997   Nationalism and the Genealogical Imagination: Oral History and Textual Authority in Tribal Jordan. Berkeley: University of California Press.

Silverstein, Michael

    1976   Shifters, Linguistic Categories, and Cultural Description. *In* Meaning in Anthropology. Keith H. Basso and Henry A. Selby, eds. Pp. 11-55. New Mexico: University of New Mexico Press.

    2005   Axes of Evals: Token versus Type Interdiscursivity. Journal of Linguistic Anthropology 15(1): 6-22.

Simpson, J. A. and E. S. C. Weiner

    1989a   The Oxford English Dictionary, Volume II, Second edition. Oxford: Clarendon Press.

    1989b   The Oxford English Dictionary, Volume III. Oxford: Clarendon Press.

    1989c   The Oxford English Dictionary, Volume V. Oxford: Clarendon Press.

Stoller, Paul

    1989   Sound in Songhay Possession. *In* The Taste of Ethnographic Things: The Senses in Anthropology. Paul Stoller, ed. Pp. 101-122,163. Philadelphia: University of Pennsylvania.

Stoller, Paul and Cheryl Olkes

    1987   In Sorcery's Shadow: A Memoir of Apprenticeship among the Songhay of Niger. Chicago: University of Chicago Press.

Strathern, Marilyn

    1988   The Gender of the Gift: Problems with Women and Problems with Society in Melanesia. Berkeley: University of California Press.

    1992   After Nature: English Kinship in the Late Twentieth Century. Cambridge: Cambridge University Press.

Symonds, Patricia V

    1991   Cosmology and the Cycle of Life: Hmong Views of Birth, Death and Gender in a Mountain Village in Northern Thailand. PhD diss., Brown University.

    2004   Calling in the Soul: Gender and the Cycle of Life in a Hmong Village. Seattle: University of Washington Press.

Taga, Akigorô

    1982   Zhongguo zongpu de yanjiu [A Study of Chinese Genealogical Books]. Tokyo: Japan Society for the Promotion of Sciences.

Tang, Chun-fang

    1986 [1959]   Miaozu hunyin ge [Marriage Songs of the Miao]. Minjian wenxue ziliao [Miao Folklore Data], Vol.17. Guiyang: Association of Chinese Folklore and Art in Guizhou.

Tarn, Nathaniel

    1975   Interview with Nathaniel Tarn. Boundary 24 (1):1-34.

Tapp, Nicholas

    1989   Hmong Religion. Asian Folklore Studies 48: 59-94.

    2001   The Hmong of China: Context, Agency and the Imaginary. Leiden: Brill.

    2003   The Hmong of China: Context, Agency, and the Imaginary. Boston and Leiden: Brill Academic Publishers.

Taussig, Michael

    1993   Mimesis and Alterity: A Particular History of the Senses. New York: Routledge.

Urban, Greg

    1996   Metaphysical Community: The Interplay of the Senses and the Intellect. Austin: University of Texas Press.

Wang, Ming-Ke

 2000 Lun panfu: Jindai Yan-Huang zisun guozu de gudai jichu [On Mimicry for Prestige: the Historical Foundation of Nation-Building and the Descendants of Yandi and Huangdi in Modern Time]. Zhongyang yenjuiyuan lishi yuyan yanjiusuo jikan [Bulletin of the Institute of History and Philology Academia Sinica], 73(3) : 583-624.

Wilkerson, James

 2003 Late Imperial Education and Control: Rural Villages in the Penghu Islands. Taiwan Journal of Anthropology 2(1): 141-169.

 2005 A New Page: Literacy and Learning as a Form of Power in Local Society. Workshop of Rethinking Boundary. Institute of Ethnology, Academia Sinica, Taipei. June 18.

Xu, Jia-Qian [Qing]

 1997 Miaojiang wenjianlu [What I've Seen and Heard in Frontier Miao]. Guiyang: Guizhou minzu chubanshe.

Yan, Y. X.

 2003 Private Life under Socialism: Love, Intimacy, and Family Change in a Chinese Village 1949-1999. Stanford: Stanford University Press.

Yang, Ting-shuo

 1998 The Historical Process of Signs in Human Groups: The Case of Miao Nationality Names. Guiyang: Guizhou Renmin Chubanshe.

Zajonc, R. B.

 1980 Feeling and Thinking: Preferences Need No Inferences. American Psychologist 35(2): 151-175.

索引

國家圖書館出版品預行編目 (CIP) 資料

貴州東部村寨物語：Hmub 人的日常、情感及語言
= Narratives of Hmub Village Life in Eastern Guizhou:
Everydayness, Emotions and Language / 簡美玲著.
-- 初版. -- 新竹市：國立陽明交通大學出版社,
2022.09
　　面；　公分. -- (族群與客家系列)
ISBN 978-986-5470-42-5(平裝)

　　1.CST: 苗族 2.CST: 民族學 3.CST: 文化研究
　　4.CST: 貴州省

536.26　　　　　　　　111010889

族群與客家系列

貴州東部村寨物語：Hmub 人的日常、情感及語言
Narratives of Hmub Village Life in Eastern Guizhou: Everydayness, Emotions and Language

作　　者：簡美玲
封面設計：柯俊仰
內頁排版：黃春香
執行編輯：陳建安
校對協力：張匯聆

出 版 者：國立陽明交通大學出版社
發 行 人：林奇宏
社　　長：黃明居
執行主編：程惠芳
編　　輯：陳建安
行　　銷：蕭芷芃
地　　址：新竹市大學路 1001 號
讀者服務：03-5712121 #50503 （週一至週五上午 8:30 至下午 5:00）
傳　　真：03-5731764
e - m a i l：press@nycu.edu.tw
官　　網：https://press.nycu.edu.tw
FB 粉絲團：https://www.facebook.com/nycupress
製版印刷：中茂分色製版印刷事業股份有限公司
出版日期：2022 年 9 月初版一刷
定　　價：480 元
I S B N：978-986-5470-42-5
G P N：1011100909

展售門市查詢：
　　陽明交通大學出版社 https://press.nycu.edu.tw
　　三民書局（臺北市重慶南路一段 61 號））
　　網址：http://www.sanmin.com.tw　電話：02-23617511
或洽政府出版品集中展售門市：
　　國家書店（臺北市松江路 209 號 1 樓）
　　網址：http://www.govbooks.com.tw　電話：02-25180207
　　五南文化廣場（臺中市西區臺灣大道二段 85 號）
　　網址：http://www.wunanbooks.com.tw　電話：04-22260330